THE OXFORD CHEKHOV

VOLUME III

—

UNCLE VANYA

THREE SISTERS

THE CHERRY ORCHARD

THE WOOD-DEMON

THE OXFORD
CHEKHOV

VOLUME III

UNCLE VANYA
THREE SISTERS
THE CHERRY ORCHARD
THE WOOD-DEMON

Translated and edited by
RONALD HINGLEY

LONDON
OXFORD UNIVERSITY PRESS
NEW YORK   TORONTO
1964

Oxford University Press, Amen House, London E.C.4

GLASGOW NEW YORK TORONTO MELBOURNE WELLINGTON
BOMBAY CALCUTTA MADRAS KARACHI LAHORE DACCA
CAPE TOWN SALISBURY NAIROBI IBADAN ACCRA
KUALA LUMPUR HONG KONG

PRINTED IN GREAT BRITAIN

CONTENTS

PREFACE

(a) Contents of this volume

VOLUME II and the present volume (Vol. III) of this edition contain Chekhov's long plays in—essentially—chronological order. The present volume therefore contains the last three plays: *Uncle Vanya*, *Three Sisters* and *The Cherry Orchard*. It also contains *The Wood-Demon*. This involves a break in chronological sequence which has been accepted because the affinities between *The Wood-Demon* and *Uncle Vanya* make it desirable to have the two plays in the same volume.[1]

Since *The Wood-Demon* is the least important of the plays in this volume, being to some extent a draft of *Uncle Vanya*, and is in any case included here out of chronological order, it has been thought best to place it after the other three plays.

(b) The text

The translations in this volume are based on the Russian text of the plays as printed in vol. xi of the twenty-volume *Complete Collection of the Works and Letters of A. P. Chekhov*, Moscow, 1944–51. This edition is here referred to as '*Works*, 1944–51'.

The choice of this edition perhaps requires explanation, since—as shown conclusively by Professor Gleb Struve—a few passages in Chekhov's letters have been deleted from the later volumes for non-literary reasons.[2] These mutilations inevitably cast doubt on the edition as a whole and naturally arouse suspicion. But no evidence of interference with the text of Chekhov's imaginative work has come to light during the preparation of the present volume, and it seems reasonably certain that the wording of Chekhov's plays (as opposed to that of the letters) in *Works*, 1944–51, has not been tampered with. Incidentally, the text used here differs at a few points from that on which some earlier English translations are based. The points in question are mainly those where Chekhov's original text, altered by him as the result of cuts imposed by the official censor, has been restored by the Soviet editors.

Since the publication of *Works*, 1944–51, further material bearing on

---

[1] For the relationship between these plays, see further pp. 1–5, below.
[2] See Gleb Struve, 'Chekhov and Soviet Doublethink', *The New Leader*, 22 Nov. 1954, pp. 22–24, and 'Chekhov in Communist Censorship', *The Slavonic and East European Review*, xxxiii, no. 81, June 1955, pp. 327–41.

the text has been published in Russia. In particular, two manuscripts of
Three Sisters unexpectedly came to light in 1953. These were published
in *Literaturnoye nasledstvo: Chekhov* ('Literary Heritage: Chekhov') in
Moscow in 1960, as was also a manuscript giving some variants to
Act Two of *The Cherry Orchard*. These new documents have been
taken into account in preparing the present volume, and the material
on early recensions in the appendixes is also based on the admirable
commentaries in *Works*, 1944–51, xi.

(c) Aims of the translation

The chief aim has been to produce versions for the stage. Though
strict accuracy has always been the aim, it is hoped that pedantry has
been avoided. Neither the 'speakability' of the lines nor the spirit of the
original has ever been knowingly sacrificed to literal faithfulness. The
versions are intended for reading as well as acting, but this has not
involved any conflict of approach, since the view has been taken that the
best stage version must automatically be the best version for reading
purposes as well. The view has also been taken that the best acting
version of a play must be the most scholarly in the true sense of the
word.

An attempt has been made to use modern English which is lively
without being slangy. Above all, an effort has been made to avoid the
kind of unthinking 'translationese' which has so often in the past
imparted to translated Russian literature a distinctive, somehow
'doughy', style of its own with little relation to anything present in the
original Russian. For example, the word философствовать, so common
in Chekhov, is not automatically rendered here as 'to philosophize'.
Nor has it been thought necessary to bring in the soul wherever the
Russian has душа, since the use of the English word 'soul' is now almost confined to theological contexts, and Chekhov's plays contain
few theological discussions.

(d) Previous translations

The plays in this volume have been translated into English many
times before. It seemed important to keep a close watch on the work of
earlier translators, and this has been done—in particular the versions
of Calderon, Fell, West, Garnett, Koteliansky, Noyes, Young, Fen,
Magarshack and Corrigan have been closely examined.[1]

[1] See Bibliography, pp. 339–41, below.

The methods and achievements of these translators have made a fascinating study on which it is tempting to report in detail. One is tempted to pick out howlers, omissions and infelicities to be found here and there in most of these works, as in almost any translation, and to hold them up to ridicule. But this temptation must be resisted, for when presenting a new translation it is impossible to discuss earlier versions in detail without sounding arrogant or patronizing, quite apart from the fact that the new translator is after all an interested party himself. Moreover, it is all too likely that howlers, omissions and infelicities occur here too, though I have tried to avoid them. But the layman does not perhaps appreciate how hard these things are to avoid when a large quantity of material is involved.

So far as comparison with previous versions is concerned, the translations in this volume must therefore be left to speak for themselves. If anyone should be sufficiently interested to compare the text in detail with that of other translators or with the original, this can only be welcomed.

(e) Transliteration

Russian proper names have been transliterated in accordance with the following table.

Russian	English	Russian	English
a	a	з	z
б	b	и	i
в	v	й	y
г	g	к	k
д	d	л	l
е	ye (as first letter of a word and after a vowel, ъ or ь) e (elsewhere)	м	m
		н	n
		о	o
		п	p
		р	r
		с	s
ё	yo, except after ж, ч, ш or щ—when it is given as 'o'	т	t
		у	u
		ф	f
		х	kh
		ц	ts
ж	zh	ч	ch

Russian	English	Russian	English
ш	sh	ь	[omitted]
щ	shch	э	e
ъ	[omitted]	ю	yu
ы	y	я	ya

The combinations ий and ый are transliterated as 'y'.

The name Родэ in *Three Sisters* is given as 'Rodé'. The accent is not intended as an indication of Russian stress, but is meant to show that the word contains two syllables.

(*f*) Treatment of first names

Russian first names often have English equivalents which resemble them fairly closely, and where this is the case the English equivalent rather than the transliterated form of the Russian name has usually been preferred. Thus Александр is rendered 'Alexander' (not 'Aleksandr'), Пётр is rendered 'Peter' (not 'Pyotr') and Елена is rendered 'Helen' (not 'Yelena').

This procedure has, however, not been followed where the English equivalent approximates less closely to the transliterated Russian name, or seems to strike the wrong note. Thus Дядя Ваня is rendered 'Uncle Vanya' (not 'Uncle Jack'), Маша is rendered 'Masha' (not 'Molly'), and Василий is rendered 'Vasily' (not 'Basil').

It has been suggested to me that this solution involves inconsistency, and that an all-or-nothing solution should have been adopted; that is, either all first names should appear in transliterated Russian form ('Aleksandr', 'Pyotr', 'Yelena', 'Vanya', 'Masha', 'Vasily' etc.), or all should appear in anglicized form ('Alexander', 'Peter', 'Helen', 'Jack', 'Molly', 'Basil' etc.).

Both all-or-nothing solutions are unsatisfactory, in particular the latter, since only the most wildly experimental theatre is ever likely to bill '*Uncle Jack* by Anthony Chekhov' in place of '*Uncle Vanya* by Anton Chekhov'. On the other hand it would seem pedantic to insist on forms such as 'Pyotr' and 'Aleksandr', which an English-speaking actor would find hard to pronounce, especially as none of us talks about 'Pyotr the Great' or 'Tsar Aleksandr II'.

My solution, though a compromise, is in fact consistent with the traditional treatment of Russian names in English, whether of rulers or of other well-known persons. We anglicize 'Catherine the Great',

'Peter the Great', and, among other Tsars, 'Paul', the 'Alexanders' and the 'Nicholases'—as also 'Alexander Pushkin' and 'Leo Tolstoy'. But we retain the Russian forms elsewhere; for example, in 'Ivan the Terrible', 'Ivan Turgenev' and 'Anton Chekhov'. A similar compromise has been adopted here.

Since no solution of such problems can satisfy all tastes, it is possible that some producers might wish to keep the Russian forms of some of the first names anglicized in the text. A list of these names is therefore appended, and the corresponding transliterated Russian forms are indicated.

Anglicized form	Russian form	Anglicized form	Russian form
Alexander	Aleksandr	Michael	Mikhail
Andrew	Andrey	Nicholas	Nikolay
Charlotte	Sharlotta	Paul	Pavel
Helen	Yelena	Peter	Pyotr
Julia	Yuliya	Simon	Semyon
Luke	Luka	Stanislaus	Stanislav
Martha	Marfa	Stephen	Stepan
Maxim	Maksim	Theodore	Fyodor

(g) Treatment of names of persons (general)

First names are only part of the larger problem which confronts us when the Russian name-system as a whole (including surnames, patronymics and affectionate forms as well as first names) is considered.

Translators from the Russian have generally been content to reproduce in transliterated or, where appropriate, anglicized form the Russian names as they appear in the original. This procedure has been rejected here as causing unnecessary hardship without compensating gain.

As students of Russian fiction in translation are aware, Russians often have too many names for the foreign reader's comfort. But the full complexity of the Russian name system is rarely consciously appreciated. We can do no more than indicate it here—by conjuring up an imaginary character called 'Alexander Andreyevich Mikhaylov'. Such a person might be referred to by this name in full, and before 1917 might also be called '*gospodin* [Mr.] Mikhaylov'. Other possibilities include:

surname alone: Mikhaylov
first name and surname: Alexander Mikhaylov
first name and patronymic: Alexander Andreyevich
first name and abbreviated patronymic: Alexander Andreich
abbreviated patronymic alone: Andreich
first name alone: Alexander
French form of first name: Alexandre
affectionate or intimate derivatives: Sasha, Sashka, Sashenka, Shura,
                                        Shurochka etc.

Derivatives can also on occasion be combined with the surname—
'Shura Mikhaylov' etc.

The disadvantages of automatically reproducing all such forms in
translation are as follows:

(i) Many of them are, for some obscure reason, thought to be vaguely
comic.

(ii) They are too numerous for easy assimilation by English-speaking
readers or audiences.

(iii) It is not immediately obvious to a foreigner—as it would be to a
Russian—that a given derivative (such as 'Sasha') relates to a per-
son whose first name may sound entirely different (in this case
'Alexander').

(iv) Some Russian modes of address—especially the first name and
patronymic—tend to sound cumbrous on the stage. Thus English-
speaking actors naturally tend to give 'Ivan Ivanovich' its full six
syllables—whereas in Russian speech such forms are enclitic as a
form of address (i.e. take no stress) and are pronounced rapidly.
'Ivan Ivanovich' may even sound like 'Vanch', and in any case there
is nothing sesquipedalian about it in normal Russian speech.

(v) Though each of the forms of address mentioned above carries, in
Russian, its own flavour of intimacy, irritation, formality and so
on, these refinements are largely lost on audiences or readers un-
familiar with Russian. There can be no doubt that this is so, since
experience shows that even advanced students of the Russian
language are by no means always attuned to these nuances when
they read the plays in the original.

(vi) The use of numerous different modes of address for a single person,
and especially of the first name and patronymic, imparts to the
English an exotic element not present in the original Russian, since
Russians, after all, call someone 'Ivan Ivanovich' as naturally as we

call someone 'John Smith'. Intrusive exoticisms are particularly unfortunate in the case of Chekhov, with his natural, apparently casual, elegance of expression and insistence on portraying 'ordinary life'. Since there is almost nothing quaint or exotic about Chekhov's plays in the original, there should be nothing quaint or exotic about them in translation, except at points where this is unavoidable or actually does correspond to something in the original.

In the translations in this volume the number of possible ways of alluding to a given character by name has normally been reduced to four:
(i) Surname preceded by title, e.g. 'Mr. Mikhaylov'.
(ii) Surname only, e.g. 'Mikhaylov'.
(iii) First name (or derivative of first name) only, e.g. either 'Alexander' or 'Sasha' or one of the other derivatives.
(iv) First name (or derivative) followed by surname, e.g. 'Alexander Mikhaylov'.

Thus Uncle Vanya, whose full name in Russian is 'Ivan Petrovich Voynitsky', is alluded to in only four ways in the translation (apart from occasions when he may be called 'Uncle', 'my dear' and so on). These are: 'Mr. Voynitsky', 'Voynitsky', 'Vanya' and 'Vanya Voynitsky'. Female surnames occurring in the text (but not in the appendixes) are given in the masculine form. Thus Vanya's mother is 'Mrs. Voynitsky', not 'Mrs. Voynitskaya'.

First names and patronymics have very occasionally been retained in the appendixes, and also at one or two points in the text where reference is made in passing to someone whose surname is not known. Also a shortened affectionate form of a first name has occasionally been admitted in addition to the long form where an English speaker can easily relate it to the long form, e.g. 'Theo' from 'Theodore'.

This austerity of approach embraces also French names, where used by Chekhov's characters to refer to Russians. For example, Chekhov sometimes causes Uncle Vanya to be addressed as '*Jean*'. He often uses this method of address to create an antipathetic, vulgar, 'genteel' (or one might wish to say 'pseudo-genteel') effect. However, this effect is not obtained if the French forms are mechanically reproduced in English, since the use of French does not perform a comparable function when interpolated in English speech. In any case there is no need to keep the French, as there is, heaven knows, no lack of stylistic means for producing a pseudo-genteel effect in English. In this connexion it must be pointed out that whole sentences spoken (sometimes inaccurately) in French have usually been retained in French. These too are sometimes introduced by Chekhov to produce an effect of pseudo-gentility, for example, when used by Natasha in *Three Sisters*. It would be a mistake for an actress to pronounce these French sentences with a good Parisian accent. On the English stage they would probably sound best spoken in some suburban English accent, which, however, like everything else connected with Chekhov, should not be overdone.

The simplification of names leaves the translator free to convey nuances of intimacy and so on by relying less on the names themselves than on other stylistic means more natural to English—just as he can preserve the distinction between the intimate second person singular (ты) and the polite second person plural (вы) without having recourse to English 'thou' and 'ye'. This method also has the advantage of enabling the translator to aim at a clarity comparable with the clarity which the original has for a Russian whose mind is trained to operate his complex and subtle system of names without effort.

My treatment of names appears to be consistent with that of Mr. McFarlane in his translations of Ibsen:

In deciding whether characters should address each other by first name or sur-name, I have chosen what seemed appropriate to the equivalent English context of situation, rather than follow the Norwegian conventions mechanically; titles such as 'Adjunkt', 'Frøken', and so on, have been similarly treated; and I have also tried to exploit this device to the point where it would, I hoped, deal relatively unobtrusively with the perennial problem of 'De' and 'du', the formal and familiar modes of address.[1]

In further support of the solution of this problem adopted here, the following two brief extracts are quoted from a recent translation of *The Cherry Orchard*. These show, admittedly in exaggerated form, the kind of unfortunate effect—and 'un-Chekhovian' atmosphere—which I have sought to avoid here.

(i) From the list of Characters:

RANYEVSKAIA, Liubov Andryeevna (Liuba), a landowner
ANIA (Anichka), her daughter, aged 17
VARIA (Varvara Mihailovna), her adopted daughter, aged 24
GAYEV, Leonid Andryeevich (Lionia), brother of Mme Ranyevskaia
LOPAHIN, Yermolai Aleksyeevich, a business-man
TROFIMOV, Piotr Serghyeevich (Pyetia), a student

---

[1] *The Oxford Ibsen*, vol. v, translated and edited by James Walter McFarlane (London, 1961), p. viii.

(ii) From Act One:

DOONIASHA. Piotr Serghyeich arrived the day before yesterday.

ANIA [*joyfully*]. Pyetia!

Before this controversial question of names is abandoned, apologies must be offered to those who find my solution unnecessarily brutal. A sentimental attachment, which one can respect, has grown up between many English-speaking readers or theatre-goers and the traditional 'Pyotr Sergeyeviches' or 'Serghyeiches' or 'Serghyeeviches' in earlier translations—whether of Chekhov, Tchehoff, Chekoff, Tchekov or Chehoff. That these evocative allocutions have an attractive flavour— and even a certain wild poetry—of their own is not disputed. But what really matters is whether this flavour gives the best possible approximation to the taste of the original. My own feeling is that it approximates more to the spirit of Ezra Pound's *Cantos* than to that of Chekhov.

(*h*) *Punctuation*

Chekhov's text follows the normal Russian conventions of punctuation by making liberal use of exclamation marks and of repeated dots, the latter being designed to indicate a tailing off or tentative flavour— or sometimes, one feels, just to vary the unbroken, even lines of Cyrillic type, which is more monotonous to the eye than the Roman.

The mechanical reproduction of these features of Russian punctuation is another way in which an undesirable exotic effect is often imparted to translations from the Russian. Though few (I believe no) translators of Chekhov have faithfully transferred all the exclamation marks and dots from the original—where they are of course perfectly natural—there are occasions when the page of a translated text appears to be suffering from a severe attack of measles. The general effect may be burlesqued in the following short (imaginary) piece of dialogue, vaguely inspired by *The Cherry Orchard*.

A. Lioobov Andryeevna . . . ! Pyotr Serghyeich . . . has arrived . . . !

B. What's that . . . Dooniasha . . . ? Not . . . Piotr Serghyeevich . . . ?

A. Yes . . . it is Pyetrooshka . . . here he comes . . . ! [*Enter* TROFIMOV.]

B. Pyetia . . . ! Good morning, Pietyenka . . . ! [*with an air of* (*not unnatural*) *disbelief*.] Can it really be you . . .?

In this translation exclamation marks are confined to points where they would be used in English. And after much thought and consultation it has been decided to omit all the dots, rendering them where necessary by dashes and by other means.

(i) Repetition

A tendency to repeat words or phrases is a feature of conversational Russian shared by English, but not to the same extent. Thus, Chekhov's characters, in moments of frustration, often say я не могу, не могу (literally, 'I cannot, I cannot'). Once again the mechanical reproduction in English of a feature of the Russian is not necessarily always consistent with the spirit of the original—though there are of course occasions when it is. For example, the above phrase is probably better rendered as something like 'I can't stand it, I tell you', rather than by 'I can't stand it, I can't stand it'.

In this matter I have consciously departed from a principle of translation put forward by Mr. Stark Young: 'Let Chekhov . . . have it his own way—let him, for example, repeat a word when he chooses to repeat it, invert the word-order when he chooses, and so on.'[1]

The acceptance of this principle would certainly save the translator a lot of hard work. But it would involve him in mechanically reproducing features of the original even when the effect produced in English runs contrary to the spirit of the original.

(j) Dates

Dates relating to Russia before 1918 are given in the 'old style'—that is, they lag behind the calendar in use in Western Europe by twelve days in the nineteenth century and by thirteen days in the twentieth century.

(k) Acknowledgements

The preparation of this volume has been greatly assisted by the advice of friends, colleagues and strangers, for whose kindness I should like to express my most sincere and heartfelt thanks.

Mr. I. P. Foote read through all the first drafts, compared them carefully with the original and made many valuable suggestions. I am more grateful than I can say for his patience and skill; also to Mr. J. S. G. Simmons who did the same for later drafts of the text and gave the benefit of his great experience in bibliographical and many other matters both technical and general; to my wife who has helped me at every stage, by typing out and criticizing early drafts, and above all by helping to purge the lines of 'translationese'; to Dr. and Mrs. H. Shukman and to Dr. A. J. Krailsheimer for their careful study and sensitive criticisms of my versions; to Mr. Max Hayward, my

---

[1] *The Three Sisters*, translated by Stark Young, p. vii.

many problems as it solves. How can two works
l in common, yet be so very different? Why
tive about the conversion of *The Wood-Demon*
d when did he actually do the work?

nconclusive evidence summarized below in Ap-
ya was written early in 1890. Yet *Uncle Vanya*
ekhov's first fully mature play, certainly as more
gull (1896). It is perhaps for this reason that scholars
to accept 1890 as the year in which *Uncle Vanya*
ve tended, in defiance of the evidence, to assign the
to 1896.[1]

literary quality between the two plays also makes
zzle. *Uncle Vanya* is one of the great masterpieces of
Wood-Demon is certainly not that, though it is more
ry curio, and has been unjustly neglected.

nterest of *The Wood-Demon* is that it is a transitional
mewhere between the light-hearted and relatively
er of Chekhov's early writings and the thoughtful,
ions of his maturity. It has some of the hall-marks of
Chekhov used to sign his short stories 'Antosha Che-
mong his dramatic works) recalls at times his 'vaude-
rces such as *The Bear* (1888) and *The Proposal* (1888–9).
early work can to some extent be considered that of a
Wodehouse. It can also be argued that, as in the case of
use, his facetiousness is worth more than many another
usness. Yet the fact remains that the differences between
arly and mature writings are much more striking than the
It is thus tempting to think of two separate Chekhovs—
hand the Chekhov of *The Bear* or *Death of an Official* and
r the Chekhov of *The Lady with the Dog* and *The Cherry*
t it is not quite the case that there were two Chekhovs, or
the twain did meet. In particular, many stories written in
he year 1887 contain both elements, often harmoniously
And *The Wood-Demon* is an example of a play in which the
mingled, not perhaps in the smoothest of mixtures, but the
far from unsuccessful.
ood-Demon also reflects certain preoccupations (not present in
anya) which troubled Chekhov in the late 1880's—a period
e allowed himself to experiment for a time with the teaching

[1] See Ernest J. Simmons, *Chekhov* (Boston, 1962), p. 200, footnote.

---

collaborator in some previous translations, for his advice on matters of policy and of detailed interpretation.

For their kindness in advising me and for helpful suggestions on points of detail I am also grateful to Dr. George Katkov, to Mr. John Fernald, to Mr. Alexander Kerensky, to Dr. and Mrs. S. V. Utechin, as also to two former pupils, Mr. K. G. Wakely and Mr. R. J. Jacoby; also to two anonymous advisers (consulted on my behalf by the publishers) whose suggestions have been most welcome; to Mrs. Olga Bowditch and Miss Josephine Reynolds for their expert typing of the final version; to Messrs. George Allen and Unwin Ltd. for kindly allowing me to reprint material on pp. 331–2 from my book *Chekhov*; to Mr. J. M. C. Davidson for his kindness in replying to queries and for his annotated editions of *Uncle Vanya*, *Three Sisters* and *The Cherry Orchard*, which helped to clear up some points covered in the Notes.

RONALD HINGLEY

Frilford, Abingdon

1964

though it perhaps sets as
have so much materia
was Chekhov so secre
into *Uncle Vanya*? An

According to the i
pendix II, *Uncle Van*
impresses one as Ch
mature than *The Sea*
have been reluctant
was written, and ha
writing of the play

The difference i
something of a pu
world theatre. Th
than a mere litera

One claim to
work, poised s
superficial manr
moving produc
the period whe
khonte', and (
villes'—short f
Chekhov's
Russian P. G.
Mr. Wodeho
writer's serio
Chekhov's e
similarities.
on the one
on the oth
Orchard. Y
that never
or near t
blended.
two are
result is
The V
Uncle V
when h

OF the
position
Uncle Var
of *Uncle V*
where betv

Nearly se
ever heard o
pendent play-
lithographed
Moscow in the
have wanted *U*
'Chekhov did no
The Wood-Demon
Vanya is a complet

On the other han
two plays from each
Demon as a play in
forgotten entirely. An
tended, the close simila
to treat them as entirel
The Wood-Demon are re
Vanya. *Uncle Vanya* also
less equated with characte
cases bear the same or simil

The Wood-D
Serebryakov
Helen
Sonya
Mrs. Voynitsky
George Voynitsky
Khrushchov
Dyadin

The comparison of the two plays
with important implications for stud

1 V. I. Nemirovich-Danchenko, *Iz proshlog*
p. 296).

of moral lessons in his fiction. This was associated with the attraction which the teaching of Tolstoy exercised over him for a few years.[1] But the inculcation of simple moral lessons proved hostile to Chekhov's art, as it has to that of other writers who have tried it. For though it may be true that we should not tell lies, steal, or behave inconsiderately, a fiction-writer is heading for disaster if he makes the direct demonstration of such truths one of his main aims.

Chekhov was already discovering this at the time when he wrote *The Wood-Demon*. But he had not yet entirely rejected the attempted inculcation of moral lessons through his art. For example, in *The Wood-Demon* the virtues of repentance, charity, and commitment to a good cause are by implication commended in the person of Michael Khrushchov, an unsuccessfully drawn character, but one of unending fascination to the student of Chekhov's thought. The eager, energetic, impulsive Khrushchov represents a shadowy and half-hearted attempt by Chekhov to create a 'positive character'—an occupational obsession of Russian writers from which he luckily soon freed himself. In *Uncle Vanya*, Khrushchov is replaced by the enigmatic and pleasantly cynical Astrov. Astrov may be a more deplorable character than Khrushchov by conventional standards, but he is a brilliant literary creation, whereas Khrushchov is only half-realized and betrays indecision and hesitation in the mind of his creator. And Astrov also gives the impression of being an adult, which cannot quite be said of Khrushchov.

Again, to take other 'moral' elements present in *The Wood-Demon*, Helen Serebryakov seems to be held out for approval because she has 'sacrificed herself' to her elderly, gout-ridden husband, whereas in *Uncle Vanya* Chekhov's attitude to Helen has become more detached. On the 'moral' plane, incidentally, we even find in *The Wood-Demon* a close anticipation (in Ivan Orlovsky's public confession) of the techniques of Moral Rearmament.

This kind of moralizing concern was only a hindrance to Chekhov's evolution as an artist. The fact that he has shed it so completely in *Uncle Vanya* is one reason why it is hard to assign this play to 1890, which would mean that the reconstruction of *The Wood-Demon* followed very hard on the heels of its composition in 1889. Could any dramatist have developed at quite this speed? One wonders.

The characters of *Uncle Vanya* have the disadvantage of presenting less edifying moral examples to the young than the equivalent characters in *The Wood-Demon*. Thus, as already indicated, Astrov is more

[1] See Ronald Hingley, *Chekhov*, pp. 89–94.

cynical than his earlier counterpart Khrushchov, and Helen has become more selfish, while her husband, Professor Serebryakov, seems even nastier and more inconsiderate than his namesake in the earlier play. But they have all become more convincing. So perhaps has Sonya, who has changed a lot from the fashionable, highbrow, upper-class girl of *The Wood-Demon* (who suffers an abrupt and implausible change of heart in Act Four) to the more deeply felt, pathetic, hard-working Sonya of *Uncle Vanya* with a hopeless love for Astrov as her leit-motiv.

Of the characters common to the two plays, Voynitsky ('George' in *The Wood-Demon*; 'Vanya' in *Uncle Vanya*) remains relatively un-changed, despite the fact that he has become the central character who gives his name to the play in place of the Wood-Demon Khrushchov (= Astrov in *Uncle Vanya*).

Conversion was largely a process of cutting—*The Wood-Demon* is half as long again as *Uncle Vanya*. The more facetious elements of the earlier play were purged, with the result that Telegin in *Uncle Vanya* has far fewer lines than Dyadin, his equivalent in *The Wood-Demon*, though his character has not been made more serious. The cast has been cut as well, four main characters (Leonid and Julia Zheltukhin, Theo-dore and Ivan Orlovsky) having disappeared entirely. These were all 'broad' characters, conceived in the spirit of the vaudevilles, and there was only a relatively small place for such in Chekhov's mature drama. Indeed, two of them—the ebullient extrovert Theodore and the super-competent Julia—might be thought by some to be disqualified by their very vigour for the twilight world, as it is sometimes described, of Chekhov's mature drama. Along with these jolly figures a lot of harm-less rubbish, such as the joke about the Tarpeian Rock on p. 229, was also pitched out.

Chekhov's chief discovery (which came between the writing of *The Wood-Demon* and *Uncle Vanya*) was the fact that his true element as a dramatist was inconclusiveness. Both in *The Wood-Demon* and *Uncle Vanya* Voynitsky fires a revolver. But it is significant that he manages to hit the target (himself) in the earlier play, whereas in the later play he misses. *Uncle Vanya* is pervaded by the poignancy—more keenly felt perhaps because so lightly and delicately handled—of unhappy love. In *The Wood-Demon*, by contrast, the two young couples are brought together at the end with almost indecent haste, leaving only the petulant Zheltukhin unmated. And Chekhov makes it clear enough that no one need feel sorry for *him*.

The Wood-Demon is by no means a negligible achievement. But its main interest is for what it shows us of Chekhov as a traveller. In *Uncle Vanya* he has already arrived.

Chekhov's 'arrival' as a dramatist was closely followed by another important event in the history of the Russian stage, the foundation of the Moscow Art Theatre in 1898. The founders of the new theatre, Konstantin Stanislavsky and Vladimir Nemirovich-Danchenko, sought to break with existing stage conventions and to start a new and lively tradition of their own. That these pioneers in the techniques of theatrical production should have been attracted to the work of Chekhov, himself a breaker of new ground in the technique of writing plays, was only natural.

The Moscow Art Theatre rescued Chekhov's *Seagull*, which had been received with hisses and jeers at its first performance in St. Petersburg in 1896, and two years later scored an outstanding success with this play in its opening season. The same theatre also gave the first important performance of *Uncle Vanya*, which had previously been staged by some Russian provincial companies, and the first performances of *Three Sisters* and *The Cherry Orchard*.

The partnership between Chekhov and the Moscow Art Theatre became one of the most celebrated examples of collaboration in the history of the drama. But it was no idyll of co-operation, since Chekhov himself was never satisfied, and became increasingly dissatisfied, with the performances of his plays by the Art Theatre.

In many ways Konstantin Stanislavsky and his colleagues deferred to their distinguished author. He was encouraged to attend rehearsals and to give advice on production and casting. Moreover, though producers are notoriously wary of interference by authors in the staging of their plays, Stanislavsky seems to have felt that Chekhov gave too little rather than too much advice. Such advice as he did give on the spot was, Stanislavsky thought, often too cryptic to be interpreted.

There seems to have been a conflict of temperament between Chekhov and Stanislavsky. It did not lead to quarrels, since both sides were too good-hearted, and probably respected each other too much, for this to happen. But it did lead to misunderstandings. Stanislavsky cuts a less dignified and impressive figure than Chekhov in these disagreements, and in particular the portraits of himself and of Chekhov contained in his memoirs are misleading. Here Stanislavsky is perhaps even more unfair to himself than he is to Chekhov, for he makes himself appear something of an overgrown schoolboy, a representation in which there may, however, have been a grain of truth.

In any case it is impossible to reconcile Stanislavsky's picture of Chekhov with what is known of Chekhov from other sources. In Stanislavsky's memoirs Chekhov appears as a kind of 'absent-minded professor', a sort of unpractical, bumbling, 'lovable' genius. This impression comes over more strongly in Stanislavsky's Russian than in the English translation because of the comic language which he puts into Chekhov's mouth. As these memoirs emphasize, Stanislavsky, though a great man of the theatre, was unimpressive as a memoirist. He was, at least in print, a great striker of the wrong note. But of course his services as the first impresario of Chekhov's plays should not be underestimated. Nor must it be forgotten that his colleague Nemirovich-Danchenko performed at least as important a role, especially by encouraging Chekhov to continue writing for the stage after his early disappointments.

The advice which Chekhov gave at rehearsals may have been cryptic, but that contained in his letters is instructive and reasonably full. This was one fortunate by-product of the tragic illness which kept him marooned in Yalta during a large part of each year when these plays were in production in Moscow, and which ended his life in 1904. The letters, addressed to his wife, Olga Knipper—herself an actress at the Moscow Art Theatre who was appearing in the plays—to Stanislavsky, Nemirovich-Danchenko and others, form an unsystematic but valuable commentary on his own view of the plays. His comments, which are particularly full in the case of *The Cherry Orchard*, are quoted at length in the appendixes. They give a vivid picture of Chekhov's philosophy of the theatre, and form a guide which no serious producer of the plays would wish to ignore. Admittedly the producer of a play will not necessarily defer to his author's wishes in every particular. But it would be a rash producer who would not at least want to know what those wishes were, certainly where an author of Chekhov's stature is concerned.

There is a curious, almost comic, paradox running through Chekhov's relations with the Moscow Art Theatre, and with Stanislavsky in particular. On the one hand Stanislavsky championed Chekhov as a new playwright of great originality. On the other hand he failed to give full weight to Chekhov's originality as a writer for the stage.

The nature of Chekhov's originality is notoriously difficult to define, but it may at least be put in crude terms by saying that Chekhov was the pioneer of the 'untheatrical' in the theatre. The most dramatic moments in his plays are often those which have least 'drama' in the conventional sense of the word. These are plays in which—to overstate the case a little—what is left unsaid may be more moving and truly dramatic than what is said or might have been said.

Stanislavsky did of course understand this—many comments in his memoirs show that the point had gone almost too far home. But it seems that all his instincts at this period of his career were in favour of the (externally) strong effect and of the grand dramatic gesture. Stanislavsky was flamboyant where Chekhov was restrained and apparently casual.

It would be an absurd and narrow-minded view which would seek to exclude the strong effect from the theatre—a view which, amongst other things, might result in the disappearance of much of Shakespeare from the repertoire. The theatre is broad. It can tolerate the resounding chords of a Shakespeare or Aeschylus as well as the subtle, carefully modulated undertones of a Chekhov. But it is important that a producer operating in one of these two different genres should not behave as if he was operating in the other. Some such schizophrenia seems to have affected Stanislavsky during Chekhov's lifetime.

An example of this approach occurred in Stanislavsky's interpretation of Act Four of *Uncle Vanya*. Here, for example, he at one stage required Astrov to address Helen in the tones of a 'passionate lover', whereas, in Chekhov's conception, Astrov's attitude was relatively uninvolved. Similarly Stanislavsky apparently wanted Tuzenbakh's body to be carried across the stage at the end of *Three Sisters*, though the facts about this dispute are not entirely clear. A further incident, in which Stanislavsky was not concerned, also emphasizes Chekhov's dislike of the 'theatrical' effect. When he heard that the actress playing Sonya in *Uncle Vanya* was going down on her knees and kissing her father's hand at a certain point in Act Three, Chekhov protested. He said: 'The whole meaning and drama of a person is inside, not in outward manifestations.'[1]

It seems that Stanislavsky was altogether too fond of noise for Chekhov's taste, and it was on this point that his most frequent clashes with Chekhov occurred. Chekhov had to remind him that the fire-alarm in Act Three of *Three Sisters* was 'only in the distance—off stage, a vague, muffled noise'.[2] Even the well-known noise of a breaking

---

[1] See below, p. 302. It must, however, be admitted that Chekhov's own stage directions require Sonya to speak the lines in question 'kneeling'.   [2] See below, p. 314.

string in *The Cherry Orchard* was being overdone, while Stanislavsky's love of choruses of singing birds, croaking frogs, and chirping crickets was a byword.

Part of the comedy of this clash between Chekhov and Stanislavsky lay in Chekhov's own diffidence (not weakness) of character, which prevented him from giving vent to his exasperation. But his letters on these points often show a strong irritation below the surface. For instance, he wrote to Stanislavsky (the play under discussion was *The Cherry Orchard*): 'Haymaking usually takes place between 20 and 25 June, at which time I think the corncrake no longer cries, and frogs also are silent at this time of year.' At about the same time Chekhov wrote to Olga Knipper that 'Stanislavsky wants to bring on a train in Act Two, but I think he must be restrained. He also wants frogs and corncrakes.'[1]

However, these questions of noise and gesture are, after all, only minor externals and the disagreements to which they gave rise between Chekhov and the directors of the Moscow Art Theatre derived from a more fundamental disagreement on the general interpretation of the plays. This revolved around the argument about whether they were 'comedies' or not.

As is abundantly documented in the appendixes, Chekhov repeatedly insisted that his last two plays were gay comedies. The following are three among many such references: 'It [*The Cherry Orchard*] hasn't turned out as a drama, but as a comedy, in places even a farce.'[2] 'The last act will be gay. Actually the whole play [*The Cherry Orchard*] is gay and frivolous.'[3] Chekhov 'was convinced that he had written a gay comedy, but at the reading everyone took the play [*Three Sisters*] for a drama and wept as they listened to it.'[4]

As play succeeded play these protestations grew louder, and were particularly numerous in the case of *The Cherry Orchard*. One almost gets the impression that by this time Chekhov was trying to convince himself, having given up hope of convincing anyone else. At all events he did not convince Stanislavsky and Nemirovich-Danchenko. They were inclined to regard the plays as 'heavy dramas of Russian life', and they continued to do so after Chekhov's death.

In talking about 'comedy' Chekhov was obviously expressing something which he felt deeply, but was perhaps not choosing the best way of making his meaning clear. Certainly his plays are not comedies

---

[1] See below, p. 329.   [2] See below, p. 319.
[3] See below, p. 320.   [4] See below, p. 314.

in the vulgar sense of having 'happy endings'. On the other hand the 'unhappy endings' of *Uncle Vanya*, *Three Sisters*, and, to some extent, *The Cherry Orchard*, scarcely qualify these plays as tragedies. There could in fact be hardly any more futile occupation than to debate whether these plays are 'farces', 'comedies', 'dramas', 'heavy dramas', or 'tragedies'. These terms, fuzzier and more imprecise than they sometimes seem, may have their uses as labels for some kinds of pre-Chekhovian drama. Certainly there is at least a valid distinction between Greek and Shakespearian 'comedy' and 'tragedy', despite instances where the two genres tend to encroach on each other's territory. But when applied to the new kind of drama evolved by Chekhov these terms tend to cause confusion.

However, this cannot have been Chekhov's own view, or he would not have argued as he did. He did not want Stanislavsky and Nemirovich-Danchenko to throw away their labels. He merely wanted them to stop using the wrong ones. And so far as he was concerned, the right label for his plays was 'comedy'.

This is baffling, at least on a superficial level. All these attempted suicides or murders, frustrated love affairs and cries of despair, all this boredom, disappointment, and misery, all these regrets for the past and hopeless yearnings for the future—can the term 'comedy', or even 'farce', really be applied to them? Surely Chekhov must have been joking when he spoke like this—and it is quite true that he was fond of pulling people's legs.

It may be said at once that this suggestion cannot be sustained. Chekhov may occasionally have told his friends that he was going to get married at times when nothing was farther from his intentions, but his art was something serious to him—especially the interpretation of his plays on the stage. If his earnest advice on this matter sometimes spread alarm and confusion, this was certainly not what he wanted.

In recommending that his plays should be treated as comedies, Chekhov was probably only trying to provide a counter-weight to an over-solemn approach which he felt to be hostile to the spirit of his drama. He was probably making just one more protest against theatrical gestures and over-acting such as he was constantly putting in more explicit terms—one more appeal in favour of the lightest possible touch and of the correct degree of detachment in interpretation. This may also have been his way of tactfully calling attention to the humour which pervades the plays. The humour is often cunningly and deliciously unobtrusive, and Chekhov perhaps feared that much of it would go unnoticed if his actors and producers showed too little sensitivity. No true humorist likes to explain his own jokes, particularly when these are as subtle as Chekhov's. Hence, perhaps, the constant emphasis on comedy.

It is difficult to exaggerate the importance of humour in these plays. But there are many other things in them besides humour, for—to judge from much of the critical material on Chekhov—his work is also deeply appreciated by that large section of the human race which entirely lacks a sense of humour, and it is from this section of humanity that many of Chekhov's critics, to judge from the evidence of their work, are drawn.

However, humour cannot be ignored when considering Chekhov, though it is a notoriously difficult subject to discuss. As a test case the scene at the end of Act Three of *Uncle Vanya* has a certain value. It will be remembered that Uncle Vanya, driven to distraction by the selfishness and insensitivity of Professor Serebryakov, fires a revolver at him and misses. It is tempting to describe this as one of the funniest scenes in Chekhov's works, particularly at the point where Vanya says: 'My life's ruined. . . . I might have been a Schopenhauer or a Dostoyevsky.' But it has to be admitted that there are individuals to whom this key scene appears more solemn than funny. One may dispute this reaction, but it would be a little arbitrary to dismiss it as wholly illegitimate, especially as the scene admittedly does have its tragic elements.

The fact is that you find as much humour in Chekhov's plays as you are qualified by your own sense of humour, or assisted by skilled interpretation, to find. The plays, like so many of the stories, are built on tension between the humorous and the serious, so that it is not really possible to assess the extent to which they are serious—quite apart from the fact that 'humorous' and 'serious' are not concepts which necessarily exclude each other.

To argue the case for Chekhov's humour at length would itself be a humourless proceeding, but it is worth briefly considering the characters in his last three plays from this point of view. In their various ways the minor characters are all more or less funny. These are mainly dependants of one kind and another—servants or 'hangers-on'. They include a number of sympathetic old dodderers who talk in peasant Russian, are full of goodwill, and have only a vague idea of what is going on around them (Marina, Anfisa, Ferapont, Firs). Then *The Cherry Orchard* provides a trio of comic young servants (Yepikhodov, Yasha, Dunyasha) and *Three Sisters* a brace of not quite so comic junior officers (Fedotik, Rodé). No less absurd are the clownish 'spongers' from the gentry class (Telegin, Chebutykin, Simeonov-Pishchik). Even if it is admitted that Anfisa and Rodé, say, are less funny than Ferapont and Simeonov-Pishchik, it is hardly an exaggeration to claim that the minor characters, as a whole, are funny.

The major characters present a more complex problem, and it would require too much space to consider the admixture of the comic and the serious in each individual case. But it seems fair to say that there are no more than seven characters in the three plays who can claim to be regarded as entirely serious:

> *Uncle Vanya*: Astrov, Sonya.
> *Three Sisters*: Olga, Masha, Irina.
> *The Cherry Orchard*: Anya, Varya.

We have referred above to the detachment which Chekhov apparently felt about his characters, and it is worth going on to consider the major characters in the three plays from this point of view. Is it true that Chekhov shared a principal characteristic of Russian 'realism', as defined by D. S. Mirsky? ('People are not good or bad; they are only more or less unhappy and deserving of sympathy.')[1] This conception accords with one long-standing presentation of Chekhov as a 'gentle, suffering soul' or 'wise observer with a wistful smile and an aching heart'.

Such formulations give altogether too sloppy an impression of Chekhov. And the idea of a gentle, dispassionate observer disappears immediately the moment one considers the character of Natasha in *Three Sisters*. Natasha's misdemeanours are domestic—she 'carries on' with Protopopov, expels other members of her family from their bedrooms, stops them having a party, drools over her infants, is rude to the servants, and so on. But there is a restrained viciousness and icy contempt in Chekhov's development of Natasha's character, which makes this one of the great denunciatory studies in Russian literature. 'There's no room for misfits in this house'—this remark, put into Natasha's mouth at the beginning of Act Three, is one of the most telling strokes in the delineation of her character, not least because, if there is one person in the absurd household of the Prozorovs who is more of a 'misfit' than any of the others, that person is Natasha herself. As the result of such master-strokes, Natasha comes over as more of a 'villain' than Dostoyevsky's Svidrigaylov or Saltykov-Shchredrin's

---

[1] D. S. Mirsky, *A History of Russian Literature* (London, 1949), p. 170.

Iudushka, to quote two of the chief bogymen in Russian fiction. We are reminded that Chekhov, on the evidence of his own fiction, was sceptical of domestic bliss, and that there was something about the thought of a competent wife and mother which exasperated him hardly less than Strindberg.

As the portrait of Natasha shows, Chekhov did not inevitably pull his punches, even if he did prefer to win on points rather than by a knock-out, and he shows himself almost equally hard-hitting when he squares up to Professor Serebryakov in *Uncle Vanya*.

So much for characters with whom he was out of sympathy. What about the other end of the scale? Are there any figures with whom he particularly identified himself? Here Astrov in *Uncle Vanya* is a possible candidate, but it is harder to be sure of Chekhov's attitude to this enigmatic figure than to feel the presence of his warm sympathy for the unfortunate Sonya in the same play. Young women seem to have been able to call on immense reserves of sympathy from Chekhov so long as they took the precaution of keeping their love lives unhappy and frustrated. The three sisters (Olga, Masha, and Irina) are a case in point, as are Varya and Anya in *The Cherry Orchard*. Let any of them have found herself a reasonable man (Anya's Peter Trofimov hardly comes in that category) and we should have seen Chekhov relegating her to the category of *persona non grata*.

In general *The Cherry Orchard* shows Chekhov taking great care not to get his sympathies involved. He shows Gayev and Lyuba Ranevsky relatively unaffected by the sale of their ancestral home over which so many words and tears had been spilt. The suggestion, embodied in Soviet criticism and in recent productions of the Moscow Art Theatre, that Peter Trofimov (as a representative of the vigorous younger generation) enjoyed Chekhov's particular sympathy, distorts the careful portrayal which Chekhov made of that loser of galoshes, and is not worth serious discussion. Trofimov is in fact one of Chekhov's great comic creations.

The fact that the plays are humorously conceived and should be played humorously—and, within reason, 'for laughs'—does not mean, of course, that they should be handled flippantly or facetiously. Quite the reverse. As a comment on human life they are immensely serious in conception and execution, and anyone who doubts whether something can be serious and humorous at the same time may have to re-educate himself if he is to understand Chekhov.

The underlying seriousness of Chekhov's approach is well brought out in the material from his letters and from the memoirs of others quoted in the appendixes. As is emphasized again and again, there was nothing which Chekhov disliked more than any kind of automatic reaction. As early as *The Wood-Demon* he was concerned not to introduce any of the stock characters to which Russian theatre-goers were accustomed. Later on he was anxious, for example, that actors and producers should not fall into the easy trap of portraying the officers in *Three Sisters* as the bluff types with clipped voices familiar to theatre-goers in most civilized countries in the world. Vershinin might be slightly laughable because he could not stop talking nonsense, but he was still a human being—not at all a 'stage colonel'.

To put the position in modern jargon, what Chekhov disliked was any kind of stereotype—an attitude illustrated in his letters bearing on the interpretation of Lopakhin in *The Cherry Orchard*. Because Lopakhin was a merchant and a self-made man he must (according to the stereotype) be a vulgar, tasteless, blustering *nouveau riche*. Chekhov simply did not think in such categories, and was exasperated by people who did. Lopakhin, he pointed out, was 'a decent person in the full sense of the words and his bearing must be that of a completely dignified and intelligent man'.[1] Lopakhin is surely one of the most attractive characters on Chekhov's pages. His admittedly unkind and tactless outburst in Act Three (after the announcement that he has bought the orchard) is a moment of selfishness excusable—one might say endearing—after all the trouble he has taken earlier to preserve the orchard for its former owners. Lopakhin certainly is not—and even more certainly was not intended by Chekhov to be—'detestable' as D. S. Mirsky claimed.[2]

Chekhov secures some of his best effects by a 'masterly economy of means'. The words are a cliché and the point has been made again and again, but is perhaps worth illustrating briefly here. For example, the following exchange from Act Three of *Uncle Vanya* is among the most characteristic in the plays:

SEREBRYAKOV. . . . Ask my mother-in-law and my wife to come here.
HELEN. I *am* here.

Here we have, as so often, a deadly comment put in language of the utmost simplicity and surface innocence. Again, a few pages later, one meets another apparently innocent remark made by Serebryakov: 'I cannot manage without the guidance of competent persons, so I appeal

---

[1] See below, p. 327.
[2] See further, Ronald Hingley, *Chekhov*, p. 212.

to you, Vanya, to you, Mr. Telegin, and to you, Mother.' The full
humour of this remark does of course at once become obvious when
one briefly reviews the 'competence' of this trio as evidenced by their
known record. These are comparatively crude examples of something
which students of Chekhov from Stanislavsky onwards have noted
repeatedly—the plays are rich in submerged or semi-submerged comment. However well one knows them, they continue to reveal new
meanings. The much abused literary term 'profound' really can be
applied to them.

Chekhov has often been praised for his economy of means, and the
impression has sometimes been created that the ideal Chekhovian play
would be one without text, characters, stage, or theatre. It is therefore
worth drawing attention to the many great harangues or tirades in the
plays when one of the characters speaks his mind, whether it is Uncle
Vanya expatiating on his dislike of Professor Serebryakov, Andrew
Prozorov castigating provincial life, or Peter Trofimov holding forth on
the future of the human race. In Russian these speeches have a compel-
ling emotional rhythm and a beauty of language which makes them the
despair of the translator. But it is worth noting that these occasions,
when a point is eloquently overstated, blend deliciously with the many
other occasions where a point is, equally eloquently, understated.

The great harangues and the great silences of Chekhov, together with
the subtle dialogue—these contain so many qualities that it is impossible
to enumerate and illustrate them in a brief introduction. In any case it
is better to let Chekhov speak for himself. There are so many elements
in his work which can only be covered by vague and unsatisfactory
words such as 'poetry', 'lyricism', 'atmosphere', 'poignancy' and the
like—words which produce an effect violently hostile to Chekhov and
one more likely to distort the nature of his genius than to illuminate it.
Such words have already been worn threadbare in criticism of Chekhov.
Moreover, there is no point in enlarging on the 'poetic atmosphere' of
Chekhov's plays in the introduction to a translation if this atmosphere
has not been conveyed at least to some extent in the text which follows.
The translations in this volume may or may not convey this atmosphere
in some degree. But if they do not they certainly cannot be rescued by
indulging here in the kind of evocative critical language which Chekhov
himself disliked.

UNCLE VANYA

[Дядя Ваня]

SCENES FROM COUNTRY LIFE
IN FOUR ACTS

(1897)

CHARACTERS

ALEXANDER SEREBRYAKOV, a retired professor

HELEN, his wife, aged 27

SONYA, his daughter by his first wife

MRS. VOYNITSKY, the widow of a high official and
    mother of the professor's first wife

VANYA VOYNITSKY, her son

MICHAEL ASTROV, a doctor

ILYA TELEGIN, an impoverished landowner

MARINA, an old nurse

A labourer

The action takes place on Serebryakov's estate

ACT ONE

The garden. Part of the house and terrace can be seen. A table, laid for tea, stands on a path under an old poplar. Benches and chairs. There is a guitar on one of the benches. Near the table is a swing. It is between two and three o'clock in the afternoon. The sky is overcast.

MARINA, a stout, elderly woman, slow in her movements, sits by the samovar knitting a stocking. ASTROV walks up and down near her.

MARINA [*pours out a glass of tea*]. Do have some tea, Doctor.

ASTROV [*reluctantly accepts the glass*]. I don't really feel like it.

MARINA. A little vodka then?

ASTROV. No, it's not every day I drink vodka. Besides it's so stuffy today. [*Pause.*] Nanny, how long have we known each other?

MARINA [*considering*]. How long? Lord, let me think. You first came to these parts—when was it? It was when Sonya's mother was still alive. You used to come and see us in her day. Now that went on for two winters, so it must have been about eleven years ago. [*After a moment's thought.*] Maybe more.

ASTROV. Have I changed much since then?

MARINA. Yes, you have. You were young and good-looking then, but you're beginning to show your age now and your looks aren't what they were either. Another thing, you like your drop of vodka.

ASTROV. Yes. In ten years I've become a different man. And I'll tell you why. It's overwork, Nanny. On my feet from morning to night with never a moment's peace, and then lying under the bed-clothes at night afraid of being dragged out to a patient. All the time we've known each other I haven't had one day off. It's enough to make anyone look old. And then life here is so dreary and stupid and sordid. It gets you down, this life does. You're surrounded by the oddest people, because that's what they all are—odd. Spend a couple of years among them, and you gradually turn into a freak yourself and don't even notice it. That's bound to happen. [*Twists his long moustache.*] Look at this, I've grown a huge moustache.

An idiotic moustache. I've become a freak, Nanny. Not that I've grown stupid yet, thank God, I still have my wits about me. But somehow I don't feel things keenly any more. I don't want anything, I don't seem to need anything and there's no one I'm fond of. Except just you perhaps. [*Kisses her head.*] I had a nanny like you when I was a little boy.

MARINA. Would you care for something to eat?

ASTROV. No thank you. A few weeks before Easter I went to Malitskoye. They had an epidemic there. Typhus. There were village people lying around all over the place in their huts. Filth, stench, smoke everywhere and calves on the floor mixed up with patients— little pigs as well. I was on the go all day—didn't so much as sit down or have a bite to eat—and even when I got home there was no rest for me. They brought someone in from the railway, a switchman. I got him on the table to operate, and damned if he didn't have to die on me under chloroform. Then just at the worst possible moment my feelings did come to life and I felt as guilty as if I'd murdered the man. I sat down and closed my eyes like this. And I thought of the men and women who will be alive a hundred or a couple of hundred years after we've gone, those we're preparing the way for. Will they have a good word to say for us? You know, Nanny, they won't even remember us.

MARINA. Men may forget, but God will remember.

ASTROV. Thank you for saying that. You put it very well.

[*Enter* VOYNITSKY.]

VOYNITSKY [*coming out of the house. He has been taking a nap after lunch and looks dishevelled. He sits on a bench and straightens his smart tie*]. Yes. [*Pause.*] Yes.

ASTROV. Had a good sleep?

VOYNITSKY. Yes. Very. [*Yawns.*] Since the professor and his wife came to live here everything's been turned upside down. I sleep at the wrong times, eat all sorts of fancy things for lunch and dinner, drink wine. It's all very bad for me. Before they came I never had a minute to myself. Sonya and I were pretty busy, I can tell you that. But now only Sonya works and I just sleep, eat and drink. It's all wrong.

MARINA [*shaking her head*]. Disgraceful, I call it. The professor doesn't get up till midday, but the samovar's kept on the boil all morning waiting his pleasure. Before they came we always had dinner about half past twelve like everyone else, but now they're here we don't have it till nearly seven. The professor sits up at night reading and writing. Then all of a sudden, past one in the morning, the bell goes. Goodness gracious, whatever can it be? Wants some tea, if you please. So you have to wake up the servants and put the samovar on. Disgraceful, I call it.

ASTROV. Are they staying here much longer?

VOYNITSKY [*whistles*]. A hundred years. The professor's decided to make his home here.

MARINA. And now look what they've done. Two hours that samovar's been on the table, and they've gone for a walk.

VOYNITSKY. They're coming, they're coming. Don't get excited.

[*Voices are heard.* SEREBRYAKOV, HELEN, SONYA *and* TELEGIN *come in from the far end of the garden on the way back from their walk.*]

SEREBRYAKOV. Wonderful, wonderful. What scenery!

TELEGIN. Magnificent indeed, sir.

SONYA. We're going to the forest reservation tomorrow, Father. Like to come?

VOYNITSKY. Let's have tea, everybody.

SEREBRYAKOV. Would you good people send some tea into the study for me, please? I have some more work to do today.

SONYA. I'm sure you'll like it out at the reservation.

[HELEN, SEREBRYAKOV *and* SONYA *go into the house.* TELEGIN *goes towards the table and sits down by* MARINA.]

VOYNITSKY. It's hot and stuffy today, but the great sage is complete with overcoat, galoshes, umbrella and gloves.

ASTROV. Obviously takes good care of himself.

VOYNITSKY. But isn't she lovely? Lovely! She's the most beautiful woman I've ever seen.

TELEGIN. When I go for a country drive, Nanny, or stroll in the shade of the garden or just gaze at this table here, I experience bliss beyond compare. The weather is enchanting, the birds are singing and we all live in peace and harmony. What more could we ask for? [*Accepting a glass of tea.*] I'm uncommonly obliged to you.

VOYNITSKY [*dreamily*]. What eyes! A marvellous woman.

ASTROV. Come on, Voynitsky. Talk to us.

VOYNITSKY [*listlessly*]. What do you want me to say?

ASTROV. Have you nothing new to tell us?

VOYNITSKY. No, I haven't. It's the same old story. I'm no different —worse, I daresay, because I've grown lazy and don't do anything apart from grousing away like an old fogy. And my dear mother, the old chatterbox, still keeps burbling on about the emancipation of women. She's got one foot in the grave, but she still reads all those solemn pamphlets and thinks they'll lead her to a new life.

ASTROV. And the professor?

VOYNITSKY. And the professor still sits in his study writing from morning till last thing at night.

'With harassed brain and furrowed brow
We pen heroic lays.
But neither we nor they till now
Have had one word of praise.'

I pity the paper he writes on. He'd do better to work on his autobiography. What a superb subject! A retired professor—an old fossil, if you see what I mean, a sort of academic stuffed trout. He suffers from gout, rheumatism, migraine and liver trouble, and he's almost bursting with envy and jealousy. The old fossil lives on his first wife's estate. Not that he wants to live here, but he can't afford to live in town. He's forever moaning about his misfortunes, though as a matter of fact he's been pretty lucky. [*Agitatedly.*] Just think what luck he's had. The son of an ordinary parish clerk and educated at a church school, he's collected academic degrees and a university chair, become a person of consequence, married a senator's daughter and so on and so forth. None of that matters, though. But you note my next point. For precisely twenty-five years the man's been lecturing and writing about art. And what does he understand about art? Nothing. For twenty-five years he's been chewing over other people's ideas on realism, naturalism and every other kind of tomfoolery. For twenty-five years he's been lecturing and writing about things which every intelligent person has known all along, and which don't interest fools anyway. In other words he's spent twenty-five years chasing his own shadow. And all the time what ghastly conceit! What presumption! Now he's retired and not a living soul knows who he is. He's totally obscure. In other words, for twenty-five years he's been in the wrong job. But you just watch him strut about as if he was God Almighty.

ASTROV. I think you're really a bit envious.

VOYNITSKY. I most certainly am. And what success with women! Casanova himself couldn't have done better. His first wife, my own sister—a beautiful, gentle creature as pure as the blue sky above us, a fine, generous girl who had more admirers than he had pupils— she loved him as only angels in heaven can love beings as pure and lovely as themselves. My own mother, his mother-in-law, still idolizes him, still goes in awe of him. His second wife—she just came through here—is a beautiful, intelligent woman, and she married him when he was already an old man and gave him her youth, her beauty, her freedom, her radiance. Whatever for? Why?

ASTROV. Is she faithful to him?

VOYNITSKY. Yes, I'm sorry to say.

ASTROV. Why sorry?

VOYNITSKY. Because she's faithful in a way that's so thoroughly bogus. Oh, it sounds impressive enough, but it just doesn't make sense. To be unfaithful to an elderly husband you can't stand, that's immoral. But if you make these pathetic efforts to stifle your own youth and the spark of life inside you, that isn't immoral at all.

TELEGIN [*in a tearful voice*]. Vanya, I hate it when you talk like that. Well, really. Anyone who betrays a wife or husband could easily be unreliable enough to betray his country as well.

VOYNITSKY [*with annoyance*]. Turn the tap off, Waffles.

TELEGIN. No, let me go on, Vanya. The day after we were married my wife ran away with another man because of my unprepossessing appearance. Since then I've always done my duty. I still love her, I'm still faithful to her, I help her as much as I can and I've spent all I had on educating her children by this other man. I've lost my happiness, but I've kept my pride. What about her, though? She's no longer young, she's lost her looks—as was bound to happen sooner or later—and her lover is dead. So what has she got left?

[SONYA *and* HELEN *come in. A little later* MRS. VOYNITSKY *comes in with a book. She sits down and reads. She is given some tea and drinks it without looking up.*]

SONYA [*rapidly, to the* NURSE]. Nanny dear, some people have turned up from the village. Go and see what they want, please, and I'll pour the tea. [*Pours the tea.*]

[*The* NURSE *goes out.* HELEN *takes her cup and drinks, sitting on the swing.*]

ASTROV [*to* HELEN]. I really came to see your husband, you know. You did write to say he was very ill with rheumatism and something else. But it seems he's as fit as a fiddle.

HELEN. He was in a bad way last night and complained of pains in his legs, but today he's all right.

ASTROV. And I've driven twenty miles at top speed to get here. Oh well, never mind, it's not the first time. Anyway, I'll stay till tomorrow now I am here and at least have a good night's rest. Just what the doctor ordered.

SONYA. And a very good idea too. You stay here so seldom. I don't suppose you've eaten.

ASTROV. No, I haven't as a matter of fact.

SONYA. Good, you can eat with us then. We dine about half past six these days. [*Drinks.*] The tea's cold.

TELEGIN. The temperature in the samovar has indeed considerably diminished.

HELEN. Never mind, Mr. Galetin, we'll drink it cold.

TELEGIN. Pardon me, madam. My name is not Galetin, madam, it's Telegin. Ilya Telegin or, as some people call me because of my pock-marked face, Waffles. I happen to be Sonya's godfather and Professor Serebryakov, your husband, knows me very well. I'm now living here on your estate, madam. And as you may possibly have noticed, I have dinner with you every day.

SONYA. Mr. Telegin is a great help and support to us. [*Affectionately.*] Would you like some more tea, Godfather dear?

MRS. VOYNITSKY. Oh!

SONYA. What's the matter, Grandmother?

MRS. VOYNITSKY. I forgot to tell Alexander, it slipped my mind. I had a letter today from Kharkov, from Paul Alekseyevich. He sent his new pamphlet.

ASTROV. Is it interesting?

MRS. VOYNITSKY. Interesting, but rather odd. He attacks the very position he was defending seven years ago. That's dreadful.

VOYNITSKY. There's nothing dreadful about it. Drink your tea, Mother.

MRS. VOYNITSKY. But I want to talk.

VOYNITSKY. For fifty years we've talked and talked and read pamphlets. And it's about time we stopped.

MRS. VOYNITSKY. For some reason you dislike the sound of my voice. I'm sorry, my boy, but this last year you've changed out of all recognition. You used to be a man of such firm principles, a shining example——

VOYNITSKY. Oh yes, I've been an example of something all right, but I haven't exactly shone. [*Pause.*] A shining example. That's a pretty poisonous sort of joke. I'm forty-seven. Until last year I was like you, I deliberately tried to befuddle myself with your brand of pedantic humbug so as not to see life as it really is. I thought I was doing the right thing, but now—if you only knew! I can't sleep at night for frustration and anger at the stupid way I've wasted time when I might have had everything I can't have now because I'm too old.

SONYA. Uncle Vanya, this is boring.

MRS. VOYNITSKY [*to her son*]. You seem to be blaming your former principles for something, but they're not to blame. You are. You're forgetting that principles on their own don't mean anything, they're just so much dead wood. You should have *done* something.

VOYNITSKY. 'Done something'? We can't all be non-stop writing machines like the learned professor.

MRS. VOYNITSKY. What exactly do you mean by that?

SONYA [*beseechingly*]. Grandmother! Uncle Vanya! Please!

VOYNITSKY. I am silent. Silent and repentant.

[*Pause.*]

HELEN. It's a perfect day. Not too hot.

[*Pause.*]

VOYNITSKY. It's a perfect day. For a man to hang himself.

[TELEGIN *tunes the guitar.* MARINA *walks about near the house calling the hens.*]

MARINA. Chuck, chuck, chuck.

SONYA. Nanny, what did those village people want?

MARINA. Same thing as before, they're still on about that bit of waste land. Chuck, chuck, chuck.

SONYA. Which one are you calling?

MARINA. Old Speckles has gone off somewhere with her chicks. The crows might get them. [*Walks away.*]

[TELEGIN *plays a polka. All listen in silence. The* LABOURER *comes in.*]

LABOURER. Is the doctor here? [*To* ASTROV.] Will you come please, Dr. Astrov? You're wanted.

ASTROV. Who by?

LABOURER. The factory.

ASTROV [*irritated*]. Much obliged, I'm sure. Oh very well then, I'll have to go. [*Looks round for his cap.*] This is a damn nuisance.

SONYA. It really is too bad. But do come back to dinner when you're finished at the factory.

ASTROV. No, it'll be too late. Where could I—? Where on earth—? [*To the* LABOURER.] Look, be a good fellow, do, and fetch me a glass of vodka. [*The* LABOURER *goes out.*] Where could I—? Where on earth—? [*Finds his cap.*] In one of Ostrovsky's plays there's a character with more whiskers than sense. That's me. Well, I must bid you all good day. [*To* HELEN.] If you ever care to look me up, you and Miss Serebryakov here, I'll be delighted to see you. I've a small estate of eighty acres or so, but if you're interested there's an orchard that's something of a show-piece and a nursery such as you won't find for hundreds of miles around. Next to my place there's the government forest reservation. The forester is getting on and his health's none too good, so I pretty well run the whole thing.

HELEN. I've already heard how fond you are of forestry work. You can do a lot of good that way of course, but doesn't it interfere with your real business in life? You are a doctor after all.

ASTROV. God alone knows what our real business in life is.

HELEN. And is it interesting?

ASTROV. It's interesting work, yes.

VOYNITSKY [*ironically*]. Oh, very!

HELEN [*to* ASTROV]. You're still young, you don't look more than —well, thirty-six or seven—and you can't really find it as interesting as all that. Nothing but trees and more trees. It must be a bit monotonous, I should think.

SONYA. No, it's extremely interesting. Dr. Astrov plants new woods every year and he's already been given a bronze medal and a certificate. He's doing his best to save the old forests from destruction. If you'll listen to what he has to say you'll agree with him completely. He says that forests are the glory of our earth, that they teach man to appreciate beauty and give him a sense of grandeur. Forests alleviate a harsh climate. In countries with a mild climate less effort is spent on the struggle for existence, so that men and women are gentler and more affectionate. In such places people are handsome, adaptable and sensitive, their speech is elegant and their movements are graceful. Art and learning flourish among them, their philosophy is cheerful and they treat their womenfolk with great courtesy and chivalry.

VOYNITSKY [*laughing*]. Loud cheers! This is all very charming, but not in the least convincing, so [*to* ASTROV] allow me, my friend, to carry on burning logs in my stoves and building my barns of wood.

ASTROV. You can burn peat in your stoves and make your barns of stone. All right, I grant your point—cut the timber if you need it. But why ruin the forests? The forests of Russia are crashing down before the axe, millions upon millions of trees perish, the homes of birds and beasts are devastated, rivers grow shallow and dry up, wonderful scenery disappears without trace, and all because man's so lazy—hasn't the sense to bend down and take his fuel from the ground. [*To* HELEN.] Don't you agree, madam? Only an unreason-ing brute could burn beauty like this in his stove, destroying what we cannot create. Man has been endowed with reason, with the power to create, so that he can add to what he's been given. But up to now he hasn't been a creator, only a destroyer. Forests keep dis-appearing, rivers dry up, wild life's become extinct, the climate's ruined and the land grows poorer and uglier every day. [*To* VOY-NITSKY.] You look at me ironically. You don't take any of this seriously, and—and perhaps I really have got a bee in my bonnet. But when I walk past our village woodlands which I've saved from the axe or hear the rustle of my own saplings, planted with my own hands, I feel that I too have some slight control over the climate and that if man is happy a thousand years from now I'll have done a bit towards it myself. When I plant a young birch and later see it covered with green and swaying in the breeze, my heart fills with pride and I—. [*Seeing the* LABOURER, *who has brought a glass of vodka on a tray.*] However, [*drinks*] I must go. Anyway, this is all a bee in my bonnet, I daresay. I bid you good day. [*Makes for the house.*]

SONYA [*takes his arm and goes with him*]. But when are you coming to see us again?

ASTROV. I don't know.

SONYA. Not for another month again?

[ASTROV *and* SONYA *go into the house.* MRS. VOYNITSKY *and* TELEGIN *remain near the table.* HELEN *and* VOYNITSKY *go towards the terrace.*]

HELEN. Once again you've behaved abominably, Vanya. Did you have to annoy your mother with that stuff about non-stop writing machines? And you had another quarrel with Alexander at lunch today. That's a pretty poor way to behave.

VOYNITSKY. But what if I hate him?

HELEN. There's no reason to hate Alexander, he's just the same as anyone else. No worse than you are, anyway.

VOYNITSKY. If you could only see your face and the way you move. It's as if life was too much for you, altogether too much.

HELEN. Dear me, it is, and I'm so bored too. They all run down my husband and look at me as if they're sorry for me. 'Poor girl, she's married to an old man.' This sympathy for me, oh how well I understand it. It's just what Astrov was saying a moment ago—you all wantonly destroy the forests, and soon there won't be anything left on earth. You destroy men and women too every bit as wantonly, and soon, thanks to you, there will be no loyalty, integrity or unselfishness left on earth. Why does it upset you so much to see a woman who doesn't belong to you? Because—and the doctor's right—there's a demon of destruction in every one of you. You don't spare anything, whether it's the trees, the birds—or women or one another.

VOYNITSKY. I hate this sort of pretentious talk. [*Pause.*]

HELEN. The doctor looks tired and highly-strung. It's an attractive face. Sonya's obviously taken with him—she's in love with him, and I can understand that. He's been here three times since I arrived, but I'm rather shy, so we've never had a proper talk and I've never been really friendly to him. He doesn't think I'm very nice. Do you know why you and I are such good friends, Vanya? It must be because we're both such abysmal bores. Yes, bores! Don't look at me in that way, I don't like it.

VOYNITSKY. How else can I look at you when I love you? You are my happiness, my life, my youth. I know there's little or no chance of your loving me, but I don't want anything from you. Only let me look at you, listen to your voice——

HELEN. Sh! Someone might hear you. [*They move towards the house.*]

VOYNITSKY [*following her*]. Let me speak of my love. So long as you don't drive me away, that's all I need to be the happiest man on earth.

HELEN. This is really too much. [*Both go into the house.*]

[TELEGIN *plucks the strings and plays a polka.* MRS. VOYNITSKY *makes a note in the margin of her pamphlet.*]

CURTAIN

ACT TWO

The dining-room of SEREBRYAKOV's *house. Night time. The watchman can be heard tapping his stick in the garden.* SEREBRYAKOV *sits dozing in an armchair by an open window while* HELEN, *also dozing, sits by his side.*

SEREBRYAKOV [*opening his eyes*]. Who's there? Sonya, is it you?

HELEN. It's me.

SEREBRYAKOV. Oh, it's you, Helen. I'm in agony.

HELEN. Your rug's fallen on the floor. [*Wraps it round his legs.*] I'd better shut the window.

SEREBRYAKOV. No, it's too stuffy. Just now I dozed off and dreamed that my left leg didn't belong to me. I woke up with an excruciating pain. It can't be gout, it's more like rheumatism. What time is it?

HELEN. Twenty past twelve. [*Pause.*]

SEREBRYAKOV. You might look out Batyushkov's poems for me in the library tomorrow. I think we have them.

HELEN. What's that?

SEREBRYAKOV. Find me a Batyushkov in the morning. I seem to remember we had one. But why do I find it so hard to breathe?

HELEN. You're tired. This is the second night you've had no sleep.

SEREBRYAKOV. That's how Turgenev is supposed to have got angina, from having gout. I'm afraid it might happen to me. Old age, what a damnable, repulsive thing it is, confound it. Since I've aged so much I've even begun to disgust myself. And obviously none of you can stand the sight of me.

HELEN. The way you go on about your age, anyone would think it was all our fault.

SEREBRYAKOV. You're the one who really can't stand me.

[HELEN *gets up and sits down farther away.*]

SEREBRYAKOV. You're right of course. I'm not such a fool I can't see it. You're a good-looking, healthy young woman and you want a bit of life. And I'm an old man more dead than alive. Well?

Do you really think I don't understand? Stupid of me of course to go on living at all. But just wait a bit, I'll soon set you all free. I shan't last much longer.

HELEN. I feel quite faint. For God's sake stop talking.

SEREBRYAKOV. What it comes to is that you're all faint and weary and you're all wasting the best years of your lives on my account. While I'm the only person who's happy and enjoys life. Obvious, isn't it?

HELEN. Do stop it. You've completely worn me out.

SEREBRYAKOV. But then I've worn everybody out, haven't I? Obviously.

HELEN [*through tears*]. I can't stand any more. Look here—what do you want from me?

SEREBRYAKOV. Nothing.

HELEN. Well, in that case stop talking. Please.

SEREBRYAKOV. It's a curious thing, but if Vanya Voynitsky or that imbecile old mother of his ever say anything, that's perfectly in order and everyone listens. But I've only to open my mouth and everyone starts feeling miserable. Even my voice disgusts you. All right, I'm disgusting, I'm selfish, I'm a tyrant. But haven't I the right to a little selfishness in my old age? Haven't I earned it? I'm asking you, have I really no right to a peaceful old age and a little considera-tion from others?

HELEN. Nobody's disputing your rights. [*The window bangs in the wind.*] There's a wind getting up, I'd better shut that window. [*Shuts it.*] It's going to rain. Nobody's disputing your rights.

[*Pause. The watchman in the garden is heard tapping his stick and singing a song.*]

SEREBRYAKOV. You give your whole life to scholarship, you get used to your study, your lecture-room and your distinguished colleagues. Then suddenly, God knows why, you turn up in this dead and alive hole where you can't get away from fools and their inane chatter. I want some life, I like success, I like to be well-known and make a bit of a stir. But here—I might just as well be exiled to the depths of Siberia. To spend every moment regretting one's past, watching others succeed and going in fear of death—

I can't stand it. It's too much! And now they won't even forgive me for growing old.

HELEN. Just wait and be patient. In five or six years I'll be old too.

[SONYA *comes in.*]

SONYA. Father, it was you who told us to send for Dr. Astrov, but now he's here you won't see him. It's not very polite. We've troubled him for nothing.

SEREBRYAKOV. What do I want with this Astrov of yours? He knows as much about medicine as I do about astronomy.

SONYA. We can hardly bring an entire medical faculty out here to attend to your gout.

SEREBRYAKOV. I won't even talk to him, he's a complete crackpot.

SONYA. Have it your own way. [*Sits down.*] I don't care.

SEREBRYAKOV. What time is it?

HELEN. Past midnight.

SEREBRYAKOV. It's stuffy in here. Sonya, will you get me that medicine from the table?

SONYA. Here you are. [*Hands him the medicine.*]

SEREBRYAKOV [*irritably*]. Oh really, not that one! It's no use asking for anything.

SONYA. Please stop behaving like a child. It may appeal to some people, but don't treat me that way, thank you very much. I dislike that sort of thing. Besides I'm too busy, I must be up early tomorrow. There's haymaking to see to.

[*Enter* VOYNITSKY *wearing a dressing-gown and carrying a candle.*]

VOYNITSKY. There's going to be a storm. [*A flash of lightning.*] Did you see that! Helen and Sonya, you go to bed. I've come to relieve you.

SEREBRYAKOV [*terrified*]. No, no! Don't leave me alone with him. No! He'll talk my head off.

VOYNITSKY. But you must let them have some rest, they were up all last night.

SEREBRYAKOV. Let them go to bed, but you go away too, thank

you very much. I implore you in the name of our past friendship, don't argue. We'll talk some other time.

VOYNITSKY [*with an ironical grin*]. Our past friendship—. Our *past* friendship——.

SONYA. Please be quiet, Uncle Vanya.

SEREBRYAKOV [*to his wife*]. My dear, don't leave me alone with him. He'll talk my head off.

VOYNITSKY. This is becoming quite ridiculous.

[MARINA *comes in carrying a candle.*]

SONYA. Why don't you go to bed, Nanny? It's late.

MARINA. I haven't cleared away the tea things. Much hope I have of getting to bed.

SEREBRYAKOV. None of you can sleep, you're all in a state of collapse. The only person who's enjoying himself is me.

MARINA [*approaching* SEREBRYAKOV, *affectionately*]. What is it, my dear? Have you got a pain? My own legs ache, they ache something terrible. [*Arranges his rug.*] It's your old trouble. Sonya's poor mother used to miss her sleep of a night worrying about it. Ever so fond of you she was. [*Pause.*] Old folks are like children, they want a bit of affection, but who feels sorry for old folks? [*Kisses* SEREBRYAKOV *on the shoulder.*] Come along to bed, my dear. Come on, my lamb, I'll give you some lime-flower tea and warm your poor feet. I'll say a prayer for you.

SEREBRYAKOV [*very touched*]. Come on then, Marina.

MARINA. My own legs ache and ache something terrible. [*Leading him with* SONYA'*s help.*] Sonya's mother used to take on so, crying all the time. You were just a little child then, Sonya, didn't understand. Come on, come on, my dear.

[SEREBRYAKOV, SONYA *and* MARINA *go out.*]

HELEN. He's completely worn me out, I can hardly stand.

VOYNITSKY. He wears you out and I wear myself out. This is the third night I've had no sleep.

HELEN. We are in a bad way in this house. Your mother hates everything except her pamphlets and the professor. The professor's overwrought, he doesn't trust me and he's afraid of you. Sonya's annoyed with her father and with me too. She hasn't spoken to me for a fortnight. You loathe my husband and openly sneer at your mother, and I'm so much on edge I've been on the verge of tears a dozen times today. We are in a bad way, aren't we?

VOYNITSKY. We can do without the moralizing, thank you.

HELEN. You're an intelligent and civilized man, Vanya. I should have thought you could see why the world's heading for disaster. It's not fire and sword we have to blame, it's hatred, malice and all these sordid little squabbles. You ought to stop grousing and try to make peace here.

VOYNITSKY. First help me make peace with my own self. My darling—. [*Bends down and kisses her hand.*]

HELEN. Leave me alone. [*Removes her hand.*] Go away.

VOYNITSKY. Soon the rain will be over. All living things will revive and breathe more freely. Except me. The storm won't revive me. Day and night my thoughts choke me, haunt me with the spectre of a life hopelessly wasted. I've never lived. My past life has been thrown away on stupid trivialities and the present is so futile, it appals me. My life and my love—well, there you have it. What can I do with them? What can I make of them? My feelings are wasted like a ray of sunlight falling in a well, and I'm running to waste too.

HELEN. When you talk about love I somehow can't think or feel— words fail me. I'm sorry, but I've nothing to say to you. [*Makes to leave.*] Good night.

VOYNITSKY [*barring her way*]. And if you only knew how it hurts me to think that in this very house another life is wasting away besides my own. I mean yours. What are you waiting for? What's stopping you, dammit? Some wretched theory or other? Do, do get it into your head that——

HELEN [*stares at him*]. Vanya, you're drunk.

VOYNITSKY. Possibly, very possibly.

HELEN. Where's the doctor?

VOYNITSKY. In there. He's sleeping in my room tonight. Possibly, very possibly. Anything's possible.

HELEN. So you've been drinking again today, have you? What do you do it for?

VOYNITSKY. It at least gives one the illusion of being alive. Don't try and stop me, Helen.

HELEN. You never used to drink. You never used to talk so much either. Go to bed. You bore me.

VOYNITSKY [*bending down to kiss her hand*]. My darling. Wonderful woman!

HELEN [*with annoyance*]. Leave me alone. This is becoming quite disgusting. [*Goes out.*]

VOYNITSKY [*alone*]. She's gone. [*Pause.*] To think that ten years ago I used to meet her at my sister's when she was only seventeen and I was thirty-seven. Why didn't I fall in love then and ask her to marry me? It would have been the most natural thing in the world. And she'd be my wife now. Yes. And tonight the storm would have woken us both. She'd be scared of the thunder and I'd hold her in my arms and whisper, 'Don't be afraid. I'm here.' Oh, what wonderful thoughts, I could laugh for sheer joy. But oh God, my head's in such a whirl. Why am I so old? Why can't she understand me? The affected way she talks, her languid moralizing, those trivial, tired ideas about the world heading for disaster—how utterly I loathe it all. [*Pause.*] Oh, I've made such a fool of myself. I used to idolize that miserable, gout-ridden professor—worked my fingers to the bone for him. Sonya and I've squeezed every drop we could out of this estate and we've haggled over our linseed oil and peas and cream cheese like a couple of miserly peasants. We've gone short ourselves so we could scrape odd savings together and send him thousands of roubles. I was proud of him and his great learning. He was the very breath of life to me. Everything he wrote or uttered seemed to me inspired. But ye gods, what does it look like now? Now he's retired you can see exactly what his life is worth. Not a page of his work will survive him. He's totally obscure, a nonentity. A soap bubble! And I've made a fool of myself, I see it now, a complete fool.

[ASTROV *comes in. He wears a frock-coat, but no waistcoat or tie. He is a bit tipsy.* TELEGIN *follows him carrying a guitar.*]

ASTROV. Play something.

TELEGIN. But everyone's asleep.

ASTROV. Play.

[TELEGIN *strums softly.*]

ASTROV [*to* VOYNITSKY]. Here on your own? None of the ladies about? [*Puts his hands on his hips and sings softly.*]

> 'Come dance, my stove, come dance, my shed.
> The master has nowhere to lay his head.'

The storm woke me up. Quite a shower. What time is it?

VOYNITSKY. How the hell should I know?

ASTROV. I thought I heard Mrs. Serebryakov speaking.

VOYNITSKY. She was in here a moment ago.

ASTROV. Gorgeous creature. [*Looks at the medicine bottles on the table.*] Medicine, eh? Prescriptions from everywhere under the sun. From Moscow, Kharkov, Tula. Every town in Russia has been plagued with his gout. Is he really ill or just putting it on?

VOYNITSKY. He's ill. [*Pause.*]

ASTROV. Why so mournful tonight? Feeling sorry for the professor or something?

VOYNITSKY. Leave me alone.

ASTROV. Or could it be that you're in love with Mrs. Professor?

VOYNITSKY. She's a friend of mine.

ASTROV. Already?

VOYNITSKY. What do you mean, 'already'?

ASTROV. A woman can become a man's friend only in the following stages—first an acquaintance, next a mistress, and only then a friend.

VOYNITSKY. That's a pretty cheap line of talk.

ASTROV. Eh? Oh, yes. But then I'm becoming a pretty cheap kind of person. Drunk too, you see. As a rule I only drink this much once a month. When I'm in this state I get terribly bumptious and impudent. I feel equal to anything. I take on the most difficult operations and do them perfectly. Draw up the most sweeping plans for the future. At such times I no longer think of myself as a freak and I believe I'm bringing humanity enormous benefits. Enormous. And at such times I have my own philosophical system and all of you, my lads, are no more than a lot of insects so far as I'm concerned. Microbes. [*To* TELEGIN.] Waffles, play on.

TELEGIN. Only too pleased to oblige, old man, but people are trying to sleep, you know.

ASTROV. Play.

[TELEGIN *strums softly.*]

ASTROV. We need a drink. Come on, I think we still have some brandy left in the other room. And as soon as it's light we'll drive over to my place. Wodger say? I have an assistant who can't say 'what do you', always says 'wodger'. A frightful rogue. So wodger say? [*Seeing* SONYA, *who is coming in.*] Excuse me, I haven't got a tie on. [*Goes out quickly.* TELEGIN *follows him.*]

SONYA. So you've been drinking with the doctor again, Uncle Vanya. The boys *have* been getting together, haven't they? All right then, he's always that way inclined, but what's got into you? It doesn't suit you at your time of life.

VOYNITSKY. My time of life is neither here nor there. When people aren't really alive they live on illusions. It's better than nothing anyway.

SONYA. The hay's all cut, there's rain every day, and it's all rotting. And you spend your time on illusions. You've completely abandoned the farm. I do all the work myself and I'm about at the end of my tether. [*Alarmed.*] Uncle, you have tears in your eyes.

VOYNITSKY. What do you mean, tears? Nothing of the sort. Rubbish. The way you looked at me just now, your poor dear mother used to look like that. My darling—. [*Eagerly kisses her hands and face.*] My sister, my darling sister—. Where is she now? If she only knew! Oh, if she only knew!

SONYA. Knew what? What do you mean, Uncle?

VOYNITSKY. It's so painful, such a wretched business. Never mind, I'll tell you later. It doesn't matter—I'll go. [*Goes.*]

SONYA [*knocks at the door*]. Dr. Astrov! You aren't asleep, are you? May I see you a moment?

ASTROV [*through the door*]. Coming. [*Comes in after a short delay. He now has his waistcoat and tie on.*] Can I help you?

SONYA. You drink as much as you like if you don't find it disgusting, but for goodness' sake don't let my uncle drink. It's bad for him.

ASTROV. All right. We won't drink any more. [*Pause.*] I'll be off home now, so that's all well and truly settled. By the time the horses are harnessed it will be light.

SONYA. It's still raining. Why not wait till morning?

ASTROV. The storm's passing over, we shall pretty well miss it. I'll be off. And please don't ask me to attend your father again. I tell him it's gout, he says it's rheumatism, and if I ask him to lie down he sits up. And today he wouldn't talk to me at all.

SONYA. He's spoilt. [*Looks in the sideboard.*] Do you want something to eat?

ASTROV. Well, yes perhaps.

SONYA. I like eating in the middle of the night. We have some food in the sideboard, I think. Father's said to have been a great ladies' man in his day. Women have spoilt him. Here, have some cheese. [*Both stand by the sideboard and eat.*]

ASTROV. I haven't eaten all day, done nothing but drink. Your father's a very difficult man. [*Takes a bottle from the sideboard.*] May I? [*Drinks a glassful.*] There's no one else here, so I can speak freely. You know, I don't think I should survive a single month in your house, this air would choke me. Your father, so obsessed with his gout and his books, Uncle Vanya with his depressions, your grand-mother, and then your step-mother——

SONYA. What about my step-mother?

ASTROV. People should be beautiful in every way—in their faces, in the way they dress, in their thoughts and in their innermost selves. She *is* beautiful, there's no question about that, but—let's face it, she does nothing but eat, sleep, go for walks and enchant us with her beauty. That's all. She has no responsibilities, and other people work for her. That's so, isn't it? But there's something wrong about a life of idleness. [*Pause.*] Well, perhaps I'm a bit harsh. I'm disappointed with life like your Uncle Vanya. He and I are turning into a couple of old grousers.

SONYA. Aren't you satisfied with life then?

ASTROV. I do like life in general, but the kind of provincial, parochial life we get in Russia—that I simply can't stand, in fact I heartily despise it. As for my own private life, well, heaven knows there's absolutely nothing good about that. You know, sometimes when you walk in a wood on a dark night there's a glimmer of light shining in the distance, isn't there? Then you don't notice how tired you are or how dark it is or how the thorns and twigs hit you in the face. As you well know, I work harder than anyone else round here, the most awful things are always happening to me and there are times when the whole business really gets me down. But for me there's no light shining in the distance. I don't expect anything for myself any more and I don't care for other people either. It's ages since I was really fond of anyone.

SONYA. You're not fond of anyone at all then?

ASTROV. No, I'm not, though I do have a soft spot for your nanny just for old time's sake. The peasants are all the same. They're uncivilized and they live in filth. And it's hard to get on with educated people. They make me so tired. These good friends of ours all think their shallow little thoughts and have their shallow little feelings, but not one of them can see farther than the end of his own nose. In fact they're just plain stupid. And the brighter ones who have a bit more to them, well, they're hysterical and go in for all this brooding and morbid introspection, all this whining, hating and slandering. They come crawling up to you, look at you sideways on and then proclaim, 'Oh, he's a psychopath,' or, 'He talks a lot of hot air.' And when they don't know how to label me they say, 'He's an odd fellow, odd.' I like forests. So that's odd. I don't eat meat, so that's odd too. They don't have straightforward, decent, free relationships any more either with nature or with other people. That's gone entirely. [*Is about to have a drink.*]

SONYA [*stops him*]. Please, I implore you, don't drink any more.

ASTROV. And why not?

SONYA. Because you're not that kind of person. You're so distinguished, you have such a gentle voice. And then again, you're so different from everyone else I know. You're a really fine man. So why ever should you want to be like ordinary people, the sort who drink and play cards? Oh don't be like that. Please! You're always saying that man doesn't create anything, that he only destroys what God has given him. Then why, oh why, destroy your own self? Don't do it, don't do it, I beg you, I implore you.

ASTROV [*holds out his hand to her*]. I'll stop drinking then.

SONYA. Give me your word.

ASTROV. My word of honour.

SONYA [*clasps his hand firmly*]. Thank you.

ASTROV. Right, that's settled. Now I'm sober. Yes, as you see, I'm now quite sober, and sober I shall remain till the end of my days.

[*Looks at his watch.*] Right, let's go on. The fact is, my time's run out and I'm rather past it all. I feel so old, I've worked myself to a standstill and become thoroughly second-rate. I don't feel things keenly any more and I don't think I could grow fond of anyone any more. There's no one I love, or ever shall love now. One thing still thrills me—beauty. That does affect me very much. I think if Helen Serebryakov wanted to for instance, she could turn my head in a day. But then that wouldn't be love or affection. [*Covers his eyes with his hand and shudders.*]

SONYA. What's the matter?

ASTROV. Nothing. Just before Easter one of my patients died under chloroform.

SONYA. It's time you forgot about that. [*Pause.*] Tell me, Dr. Astrov, suppose I had a friend or a younger sister and you found out that she—well, let's say she loved you. What would be your attitude?

ASTROV [*shrugging his shoulders*]. I don't know. I don't suppose I'd have an attitude. I should make it clear to her I couldn't love her. After all I do have other things to think about. Anyway, if I'm to go it's time I went. I'll say good-bye, my dear, or else we shan't be finished till the sun's up. [*Shakes hands with her.*] I'll go out through the drawing-room if I may, otherwise your uncle might keep me back. [*Goes out.*]

SONYA [*alone*]. He didn't say anything to me. I still don't know what his real feelings are, but why, why do I feel so happy? [*Laughs happily.*] I told him, 'You're so distinguished, such a fine man, you have such a gentle voice.' Surely that didn't sound out of place. His voice vibrates so tenderly, I can still hear it ringing in the air. But when I spoke about a younger sister he didn't understand. [*Wringing her hands.*] Oh, how dreadful not to be beautiful. It's dreadful. And I know I'm not beautiful, I know, I know, I know. Coming out of church last Sunday I heard some people talking about me and one woman said, 'She's such a nice, kind girl. What a pity she's so plain.' So plain.

[HELEN *comes in.*]

HELEN [*opens the windows*]. The storm's over. What wonderful air. [*Pause.*] Where's the doctor?

SONYA. Gone home. [*Pause.*]

HELEN. Sonya.

SONYA. What?

HELEN. When are you going to stop sulking? We've done each other no harm, so why should we be enemies? Can't we call it off?

SONYA. I've wanted to myself. [*Embraces her.*] Let's not be angry any more.

HELEN. That's splendid. [*Both are very moved.*]

SONYA. Has Father gone to bed?

HELEN. No, he's in the drawing-room. We don't speak to each other for weeks on end and heaven knows why. [*Noticing that the sideboard is open.*] What's this?

SONYA. Dr. Astrov has been having some supper.

HELEN. There's wine too. Let's drink to our friendship.

SONYA. Yes, let's.

HELEN. From the same glass. [*Fills it.*] That's better. So we're friends now, Sonya?

SONYA. Friends, Helen. [*They drink and kiss each other.*] I've wanted to make it up for ages, but I felt too embarrassed somehow. [*Cries.*]

HELEN. But why are you crying?

SONYA. Never mind, it's nothing.

HELEN. There, there, that'll do. [*Cries.*] You silly girl, now I'm crying too. [*Pause.*] You're angry with me because you think I married your father for selfish reasons. I give you my word of honour, if that means anything to you, that I married him for love. He attracted me as a scholar and public figure. It wasn't real love, it was quite artificial, but it seemed real enough at the time. It wasn't my fault. But since the day we were married you've been tormenting me by looking as if you knew what I was up to and didn't much like it.

SONYA. Please, please, remember we're friends now. Let's forget all that.

HELEN. You shouldn't look at people like that, it doesn't suit you. One must trust people or life becomes impossible. [*Pause.*]

SONYA. Tell me honestly as a friend. Are you happy?

HELEN. No.

SONYA. I knew it. Another question. Tell me frankly, do you wish you were married to somebody younger?

HELEN. What a child you are. Of course I do. [*Laughs.*] All right, ask me something else, go on.

SONYA. Do you like the doctor?

HELEN. Yes I do, very much.

SONYA [*laughs*]. I have a foolish expression on my face, haven't I? He's just left, but I can still hear his voice and footsteps. And if I look into a dark window I seem to see his face in it. Let me finish what I have to say. But I can't say it out loud like this, I feel too embarrassed. Let's go to my room and talk there. Do you think I'm silly? You do, don't you? Tell me something about him.

HELEN. All right.

SONYA. He's so intelligent. He can do anything, he's so clever. He practises medicine, plants trees——

HELEN. There's a bit more to it than medicine and trees. Don't you see, my dear? He's a brilliant man. And you know what that means? It means he has courage, flair, tremendous vision. When he plants a tree he's already working out what the result will be in a thousand years' time, already glimpsing man's future happiness. People like that are rare and should be cherished. He drinks and is sometimes a bit rude, but never mind that. In Russia a brilliant man can't exactly be a saint. Just think what the doctor's life is like. Roads deep in mud, freezing cold, blizzards, enormous distances, coarse, brutal peasants, poverty and sickness on all sides. If a man does his job and battles on day in day out in conditions like these, you can't expect that at the age of forty he'll still be a good little boy who doesn't drink. [*Kisses her.*] I wish you happiness with all my heart. You deserve it. [*Stands up.*] As for me, I'm just a tiresome character and not a very important one. In my music, in my husband's house, in all my romantic affairs—in everything, that is—I've always played a minor role. Come to think of it, Sonya, I'm really very, very unhappy. [*Walks agitatedly up and down the stage.*] There's no happiness for me in this world. None at all. What are you laughing at?

SONYA [*laughing and hiding her face*]. I'm so happy. So happy.

HELEN. I feel like playing the piano. I'd like to play something now.

SONYA. Yes, do. [*Embraces her.*] I can't sleep. Do play something.

HELEN. Just a minute, your father's still awake. Music annoys him when he's unwell. Go and ask him and I'll play something if he doesn't mind. Go on.

SONYA. All right. [*Goes out.*]

[*The watchman is heard tapping his stick in the garden.*]

HELEN. It's ages since I played anything. I'll play and cry, cry my eyes out like a silly girl. [*Through the window.*] Is that you knocking, Yefim?

WATCHMAN [*off stage*]. Yes madam.

HELEN. Stop it then. The master's unwell.

WATCHMAN [*off stage*]. I'm just going. [*Whistles under his breath.*] Hey there, good dogs. Come, boy! Good dog! [*Pause.*]

SONYA [*returning*]. He says no.

CURTAIN

ACT THREE

The drawing-room of SEREBRYAKOV'*s house. Three doors, right, left and centre. It is early afternoon.*
    VOYNITSKY *and* SONYA *are seated.* HELEN *walks up and down, deep in thought.*

VOYNITSKY. The learned professor has graciously desired us all to assemble in the drawing-room here at one o'clock today. [*Looks at his watch.*] It's a quarter to. He has some message for the world.

HELEN. It's more likely a business matter.

VOYNITSKY. He never deals in such things. All he ever does is write nonsense, grumble and feel jealous.

SONYA [*reproachfully*]. Uncle!

VOYNITSKY. All right, all right. I'm sorry. [*Points to* HELEN.] Look at the way she goes around, nearly falling over from sheer laziness. A charming sight, I must say.

HELEN. Really, you do keep on and on so the whole day. Don't you ever get tired? [*Miserably.*] I'm bored to death, I don't know what to do.

SONYA [*shrugging her shoulders*]. There's plenty to do if you wanted to.

HELEN. Well, what for example?

SONYA. You could help to run the farm. You could do some teaching or nursing, there's plenty to do. For instance, before you and Father lived here Uncle Vanya and I used to go to market and sell our own flour.

HELEN. I'm no good at that sort of thing, and besides I'm not interested. It's only in a certain kind of earnest novel that people go in for teaching and dosing peasants. And do you really see me suddenly dropping everything to run round nursing and teaching?

SONYA. What I don't understand is how you can help wanting to go and teach. You'd get used to it after a bit. [*Embraces her.*] Don't be bored, dear. [*Laughing.*] You're bored, you don't know what to do with yourself and boredom and idleness are infectious. Look— Uncle Vanya does nothing but trail round after you like a shadow.

I've left my work and rushed along here to talk to you. And I've grown so impossibly lazy. Then Dr. Astrov used to come here very seldom, once a month—it was hard to get him here at all—but now he visits us every day and he's quite abandoned his trees and his patients. You must be a witch.

VOYNITSKY. Why so downhearted? [*Vigorously.*] No really, my dear, splendid creature, do be sensible. There's mermaid's blood flowing in your veins. So go on, be a mermaid. Let yourself go for once in your life and fall madly in love with a river-god, dive head first into deep water and leave the learned professor and the rest of us gasping on the shore.

HELEN [*angrily*]. Leave me alone. How can you be so cruel? [*Makes to leave.*]

VOYNITSKY [*preventing her*]. Very well, my dear, forgive me. I'm sorry. [*Kisses her hand.*] Let's be friends.

HELEN. You'd try the patience of a saint, you know.

VOYNITSKY. I'll fetch you a bunch of roses as a peace offering. I got them for you this morning. Autumn roses, beautiful and sad—. [*Goes out.*]

SONYA. Autumn roses, beautiful and sad—. [*Both look out of the window.*]

HELEN. September already. How ever shall we get through the winter here? [*Pause.*] Where's the doctor?

SONYA. In Uncle Vanya's room, writing. I'm glad Uncle went out, I must talk to you.

HELEN. What about?

SONYA. What about? [*Puts her head on* HELEN'*s breast.*]

HELEN. There there, that'll do. [*Strokes her hair.*] There now.

SONYA. I'm not beautiful.

HELEN. You have lovely hair.

SONYA. No. [*Turns round and looks in the mirror.*] No. When a woman isn't beautiful, people always say, 'You have lovely eyes, you have lovely hair.' I've loved him for six years. I love him more than I loved my own mother. Every moment I seem to hear his voice or feel his hand in mine. I keep looking at the door, expecting him, thinking he's just going to come in and now, as you see, I'm always coming to you to talk about him. He visits us every day now, but he doesn't look at me, doesn't even see me. It's breaking my heart. There's no hope for me, no hope at all. [*Desperately.*] God, give me strength. I spent the whole night praying. I often go up to him, start talking to him, look into his eyes. I've no pride left, no self-control. Yesterday I couldn't help telling Uncle Vanya I was in love, and all the servants know. Everyone knows.

HELEN. Does he know?

SONYA. No. He doesn't even notice me.

HELEN [*thoughtfully*]. He's a strange man. I tell you what, let me talk to him. I'll be most discreet, I'll only drop a hint or two. [*Pause.*] Really, how much longer is this uncertainty to go on? Do let me.

[SONYA *nods.*]

HELEN. Well, that's settled. It won't be hard to find out whether he loves you or not. Now don't be embarrassed, my dear, don't worry, I'll question him so carefully he won't even notice. We only need to find out whether it's yes or no. [*Pause.*] If it's no he'd better stop coming here, don't you think?

[SONYA *nods.*]

HELEN. It'll be easier for you if you don't see him. Now we won't keep putting it off, we'll question him straight away. He was going to show me some maps. You go and tell him I want to see him.

SONYA [*very agitated*]. You will tell me the whole truth, won't you?

HELEN. Of course I will. It's always better to know the truth, however bad, or that's what I think. Better than not knowing, anyway. Depend on me, dear.

SONYA. Yes, yes, I'll say you want to see his maps. [*Starts to leave, then stops by the door.*] No, not knowing *is* better. At least there's still hope.

HELEN. What did you say?

SONYA. It doesn't matter. [*Goes out.*]

HELEN [*alone*]. There's nothing worse than knowing someone else's secret and not being able to help. [*Meditatively.*] He's not in love with her, that's obvious, but why shouldn't he marry her? She isn't beautiful, but for a country doctor at his time of life she'd make an excellent wife. She's such a clever girl, so kind and unspoilt. But no, that's not really the point at all. [*Pause.*] I understand the poor child so well. In the middle of all this ghastly boredom, where there are no real people, but just dim, grey shapes drifting round, where you hear nothing but vulgar trivialities, where no one does anything but eat, drink and sleep—*he* appears from time to time, so different from the others, so handsome, charming and fascinating, like a bright moon rising in the darkness. To fall under the spell of such a man, to forget everything—. I do believe I'm a little attracted myself. Yes, I'm bored when he's not about and here I am smiling as I think of him. And Uncle Vanya says I've mermaid's blood in my veins. 'Let yourself go for once in your life.' Well, and why not? Perhaps that would be the thing. Oh to fly away, free as a bird, away from you all, away from your sleepy faces and your talk, to forget that you so much as exist! But I'm such a coward, I'm so shy. My conscience would torment me. He comes here every day now. I can guess why, and I already feel guilty. I want to kneel down and cry and ask Sonya to forgive me.

ASTROV [*entering with map*]. Good afternoon. [*Shakes hands.*] You wanted to see these works of art?

HELEN. You did promise yesterday to show me some of your work. Can you spare the time?

ASTROV. Why, of course. [*Spreads the map on a card table and fixes it with drawing-pins.*] Where were you born?

HELEN [*helping him*]. In St. Petersburg.

ASTROV. And where were you educated?

HELEN. At the College of Music.

ASTROV. Then I don't suppose this will interest you.

HELEN. Why not? It's true I know nothing about country life, but I've read a great deal.

ASTROV. I have my own table in this house, in Voynitsky's room. When I'm worn out, absolutely dead beat, I drop everything, run along here and spend an hour or two amusing myself with this stuff. Voynitsky and Miss Serebryakov click away on their counting frame while I sit near by at my table messing about with my paints. It's warm and peaceful and the cricket chirps. But I don't allow myself this pleasure very often, only once a month. [*Pointing to the map.*] Now look at this. This gives a picture of our district as it was fifty years ago. Dark green and light green stand for woodlands, and half the entire area was wooded. Where I have this red cross-hatching over the green, that was the home of elk and wild goat. I show both flora and fauna. This lake here was the home of swans, geese and wild duck, and they made 'a powerful lot of birds', as the old peasants say, no end of them—whole clouds swarming overhead. Besides the villages and larger settlements there were, as you see, isolated hamlets all over the place, odd farmsteads, hermitages and watermills. There were lots of cattle and horses. Those are shown in blue. Do you see this area where there's such a lot of blue? There were any number of horses here, an average of three per household. [*Pause.*] Now let's look lower down and see what things were like twenty-five years ago. Here only a third of the area's under timber. There are no more wild goats, but there are still some elk. The green and blue colouring is less in evidence. And so it goes on, so it goes on. Now let's move on to part three, a picture of the district as it is today. There are odd bits of green here and there in patches, but no continuous stretches. The elk, swans and woodgrouse are no more. The old hamlets, farmsteads, hermitages and mills have vanished without trace. The general picture is one of a gradual and unmistakable decline, and it obviously needs only another ten or fifteen years to become complete. You'll tell me it's the influence of civilization, that the old life obviously had to make way for the new. All right, I see what you mean. If roads and railways had been built in place of the ravaged woodlands, if we had factories, workshops and schools, the peasants would have become healthier, better off and more intelligent. But you see, nothing of the sort has happened. Our district still has the same old swamps and mosquitoes, the same terrible roads, the same poverty, typhus, diphtheria, the same fires breaking out all over the place. The point is, everything's gone downhill because people have found the struggle for existence too much for them, because they're backward and ignorant, because they haven't the faintest idea what they're doing. Shivering with cold, hungry and ill, man wants to hang on to what's left of his life, wants to protect his children, and so he clutches instinctively and blindly at anything that might fill his belly and keep him warm. He destroys everything with no thought for the morrow. And now pretty well everything has been destroyed, but so far nothing new has been put in its place. [*Coldly.*] I can see this bores you.

HELEN. But I understand so little about these things.

ASTROV. It's not a question of understanding, you're just not interested.

HELEN. To be perfectly honest, I was thinking about something else. I'm sorry, I have to put you through a sort of cross-examination and I feel a bit embarrassed. I don't know how to begin.

ASTROV. A cross-examination?

HELEN. Yes, but—a fairly harmless one. Let's sit down. [*They sit down.*] It concerns a certain young person. Let's be honest with each other like good friends and come straight to the point. We'll talk it over and then forget about it. All right?

ASTROV. All right then.

HELEN. It's about my step-daughter Sonya. Do you like her?

ASTROV. Yes I do, I think very highly of her.

HELEN. Does she attract you as a woman?

ASTROV [*after a short pause*]. No.

HELEN. I've very nearly finished. Haven't you noticed anything?

ASTROV. No.

HELEN [*taking him by the arm*]. You don't love her, I can see it in your eyes. She's so unhappy. Do understand that and—stop coming here.

ASTROV [*standing up*]. I'm a bit past all that. I have too much to do anyway. [*Shrugs his shoulders.*] You know how busy I am. [*Is embarrassed.*]

HELEN. Really, what a disagreeable conversation. I'm so upset, I feel as if I'd been dragging a ton weight about. Anyway, thank heavens it's over. Let's forget it, let's pretend nothing's been said, and you—you go away. You're a sensible man, you can understand. [*Pause.*] It's even made me blush.

ASTROV. If you'd told me a month or two ago I might perhaps have considered it, but now—. [*Shrugs his shoulders.*] But if she's unhappy, then of course—. There is one thing I don't understand, though— why did you bring this business up at all? [*Looks into her eyes and wags a finger at her.*] You're quite a little box of tricks, aren't you?

HELEN. What do you mean?

ASTROV [*laughing*]. You've got it all worked out, haven't you? All
right, Sonya may be unhappy, I'll grant you that—but why interro-
gate me? [*Vigorously, preventing her from speaking.*] Now don't try
and look so surprised. You know perfectly well why I come here
every day. Why I come and who I come to see, that you know perfectly well. Don't look at me like that, you little vampire, I'm not
exactly new to this game.

HELEN [*bewildered*]. Vampire? I don't understand at all.

ASTROV. You beautiful furry little weasel. You must have your prey.
For a whole month I do nothing at all, let everything slide because
I simply have to see you. And you like that, don't you, oh yes
you like that very much indeed. Well now, what am I to say? I'm
conquered, as you very well knew without cross-examining me at
all. [*Folding his arms and bowing his head.*] I surrender. Come on,
eat me.

HELEN. You must be out of your mind.

ASTROV [*laughing through clenched teeth*]. Quite standoffish, aren't you?

HELEN. Oh, I'm not quite so bad or so despicable as you think, I can
tell you. [*Makes to leave.*]

ASTROV [*barring her way*]. I'll go away today, I won't come here any
more, but—. [*Takes her by the hand and looks around.*] Where can
I see you? Tell me quickly, where? Someone may come in, tell me
quickly. [*Passionately.*] You splendid, glorious creature. One kiss—
just let me kiss your hair, your fragrant hair.

HELEN. I do assure you that——

ASTROV [*preventing her from speaking*]. You assure me, do you? No
need for that. No need to say anything either. Oh, how beautiful
you are. What lovely hands! [*Kisses her hands.*]

HELEN. That's quite enough. Really! Go away. [*Withdraws her hands.*]
You're forgetting yourself.

ASTROV. But tell me, tell me, where can we meet tomorrow? [*Puts
his arm round her waist.*] You see, Helen, there's no getting away from
it, we must meet. [*Kisses her just as* VOYNITSKY *comes in with a bunch
of roses and stops near the door.*]

HELEN [*not seeing* VOYNITSKY]. Please let me go. Leave me alone.
[*Lays her head on* ASTROV'*s chest.*] No! [*Tries to get away.*]

ASTROV [*holding her by the waist*]. Come to the forest reservation to-morrow. Be there by two o'clock. You will come, won't you? For God's sake say you'll come.

HELEN [*seeing* VOYNITSKY]. Let me go. [*Goes towards the window in great agitation.*] This is dreadful.

VOYNITSKY [*puts the roses on a chair, then agitatedly wipes his face and neck with a handkerchief*]. Never mind, that is—. It doesn't matter.

ASTROV [*inwardly fuming*]. Today's weather, my dear Voynitsky, isn't bad at all. It was dull and looked like rain this morning, but now the sun's come out. It certainly has been a splendid autumn, and the winter corn isn't doing too badly. [*Rolls up the map.*] The trouble is, though, the days are drawing in. [*Goes out.*]

HELEN [*going quickly up to* VOYNITSKY]. You must do everything you can, everything in your power, to get my husband and me away from this place. And it must be today. Do you hear? Today!

VOYNITSKY [*wiping his face*]. What? Oh, yes—of course. Helen, I saw what happened, I——

HELEN [*excitedly*]. Do you hear what I say? I must get away from this place today.

[*Enter* SEREBRYAKOV, SONYA, TELEGIN *and* MARINA.]

TELEGIN. I'm a bit out of sorts myself, Professor, been poorly these last two days. Something the matter with my head, er——

SEREBRYAKOV. But where are the others? I hate this house. It's such a labyrinth, twenty-six enormous rooms with people wandering off in all directions so you can never find anyone. [*Rings.*] Ask my mother-in-law and my wife to come here.

HELEN. I *am* here.

SEREBRYAKOV. Ladies and gentlemen, pray be seated.

SONYA [*going up to* HELEN, *impatiently*]. What did he say?

HELEN. I'll tell you later.

SONYA. You're trembling, aren't you? You're quite upset. [*Looks inquiringly into her face.*] I see. He said he wouldn't be coming here again. Is that it? [*Pause.*] Tell me, is it that?

[HELEN *nods.*]

SEREBRYAKOV [*to* TELEGIN]. One can put up with ill health. What does it matter anyway? But what I can't stand is the whole pattern of country life. I feel as if I'd left the earth entirely and got stuck on some strange planet. Do sit down, everyone, please. Sonya! [SONYA *does not hear him, but stands sadly hanging her head.*] Sonya! [*Pause.*] She doesn't hear. [*To* MARINA.] And you sit down too, Nanny. [MARINA *sits down and knits a stocking.*] Now! Friends, ladies, gentlemen, lend me your ears, as the saying goes. [*Laughs.*]

VOYNITSKY [*agitated*]. You don't need me, do you? Do you mind if I go?

SEREBRYAKOV. Yes, I need you more than anyone else.

VOYNITSKY. What exactly do you require of me?

SEREBRYAKOV. 'Require of you'? But what are you so annoyed about? [*Pause.*] If I've offended you somehow, please forgive me.

VOYNITSKY. Oh, don't be so pompous and let's get down to business. What do you want?

[MRS. VOYNITSKY *comes in.*]

SEREBRYAKOV. Ah, here is Mother. Ladies and gentlemen, I'll begin. [*Pause.*] Ladies and gentlemen, I have invited you here to announce that a government inspector is on his way. Actually, joking apart, I do have something serious to say. I have gathered you all here to ask for your help and advice. And, aware as I am of your unfailing kindness, I trust I shall receive the same. I'm an academic person, a man of books, and I've always been out of my depth in practical affairs. I cannot manage without the guidance of competent persons, so I appeal to you, Vanya, to you, Mr. Telegin, and to you, Mother. The thing is that *manet omnes una nox.* In other words none of us is going to live for ever. I'm old and ill, so it seems to me high time to put my property and affairs in order in so far as they affect my family. My own life is over and I'm not thinking of myself, but I do have a young wife and an unmarried daughter. [*Pause.*] I simply cannot go on living in the country. We are not cut out for country life. But we can't live in town either on the income from this estate. Let's say we sell some of the timber—well, that's an abnormal measure which can't be repeated every year. We must find some procedure that guarantees us a constant, more or less stable income. Such a procedure has occurred to me and I have the honour to submit it for your consideration. I'll leave out the details and explain it in general terms. Our estate gives an average return of no more than two per cent on its capital value. I propose we sell it. If we invest the proceeds in securities we should get from four to five per cent on them and there may even be a few thousand roubles to spare, so that we can buy a cottage near St. Petersburg.

VOYNITSKY. Just a moment. My ears must be deceiving me. Say that again.

SEREBRYAKOV. Invest the money in securities and buy a cottage near St. Petersburg with what's left over.

VOYNITSKY. No, it wasn't the bit about St. Petersburg. It was something else you said.

SEREBRYAKOV. I propose selling the estate.

VOYNITSKY. Ah, that was it. You're going to sell the estate. Wonderful. A very bright idea. And what do you suggest my old mother and I should do with ourselves? And what about Sonya here?

SEREBRYAKOV. We'll discuss that all in good time. One can't do everything at once.

VOYNITSKY. Just a moment. It looks as if I've never had a scrap of ordinary common sense. Till now I've been stupid enough to think this estate belonged to Sonya. This estate was bought by my father as a dowry for my sister. So far I've been simple-minded enough to imagine that our laws weren't made in Turkey and I thought the estate had passed from my sister to Sonya.

SEREBRYAKOV. Yes, the estate does belong to Sonya. Nobody denies that. Without Sonya's consent I shouldn't venture to sell it. Besides, it's in the girl's own best interests that I propose to do so.

VOYNITSKY. But this is fantastic, utterly fantastic. Either I've gone stark, staring mad or—. Or else——

MRS. VOYNITSKY. Vanya dear, don't contradict Alexander. He knows better than we do what's right and what's wrong, believe me.

VOYNITSKY. Oh, give me some water. [*Drinks water.*] Say what you like then, I give up.

SEREBRYAKOV. I don't know why you're so worked up. I'm not claiming my scheme is ideal. If you all decide it's no good I shan't insist on it. [*Pause.*]

TELEGIN [*embarrassed*]. I revere scholarship, Professor, and even have a kind of family feeling for it. My brother Gregory's wife's brother, a Mr. Konstantin Lakedemonov—you may possibly know him—was a Master of Arts.

VOYNITSKY. One moment, Waffles, this is serious. Wait a bit, you can tell us later. [*To* SEREBRYAKOV.] Here, ask him. This estate was bought from his uncle.

SEREBRYAKOV. Oh indeed, and why should I ask him? Where would that lead us?

VOYNITSKY. This estate was bought for ninety-five thousand roubles as prices went in those days. My father paid only seventy thousand down and left twenty-five thousand on mortgage. Now listen to me. The estate would never have been bought at all if I hadn't given up my own share of the inheritance to my sister, whom I loved dearly. What's more, I slaved away for ten years and paid off the whole mortgage.

SEREBRYAKOV. I'm sorry I ever started this conversation.

VOYNITSKY. This estate is free from debt and in good order solely through my own personal efforts. And now I've grown old I'm to be pitched out of it neck and crop!

SEREBRYAKOV. I don't know what you're getting at.

VOYNITSKY. For twenty-five years I've run this estate. I've worked and sent the money to you. The best manager in the world couldn't have done more. And all this time you haven't thanked me once. All this time, when I was young and just the same today, I've been getting a salary of five hundred roubles a year from you—a miserable pittance! And not once has it occurred to you to give me a single extra rouble.

SEREBRYAKOV. But how was I to know, my dear man? I'm not a practical person, I don't understand these things. You could have helped yourself to as much as you liked, couldn't you?

VOYNITSKY. Why didn't I steal, you mean? Why don't you all despise me for not stealing? It would have been only fair if I had and I shouldn't be a pauper now.

MRS. VOYNITSKY [*sternly*]. Vanya!

TELEGIN [*agitatedly*]. Vanya, my dear chap, don't talk like this, for heaven's sake. I'm trembling all over. Why spoil good relations? [*Kisses him.*] Please don't.

VOYNITSKY. For twenty-five years I've been cooped up in this place with this mother of mine. All our thoughts and feelings were for you alone. In the daytime we talked of you and your writings, we were proud of you and worshipped the very sound of your name. And we wasted our nights reading books and journals that I now utterly despise.

TELEGIN. Oh stop it, Vanya, please, I can't stand this.

SEREBRYAKOV [*angrily*]. What are you driving at? That's what I don't see.

VOYNITSKY. We thought of you as a superior being and we knew your articles by heart. But now my eyes have been opened. Everything's perfectly clear. You write about art, but you haven't the faintest idea what art is all about. Your entire works, which once meant so much to me, aren't worth a brass farthing. You've made fools of us all.

SEREBRYAKOV. My friends, can't you stop him? Really! I'll go away.

HELEN. Vanya, I insist you keep quiet. Do you hear me?

VOYNITSKY. I will not keep quiet. [*Barring* SEREBRYAKOV'*s way.*] Wait, I haven't finished yet. You've ruined my life! I've not lived, not lived, I tell you. Thanks to you the best years of my life have been thrown down the drain. You are my worst enemy!

TELEGIN. I can't stand this, I really can't. I'm going. [*Goes out in terrible agitation.*]

SEREBRYAKOV. What do you want from me? And what right have you to talk to me like that? Nonentity! If the estate is yours take it. I don't want it.

HELEN. I'm getting out of this madhouse this instant. [*Shouting.*] I've had about as much as I can stand.

VOYNITSKY. My life's ruined. I'm gifted, intelligent, courageous. If I'd had a normal life I might have been a Schopenhauer or a Dostoyevsky. But I'm talking nonsense, I'm going mad. Mother dear, I'm desperate. Mother!

MRS. VOYNITSKY [*sternly*]. Do as Alexander says.

SONYA [*kneeling down in front of* MARINA *and pressing close to her*]. Nanny! Nanny, darling!

VOYNITSKY. Mother! What am I to do? Never mind, don't tell me. I know what to do all right. [*To* SEREBRYAKOV.] I'll give you something to remember me by! [*Goes out through centre door.*]

[MRS. VOYNITSKY *follows him.*]

SEREBRYAKOV. Really, everybody, what on earth is all this? Rid me of this maniac! I cannot live under the same roof with him. His room is here [*points to centre door*], almost next to mine. Let him move into the village, into a cottage in the grounds, or I'll move out myself, but I cannot stay in the same house.

HELEN [*to her husband*]. We're leaving this place today. We must arrange it at once.

SEREBRYAKOV. Utter nonentity!

SONYA [*kneeling, addresses her father excitedly through her tears*]. Do show some understanding, Father. Uncle Vanya and I are so unhappy. [*Trying to hold back her despair.*] You must be charitable. Remember, when you were younger Uncle Vanya and Grandmother used to translate books for you at night, copy out your papers—every night, every single night. Uncle Vanya and I worked without a moment's rest, afraid to spend anything on ourselves, and sent everything to you. We did earn our keep, you know. Oh, I'm not putting it the right way at all, but you've got to understand us, Father. You must show some sympathy.

HELEN [*very upset, to her husband*]. Alexander, for heaven's sake sort the thing out with him. Please!

SEREBRYAKOV. Very well, I'll talk to him then. I am not accusing him of anything and I am not angry, but you must admit his conduct is, to put it mildly, odd. All right then, I'll go and see him. [*Goes out through centre door.*]

HELEN. Be gentle with him, calm him down. [*Follows him out.*]

SONYA [*nestling up to* MARINA]. Nanny! Nanny, darling!

MARINA. It's all right, my child. The geese will cackle for a while and then they'll stop. They'll cackle a bit and then they'll stop their cackling.

SONYA. Nanny!

MARINA [*stroking her hair*]. You're shivering as if you'd been out in the cold. There there, my darling, God is merciful. A drink of lime-flower tea or some raspberry juice and it'll pass off. Don't grieve, my poor darling. [*Looking at the centre door, angrily.*] Dear me, the feathers are flying. A plague on those geese!

[*A shot off stage.* HELEN *is heard to scream.* SONYA *shudders.*]

MARINA. Oh, a curse upon you!

SEREBRYAKOV [*runs in, staggering and terrified*]. Stop him, stop him! He's gone mad!

[HELEN *and* VOYNITSKY *are seen struggling in the doorway.*]

HELEN [*trying to take the revolver from him*]. Give it to me. Give it to me, I tell you!

VOYNITSKY. Let me go, Helen. Let go of me. [*Frees himself, runs in and looks round for* SEREBRYAKOV.] Where is he? Ah, there he is. [*Fires at him.*] Bang! [*Pause.*] Missed him, did I? Missed him again, eh? [*Angrily.*] Oh, hell, hell! Hell and damnation! [*Bangs the revolver on the floor and sinks exhausted in a chair.* SEREBRYAKOV *looks stunned.* HELEN *leans against a wall almost fainting.*]

HELEN. Get me away from here. Take me away, I don't care if you kill me, but I can't stay here. I can't.

VOYNITSKY [*desperately*]. Oh, what am I doing? What am I doing?

SONYA [*quietly*]. Nanny darling! Nanny!

CURTAIN

ACT FOUR

VOYNITSKY's *room, which serves as his bedroom and the estate office. Near the window is a large table covered with ledgers and various papers, also a bureau, cupboards and a pair of scales. There is a smaller table for* ASTROV *with drawing materials and paints on it. Near them a portfolio. A cage containing a starling. On the wall hangs a map of Africa which is obviously quite out of place here. A huge sofa upholstered in American cloth. A door, left, leading to the rest of the house. A door, right, into the hall. Near the door, right, is a mat for the peasants to wipe their boots on.*

It is an autumn evening and very quiet.

TELEGIN *and* MARINA *sit facing each other, winding wool.*

TELEGIN. Hurry up, Marina, they'll be calling us to say good-bye soon. They've already ordered their carriage.

MARINA [*tries to wind more quickly*]. There's not much wool left.

TELEGIN. They're going to Kharkov, going to live there.

MARINA. A good thing too.

TELEGIN. They've properly got the wind up. There's Mrs. Serebryakov. 'I won't spend another hour in this place,' says she. 'We'll go away altogether,' she says. 'We'll go to Kharkov for a bit and have a look round, then send for our things.' They're not taking much with them. So they're not going to live here after all, Marina, so that's how things have worked out. Such are the dictates of destiny.

MARINA. And a good thing too. The row they made this afternoon and all that shooting, a thorough disgrace I call it.

TELEGIN. Yes, it was a subject worthy of the brush of Ayvazovsky.

MARINA. It was no sight for my old eyes. [*Pause.*] We'll go back to our old way of doing things, with breakfast at eight o'clock and dinner at one. And we'll sit down to supper in the evenings. We'll do everything properly like other self-respecting people, in a decent Christian manner. [*With a sigh.*] I haven't tasted noodles for ages, old sinner that I am.

TELEGIN. Yes, it's quite a while since noodles were cooked in this house. [*Pause.*] Quite a while. I was going through the village this morning, Marina, and a shopkeeper shouted after me, 'Hey there, you useless scrounger!' It quite upset me, I can tell you.

MARINA. Don't take any notice, my dear. In God's eyes we're all scroungers. You and Sonya and Mr. Voynitsky are all the same. You none of you sit around doing nothing. All of us work. Where's Sonya?

TELEGIN. In the garden with the doctor. They're looking for Vanya, they're afraid he might do himself an injury.

MARINA. But where's his pistol?

TELEGIN [*in a whisper*]. I hid it in the cellar.

MARINA [*with a grin*]. What a business!

[VOYNITSKY *and* ASTROV *come in from outside*.]

VOYNITSKY. Leave me alone. [*To* MARINA *and* TELEGIN.] Go away. Can't you leave me alone for a single hour? I'm fed up with people watching me.

TELEGIN. All right then, Vanya. [*Creeps away*.]

MARINA. You old gander. Cackle, cackle, cackle! [*Picks up her wool and goes out*.]

VOYNITSKY. Leave me alone.

ASTROV. With the greatest pleasure. I ought to have gone long ago, but I tell you once more, I shan't leave till you give me back what you took from me.

VOYNITSKY. I haven't taken anything from you.

ASTROV. I mean what I say. Don't keep me waiting, please. I should have left ages ago.

VOYNITSKY. I didn't take anything from you. [*Both sit down*.]

ASTROV. Oh no? Right, I'll give you a bit longer, and then I'm sorry, but we'll have to use force. We shall tie you up and search you. I mean what I say, I can tell you.

VOYNITSKY. Have it your own way. [*Pause*.] How could I be such a fool—fire twice and miss both times? I'll never forgive myself.

ASTROV. If you were so keen on shooting someone why didn't you blow your own brains out?

VOYNITSKY [*shrugging his shoulders*]. It's very funny. I've just tried to murder somebody, but no one thinks of arresting me or putting me on trial. So they must think I'm mad. [*Laughs unpleasantly.*] I'm a madman. But those who dress themselves up as professors and learned pundits, so people can't see how cheap, stupid and utterly callous they are—they aren't mad at all. And women who marry old men and openly deceive them, they aren't mad either. I saw you. I saw you kissing her.

ASTROV. Yes. I did kiss her, and my answer to you, sir, is this. [*Thumbs his nose.*]

VOYNITSKY [*looking at the door*]. No, it's the earth itself which must be mad for still putting up with you.

ASTROV. That's a stupid thing to say.

VOYNITSKY. What of it? I'm mad, aren't I? I'm not responsible for my actions, so I have the right to say stupid things.

ASTROV. That line's as old as the hills. You're no madman, you just have no sense. You're an old clown. I used to think anyone like that was ill and abnormal, but my view now is that having no sense is man's normal condition. You're perfectly normal.

VOYNITSKY [*hiding his head in his hands*]. I'm ashamed of myself, so ashamed, if you did but know. This feeling of shame, it hurts so much. It's worse than any pain. [*With anguish.*] I can't stand it. [*Bends over the table.*] What am I to do? What am I to do?

ASTROV. Nothing.

VOYNITSKY. Give me some medicine or something. Oh my God, I'm forty-seven. Suppose I live to be sixty, that means I have still thirteen years to go. It's too long. How am I to get through those thirteen years? What am I to do? How do I fill the time? Oh, can you think—? [*Feverishly clutches ASTROV's arm.*] Can you think what it would be like to live the rest of one's life in a new way? Oh, to wake up some fine, clear morning feeling as if you'd started living all over again, as if the past was all forgotten, gone like a puff of smoke. [*Weeps.*] To begin a new life—. Tell me, how should I begin? Where do I start?

ASTROV [*annoyed*]. Oh, get away with you. New life indeed. Our situation's hopeless, yours and mine.

VOYNITSKY. Is it?

ASTROV. I'm perfectly certain of it.

VOYNITSKY. Please give me something. [*Pointing to his heart.*] I've a burning feeling here.

ASTROV [*shouts angrily*]. Oh, shut up! [*More gently.*] Those who live a century or two after us and despise us for leading lives so stupid and tasteless, perhaps they'll find a way to be happy, but as for us—. There's only one hope for you and me, that when we're resting in our graves we may have visions. Even pleasant ones perhaps. [*Sighs.*] Yes, my dear fellow. In our whole district there were only two decent, civilized people—you and I. But ten years or so of this contemptible, parochial existence have completely got us down. This filthy atmosphere has poisoned our blood and we've become as second-rate as the rest of them. [*Vigorously.*] Anyhow, don't you try and talk your way out of it. You give me back what you took.

VOYNITSKY. I didn't take anything.

ASTROV. You took a small bottle of morphia out of my medical case. [*Pause.*] Look here, if you're so terribly keen on doing yourself in, why not go into the woods and blow your brains out there? But do give me back that morphia or people will start talking and putting two and two together and they'll end up thinking I gave it you. It'll be quite bad enough having to do the post mortem. You don't suppose that will be exactly fun, do you?

[SONYA *comes in.*]

VOYNITSKY. Leave me alone.

ASTROV [*to* SONYA]. Sonya, your uncle has taken a bottle of morphia from my case and he won't give it back. Tell him that this is—well, not particularly bright of him. Besides, I'm in a hurry, I ought to be off.

SONYA. Uncle Vanya, did you take the morphia? [*Pause.*]

ASTROV. He took it all right.

SONYA. Give it back. Why frighten us like this? [*Affectionately.*] Give it back, Uncle Vanya. I daresay I'm no less unhappy than you, but I don't give way to despair. I put up with things patiently and that's how I mean to go on till my life comes to its natural end. You must be patient as well. [*Pause.*] Give it back. [*Kisses his hands.*] Uncle, darling Uncle, do give it back. [*Weeps.*] You're kind, you'll have pity on us and give it back. You must be patient, Uncle. Please.

VOYNITSKY [*gets the bottle from the table drawer and gives it to* ASTROV]. There you are, take it. [*To* SONYA.] But we must hurry up and start work, we must do something quickly, or else I just can't carry on.

SONYA. Yes, yes, we'll do some work. As soon as we've seen the others off we'll get down to work. [*Agitatedly moves some papers about on the table.*] We've let everything go here.

ASTROV [*puts the bottle in his case and tightens the straps*]. Now I can be on my way.

HELEN [*comes in*]. Vanya, are you here? We're just leaving. Go and see Alexander, he wants a word with you.

SONYA. Come on, Uncle Vanya. [*Takes* VOYNITSKY *by the arm.*] Come with me. You and Father must make it up and be friends, you really must.

[SONYA *and* VOYNITSKY *go out.*]

HELEN. I'm just leaving. [*Gives her hand to* ASTROV.] Good-bye.

ASTROV. So soon?

HELEN. The carriage is at the door.

ASTROV. Good-bye then.

HELEN. This afternoon you promised me you'd go away.

ASTROV. I haven't forgotten. And I'm just off. [*Pause.*] Got cold feet, have you? [*Takes her by the hand.*] Are you really quite so scared?

HELEN. Yes, I am.

ASTROV. Why not stay on after all? How about it? Tomorrow at the forest reservation——

HELEN. No. It's all settled. And that's why I can look you in the face now, just because we definitely *are* leaving. One thing I do ask you, don't think too badly of me. I'd like to feel you respected me.

ASTROV. Oh, really! [*Makes an impatient gesture.*] Do stay, please. You have nothing in the world to do, you may as well admit it—no object in life, nothing to occupy your mind—and sooner or later your feelings are going to be too much for you, that's bound to happen. Well, it would be a lot better for it to happen here in the depths of the country than in Kharkov or Kursk or somewhere like that. At least this is a romantic sort of place and it's even beautiful in autumn. We've the forest reservation and tumble-down country houses and gardens like those in Turgenev.

HELEN. You really are absurd. I'm angry with you, but all the same—I shall remember you with pleasure. You're an interesting man, you're different somehow. We shall never meet again, you and I, so—I may as well admit it—I did find you rather attractive, actually. Let's shake hands then and part as friends. No hard feelings.

ASTROV [*after shaking hands*]. Yes, you'd better leave. [*Thoughtfully.*] You're quite a decent, sensitive person in your way, but everything about you seems odd somehow. No sooner do you and your husband turn up in this place than people here who were getting on with their work, all busy creating something, have to drop everything and do nothing all summer but attend to you and your husband's gout. You two have infected us all with your idleness. I've been under your spell and I've done nothing for a whole month while all the time people have been falling ill and the villagers have been grazing their cattle in my newly-planted woods. So you see, you and your husband bring havoc wherever you go. I'm joking of course, but still—it is odd. And I'm quite sure of this. If you'd stayed on here we'd have had a full-scale disaster on our hands. It would have been the end of me and you wouldn't have come out of it too well either. All right then, off with you. The show is over.

HELEN [*takes a pencil from his table and quickly hides it*]. I'm taking this pencil to remember you by.

ASTROV. It's strange somehow. We've been friends and now suddenly for no good reason we shall never meet again. It's the way things happen in this world. Before anyone comes in, before Uncle Vanya turns up with his bunch of flowers, allow me—to kiss you goodbye. May I? [*Kisses her cheek.*] Well, there you are. And very nice too.

HELEN. I wish you every happiness. [*Looks round.*] Oh, all right then, just for once in a lifetime. [*Embraces him impulsively, after which they quickly move away from each other.*] I must go.

ASTROV. Hurry up and go then. If the carriage is ready you'd better be off.

HELEN. I think someone's coming. [*Both listen.*]

ASTROV. The show is over.

[*Enter* SEREBRYAKOV, VOYNITSKY, MRS. VOYNITSKY *carrying a book*, TELEGIN *and* SONYA.]

SEREBRYAKOV [*to* VOYNITSKY]. We'll let bygones be bygones. So much has happened and I've been through so much and thought so many thoughts these last few hours, I could probably write a whole treatise on the art of living for the benefit of posterity. I gladly accept your apologies and beg you to accept mine. Good-bye. [*He and* VOYNITSKY *kiss each other three times.*]

VOYNITSKY. You'll be receiving a regular amount as before. Everything will be just as it was.

[HELEN *embraces* SONYA.]

SEREBRYAKOV [*kissing* MRS. VOYNITSKY'*s hand*]. Mother——.

MRS. VOYNITSKY [*kissing him*]. Do have your photograph taken again, Alexander, and send me it. You know how fond I am of you.

TELEGIN. Good-bye, sir. Think of us sometimes.

SEREBRYAKOV [*kisses his daughter*]. Good-bye. Good-bye, all. [*Shaking hands with* ASTROV.] Thank you for the pleasure of your company. I respect your way of thinking, your enthusiasm and your eager impulses, but permit an old man to include one suggestion among his farewell wishes. You should get down to work, gentlemen. What we need is a bit of action. [*Everyone bows.*] I wish you all the best. [*Goes out followed by* MRS. VOYNITSKY *and* SONYA.]

VOYNITSKY [*kisses* HELEN'*s hand with great feeling*]. Good-bye. Forgive me. We shall never meet again.

HELEN [*very touched*]. Good-bye, Vanya. [*Kisses him on the head and goes out.*]

ASTROV [*to* TELEGIN]. Waffles, would you mind telling them to bring my carriage round as well while they're about it?

TELEGIN. At your service, old man. [*Goes out.*]

[*Only* ASTROV *and* VOYNITSKY *are left.*]

ASTROV [*removes his paints from the table and puts them in a suitcase*]. Why don't you go and see them off?

VOYNITSKY. Let them go, I—. It's all a bit too much for me. I feel so depressed. I must get down to work quickly. To work then. Must work. [*Rummages among the papers on the table.*]

[*Pause. Harness bells can be heard.*]

ASTROV. They've gone. I bet the professor's pleased. You won't catch him coming back here in a hurry.

MARINA [*coming in*]. They've gone. [*Sits in an armchair and knits a sock.*]

SONYA [*coming in*]. They've gone. [*Wipes her eyes.*] I hope to God they'll be all right. [*To her uncle.*] Well, Uncle Vanya, how about getting down to something?

VOYNITSKY. Work—must work.

SONYA. It's ages since we sat at this table together. [*Lights the lamp on the table.*] There doesn't seem to be any ink. [*Takes the inkstand, goes to the cupboard and fills it with ink.*] I feel so sad now they've gone.

MRS. VOYNITSKY [*coming in slowly*]. They've gone. [*Sits down and becomes absorbed in her reading.*]

SONYA [*sitting down at the table and turning the leaves of a ledger*]. First we'll make out the accounts, Uncle Vanya. We really have let things slide. Today someone sent for his account again. Start writing. You do one lot and I'll do another.

VOYNITSKY [*writing*]. To the account—of Mr. —. [*Both write silently.*]

MARINA [*yawning*]. Well, I'm ready for bed.

ASTROV. How quiet it is. Pens scratching, the cricket chirping. It's warm and cosy, I don't feel like leaving. [*Harness bells can be heard.*] Ah, there's my carriage. So it remains for me to say good-bye to you, my friends, to say good-bye to my table and—be off. [*Puts his maps in the portfolio.*]

MARINA. What's the great rush? Why not stay on a bit longer?

ASTROV. I can't.

VOYNITSKY [*writing*]. And two roubles seventy-five brought forward from your previous account——

[*The LABOURER comes in.*]

LABOURER. Your carriage is ready, Doctor.

ASTROV. I heard it. [*Hands him the medicine case, suitcase and portfolio.*] Here, take these things. And mind you don't squash the portfolio.

LABOURER. Very good, sir. [*Goes out.*]

ASTROV. Well now—. [*Comes forward to say good-bye.*]

SONYA. When shall we see you again?

ASTROV. Probably not before next summer. Not this winter, I imagine. If anything happens of course, let me know and I'll come over. [*Shakes hands.*] Thanks for all your hospitality and kindness—for everything in fact. [*Goes up to* MARINA *and kisses her on the head.*] Good-bye, old girl.

MARINA. You're not going off without any tea?

ASTROV. I don't want any, Nanny.

MARINA. A little vodka then?

ASTROV [*hesitantly*]. Well, perhaps——.

[MARINA *goes out.*]

ASTROV [*after a pause*]. My trace horse has gone a bit lame. I noticed it yesterday when Petrushka was taking him to water.

VOYNITSKY. You'll have to get him reshod.

ASTROV. I'd better call at the blacksmith's in Rozhdestvennoye. There's nothing else for it. [*Goes up to the map of Africa and looks at it.*] Down there in Africa the heat must be quite something. Terrific!

VOYNITSKY. Very probably.

MARINA [*returning with a glass of vodka and a piece of bread on a tray*]. Here you are.

[ASTROV *drinks the vodka.*]

MARINA. Your health, my dear. [*Bows low.*] Why not have a little bread with it?

ASTROV. No, it'll do as it is. All the best to you then. [*To* MARINA.] Don't bother to see me to the door, Nanny, there's no need.

[*He goes out.* SONYA *goes after him with a candle to see him off.* MARINA *sits down in her armchair.*]

VOYNITSKY [*writing*]. February second, three gallons of linseed oil—. February sixteenth, another three gallons of linseed oil—. Buckwheat—. [*Pause.*]

[*Harness bells are heard.*]

MARINA. He's gone.

[*Pause.*]

SONYA [*returning, puts the candle on the table*]. He's gone.

VOYNITSKY [*making a calculation on the counting frame and writing it down*]. That makes—fifteen—twenty-five.

[SONYA *sits down and writes.*]

MARINA [*yawns*]. Oh dearie me.

[TELEGIN *comes in on tip-toe, sits down near the door and quietly tunes his guitar.*]

VOYNITSKY [*to* SONYA, *running his hand over her hair*]. I'm so depressed, Sonya, you can't think how depressed I feel.

SONYA. Well, it can't be helped. Life must go on. [*Pause.*] And our life will go on, Uncle Vanya. We shall live through a long succession of days and endless evenings. We shall bear patiently the trials fate has in store for us. We shall work for others—now and in our old age—never knowing any peace. And when our time comes we shall die without complaining. In the world beyond the grave we shall say that we wept and suffered, that our lot was harsh and bitter, and God will have pity on us. And you and I, Uncle dear, shall behold a life which is bright and beautiful and splendid. We shall rejoice and look back on our present misfortunes with feelings of tenderness, with a smile. And we shall find peace. We shall, Uncle, I believe it with all my heart and soul. [*Kneels down in front of him and places her head on his hands, continuing in a tired voice.*] We shall find peace.

[TELEGIN *quietly plays the guitar.*]

SONYA. We shall find peace. We shall hear the angels, we shall see the sky sparkling with diamonds. We shall see all the evils of this life, all our own sufferings, vanish in the flood of mercy which will fill the whole world. And then our life will be calm and gentle, sweet as a caress. I believe that, I do believe it. [*Wipes away his tears with a handkerchief.*] Poor, poor Uncle Vanya, you're crying. [*Through tears.*] There's been no happiness in your life, but wait, Uncle Vanya, wait. We shall find peace. [*Embraces him.*] We shall find peace.

[*The watchman taps.*]

[TELEGIN *quietly strums.* MRS. VOYNITSKY *writes something in the margin of her pamphlet.* MARINA *knits her stocking.*]

SONYA. We shall find peace.

THE CURTAIN SLOWLY FALLS

THREE SISTERS

[*Три сестры*]

A DRAMA IN FOUR ACTS

(1900–1901)

CHARACTERS

ANDREW PROZOROV

NATASHA, his fiancée, later his wife

OLGA ⎫
MASHA ⎬ his sisters
IRINA ⎭

THEODORE KULYGIN, a schoolmaster, Masha's husband

ALEXANDER VERSHININ, a lieutenant-colonel and battery commander

BARON NICHOLAS TUZENBAKH, a lieutenant

CAPTAIN VASILY SOLYONY

IVAN CHEBUTYKIN, an army doctor

ALEKSEY FEDOTIK, a second lieutenant

VLADIMIR RODÉ, a second lieutenant

FERAPONT, a caretaker at the county council offices, an old man

ANFISA, an old nurse, aged 80

The action takes place in a county town

ACT ONE

The PROZOROVS' *house. A drawing-room with columns beyond which a ballroom can be seen. Midday. Outside the sun is shining cheerfully. A table in the ballroom is being laid for lunch.*

OLGA, *wearing the regulation dark-blue dress of a high-school teacher, carries on correcting her pupils' exercise books, standing up or walking about the room.* MASHA, *in a black dress, sits with her hat on her lap reading a book.* IRINA, *in a white dress, stands lost in thought.*

OLGA. It's exactly a year ago today since Father died—on the fifth of May, your name-day, Irina. It was very cold then, and snowing. I thought I'd never get over it and you actually passed out, fainted right away. But now a year's gone by and we don't mind talking about it any more. You're wearing white again and you look radiant. [*The clock strikes twelve.*] The clock struck twelve then too. [*Pause.*] I remember the band playing when they took Father to the cemetery, and they fired a salute. He was a general, commanded a brigade. All the same, not many people came—it was a wet day of course, with heavy rain and sleet.

IRINA. Why bring up old memories?

[BARON TUZENBAKH, CHEBUTYKIN *and* SOLYONY *appear beyond the columns near the table in the ballroom.*]

OLGA. It's warm today and we can have the windows wide open, but the birch trees aren't in leaf yet. It's eleven years now since Father got his brigade and we all left Moscow. I remember it so well. It was early May, as it is now, and in Moscow everything was in blossom, it was warm and there was sunshine everywhere. Eleven years ago, but I remember it all as though we'd only left yesterday. Heavens, how marvellous! When I woke up this morning and saw the great blaze of light and knew that spring had come—I felt so happy and excited, I felt I just had to go back home to Moscow.

CHEBUTYKIN [*to* SOLYONY *and* TUZENBAKH]. Not a chance in hell.

TUZENBAKH. Absolute nonsense of course.

[MASHA, *absorbed in her reading, softly whistles a tune.*]

OLGA. Do stop whistling, Masha. Really! [*Pause.*] Being at school every day and then giving lessons till late in the evening, I'm always having headaches and the things that run through my mind—why, I might be an old woman already. And it's true that these four years I've been at the high school, I've felt my youth and energy draining away drop by drop each day. Only one thing grows stronger and stronger, a certain longing——

IRINA. To go to Moscow, to sell the house, have done with everything here and go to Moscow.

OLGA. Yes, to Moscow! As soon as we can.

[CHEBUTYKIN *and* TUZENBAKH *laugh.*]

IRINA. Andrew's probably going to be a professor and he won't live here anyway. There's nothing stopping us except poor Masha here.

OLGA. Masha can come and spend the whole summer in Moscow every year.

[MASHA *softly whistles a tune.*]

IRINA. I only pray it will work out all right. [*Looks out of the window.*] What a marvellous day! I'm in such a good mood, I don't know why. This morning I remembered it was my name-day and I suddenly felt happy, I remembered when we were children and Mother was still alive. And such wonderful thoughts passed through my head, I felt so excited.

OLGA. You're perfectly radiant today, I've never seen you look so beautiful. Masha's beautiful too. Andrew wouldn't be bad-looking either, only he's put on so much weight and it doesn't suit him. But I've aged and grown terribly thin—because I'm always losing my temper with the girls at school, I suppose. Now I have the day off, I'm here at home, my headache's gone and I feel younger than I did yesterday. I'm twenty-eight, that's all. God's in his heaven, all's right with the world, but I think if I got married and stayed at home all day it might be even better. [*Pause.*] I'd love my husband.

TUZENBAKH [*to* SOLYONY]. You talk such nonsense, I'm tired of listening to you. [*Comes into the drawing-room.*] Oh, I forgot to tell you—do you know who's going to call on you today? Our new battery commander, Vershinin. [*Sits down at the piano.*]

OLGA. Oh, is he? How nice.

IRINA. Is he old?

TUZENBAKH. No, not really. Forty or forty-five at the most. [*Plays softly.*] Seems a good chap. He's no fool, you can take my word for it, only he does talk rather a lot.

IRINA. Is he an interesting man?

TUZENBAKH. Oh, he's all right, but he has a wife and mother-in-law and two little girls—his second wife, by the way. He goes round calling on people and tells everyone he has a wife and two little girls. He'll tell you the same thing. His wife's not quite all there, she has a long pigtail like a school-girl and her conversation's rather up in the air, lot of philosophical stuff. And then she tries to commit suicide every so often, obviously just to annoy her husband. I'd have left a woman like that long ago, but he puts up with it and just goes round feeling sorry for himself.

SOLYONY [*comes into the drawing-room from the ballroom with* CHE-BUTYKIN]. With one hand I can only lift half a hundredweight, but if I use both hands I can lift two or even two-and-a-half hundred-weight. From which I conclude that two men aren't just twice as strong as one, but three times as strong, if not more.

CHEBUTYKIN [*reading a newspaper as he comes in*]. If your hair starts falling out, take two drams of naphthalene to half a bottle of spirit. To be dissolved and applied daily—. [*Writes in his notebook.*] Must note that down. [*To* SOLYONY.] Well, as I was saying, you cork up the bottle and you have a little glass tube running through it. Then you take a pinch of ordinary, common-or-garden powdered alum——

IRINA. Doctor, Doctor, dearest Doctor!

CHEBUTYKIN. What is it, my precious?

IRINA. Tell me, why am I so happy today? I feel as if I was sailing along with a great blue sky above me and huge white birds soaring about. Tell me, why?

CHEBUTYKIN [*kisses both her hands, tenderly*]. You're like a white bird yourself, my dear.

IRINA. Today I woke up, got out of bed and had a wash. And then I suddenly felt as if everything in the world made sense, I seemed to know how to live. I know everything, dearest Doctor. Man should work and toil by the sweat of his brow, whoever he is—that's the whole purpose and meaning of his life, his happiness and his joy.

How wonderful to be a workman who gets up at dawn and breaks stones in the road, or a shepherd, or a schoolmaster who teaches children or an engine-driver. Heavens, better not be a human being at all—better be an ox or just a horse, so long as you can work, rather than the kind of young woman who wakes up at noon, has her coffee in bed and then spends two hours getting dressed. Oh, that's so awful. You know how you sometimes long for a drink on a hot day—well that's how I long to work. And if I don't start getting up early and working you must stop being my friend, Doctor.

CHEBUTYKIN [*affectionately*]. I will, I will.

OLGA. Father taught us to get up at seven o'clock. Now Irina wakes at seven and lies in bed at least till nine, just thinking. And looks so serious too. [*Laughs.*]

IRINA. You're so used to seeing me as a little girl, you think it's funny when I look serious. I am twenty, you know.

TUZENBAKH. This great urge to work, heavens, how well I understand it. I've never done a hand's turn all my life. I was born in St. Petersburg—that bleak, idle place—and grew up in a family that never knew the meaning of work or worry. I remember how I used to come home from my cadet school. The footman would pull off my boots while I'd make a thorough nuisance of myself, watched by my mother who thought I was just wonderful and couldn't see why others took a rather different view. They tried to protect me from work. Only I doubt if their protection is going to prove all that effective. I doubt it. The time has come, an avalanche is moving down on us and a great storm's brewing that'll do us all a power of good. It's practically on top of us already and soon it's going to blast out of our society all the laziness, complacency, contempt for work, rottenness and boredom. I'm going to work and in twenty-five or thirty years' time everyone will work. Everyone.

CHEBUTYKIN. Well, I shan't for one.

TUZENBAKH. You don't count.

SOLYONY. In twenty-five years you won't be here at all, thank God. In a couple of years or so you'll have a stroke and die or I'll lose my temper and put a bullet through your head, my good friend. [*Takes a bottle of scent from his pocket and sprinkles his chest and hands.*]

CHEBUTYKIN [*laughs*]. You know, I've never done a thing and that's a fact. Since I left the university I haven't lifted a finger, I've never even read a book. I've read nothing but newspapers. [*Takes another newspaper out of his pocket.*] See what I mean? I know from newspapers that there was someone called Dobrolyubov, for instance, but what the fellow wrote I've no idea. I can't say I greatly care either. [*There is a banging on the floor from below.*] Aha! They want me down there, someone must have come to see me. I'll be with you in a moment. Just a second. [*Hurries out combing his beard.*]

IRINA. He's up to something.

TUZENBAKH. That's right. He went out looking terribly solemn, he's obviously going to bring you a present.

IRINA. How dreadful.

OLGA. Yes, isn't it awful? He's always playing these stupid tricks.

MASHA.   'A green oak by a curving shore,
       And on that oak a chain of gold—
       And on that oak a chain of gold.'
       [*Stands up and hums quietly.*]

OLGA. You're not very cheerful today, Masha.

[MASHA, *humming, puts on her hat.*]

OLGA. Where are you going?

MASHA. Home.

IRINA. That's a bit odd, isn't it?

TUZENBAKH. What! Leaving your sister's party?

MASHA. It doesn't matter, I'll be back this evening. Good-bye, darling. [*Kisses* IRINA.] Once again, many happy returns. In the old days when Father was alive there'd be thirty or forty officers at our parties and it was all great fun, but today there's only one man and a boy and the place is like a graveyard. I must go—I'm down in the dumps today, I feel so depressed, so don't you listen to me. [*Laughing through her tears.*] We'll talk later, but good-bye for now, darling. I'll go out somewhere.

IRINA [*displeased*]. Why, what's the matter with you?

OLGA [*crying*]. I know how you feel, Masha.

SOLYONY. When a man starts philosophizing that's what's termed philosophistics or just plain sophistics, but when a woman or a couple of women start doing it then it's just a case of them talking through their hats.

MASHA. What do you mean by that, you terrible, terrible man?

SOLYONY. Never mind.
'Before he'd time to turn a hair
He'd been knocked over by a bear.' [*Pause.*]

MASHA [*to* OLGA, *angrily*]. Oh, stop that crying!

[*Enter* ANFISA *and* FERAPONT *with a large cake.*]

ANFISA. In here, old fellow. Come in, your boots aren't dirty. [*To* IRINA.] This is from the county council offices. Mr. Michael Protopopov sent it. A cake.

IRINA. Thank you. Please thank him. [*Accepts the cake.*]

FERAPONT. Eh?

IRINA [*in a louder voice*]. Will you please thank him?

OLGA. Nanny dear, give him some cake. You can go, Ferapont, you'll get a piece of cake out there.

FERAPONT. Eh?

ANFISA. Come on, Ferapont. Come on, old fellow.

[*Goes out with* FERAPONT.]

MASHA. I don't like that Protopopov—Michael or Matthew or whatever he calls himself. We shouldn't ask him here.

IRINA. I didn't ask him.

MASHA. Well, I'm glad to hear that.

[CHEBUTYKIN *comes in followed by a* SOLDIER *carrying a silver samovar. There is a buzz of astonishment and displeasure.*]

OLGA [*covers her face with her hands*]. A samovar! How frightful!

[*Goes off towards the table in the ballroom.*]

IRINA. My dear good Dr. Chebutykin, how could you?

TUZENBAKH [*laughs*]. What did I say?

MASHA. You ought to be thoroughly ashamed of yourself.

CHEBUTYKIN. My darling girls, I've no one else but you, you're more precious to me than anything in the world. I'll soon be sixty and I'm an old man, a lonely, insignificant old man. My love for you is the only good thing about me and if it wasn't for you I'd have departed this life long ago. [*To* IRINA.] I've known you since the day you were born, dear child, I used to hold you in my arms. And I loved your mother, God rest her soul.

IRINA. But why these expensive presents?

CHEBUTYKIN [*through tears, angrily*]. Expensive presents! Oh, get away with you! [*To the* SOLDIER.] Take the samovar in there. [*Mocking her.*] Expensive presents! [*The* SOLDIER *takes the samovar into the ballroom.*]

ANFISA [*on her way through the drawing-room*]. My dears, a colonel's just arrived, someone we don't know. He's taken his coat off, girls, and he's on his way in here. Irina dear, mind you're nice and polite to him. [*Going out.*] You should have started lunch long ago, goodness me you should.

TUZENBAKH. Must be Vershinin.

[VERSHININ *comes in.*]

TUZENBAKH. Lieutenant-Colonel Vershinin.

VERSHININ [*to* MASHA *and* IRINA]. May I introduce myself? I'm Vershinin. Delighted, absolutely delighted to be here at last. Well, you *have* grown up and no mistake.

IRINA. Please sit down. This is a great pleasure.

VERSHININ [*gaily*]. I'm more pleased than I can say, I really am. But there should be three of you sisters. I remember three little girls. Can't remember your faces, but that your father, Colonel Prozorov, had three little girls I remember quite clearly, saw you with my own eyes. How times flies, dear me, how time does fly.

TUZENBAKH. The Colonel comes from Moscow.

IRINA. From Moscow? You come from Moscow?

VERSHININ. Yes, I do. Your father was battery commander there and I served in the same brigade. [*To* MASHA.] Now I think I do just remember your face.

MASHA. I don't remember you, I'm afraid.

IRINA. Olga! Olga! [*Shouts into the ballroom.*] Olga, do come here. [OLGA *comes into the drawing-room from the ballroom.*]

IRINA. We've just heard that Colonel Vershinin comes from Moscow.

VERSHININ. You must be Olga Prozorov, the eldest. You're Masha. And you'll be Irina, the youngest.

OLGA. Do you come from Moscow?

VERSHININ. Yes. I was at school in Moscow and that's where I joined the service. I was stationed there for a long time and ended up getting a battery here and moving here, as you see. I don't really remember you actually, I only remember there were three sisters. I remember your father all right, I only have to close my eyes to see him just as he was. I used to visit you in Moscow.

OLGA. I thought I remembered everyone, and now suddenly——

VERSHININ. My name is Vershinin.

IRINA. Colonel Vershinin, you're from Moscow. That really is a surprise.

OLGA. You see, we're moving to Moscow.

IRINA. We hope to be there by autumn. It's our home town. We were born there, in the Old Basmanny Road. [*Both laugh happily.*]

MASHA. Fancy meeting someone from home. [*Eagerly.*] Now I remember. Olga, you remember how we used to talk about 'the lovesick major'. You were a lieutenant then and you were in love, and everyone teased you and called you a major for some reason.

VERSHININ [*laughs*]. Oh yes, the lovesick major. You're quite right.

MASHA. You only had a moustache in those days. Oh, you look so much older. [*Through tears.*] So much older.

VERSHININ. Yes, when I was known as the lovesick major I was young and in love. Things have changed since then.

OLGA. But you haven't a single grey hair. You may look older, but no one could call you old.

VERSHININ. I'm nearly forty-three all the same. Is it long since you left Moscow?

IRINA. Eleven years. But why are you crying, Masha, you silly girl? [*Through tears.*] You'll have me crying too.

MASHA. Never mind me. Do tell me, what street did you live in?

VERSHININ. The Old Basmanny Road.

OLGA. But that's where we lived!

VERSHININ. I lived in Nemetsky Street at one time. Used to walk to the Red Barracks from there. You cross a gloomy-looking bridge on the way and you can hear the water rushing underneath it— a depressing place when you're on your own. [*Pause.*] But what a magnificent wide river you have here. It's a splendid river.

OLGA. Yes, but it's so cold. It's cold here and there are mosquitoes.

VERSHININ. Oh, you mustn't say that. You have a good healthy climate, what I call a real Russian climate. There are the woods and the river, and you've silver birches too. Charming, modest birches, they're my favourite tree. This is a good place to live. Only what's so odd is, the railway station's twelve miles out of town and nobody knows why.

SOLYONY. Well, I know why. [*Everyone looks at him.*] Because if the station was near it wouldn't be far away. And if it's far away it can't be near, can it?

[*An awkward pause.*]

TUZENBAKH. Captain Solyony likes his little joke.

OLGA. Now I do remember you. Yes, I do.

VERSHININ. I knew your mother.

CHEBUTYKIN. She was a wonderful woman, may she rest in peace.

IRINA. Mother's buried in Moscow.

OLGA. In the Novo-Devichy cemetery.

MASHA. Do you know, I'm already beginning to forget her face? Not that anyone will remember us either. We'll be forgotten too.

VERSHININ. Yes, we'll be forgotten. Such is our fate and we can't do anything about it. And the things that strike us as so very serious and important, they'll all be forgotten one day or won't seem to matter. [*Pause.*] The curious thing is, we can't possibly know now just what will be thought significant and important, or what will seem pathetic and absurd. Take the discoveries of Copernicus or Columbus, say. Didn't they look pointless and absurd at first? While the crazy rubbish put out by some nonentity seemed a great revelation. And it may turn out the same with our present way of life—it suits us all right, but one day it may look odd, inconvenient, foolish, and not all that reputable either. It may even seem terribly sinful.

TUZENBAKH. Who can say? Or perhaps people will think our life was lofty and sublime, and remember it with respect. There are no tortures, public executions or invasions nowadays, but there's a lot of suffering for all that.

SOLYONY [*in a high-pitched voice, as if calling chickens*]. Chuck, chuck, chuck. The baron wouldn't mind starving so long as you let him say his little piece.

TUZENBAKH. Kindly leave me alone, Solyony. [*Sits down in another chair.*] It gets a bit boring, you know.

SOLYONY [*in a high-pitched voice*]. Chuck, chuck, chuck.

TUZENBAKH [*to* VERSHININ]. The suffering we see around us these days—and there's plenty of it—is at least a sign that society has reached a certain moral level.

VERSHININ. Yes, yes of course.

CHEBUTYKIN. Baron, you just said that people would think of our life as something lofty. But people are a pretty low-down lot all the same. [*Stands up.*] Look what a low fellow I am. It's only to console me that my life has to be called lofty, that's quite plain.

[*A violin is played off stage.*]

MASHA. That's Andrew playing, our brother.

IRINA. He's the clever one of the family. He's bound to become a professor. Father was a soldier, but his son's chosen an academic career.

MASHA. Which was what Father wanted.

OLGA. We did tease him terribly today. We think he's a bit in love.

IRINA. With one of the local young ladies. She'll be visiting us today, very likely.

MASHA. Oh dear, the way she dresses. It's not merely ugly and unfashionable, it's downright pathetic. She wears a weird skirt in a kind of bright yellow with such a vulgar fringe, my dear, and a red blouse. And her cheeks always look as if they've been scrubbed and scrubbed. Andrew isn't in love, that I just won't believe. I mean to say, he has got some taste. He's only having us on, it's just his little game. Yesterday I heard she's going to marry Protopopov, the chairman of the local council. And a good thing too. [*Speaking into the side door.*] Andrew, come here. Come here a moment, dear.

[ANDREW *comes in.*]

OLGA. This is my brother Andrew.

VERSHININ. My name's Vershinin.

ANDREW. I'm Prozorov. [*Wipes the sweat off his face.*] You're the new battery commander here, aren't you?

OLGA. Colonel Vershinin comes from Moscow, believe it or not.

ANDREW. Really? Then I must congratulate you. Now my dear sisters won't give you a moment's peace.

VERSHININ. I'm afraid your sisters must be rather bored with me already.

IRINA. Look what Andrew gave me today, this little picture frame. [*Shows him the frame.*] He made it himself.

VERSHININ [*looking at the frame and not knowing what to say*]. Yes. Quite something, isn't it?

IRINA. And you see that frame above the piano? That's his work too.

[ANDREW *makes an impatient gesture and moves away.*]

OLGA. He's the clever one of the family, he plays the violin and does all this fretwork—in fact he's good at everything. Don't go away, Andrew. He's always going off like this. You come back.

[MASHA *and* IRINA *take him by the arms and bring him back, laughing.*]

MASHA. Now just you come here.

ANDREW. Leave me alone, please.

MASHA. Isn't he a funny boy? They used to call Colonel Vershinin the lovesick major and he didn't mind a bit.

VERSHININ. No, not a bit.

MASHA. And I want to call you the lovesick fiddler.

IRINA. Or the lovesick professor.

OLGA. He's in love. Andrew's in love.

IRINA [*clapping her hands*]. Three cheers for Andrew! Encore! He's in love!

CHEBUTYKIN [*coming up behind* ANDREW *and putting both arms round his waist*].
          'That love alone might rule the earth,
               Kind nature gave us mortals birth.' [*Laughs loudly.*
He keeps his newspaper with him all the time.]

ANDREW. All right, that's enough of that. [*Wipes his face.*] I couldn't
get to sleep last night and now I don't feel too grand, as they say.
I was reading till four o'clock, then I went to bed, but it was no use.
I kept thinking about one thing and another—then it gets light so
early and the sun comes streaming right into my room. There's an
English book I want to translate while I'm here this summer.

VERSHININ. So you know English, do you?

ANDREW. Oh yes. Our father, God rest his soul, inflicted education
on us. It's a funny thing, sounds silly in fact, but I must confess that
since he died I've started putting on weight and in one year I've
filled out like this, just as if my body had shaken off some kind of
burden. Thanks to Father, my sisters and I know French, German
and English, and Irina knows Italian too. But what an effort!

MASHA. Knowing three languages is a useless luxury in this town. It's
not even a luxury, but a sort of unwanted appendage like having
a sixth finger. We know much too much.

VERSHININ. Oh, what a thing to say! [*Laughs.*] You know much too
much. I don't think there exists, or ever could exist, a town so dull
and dreary that it has no place for intelligent, educated men and
women. Let's suppose that among the hundred thousand inhabitants
of this town—oh, I know it's a backward, rough sort of place—
there's no one else like you three. Well, you obviously can't hope
to prevail against the forces of ignorance around you. As you go on
living you'll have to give way bit by bit to these hundred thousand people and be swallowed up in the crowd. You'll go under,
but that doesn't mean you'll sink without trace—you will have some
effect. Perhaps when you're gone there will be six people like you,
then twelve and so on, and in the end your kind will be the majority.
In two or three hundred years life on this earth will be beautiful
beyond our dreams, it will be marvellous. Man needs a life like that,
and if he hasn't yet got it he must feel he's going to get it, he must
look forward to it, dream about it, prepare for it. That means he
must have more vision and more knowledge than his father or
grandfather ever had. [*Laughs.*] And here are you complaining you
know much too much.

MASHA [*takes off her hat*]. I'm staying to lunch.

IRINA [*with a sigh*]. You know, what you've just said ought really to be
written down.

[ANDREW *has slipped away unobserved.*]

TUZENBAKH. Many years from now, you tell us, life on this earth will be beautiful and marvellous. That's quite true. But if we're to play a part in it now, even at this distance, we must get ready for it and work for it.

VERSHININ [*stands up*]. Yes. I say, what a lot of flowers you have. [*Looking round.*] And what a splendid house! How I envy you. All my life I've been knocking round from one lot of rooms to another, with a couple of chairs and a sofa and stoves smoking all the time. Why, they're just what I've been missing all my life, flowers like these. [*Rubs his hands.*] Ah well, never mind.

TUZENBAKH. Yes, we must work. I'm sure you think that's a bit of sloppy German sentimentality, but I'm a Russian, you can take my word for it, and I can't even speak a word of German. My father belonged to the Orthodox Church. [*Pause.*]

VERSHININ [*walking up and down*]. I often wonder what it would be like if we could start living all over again, knowing exactly what we were doing. Suppose our past life could be just the rough draft, so to speak, and we could start the new one on a fresh sheet of paper. Then we'd all try hard not to repeat ourselves, I imagine. We'd create different surroundings for ourselves anyway, and see we had somewhere to live like this with these flowers and all this light. I have a wife and two little girls, my wife is in poor health and so on and so forth—and, well, if I could start my life again, I wouldn't get married. No, I would not.

[*Enter* KULYGIN *wearing a teacher's uniform.*]

KULYGIN [*goes up to* IRINA]. Permit me, Irina dear, to wish you many happy returns, and to add from the bottom of my heart sincere wishes for your good health and everything else one may wish a girl of your age. And now may I present you with this little book? [*Hands over a book.*] The history of our high school during the last fifty years. I wrote it myself. A trifling work, written because I had nothing better to do, but do read it all the same. Good morning to you all. [*To* VERSHININ.] My name is Kulygin and I teach at the local high school, I'm a senior assistant master. [*To* IRINA.] In this book you'll find a list of all the pupils who've been through our school in the last fifty years. *Feci quod potui, faciant meliora potentes.* [*Kisses* MASHA.]

IRINA. But you've given me this book before, last Easter.

KULYGIN [*laughs*]. Oh, surely not. In that case give it back. Or better still, give it to the colonel here. Here you are, Colonel. You can read it some time when you're at a loose end.

VERSHININ. I thank you. [*Prepares to leave.*] I really am glad to have met you.

OLGA. You aren't going, are you? We can't allow that.

IRINA. You must stay to luncheon. Please do.

OLGA. Yes, do stay.

VERSHININ [*with a bow*]. I believe I've intruded on a family occasion. Please excuse me. I didn't know, so I haven't offered my good wishes. [*Goes into the ballroom with* OLGA.]

KULYGIN. My friends, today is Sunday, the day of rest. Let us therefore relax and enjoy ourselves, each in the manner befitting his age and station. We'll have to take the carpets up for the summer and put them away till winter. We'll need some insect powder or mothballs. The Romans were healthy because they knew how to work *and* how to relax, what they had was a *mens sana in corpore sano*. Their life followed a definite pattern. Our headmaster says the important thing about life is its pattern or shape. A thing that loses its shape is finished, and that's true of our everyday life as well. [*Puts his arm round* MASHA's *waist, laughing.*] Masha loves me, my wife loves me. We must put the curtains away as well, along with the carpets. I'm happy today, I'm on top of the world. We're due at the headmaster's at four this afternoon, Masha. An outing has been fixed up for the teachers and their families.

MASHA. I'm not going.

KULYGIN [*dismayed*]. My dear, why ever not?

MASHA. I'll tell you later. [*Angrily.*] All right then, I'll go, but please leave me alone. [*Moves away.*]

KULYGIN. And after that we're to spend the evening at the headmaster's. In spite of poor health our head does do his best to be sociable. What a wonderful inspiration to us all—a thoroughly first-rate chap. After the staff meeting yesterday he said to me, 'I'm tired, Kulygin. Tired.' [*Looks at the clock, then at his watch.*] Your clock's seven minutes fast. 'Yes', he said. 'I'm tired!'

[*The sound of a violin is heard from off stage.*]

OLGA. Come along please, everyone, let's start luncheon. There's a pie.

KULYGIN. Ah, Olga my dear! Last night I worked right up to eleven o'clock and got very tired, and today I feel happy. [*Goes to the table in the ballroom.*] My dear——

CHEBUTYKIN [*puts his newspaper in his pocket and combs his beard*]. Did somebody say pie? Splendid.

MASHA [*to* CHEBUTYKIN, *sternly*]. You mind you don't drink today, do you hear? It's bad for you.

CHEBUTYKIN. Oh, stuff and nonsense! That's a thing of the past. It's two years since I really pushed the boat out. [*Impatiently.*] Anyway, old girl, what does it matter?

MASHA. All the same, don't you dare drink. Don't you dare. [*Angrily, but making sure that her husband cannot hear.*] This means another dismal evening at the headmaster's, damn it.

TUZENBAKH. I wouldn't go if I were you, it's perfectly simple.

CHEBUTYKIN. Just don't go, my dear.

MASHA. Don't go, indeed. Oh, damn this life, it's the absolute limit. [*Goes into the ballroom.*]

CHEBUTYKIN [*going up to her*]. There, there.

SOLYONY [*going through to the ballroom*]. Chuck, chuck, chuck.

TUZENBAKH. That'll do, Solyony. Give it a rest.

SOLYONY. Chuck, chuck, chuck.

KULYGIN [*gaily*]. Your health, Colonel. I'm a schoolmaster and quite one of the family here, being Masha's husband. She's a good, kind girl.

VERSHININ. I think I'll have a little of this dark vodka. [*Drinks.*] Your health. [*To* OLGA.] It's so good to be here. [*Only* IRINA *and* TUZENBAKH *are left in the drawing-room.*]

IRINA. Masha's in a bad mood today. She got married at eighteen when she thought him the wisest of men. Now things have changed. He's the kindest of men, but hardly the wisest.

OLGA [*impatiently*]. Andrew, when are you coming?

ANDREW [*off stage*]. Coming. [*Comes in and goes up to the table.*]

TUZENBAKH. What are you thinking about?

IRINA. Oh, nothing much. I don't like your friend Solyony, he frightens me. He says such stupid things.

TUZENBAKH. He's a strange man. I'm sorry for him—he annoys me too, but I feel more sorry than annoyed. I think he's shy. He's always sensible and friendly when we're alone together, but in company he's rude and throws his weight about. Don't go in just yet, let's wait till they've all sat down. Just let me be with you for a bit. What are you thinking about? [*Pause.*] You're twenty and I'm not yet thirty. What a lot of years we have ahead of us—so many, many days, all full of my love for you.

IRINA. Don't talk to me about love, Nicholas dear.

TUZENBAKH [*not listening*]. I feel such a tremendous zest for life. I want to work and struggle, and this urge has become part of my love for you, Irina. And just because you're so beautiful I find life beautiful too. What are you thinking about?

IRINA. You say life is beautiful. But what if it only seems so? As far as we three girls are concerned there hasn't been any beauty in our lives so far, life has been choking us like weeds in a garden. I'm crying. I mustn't. [*Quickly dries her eyes and smiles.*] We must work, work, work. That's why we're so miserable and take such a gloomy view of things—because we don't know the meaning of work. We're descended from people who despised it.

[NATASHA *comes in wearing a pink dress with a green sash.*]

NATASHA. They've gone into lunch already. I'm late. [*Glances at the mirror and tidies herself.*] My hair looks all right. [*Seeing* IRINA.] Many happy returns, Irina dear. [*Gives her a vigorous and prolonged kiss.*] You've got so many guests, I feel quite shy, really. Good morning, Baron.

OLGA [*coming into the drawing-room*]. Oh, here's Natasha. How are you, dear? [*They kiss.*]

NATASHA. Many happy returns. You have so many people here, I feel awfully nervous.

OLGA. Don't worry, they're all old friends. [*In a horrified undertone.*] You're wearing a green sash. That's quite wrong, my dear.

NATASHA. Why? You mean it's unlucky?

OLGA. No, but it just doesn't go with your dress, it looks odd somehow.

NATASHA [*in a tearful voice*]. Does it? But it isn't really green, you know, it's more a sort of dull colour. [*Follows* OLGA *into the ballroom.*]

[*They all sit down to luncheon in the ballroom. The drawing-room is empty.*]

KULYGIN. You know, I wish you'd find yourself a nice young man, Irina. It's high time you were married.

CHEBUTYKIN. And I wish you the same, Natasha.

KULYGIN. Natasha already has a young man.

MASHA. I'm going to have a little glass of something. Eat, drink and be merry—after all, we only live once.

KULYGIN. Take a black mark for conduct.

VERSHININ. I say, this wine is good. What's it made of?

SOLYONY. Black-beetles.

IRINA [*in a tearful voice*]. Oh! How disgusting!

OLGA. We're having roast turkey and apple pie for dinner tonight. Thank goodness I'll be home all day today, and this evening too. Do come and see us this evening, all of you.

VERSHININ. Am I invited too?

IRINA. Yes, please do come.

NATASHA. It's ever so informal here.

CHEBUTYKIN. 'That love alone might rule this earth,
            Kind nature gave us mortals birth.' [*Laughs.*]

ANDREW [*angrily*]. Oh, can't you all stop it? I wonder you don't get tired.

[FEDOTIK *and* RODÉ *come in with a large basket of flowers.*]

FEDOTIK. I say, they've already started.

RODÉ [*speaks in a loud voice and pronounces the letter 'r' in his throat in the manner affected by some Russian cavalry regiments*]. Started lunch already, have they? Yes, they have.

FEDOTIK. Half a second! [*Takes a snapshot.*] One. Half a second again. [*Takes another snapshot.*] Two. Now that's done.

[*They take the basket and go into the ballroom where they are greeted noisily.*]

RODÉ [*in a loud voice*]. Many happy returns and all possible good wishes. Marvellous weather today, simply magnificent. I've been out walking with the boys all morning. I teach gymnastics at the high school here.

FEDOTIK. You can move now if you want to, Irina. [*Takes another snapshot.*] You do look nice today. [*Takes a humming-top from his pocket.*] By the way, here's a top. It's got a wonderful hum.

IRINA. Oh, how lovely!

MASHA.   'A green oak by a curving shore,
            And on that oak a chain of gold—
            And on that oak a chain of gold.'

[*Tearfully.*] But why do I keep saying that? Those words have been going through my head all day.

KULYGIN. Thirteen at table!

RODÉ [*in a loud voice*]. I say, you surely aren't superstitious, are you? [*Laughter.*]

KULYGIN. When there are thirteen at table it means someone's in love. I suppose it wouldn't be you by any chance, Chebutykin? [*Laughter.*]

CHEBUTYKIN. Oh, I'm an old sinner, but why Natasha looks so embarrassed I really can't imagine.

[*Loud laughter.* NATASHA *runs from the ballroom into the drawing-room followed by* ANDREW.]

ANDREW. Please—don't take any notice of them. Stop. Wait a moment, please.

NATASHA. I feel so ashamed. I don't know what's the matter with me and they keep making fun of me. It was awful of me, getting up like that, but I couldn't help it, I really couldn't. [*Covers her face with her hands.*]

ANDREW. Please don't be upset, Natasha. Please. Believe me, they're only joking, it's all meant kindly. Natasha, darling, they're all kind, good-hearted people and they're fond of you and me. Come over to the window here where they can't see us. [*Looks round.*]

NATASHA. I'm just not used to meeting people.

ANDREW. Oh, how young you are, Natasha, how marvellously, splendidly young! My dearest, my darling, don't be so upset. Believe me, trust me. I feel so wonderful, my heart is full of love and joy. Oh, they can't see us, they really can't. How, oh how did I come to fall in love with you and when did it happen? Oh, I don't understand at all. My dear, innocent darling, I want you to be my wife. I love you, I love you. I've never loved anyone like this before. [*They kiss.*]

[*Two officers come in and, seeing* NATASHA *and* ANDREW *kissing, stand and stare in amazement.*]

CURTAIN

ACT TWO

The scene is the same as in Act One.
    It is eight o'clock in the evening. From the street comes the faint sound of an accordion. The stage is unlit. NATASHA *comes in wearing a dressing-gown and carrying a candle. She crosses the stage and stops by the door leading into* ANDREW'*s room.*

NATASHA. What are you doing, Andrew? Reading, are you? It's all right, I only wondered. [*Goes and opens another door, glances through the doorway, then closes it.*] I thought someone might have left a light burning.

ANDREW [*comes in carrying a book*]. What's that, Natasha?

NATASHA. I was seeing if there were any lights on. It's carnival week and the servants are in such a state anything might happen—you need eyes in the back of your head. Last night I went through the dining-room about midnight and found a candle burning. But who lit it? That's what I couldn't find out. [*Puts down the candle.*] What time is it?

ANDREW [*with a glance at his watch*]. A quarter past eight.

NATASHA. Olga and Irina aren't here yet. They're still not back from work, poor things. Olga's at a staff meeting and Irina's at the post office. [*Sighs.*] I was telling that sister of yours only this morning. 'You look after yourself, Irina dear,' I said. But she won't listen. A quarter past eight, you say? I'm afraid little Bobik isn't at all well. Why does he get so chilly? Yesterday he had a temperature and today he's cold all over. I'm so worried.

ANDREW. It's all right, Natasha, the child's well enough.

NATASHA. Still, he'd be better on a special diet. I'm so worried. And I'm told there are some people calling here about half past nine, a fancy dress party from the carnival. I'd much rather they didn't come, dear.

ANDREW. I don't quite know what to say. After all, they were asked.

NATASHA. The sweet little thing woke up this morning and looked at me, and suddenly he smiled. He knew who I was, you see. 'Good morning, Bobik,' I said. 'Good morning, darling.' And he laughed. Babies do understand, oh yes, they understand very well. All right then, dear, I'll say those carnival people aren't to be asked in.

ANDREW [*indecisively*]. Isn't that rather up to my sisters? It is their house, you know.

NATASHA. Yes, it's their house too. I'll have a word with them, they're so kind. [*Moves off.*] I've ordered some yogurt for supper. The doctor says you shouldn't eat anything but yogurt or you'll never lose weight. [*Stops.*] Bobik gets so chilly. I'm afraid his room may be too cold. We ought to put him somewhere else, at least till the weather's warmer. Irina's room, for instance, is just right for a baby, it's not damp and it gets the sun all day. We must have a word with her, she can go in with Olga for the time being. She's never at home during the day anyway, she only sleeps here. [*Pause.*] Andrew, sweetie-pie, why don't you say something?

ANDREW. I was thinking. There's nothing to say anyway.

NATASHA. Now I had something to tell you. Oh yes, Ferapont's here from the council offices, he wants to see you.

ANDREW [*yawns*]. Ask him to come in, please.

[NATASHA *goes out.* ANDREW *bends over the candle, which she has left behind, and starts reading his book.* FERAPONT *comes in wearing a shabby old overcoat with the collar up and a scarf round his ears.*]

ANDREW. Hallo, my good fellow. What is it?

FERAPONT. A book and some papers from the chairman. Here. [*Hands over a book and a packet.*]

ANDREW. Thank you. Good. But why so late? It's getting on for nine o'clock.

FERAPONT. Eh?

ANDREW [*raising his voice*]. You're late, I tell you. It's nearly nine.

FERAPONT. As you say, sir. I did get here before dark, but they wouldn't let me in. The master's busy, they told me. Ah well, if you were busy you were busy. I wasn't in a hurry. [*Thinking* ANDREW *is asking him something.*] Eh?

ANDREW. Nothing. [*Examining the book.*] Tomorrow's Friday and the office will be closed, but I'll go in and work anyway. I get so bored at home. [*Pause.*] Isn't it funny, my dear old fellow, how things change? And isn't life a swindle? Today I was bored and at a loose end, so I picked up this book, my old university lecture notes, and couldn't help laughing. God, I'm secretary of the county council and the chairman's Protopopov. I'm secretary, and the most I can ever hope for is to get on the council myself. Me—stuck here as a councillor, when every night I dream I'm a professor at Moscow University, a distinguished scholar, the pride of all Russia.

FERAPONT. I don't know, sir, I'm a bit hard of hearing.

ANDREW. If you could hear properly I don't suppose I'd talk to you at all. I must to talk to someone, but my wife doesn't understand me and I'm somehow afraid of my sisters, afraid they'll laugh at me and make me look a complete fool. I don't drink and I don't like going into bars, but if I could drop in at Testov's in Moscow right now, or the Great Muscovite Hotel—why, it would suit me down to the ground, old boy.

FERAPONT. There was a contractor at the office a few days back telling us about some businessmen in Moscow. They were eating pancakes, and one of them ate forty and died, or so he said. It was either forty or fifty, I don't rightly remember.

ANDREW. When you sit down in a big Moscow restaurant you don't know anyone and nobody knows you, but you still don't feel out of things. Now here you know everybody and everybody knows you, but you don't seem to belong at all. You're the odd man out all right.

FERAPONT. What's that? [*Pause.*] The same man was saying—he may have been having me on of course—that there's an enormous rope stretched right across Moscow.

ANDREW. What for?

FERAPONT. I don't know, sir. It's what the man said.

ANDREW. Nonsense. [*Reads the book.*] Have you ever been to Moscow?

FERAPONT [*after a pause*]. No, the chance never came my way. [*Pause.*] Shall I go now?

ANDREW. Yes, you can go. Good night. [FERAPONT *goes.*] Good night. [*Reading.*] You might come and fetch some papers tomorrow morning. Off with you then. [*Pause.*] He's gone. [*A bell rings.*]

Oh, what a life. [*Stretches himself and goes off slowly to his own room.*]

> [*Singing is heard off stage—the nanny is rocking the baby to sleep. MASHA and VERSHININ come in. While they talk to each other the MAID lights the lamp and candles.*]

MASHA. I don't know. [*Pause.*] I don't know. A lot depends on habit of course. After Father's death for instance it was ages before we got used to having no orderlies about the place. But quite apart from what one's used to, I still think what I'm saying's perfectly fair. Other places may be different, but in this town the most decent, the most civilized and cultivated people are the military.

VERSHININ. I'm a bit thirsty, I could do with some tea.

MASHA [*glancing at her watch*]. They'll be bringing some in a minute. I got married when I was eighteen, and I was scared of my husband because he was a schoolmaster and I'd only just left school myself. I thought he was terribly clever, and oh so learned and important. But things have changed since then, I'm sorry to say.

VERSHININ. Yes, I see.

MASHA. Anyway, I'm not talking about my husband. I'm used to him. But civilians in general are often so rude, disagreeable and bad-mannered. Rudeness bothers me, really upsets me. It's painful to meet people who aren't as considerate, or as kind and polite, as they might be. As for schoolteachers, my husband's colleagues, I find their company sheer torture.

VERSHININ. Yes. Though I should have thought there was nothing to choose between civilians and soldiers, at least in this town. It's six of one and half a dozen of the other. Listen to any educated person in this place—soldier or civilian, it makes no difference—and you'll find he's fed up with his wife, fed up with his house, fed up with his estate and fed up with his horses. A Russian feels so much at home when his thoughts are up in the clouds, but tell me—why is his every-day life so very earthbound? Why?

MASHA. Why?

VERSHININ. Why is he fed up with his children and fed up with his wife? Why are his wife and children fed up with him?

MASHA. You're in rather a bad mood today.

VERSHININ. Perhaps I am. I missed lunch, had nothing to eat since breakfast. One of the girls is a bit unwell, and when my children are ill I always get worried and feel so guilty because their mother's the way she is. Oh, if you could have seen her this morning, she really is beneath contempt. We started quarrelling at seven o'clock, and at nine I walked out and slammed the door. [*Pause.*] I never talk about it, the funny thing is I never complain to anyone but you. [*Kisses her hand.*] Don't be angry with me. Apart from you I have no one, no one in the world. [*Pause.*]

MASHA. What a noise the stove's making. The wind howled in the chimney before Father died, made a noise just like that.

VERSHININ. Are you superstitious then?

MASHA. Yes.

VERSHININ. How strange. [*Kisses her hand.*] You're a wonderful, marvellous woman. You're wonderful, marvellous. It's dark in here, but I can see your eyes shining.

MASHA [*moving to another chair*]. There's more light over here.

VERSHININ. I love you, love you, love you. I love your eyes, I love the way you move, I dream about you. You're a wonderful, marvellous woman.

MASHA [*laughing softly*]. When you talk like this it somehow makes me laugh, though it frightens me as well. Please don't talk that way again. [*In an undertone.*] No, it's all right, go on, I don't care. [*Covers her face with her hands.*] I don't care. There's somebody coming, you'd better talk about something else. [IRINA *and* TUZENBAKH *come in through the ballroom.*]

TUZENBAKH. I have a triple-barrelled name, Baron Tuzenbakh-Krone-Altschauer, but I'm just as much of a Russian as you are. There's not much trace of any German ancestry about me, except perhaps that I'm so persistent and stubborn about inflicting myself on you. I walk home with you every evening.

IRINA. I'm so tired.

TUZENBAKH. And I shall go on calling for you at the post office and bringing you home every evening. I'll keep it up for the next ten or twenty years if you don't tell me to go away. [*Noticing* MASHA *and* VERSHININ, *delightedly.*] Oh, it's you. Hallo.

IRINA. Well, here I am, home at last. [*To* MASHA.] Just now a woman came into the post office and wanted to send a telegram to her brother in Saratov to tell him her son died today, but couldn't remember the address. So she sent it without a proper address, just sent it to Saratov. She was crying. And I was rude to her for no reason at all, told her I'd no time to waste. Wasn't that stupid of me? Are those carnival people calling tonight?

MASHA. Yes.

IRINA [*sitting down in an armchair*]. Must have a rest. I'm so tired.

TUZENBAKH [*with a smile*]. When you come back from work you always look so young and pathetic somehow. [*Pause.*]

IRINA. I'm tired. Oh dear, I don't like working at the post office, I really don't.

MASHA. You've got thin. [*Whistles.*] You seem younger too and you've begun to look like a little boy.

TUZENBAKH. It's the way you do your hair.

IRINA. I must find another job because this one doesn't suit me. The things I'd hoped for and wanted so much—they're just what it doesn't give me. It's sheer drudgery with nothing romantic or intellectual about it. [*There is a knock on the floor from below.*] That's the doctor banging. [*To* TUZENBAKH.] Would you give him a knock, Nicholas? I can't, I'm too tired.

[TUZENBAKH *knocks on the floor.*]

IRINA. He'll be up here in a moment. Something ought to be done about this business. The doctor went to the club with Andrew yesterday and they lost again. I heard Andrew was two hundred roubles down.

MASHA [*apathetically*]. It's a bit late to do anything about that now.

IRINA. He lost money a fortnight ago and also in December. The sooner he loses the lot the better, it might mean we'd leave this place. My God, do you know, I dream about Moscow every night? I feel as if I'd gone out of my mind. [*Laughs.*] We're moving there in June, but it's, let me see—February, March, April, May—almost six months till June.

MASHA. The only thing is, Natasha mustn't find out about his gambling.

IRINA. I shouldn't think she'd care.

[CHEBUTYKIN, *who has just got out of bed after an afternoon nap, comes into the ballroom and combs his beard, then sits down at the table and takes a newspaper out of his pocket.*]

MASHA. Oh, look who's come. Has he paid his rent?

IRINA [*laughing*]. No. We haven't had a thing from him for eight months. He's obviously forgotten.

MASHA [*laughing*]. He looks so pompous sitting there.

[*Everyone laughs. Pause.*]

IRINA. Why don't you say anything, Colonel?

VERSHININ. I don't know. I'd like some tea. My kingdom for a glass of tea! I've had nothing since breakfast.

CHEBUTYKIN. Irina.

IRINA. What is it?

CHEBUTYKIN. Please come here. *Venez ici.* [IRINA *goes over and sits at the table.*] I can't do without you. [IRINA *lays out the cards for a game of patience.*]

VERSHININ. Ah well, if there's not going to be any tea we may as well have a bit of a discussion.

TUZENBAKH. All right then, what about?

VERSHININ. Let me see. Well, for instance, let's try and imagine life after we're dead and buried, in two or three hundred years, say.

TUZENBAKH. Very well then. When we're dead people will fly around in balloons, there will be a new style in men's jackets and a sixth sense may be discovered and developed, but life itself won't change, it will still be as difficult and full of mystery and happiness as it is now. Even in a thousand years men will still be moaning away about life being a burden. What's more, they'll still be as scared of death as they are now. And as keen on avoiding it.

VERSHININ [*after some thought*]. Now how can I put it? I think everything on earth is bound to change bit by bit, in fact already is changing before our very eyes. Two or three hundred years, or a thousand years if you like—it doesn't really matter how long—will bring in a new and happy life. We'll have no part in it of course, but it is what we're now living for, working for, yes and suffering for. We're creating it, and that's what gives our life its meaning, and its happiness too if you want to put it that way.

[MASHA *laughs quietly.*]

TUZENBAKH. What's the matter?

MASHA. I don't know. I've been laughing all day.

VERSHININ. I went to the same cadet school as you, though I didn't go on to staff college. I do a lot of reading, but I'm not much good at choosing books and I daresay I read all the wrong things. But the longer I live the more I want to know. My hair's going grey now and I'm growing old, but the trouble is I know so precious little. Still, when it comes to the things that really matter, there I do know my stuff pretty well, I think. And I only wish I could make you see that happiness—well, we haven't got it, we've no right to it, in fact it isn't meant for us at all. Our business is to work and go on working, and our distant descendants will have any happiness that's going. [*Pause.*] I won't have it, but my children's children may.

[FEDOTIK *and* RODÉ *appear in the ballroom. They sit down and sing quietly, one of them strumming on a guitar.*]

TUZENBAKH. You seem to think we shouldn't even dream of happiness, but what if I'm happy already?

VERSHININ. You're not.

TUZENBAKH [*throwing up his arms and laughing*]. We obviously don't speak the same language. Now how can I convince you?

[MASHA *laughs quietly.*]

TUZENBAKH [*holding up a finger to her*]. Laugh at that then. [*To* VERSHININ.] Forget your two or three hundred years, because even in a million years life will still be just the same as ever. It doesn't change, it always goes on the same and follows its own laws. And those laws are none of our business. Or at least you'll never understand them. Think of the birds flying south for the winter, cranes for instance. They fly on and on and on, and it doesn't matter what ideas, big or small, they may have buzzing about inside their heads, they'll still keep on flying without ever knowing why they do it or where they're going. They fly on and on, and what if they do throw up a few philosophers? Let them keep their philosophy so long as they don't stop flying.

MASHA. But what's the point of it all?

TUZENBAKH. The point? Look, it's snowing out there. What's the point of that? [*Pause.*]

MASHA. I feel that man should have a faith or be trying to find one, otherwise his life just doesn't make sense. Think of living without knowing why cranes fly, why children are born or why there are stars in the sky. Either you know what you're living for, or else the whole thing's a waste of time and means less than nothing. [*Pause.*]

VERSHININ. Still, I'm sorry I'm not young any more.

MASHA. As Gogol said, 'Life on this earth is no end of a bore, my friends.'

TUZENBAKH. What I say is, arguing with you is no end of a job, my friends. Oh, I give up.

CHEBUTYKIN [*reading the newspaper*]. Balzac got married in Berdichev.

[IRINA *sings softly.*]

CHEBUTYKIN. I really must put that down in my little book. [*Makes a note.*] Balzac got married in Berdichev. [*Carries on reading the newspaper.*]

IRINA [*playing patience, thoughtfully*]. Balzac got married in Berdichev.

TUZENBAKH. Well, I've burnt my boats. Did you know I'd resigned my commission, Masha?

MASHA. So I'd heard, but what's so good about that? I don't like civilians.

TUZENBAKH. Never mind. [*Gets up.*] I'm not handsome, so what business have I got in the army? And what does it matter anyway? I'm going to get a job. For once in my life I'd like to put in a hard day's work that would bring me home in the evening ready to drop down on my bed dead tired and fall straight asleep. [*Going into the ballroom.*] I'm sure labourers must sleep well.

FEDOTIK [*to* IRINA]. I've just bought you some crayons at Pyzhikov's in the Moscow Road. And this pen-knife.

IRINA. You always treat me like a child, but I am grown up, you know. [*Takes the crayons and pen-knife, delightedly.*] Oh, aren't they lovely!

FEDOTIK. And I bought a knife for myself. Just take a look at this. One blade, two blades, three blades, and here's a thing to clean your ears out with. These are some little scissors and this is a sort of nail-file.

RODÉ [*in a loud voice*]. Doctor, how old are you?

CHEBUTYKIN. Me? Thirty-two. [*Laughter.*]

FEDOTIK. Now let me show you another kind of patience. [*Lays out the cards.*]

[*The samovar is brought in and* ANFISA *attends to it. A little later* NATASHA *comes in and also busies herself at the table.* SOLYONY *comes in, greets everybody and sits down at the table.*]

VERSHININ. I say, there's quite a wind.

MASHA. Isn't there? I'm fed up with winter, I've forgotten what summer's like.

IRINA. It's going to come out, this game of patience. So we shall go to Moscow.

FEDOTIK. No it isn't. You see, that eight's on top of the two of spades. [*Laughs.*] Which means no Moscow for you.

CHEBUTYKIN [*reads his newspaper*]. 'Tsitsihar. A smallpox epidemic is raging here.'

ANFISA [*going up to* MASHA]. Tea's ready, Masha dear. [*To* VERSHININ.] Come and have tea, Colonel. I'm sorry, I've forgotten your name.

MASHA. Bring some here please, Nanny, I'm not going in there.

IRINA. Nanny!

ANFISA. Coming, coming.

NATASHA [*to* SOLYONY]. Tiny babies understand very well. 'Hallo Bobik,' I said. 'Hallo, dear.' And he gave me a special kind of look. You think I only say that because I'm his mother, but that's not it, you know, it really isn't. He's no ordinary baby.

SOLYONY. If that child was mine I'd fry it up in a frying-pan and eat it. [*Takes his glass of tea into the drawing-room and sits in a corner.*]

NATASHA [*covering her face with her hands*]. What a rude, ill-bred man!

MASHA. People don't notice whether it's winter or summer when they're happy. If I lived in Moscow I don't think I'd care what the weather was like.

VERSHININ. The other day I was reading the diary of a French minister written in prison—he'd been sentenced over the Panama swindle. He gets quite carried away with enthusiasm writing about the birds he sees from his cell window, the birds he'd never even noticed when he was a minister. Now he's been let out and of course he takes no more notice of birds than he did before. Just as you won't notice Moscow when you live there. We have no happiness. There's no such thing. It's only something we long for.

TUZENBAKH [*takes a chocolate box from the table*]. I say, what happened to the chocolates?

IRINA. Solyony ate them.

TUZENBAKH. What, the whole lot?

ANFISA [*handing round tea*]. A letter for you, sir.

VERSHININ. For me? [*Takes the letter.*] It's from my daughter. [*Reads it.*] Of course, in that case. I'm sorry, Masha, I must slip away quietly, I won't have tea. [*Stands up in agitation.*] It's the same old story again.

MASHA. What's the matter? Or is it something private?

VERSHININ [*quietly*]. My wife's taken poison again. I must go, I'll slip out so nobody notices. How frightfully unpleasant. [*Kisses* MASHA'*s hand.*] My darling, you splendid, marvellous woman. I'll slip out quietly this way. [*Goes out.*]

ANFISA. Where's he off to? And I'd just poured him some tea. A fine way to behave.

MASHA [*losing her temper*]. Oh, be quiet. You're on at people all the time—why can't you leave anyone in peace? [*Goes towards the table carrying her cup.*] I'm fed up with you, wretched old woman.

ANFISA. But what have I done wrong, dear?

ANDREW [*off stage*]. Anfisa!

ANFISA [*mimicking him*]. Anfisa! Sits in there—. [*Goes out.*]

MASHA [*by the table in the ballroom, angrily*]. Well, do let me sit down. [*Jumbles up the cards on the table.*] Playing cards all over the place. Drink your tea.

IRINA. You *are* in a bad temper, Masha.

MASHA. Don't talk to me then, if I'm so bad-tempered. You leave me alone.

CHEBUTYKIN [*laughing*]. Leave her alone, mind you leave her alone.

MASHA. You're sixty years old, but you might just as well be a school-boy with your incessant jabber about absolutely damn all.

NATASHA [*sighs*]. Need you really use such language, Masha? A nice-looking girl like you, why, you could appear in the very best society —yes, I really mean it—and be thought quite charming if only you didn't use words like that. *Je vous prie, pardonnez-moi, Marie, mais vous avez des manières un peu grossières.*

TUZENBAKH [*trying not to laugh*]. Please, give me some—. I think there's some brandy somewhere.

NATASHA. *Il paraît que mon Bobik déjà ne dort pas*, the little chap's woken up. He's a bit off colour today. I must see to him, excuse me. [*Goes out.*]

IRINA. Where did Colonel Vershinin go?

MASHA. Home. There's been another of those peculiar episodes with his wife.

TUZENBAKH [*approaches* SOLYONY *carrying a decanter of brandy*]. You always sit by yourself brooding about something, heaven knows what. Come on, let's make it up and be friends. Let's have a brandy. [*They drink.*] I suppose I'll have to play a lot of rubbish on the piano all night. Oh, what does it matter?

SOLYONY. Why should we make it up? We haven't quarrelled.

TUZENBAKH. You always give me the feeling there's something wrong between us. You are an odd specimen and no mistake.

SOLYONY [*reciting*]. 'I may be odd, but who is not?' Aleko, be not angry.

TUZENBAKH. What has Aleko got to do with it? [*Pause.*]

SOLYONY. When I'm alone with someone I'm perfectly all right, I'm no different from anyone else, but in a group of people I feel un-happy and awkward and—talk a lot of rubbish. For all that I'm a sight more honest and decent than many other people. What's more, I can prove it.

TUZENBAKH. You often make me angry and you keep picking on me in company, but somehow I like you all the same. Oh, what does it matter? I'm going to get drunk tonight. Drink up.

SOLYONY. All right. [*They drink.*] I've never had anything against you, Baron, but I'm rather the Lermontov type. [*Quietly.*] I even look a bit like Lermontov, or so people say. [*Takes a bottle of scent from his pocket and puts some on his hands.*]

TUZENBAKH. I'm resigning my commission and that's the end of that. I've been thinking of doing it for five years and at last I've taken the plunge. I'm going to get a job.

SOLYONY [*declaiming*]. Aleko, be not angry. Forget, forget your dreams. [*While they are speaking* ANDREW *comes in quietly with a book and sits down near a candle.*]

TUZENBAKH. I'm going to get a job.

CHEBUTYKIN [*coming into the drawing-room with* IRINA]. They gave us real Caucasian food too—onion soup followed by a meat dish, a kind of *escalope*.

SOLYONY. A shallot isn't meat at all, it's a plant rather like an onion.

CHEBUTYKIN. You're wrong, my dear man. *Escalope* isn't an onion, it's a sort of grilled meat.

SOLYONY. Well, I'm telling you a shallot is an onion.

CHEBUTYKIN. Well, I'm telling you *escalope* is meat.

SOLYONY. Well, I'm telling you a shallot is an onion.

CHEBUTYKIN. Why should I argue with you? You've never been to the Caucasus or eaten *escalope*.

SOLYONY. I've never eaten them because I can't stand them. Shallots smell just like garlic.

ANDREW [*imploringly*]. That's enough, you two, please.

TUZENBAKH. When's the carnival party coming?

IRINA. About nine, they said, so they'll be here any moment.

TUZENBAKH [*embracing* ANDREW]. 'Oh, my porch, my nice new porch——'

ANDREW [*dancing and singing*]. 'My nice new porch of maple wood——'

CHEBUTYKIN [*dancing*]. 'With fancy carving everywhere!' [*Laughter.*]

TUZENBAKH [*kisses* ANDREW]. Damn it, let's have a drink. Let's drink to our friendship, Andrew. And I'll go to Moscow University with you, Andrew my boy.

SOLYONY. Which university? Moscow's got two.

ANDREW. Moscow has only one university.

SOLYONY. Well, I'm telling you it has two.

ANDREW. Why not make it three while you're about it? The more the merrier.

SOLYONY. Moscow has two universities. [*Sounds of protest and murmurs of 'hush'.*] Moscow has two universities, one old and one new. And if you don't choose to listen, if what I say irritates you, I can keep my mouth shut. In fact I can go into another room. [*Goes out through one of the doors.*]

TUZENBAKH. And a very good thing too. [*Laughs.*] Ladies and gentlemen, take your partners, I'll play you something. He's a funny chap is friend Solyony. [*Sits down at the piano and starts playing a waltz.*]

MASHA [*waltzing without a partner*]. The baron is drunk, is drunk, is drunk.

[NATASHA *comes in.*]

NATASHA [*to* CHEBUTYKIN]. Doctor! [*Says something to* CHEBUTYKIN, *then goes out quietly.* CHEBUTYKIN *touches* TUZENBAKH *on the shoulder and whispers to him.*]

IRINA. What's the matter?

CHEBUTYKIN. It's time we were going. Good-night.

TUZENBAKH. Good-night. Time to go.

IRINA. But look here, what about the carnival party?

ANDREW [*embarrassed*]. There won't be any carnival party. The fact is, my dear, Natasha says Bobik's not very well and so—oh really, I don't know and I certainly don't care either.

IRINA [*shrugging her shoulders*]. Bobik's unwell.

MASHA. Oh, what's the odds! If we're being chucked out we'd better go. [*To* IRINA.] It isn't Bobik that's ill, it's his mother. In the upper storey. [*Taps her forehead.*] Vulgar creature.

[ANDREW *goes off through the door, right, to his own room, followed by* CHEBUTYKIN. *In the ballroom everyone is saying good-bye.*]

FEDOTIK. What a shame. I was looking forward to a pleasant evening, but if the baby's ill, then of course—. I'll bring him some toys tomorrow.

RODÉ [*in a loud voice*]. I took a nap after lunch today specially—thought I'd be dancing all night. Why, it's only nine o'clock.

MASHA. Let's go out in the street and talk it over. We can decide what to do there.

[*Voices are heard saying, 'Good-bye, take care of yourself.'* TUZEN-BAKH *is heard laughing happily. Everyone goes out.* ANFISA *and the* MAID *clear the table and put the lights out. The nanny can be heard singing off stage.* ANDREW, *wearing an overcoat and hat, and* CHEBUTYKIN *come in quietly.*]

CHEBUTYKIN. I never got round to marrying because my life has just flashed past like lightning, and besides I was madly in love with your mother and she was married already.

ANDREW. One shouldn't get married, indeed one shouldn't. It's a bore.

CHEBUTYKIN. Yes, yes, that's a point of view, but there is such a thing as loneliness. You can argue about it as much as you like, my boy, but loneliness is a terrible thing. Though actually of course it doesn't matter a damn.

ANDREW. Let's hurry up and get out of here.

CHEBUTYKIN. What's the great rush? There's plenty of time.

ANDREW. I'm afraid my wife might stop me.

CHEBUTYKIN. Oh, I see.

ANDREW. I shan't play cards tonight, I'll just sit and watch. I feel a bit unwell. I get so out of breath, is there anything I can do for it, Doctor?

CHEBUTYKIN. Why ask me? I don't know, dear boy. Don't remember.

ANDREW. Let's go through the kitchen. [*They go out.*]

[*The door-bell rings. There is a pause and then it rings again. Voices and laughter are heard.*]

IRINA [*comes in*]. What's that?

ANFISA [*in a whisper*]. The carnival party. [*The bell rings again.*]

IRINA. Tell them there's no one at home, Nanny. They'll have to excuse us.

[ANFISA *goes out.* IRINA *walks up and down the room, deep in thought. She is upset. Enter* SOLYONY.]

SOLYONY [*in amazement*]. No one here. But where is everybody?

IRINA. They've gone home.

SOLYONY. That's funny. Are you on your own then?

IRINA. Yes. [*Pause.*] Good-night.

SOLYONY. I rather let myself go just now and was a bit tactless. But you're different from the rest, you're such a fine, decent person, and you have so much insight. You're the only one who really understands me, no one else can. I love you so profoundly, so infinitely much——

IRINA. Good-bye. Do please go.

SOLYONY. I can't live without you. [*Following her.*] My happiness! [*Through tears.*] My joy! Your glorious, wonderful, dazzling eyes, I've never seen another woman with eyes like yours.

IRINA [*coldly*]. Please stop, Captain Solyony.

SOLYONY. It's the first time I've ever told you how I love you, and I feel like a being on another planet. [*Rubs his forehead.*] Oh, what does it matter anyway? I can't make you love me of course. But I'm not having any successful rivals, let that be quite clear. And by God I mean it, if there's anybody else I'll kill him. Oh, you are so marvellous!

[NATASHA *starts to cross the stage, carrying a candle.*]

NATASHA [*looks through one door, then another, and goes past the door leading to her husband's room*]. Andrew's in there. He may as well go on reading. Excuse me, Captain Solyony, I didn't know you were here. I'm not dressed for visitors.

SOLYONY. I don't care. Good-night. [*Goes out.*]

NATASHA. Oh, you are tired, poor child. [*Kisses* IRINA.] You should go to bed a bit earlier.

IRINA. Is Bobik asleep?

NATASHA. Yes, but he's rather restless. By the way, dear, I keep meaning to ask you, but either you've been out or I've been too busy. I think Bobik's nursery's too cold and damp. But your room's just right for a baby. Darling, would you mind moving in with Olga for a bit?

IRINA [*not understanding*]. Move in where?

[*A troika with bells is heard driving up to the house.*]

NATASHA. You can share Olga's room for the time being and Bobik can have yours. He's such a sweet little fellow. This morning I said to him, 'Bobik, you're mine, my very own.' And he just looked at me with his dear little eyes. [*The door-bell rings.*] That must be Olga. Isn't she late!

[*The* MAID *comes in and whispers in* NATASHA's *ear.*]

NATASHA. Protopopov? Oh, isn't he a scream? Protopopov's turned up, wants to know if he can take me for a drive. [*Laughs.*] Aren't men funny! [*The door-bell rings again.*] And there's someone else. Perhaps I might go for a little spin just for a quarter of an hour. [*To the* MAID.] Tell him I'm coming. [*The door-bell rings.*] There goes the bell again, it must be Olga. [*Goes out.*]

[*The* MAID *runs out.* IRINA *sits deep in thought.* KULYGIN *and* OLGA *come in followed by* VERSHININ.]

KULYGIN. Well, this is a surprise. They said they were having a party.

VERSHININ. It's very funny. I only left half an hour ago, and they were expecting some people from the carnival then.

IRINA. They've all gone away.

KULYGIN. Has Masha gone too? Where did she go? And what is Protopopov doing outside in a carriage? Who's he waiting for?

IRINA. Don't ask questions. I'm tired.

KULYGIN. Oh dear, isn't she a naughty little girl!

OLGA. The meeting's only just ended. I'm absolutely worn out. Our headmistress is ill and I have to take her place. My head, my head, my poor, poor head, how it aches. [*Sits down.*] Andrew lost two hundred roubles at cards last night, the whole town's talking about it.

KULYGIN. Yes, I got tired at the meeting too. [*Sits down.*]

VERSHININ. My wife has just decided to give me a little scare and almost managed to poison herself. It's all right now, thank goodness, and I can relax. So we've got to go, have we? Very well, I wish you all good evening. Shall we go somewhere together, Kulygin? I can't sit at home, I really can't. What do you say?

KULYGIN. I'm tired, you'd better count me out. [*Stands up.*] I'm so tired. Has my wife gone home?

IRINA. She must have.

KULYGIN [*kisses* IRINA's *hand*]. Good-night. For the next two days we can take it easy. All the best then. [*Moves off.*] I would have liked some tea. I was looking forward to a pleasant social evening, but *o, fallacem hominum spem!* Accusative of exclamation.

VERSHININ. I'll have to go off on my own then. [*Goes out with* KULYGIN, *whistling.*]

OLGA. How my head does ache. Andrew lost at cards, the whole town's talking about it. I'll go to bed. [*Moves off.*] I've got the day off tomorrow. My goodness, isn't that nice! I have the day off to-morrow and the day after too. How my head does ache. [*Goes out.*]

IRINA [*alone*]. Everyone's gone away. There's nobody left.

[*There is the sound of an accordion in the street and of the nanny singing a song.*]

NATASHA [*crosses the ballroom wearing a fur coat and a fur hat. She is followed by the* MAID]. I'll be back in half an hour, I'm just going for a little airing. [*Goes out.*]

IRINA [*alone on the stage, with intense longing*]. Moscow, Moscow, Moscow!

CURTAIN

ACT THREE

The bedroom shared by OLGA *and* IRINA. *There are beds, left and right, with screens round them. It is between two and three o'clock in the morning. Off stage church bells are ringing the alarm, a fire having broken out some time previously. Obviously no one in the house has gone to bed yet.* MASHA *is lying on a sofa wearing a black dress as usual.* OLGA *and* ANFISA *come in.*

ANFISA. They're sitting down there under the stairs now. 'Please come upstairs', I tell them. 'We can't have this, can we?' They're crying. 'We don't know where Father is,' they say. 'He might have been burnt to death.' What an idea! Then there are those other people out in the yard as well, they're in their nightclothes too.

OLGA [*takes some dresses out of a wardrobe*]. Take this grey one. And this one too. And the blouse. And take this skirt as well, Nanny. Oh heavens, what a business! Kirsanovsky Street must be burnt to the ground. Take this. And this. [*Throws the clothes into* ANFISA'*s arms.*] The Vershinins had a fright, poor things, their house only just escaped. They'd better spend the night here, we can't let them go home. And poor Fedotik's lost everything, it's all gone up in smoke.

ANFISA. You'd better call Ferapont, dearie, I can't manage all this.

OLGA [*rings*]. They don't come when you ring. [*Calls through the door.*] Come here, please. Is anyone there? [*The red glare of a window is seen through the open door. A fire engine is heard passing the house.*] How horrible. And how thoroughly tiresome too.

[FERAPONT *comes in.*]

OLGA. Here, take all this down, please. The Kolotilin girls are down there under the stairs, give it to them. And give them this too.

FERAPONT. Very well, miss. Moscow had a fire as well, in 1812. Dear oh dear, the French did get a surprise.

OLGA. Run along now, be off with you.

FERAPONT. Very well, madam. [*Goes out.*]

OLGA. Give them everything we have, Nanny dear. We don't need it, give it all away. I'm so tired, I can hardly stand. We can't possibly let the Vershinins go home. The little girls can sleep in the drawing-

room, and the colonel had better go in with Baron Tuzenbakh downstairs. Fedotik can go in with the baron as well or have the dining-
room if he likes. The doctor has to go and get hopelessly drunk at
this of all times, so we can't put anyone in with him. And Vershinin's
wife had better go in the drawing-room too.

ANFISA [*in a tired voice*]. Don't send me away, Miss Olga, please don't
send me away.

OLGA. That's silly talk, Nanny. There's no question of sending you
away.

ANFISA [*resting her head on* OLGA'*s breast*]. I do work hard, Miss Olga,
my precious, I really do. If I grow too weak to manage I'll be told
to go. But where can I go, you tell me that. I'm over eighty. Eighty-
one I am——

OLGA. Sit down a bit, Nanny. You're worn out, poor thing. [*Helps
her to sit down.*] Have a rest, dear, you look so pale.

[NATASHA *comes in.*]

NATASHA. They're saying we ought to set up a relief committee at
once for the fire victims. You know, that's not a bad idea. In fact
we should always be ready to help the poor. It's up to the rich, isn't
it? Bobik and little Sophie are sound asleep in bed just as if nothing
had happened. There's such a crowd in the house, with people everywhere whichever way you turn. And now there's 'flu about in town
I'm afraid the children might catch it.

OLGA [*not listening to her*]. You can't see the fire from this room, it's
peaceful here.

NATASHA. Isn't it? I must look a sight. [*Stands in front of the mirror.*]
People say I've put on weight. But it's not true, not a bit of it.
Masha's asleep—tired out, poor girl. [*To* ANFISA, *coldly.*] How dare
you be seated in my presence? Stand up! Be off with you! [ANFISA
goes out. Pause.] Why you keep that old woman I don't understand.

OLGA [*taken aback*]. I'm sorry, I don't quite understand either.

NATASHA. There's no place for her here. She came from a village and
she should go back to her village. This is sheer extravagance. I like
to see a house run properly, there's no room for misfits in this house.
[*Strokes* OLGA'*s cheek.*] Poor thing, you're tired out. Our headmistress is tired. You know, when little Sophie grows up and goes
to school I'll be quite scared of you.

OLGA. I shan't be a headmistress.

NATASHA. But they're appointing you, dear, it's all settled.

OLGA. I shall turn it down. I can't do it, it's more than I can manage. [*Drinks some water.*] A few moments ago you were very rude to Nanny. I'm sorry, I can't stand that kind of thing, it made me feel quite faint.

NATASHA [*very upset*]. Forgive me, Olga, forgive me. I didn't mean to upset you.

[MASHA *stands up, takes a pillow and goes out angrily.*]

OLGA. Try to understand, my dear. It may be the strange way we were brought up, but I can't stand that attitude. It really depresses me, actually makes me ill. I feel simply awful about it.

NATASHA. Forgive me, please. [*Kisses her.*]

OLGA. The least rudeness, a single word spoken unkindly—and I get upset.

NATASHA. I often say the wrong thing, I admit, but you must agree, dear, she could go and live in her village.

OLGA. She's been with our family for thirty years.

NATASHA. But the point is she can't work any more. Either I don't understand you or you've made up your mind not to understand me. She can't do a proper job, all she does is sleep or sit around.

OLGA. Then let her sit around.

NATASHA [*astonished*]. What? Let her sit around! She's a servant, isn't she? [*Through tears.*] I can't make you out, Olga. I keep a nanny myself and a wet nurse for the baby, and we have a maid and a cook. But what do we need that old woman for? That's what I don't see.

[*The fire-alarm is sounded off stage.*]

OLGA. Tonight seems to have put ten years on my life.

NATASHA. We must get this straight once and for all, Olga. Your place is the school, mine is the home. You teach. I run the house. And if I happen to pass a remark about the servants I know what I'm talking about. And the sooner you get that into your head the better. So you mind that thieving old hag gets her marching orders for tomorrow. [*Stamps her feet.*] The old bitch! How dare you exasperate me like this, how dare you? [*Regaining her self-control.*] Really, if you don't move downstairs we'll never stop quarrelling. It's perfectly horrible.

[KULYGIN *comes in.*]

KULYGIN. Where's Masha? It really is time we went home. I'm told the fire's dying out. [*Stretches himself.*] Only one row of houses burnt down, but there was a wind, you know, and it looked at one time as if the whole town was on fire. [*Sits down.*] I'm tired out. Dear Olga, I often think, if it hadn't been for Masha I'd have married you, dear. You're a wonderful person. I'm all in. [*Listens.*]

OLGA. What is it?

KULYGIN. The doctor has to pick a time like this to get roaring drunk. A time like this. [*Gets up.*] I think he's coming up here. Can you hear anything? Yes, he is. [*Laughs.*] Really, what a character. I'm going to hide. [*Goes towards the cupboard and stands in the corner.*] The old pirate.

OLGA. He hasn't touched a drop for two years and now he has to go and get drunk. [*Moves to the back of the room with* NATASHA.]

[CHEBUTYKIN *comes in. He walks across the room as steadily as if he was sober, stops, stares, then goes to the washstand and begins to wash his hands.*]

CHEBUTYKIN [*morosely*]. Damn the whole lot of them. To hell with them. They think I'm a doctor and can cure diseases, but I know absolutely nothing. What I did know I've forgotten, I don't remember a thing, my mind's a blank. [OLGA *and* NATASHA *go out, unnoticed by him.*] To hell with them. I had a patient at Zasyp last Wednesday, a woman. She died, and it was all my fault. Yes indeed. I did know a thing or two about twenty-five years ago, but now I've forgotten it all, it's all gone. Perhaps I'm not even a human being, perhaps I only pretend to have arms and legs and a head, perhaps I don't even exist at all, and only imagine I walk about and eat and sleep. [*Weeps.*] Oh, how nice not to exist. [*Stops weeping, morosely.*] Who the hell cares? A couple of days ago at the club they were talking about Shakespeare and Voltaire. I've never read them, never read a word of them, but I managed to look as if I had and everyone else did the same. Could anything be more vulgar? Or more sordid? Then I suddenly remembered the woman I killed on

Wednesday, it all came back to me and I felt rotten, dirty, twisted inside. So I went and got drunk.

[IRINA, VERSHININ *and* TUZENBAKH *come in.* TUZENBAKH *is wearing a new and fashionable suit.*]

IRINA. Let's sit here a bit. No one will come in here.

VERSHININ. If it hadn't been for the troops the whole town would have gone up in flames. Good for them! [*Rubs his hands with pleasure.*] What a grand lot of chaps! Absolutely splendid!

KULYGIN [*going up to them*]. I say, what's the time?

TUZENBAKH. Well after three. It's starting to get light.

IRINA. They're all sitting in the dining-room, nobody seems to be going. Your friend Solyony's there as well. [*To* CHEBUTYKIN.] Why don't you go to bed, Doctor?

CHEBUTYKIN. I'm all right. Thanking you very much. [*Combs his beard.*]

KULYGIN [*laughs*]. Thoroughly plastered, aren't you, Doctor? [*Claps him on the shoulder.*] Well done, my boy. *In vino veritas*, as the ancients used to say.

TUZENBAKH. Everyone's asking me to get up a concert in aid of the fire victims.

IRINA. Oh, I shouldn't have thought anyone would——

TUZENBAKH. We could do it if we wanted. Masha for instance plays the piano beautifully.

KULYGIN. Indeed she does. Beautifully.

IRINA. She's forgotten how to. She hasn't played for three or four years.

TUZENBAKH. Nobody in this town appreciates music, nobody at all. But I do, I really do, and believe me, Masha plays magnificently. Brilliantly almost.

KULYGIN. Quite right, Baron. I'm so fond of Masha. She's wonderful.

TUZENBAKH. Imagine being able to play so gloriously, knowing all the time that not one living soul appreciates you.

KULYGIN [*sighs*]. True enough. But would it be quite the thing for her to play in a concert? [*Pause.*] Of course I'm a child in these matters, you know. I daresay it's quite all right. But to be perfectly honest, though our head's a decent enough chap—first rate in fact, quite outstanding—still he does hold certain views. This is nothing to do with him of course, but still I could have a word with him if you liked.

[CHEBUTYKIN *picks up a porcelain clock and examines it.*]

VERSHININ. I got terribly dirty at the fire, must look like nothing on earth. [*Pause.*] Yesterday I heard a rumour that our brigade's in for a transfer to the back of beyond. Some say it's Poland. Others reckon it's the far side of Siberia.

TUZENBAKH. I heard the same. Ah well, the town will be deserted and no mistake.

IRINA. We're going away as well.

CHEBUTYKIN [*drops the clock and breaks it*]. Smashed to smithereens.

[*Pause. Everyone is distressed and embarrassed.*]

KULYGIN [*picking up the pieces*]. A valuable object like that—good heavens, Doctor, whatever next! Take nought out of ten for conduct.

IRINA. That clock belonged to Mother.

CHEBUTYKIN. Very possibly. No doubt it was your mother's if you say so, but what if I didn't really break it, what if we only think I did? What if we only think we exist and aren't really here at all? I know nothing and nobody else knows anything either. [*Stands by the door.*] What are you all staring at? Natasha's carrying on with Protopopov and a lot of notice you take. You sit around as if you'd lost the use of your eyes while Natasha carries on with Protopopov. [*Sings.*] 'Be so good as to accept one of these dates.' [*Goes out.*]

VERSHININ. Well, well. [*Laughs.*] A funny business all this, it really is. [*Pause.*] When the fire broke out I ran home as fast as I could. I reached the house and saw it was quite all right, not in any danger or anything. My two little girls were standing by the front door in their nightclothes, their mother wasn't there, people were rushing about, horses and dogs were charging around, and you should have seen the children's faces. They looked frightened out of their wits, terribly pathetic and goodness knows what else. When I saw those faces my heart sank. My God, I thought, how much more have the children got to live through before they're finished? I grabbed them and rushed off, and I could think only of one thing—how much more will they have to put up with in this world? [*The alarm sounds. Pause.*] I arrive here and find their mother shouting and in a filthy temper.

[MASHA *comes in with a pillow and sits down on the sofa.*]

VERSHININ. The children were standing by the front door in their nightclothes, the street was all red with flames, there was a most appalling din. It struck me that it must have been rather like this in the old days of sudden enemy invasions, with all the looting and burning. But what a difference between then and now, come to think of it. Before very long—in two or three hundred years, say—people will look back on our way of life with the same horror and contempt, they'll regard our times as tough, hard, strange and most uncomfortable. Why, life is going to be absolutely wonderful, it really is. [*Laughs.*] Sorry, I'm laying down the law again. Does anyone mind if I go on? I'm in just the mood to air my views at the moment, I can't help it. [*Pause.*] Everyone seems to be asleep. Well, as I say, life is going to be wonderful. Just imagine it. The point is, just now there are only three people like you in this town, but in future generations there will be more and more of them. Things will change in course of time and everything will be done your way. People will live your way too and after that you'll become back numbers in your turn, and a new and better breed will arise. [*Laughs.*] I'm in a funny sort of mood tonight, I feel ready to take on anything. [*Sings.*]

'As everyone has always found,
It's love that makes the world go round.' [*Laughs.*]

MASHA. Ti tum ti tum ti——

VERSHININ. Tum tum tum——

MASHA. Tara tarara.

VERSHININ. Tum ti tum. [*Laughs.*]

[FEDOTIK *comes in.*]

FEDOTIK [*dances about*]. Burnt to a cinder. Not a thing left! [*Laughter.*]

IRINA. It isn't exactly funny. Have you really lost everything?

FEDOTIK [*laughs*]. The whole lot. The cupboard's bare. My guitar, my photographic stuff, my letters—all gone up in smoke. I was going to give you a little notebook, but that went up as well.

[SOLYONY *comes in.*]

IRINA. Oh, please go away, Captain Solyony. You can't come in here.

SOLYONY. No? And why is the baron allowed in here when I'm not?

VERSHININ. We really should be going. What news of the fire?

SOLYONY. I was told it's dying down. I must say it's decidedly odd that the baron can come in here when I can't. [*Takes out a bottle of scent and sprinkles himself with it.*]

VERSHININ. Ti tum ti tum.

MASHA. Tum tum.

VERSHININ [*laughing, to* SOLYONY]. Let's go into the dining-room.

SOLYONY. Very well, I'll take a note of it.
'I could develop my idea,
But might annoy the geese, I fear.'

[*Looking at* TUZENBAKH.] Chuck, chuck, chuck. [*Goes out with* VERSHININ *and* FEDOTIK.]

IRINA. That beastly Solyony's filled the place with scent. [*Bewildered.*] The baron's gone to sleep. Hey, Baron!

TUZENBAKH [*opening his eyes*]. I say, I am tired. A brick-works. No, I'm not talking in my sleep, I'm actually going to a brick-works very shortly, going to do a job there. I've already spoken to them. [*To* IRINA, *tenderly.*] You look so pale and beautiful, so enchanting. Your pale face seems to light up the darkness around you. You're depressed and dissatisfied with life. Oh, why not come with me? We'll go away and get a job together.

MASHA. Oh Nicholas, I wish you would go away.

TUZENBAKH [*laughing*]. So you're here, are you? I can't see. [*Kisses* IRINA's *hand.*] Good-bye then, I'll be off. Looking at you now, I remember a long time ago—it was on your name-day—when you spoke about the thrill of doing a real job of work. You were so cheerful and confident then and I seemed to see a happy future ahead of me. Where's all that gone now? [*Kisses her hand.*] There are tears in your eyes. You'd better go to bed, it's already getting light. It's almost morning. How I wish I could give my life for you.

MASHA. Do go, Nicholas. This really is too much.

TUZENBAKH. I'm going. [*Goes.*]

MASHA [*lying down*]. Theodore, are you asleep?

KULYGIN. Eh?

MASHA. Why don't you go home?

KULYGIN. Darling Masha, Masha my dear one——

IRINA. She's tired out. Better let her rest, Theodore.

KULYGIN. All right, I'll go. My splendid, wonderful wife—I love you, I love no one but you.

MASHA [*angrily*]. *Amo, amas, amat, amamus, amatis, amant.*

KULYGIN [*laughs*]. Oh, isn't she marvellous! You and I've been man and wife for seven years, but I feel as if we were married only yesterday, I do honestly. You really are a marvellous creature. I'm happy, happy, oh so happy.

MASHA. I'm bored, bored, oh so bored. [*Sits up.*] And there's something else I can't get out of my mind, something quite revolting. It's become an obsession, I can't keep it to myself any longer. It's about Andrew. He's mortgaged this house to the bank and his wife's pocketed the money. But the point is the house isn't his alone, it belongs to all four of us. He must surely realize that if he has any decency at all.

KULYGIN. Steady on, Masha. Why bring all that up? Andrew's in debt all round, so leave the poor fellow alone.

MASHA. Well, anyway, it's revolting. [*Lies down.*]

KULYGIN. You and I aren't poor. I have my job at the high school and I give private lessons as well. I'm a plain straightforward chap. *Omnia mea mecum porto*, as the saying goes.

MASHA. It's not that I want anything for myself. It's so unfair, that's what infuriates me. [*Pause.*] Theodore, why don't you go home?

KULYGIN [*kisses her*]. You're tired. Have half an hour's rest, and I'll just sit and wait. Go to sleep. [*Moves off.*] I'm happy, happy, oh so happy. [*Goes out.*]

IRINA. I must say, poor old Andrew has gone to seed. Living with that wretched woman has put years on his life and knocked all the stuffing out of him. At one time he was aiming to be a professor, and there he was yesterday boasting he'd got on the county council at long last. He's on the council and Protopopov's the chairman. The whole town's talking about it, everyone's laughing at him and he's the only one who doesn't know or see what's going on. And when everyone rushed off to the fire just now, there was he sitting in his room not taking the slightest notice and just playing his violin. [*Upset.*] Oh, it's frightful, absolutely frightful. [*Cries.*] I've had as much as I can take, I just can't stand any more.

[OLGA *comes in and starts tidying her bedside table.*]

IRINA [*sobs loudly*]. Why don't you get rid of me, throw me out? I can't stand it any more.

OLGA [*frightened*]. But what's the matter, darling?

IRINA [*sobbing*]. What's become of everything, where's it all gone? Where is it? Oh my God, I've forgotten, forgotten everything, my head's in such a whirl. I can't remember the Italian for 'window'— or 'ceiling' either. I'm always forgetting things, I forget something every day. And life is slipping away, it will never, never come back again, and we shall never go to Moscow either, I just know we shan't.

OLGA. Don't, dear, don't.

IRINA [*trying to control herself*]. Oh, I'm so miserable. I can't, I won't, I will not work. I've had enough. I used to be at the post office and now I work for the town council, and I loathe and despise everything they give me to do. I'm twenty-three, I've been working all this time and my brain's shrivelled up. I've grown thin and ugly and old and I've nothing to show for it, nothing, no satisfaction of any kind, while time passes by and I feel I'm losing touch with everything fine and genuine in life. It's like sinking down, down into a bottomless pit. I'm desperate. Why am I still alive, why haven't I done away with myself? I don't know.

OLGA. Don't cry, child, please, it upsets me so.

IRINA. I'm not crying, I'm not. I won't. Look, I've stopped now. I must stop, I really must.

OLGA. My dear, let me tell you something as your sister and your friend. If you want my advice, marry the baron.

[IRINA *cries quietly.*]

OLGA. After all you do respect him, you think so much of him. He may not be all that good-looking, but he's a fine, decent man. One doesn't marry for love, you know, it's only a matter of doing one's duty. That's what I think anyway, and I'd marry without love. I'd marry the first man who came along provided it was someone honest and decent. I'd even marry an old man.

IRINA. I've been waiting for us to move to Moscow all this time, thinking I'd meet my true love there. I've dreamed about him, loved him, but that was sheer foolishness as it's turned out.

OLGA [*embraces her sister*]. I understand, Irina darling, I do understand. When the baron resigned his commission and came to see us in his civilian suit, he looked so ugly it actually brought tears to my eyes. He asked me why I was crying. How could I tell him? But if he did marry you, if such was God's will, I'd be happy. That's an altogether different thing, you see.

[NATASHA *comes in through the door, right, carrying a candle, crosses the stage and goes out through the door, left, without saying anything.*]

MASHA [*sits up*]. The way she goes about you'd think it was she who started the fire.

OLGA. Masha, you're silly. You're the silliest person in the whole family. Forgive me saying so. [*Pause.*]

MASHA. My dears, I've a confession to make. I feel I must get it off my chest. I'll tell you two and then never breathe another word about it to anyone, I'll tell you right away. [*Quietly.*] It's my secret, but I want you to know it, I can't keep it to myself. [*Pause.*] I'm in love, in love with that man. He was in here just now. Oh, what's the use? What I'm saying is, I love Vershinin.

OLGA [*goes behind her screen*]. That's enough of that. I'm not listening anyway.

MASHA. It's hopeless. [*Clutches her head.*] I found him strange at first, then felt sorry for him, then fell in love with him—with him, with his voice, his conversation, his misfortunes and his two little girls.

OLGA [*from behind the screen*]. Anyway, I'm not listening. I don't care what rubbish you talk, I'm just not listening.

MASHA. Oh, you are funny, Olga. Since I love him it must be my fate, it must be my destiny. And he loves me. It's terrifying, isn't it? Isn't it? [*Takes* IRINA *by the hand and draws her towards herself.*] Oh darling, how shall we spend the rest of our lives, and what's to become of us? When you read a novel this sort of thing all seems so trite and obvious, but when you fall in love yourself you see that nobody knows anything and we all have to decide these things for ourselves. My dears, now I've confessed I'll say no more. Now I'll be like the madman in Gogol's story. I'll keep quiet and say nothing.

[ANDREW *comes in followed by* FERAPONT.]

ANDREW [*angrily*]. What do you want? I don't understand.

FERAPONT [*standing in the doorway, impatiently*]. I must have told you ten times already, Mr. Andrew.

ANDREW. Well, don't call me Mr. Andrew for a start. Call me sir.

FERAPONT. It's the firemen, sir, they say can they please go to the river through your garden. They've been going the long way round all this time and it's more than flesh and blood can stand.

ANDREW. All right. Tell them it's all right. [FERAPONT *goes out.*] Confound them. Where's Olga? [OLGA *comes out from behind the screen.*] It's you I wanted to see. Would you mind giving me the key of the cupboard? I've lost mine. You know that little key you've got. [OLGA *silently hands him the key.* IRINA *goes behind her screen. Pause.*]

ANDREW. Well, it's been quite a fire, hasn't it? It is dying down now. That wretched Ferapont made me lose my temper, dammit, and say something silly. I told him to call me sir. [*Pause.*] Why don't you speak, Olga? [*Pause.*] Isn't it time you stopped being so silly, there's nothing to sulk about. You're here, Masha, and Irina's here. Well, that's fine, we can clear the air once and for all. What have you all got against me, eh?

OLGA. Don't start that, Andrew. We can talk about it tomorrow. [*With feeling.*] What a dreadful night.

ANDREW [*greatly put out*]. There's no need to get excited. I'm asking you quite calmly what it is you have against me, and I want a straight answer.

VERSHININ [*off stage*]. Tum ti ti.

MASHA [*getting up, in a loud voice*]. Tum tum tum. [*To* OLGA.] Goodnight, Olga, look after yourself. [*Goes behind the screen and kisses* IRINA.] Pleasant dreams. Good-night, Andrew. Do go away, they're worn out. You can sort this all out tomorrow. [*Goes out.*]

OLGA. Yes, really, Andrew, let's leave it till tomorrow. [*Goes behind her screen.*] It's time we were in bed.

ANDREW. I'll say what's on my mind and go. Right. In the first place, you all seem to have it in for Natasha. Oh yes, I've noticed it since the day we were married. My wife, in case you want to know, is a fine, decent, straight-forward, honourable woman. Or that's what I think. I love my wife and respect her. I respect her, I tell you, and I require others to do the same. I repeat—she's a decent, honourable woman, and you'll forgive my saying that all your objections to her are sheer childishness. [*Pause.*] And in the second place, you seem annoyed with me because I'm not a professor and don't do academic work. But I happen to work for the county council. I'm a county councillor and I consider that work every bit as honourable and worth-while as any academic job. I'm on the county council and proud of it, in case you're interested. [*Pause.*] And in the third place I've something else to say. I know I mortgaged this house without getting your permission. That was wrong, I admit, and I apologize. I had to do it because of all that money I owed, thirty-five thousand roubles of it. I don't gamble any more, I gave that up long ago, but the main point in my defence is that you girls have an annuity, whereas I've had no such source of—income, so to speak. [*Pause.*]

KULYGIN [*through the door*]. Isn't Masha here? [*Agitated.*] Where can she have got to? This is all very odd. [*Goes out.*]

ANDREW. They won't listen. Natasha's a fine, decent woman, I tell you. [*Walks silently up and down the stage, then stops.*] When we got married I thought we were going to be happy, all of us. But oh my God! [*Cries.*] My dear sisters, my darling sisters, don't believe what I've been saying, don't believe a word of it. [*Goes out.*]

KULYGIN [*through the door, agitatedly*]. Where's Masha? Isn't she here? This is most peculiar. [*Goes away.*]

[*The alarm sounds. The stage is empty.*]

IRINA [*from behind the screen*]. Olga, who's that knocking on the floor?

OLGA. The doctor. He's drunk.

IRINA. It's been one thing after another all night. [*Pause.*] Olga! [*Looks out from behind the screen.*] Have you heard? They're moving our brigade, posting it somewhere far away.

OLGA. That's only a rumour.

IRINA. Then we'll be all on our own. Olga!

OLGA. Yes?

IRINA. I respect the baron, Olga darling, I think very highly of him, he is a very good man and I will marry him, I will, I will, only do let's go to Moscow. We must go. Please! There's nowhere in the world like Moscow. Let's go, Olga, do let's go!

CURTAIN

ACT FOUR

The old garden belonging to the PROZOROVS' *house. A long avenue of firs with a view of the river at the end. A wood on the far side of the river. On the right the terrace of the house. On it a table with bottles and glasses—someone has obviously just been drinking champagne. Midday. From time to time people from the street go through the garden towards the river. Five or six soldiers march briskly past.*

*   CHEBUTYKIN, who remains in a genial mood throughout the Act, is sitting in an armchair in the garden waiting for someone to call him. He has his army cap on and holds a stick.* IRINA, KULYGIN—*who wears a decoration on a ribbon round his neck and has shaved off his moustache—and* TUZENBAKH *are standing on the terrace saying good-bye to* FEDOTIK *and* RODÉ, *who are coming down the steps. Both officers are in service dress.*

TUZENBAKH [*embraces* FEDOTIK]. You're a good fellow, we've always got on well together. [*Embraces* RODÉ.] Once more then. Good-bye, my dear fellow.

IRINA. *Au revoir.*

FEDOTIK. It isn't *au revoir*, it's good-bye. We'll never see each other again.

KULYGIN. Who knows? [*Wipes his eyes and smiles.*] Now I'm crying too.

IRINA. We'll meet again some time.

FEDOTIK. You mean in ten or fifteen years? By then we'll hardly know each other, we'll meet as strangers. Stand still, please. [*Takes a snapshot.*] Now, just once more.

RODÉ [*embraces* TUZENBAKH]. This is the last time we'll see each other. [*Kisses* IRINA'*s hand.*] Thank you for all you've done.

FEDOTIK [*annoyed*]. Oh, can't you stand still a moment?

TUZENBAKH. We shall meet again with luck. And be sure to write to us, don't forget.

RODÉ [*looking round the garden*]. Good-bye, trees. [*Shouts.*] Halloo-oo! [*Pause.*] Good-bye, echo.

KULYGIN. You'll get married over in Poland, very likely. Your wife will put her arms round you and call you 'darling' in Polish. [*Laughs.*]

FEDOTIK [*with a glance at his watch*]. There's less than an hour to go. Solyony's the only one from our battery on the barge party, the rest of us go with the marching column. There's a unit of three batteries leaving today and three more going tomorrow, and then the town will have a bit of peace and quiet.

TUZENBAKH. And an awful dose of boredom.

RODÉ. I say, where's Masha?

KULYGIN. In the garden somewhere.

FEDOTIK. We must say good-bye to her.

RODÉ. Good-bye. I must go or I'll start crying. [*Quickly embraces* TUZENBAKH *and* KULYGIN, *kisses* IRINA'*s hand*.] We've had a wonderful time here.

FEDOTIK [*to* KULYGIN]. Here's something to remember me by, a note-book and pencil. We'll take this way down to the river. [FEDOTIK *and* RODÉ *move off, glancing back*.]

RODÉ [*shouts*]. Halloo-oo!

KULYGIN [*shouts*]. Good-bye.

[FEDOTIK *and* RODÉ *meet* MASHA *at the back of the stage and say good-bye to her. She goes off with them.*]

IRINA. They've gone. [*Sits down on the bottom step of the terrace.*]

CHEBUTYKIN. And forgotten to say good-bye to me.

IRINA. Well, what about you?

CHEBUTYKIN. That's true, I forgot to myself. Still, I'll be seeing them again before long. I'm off tomorrow. Yes. I have just one day left. A year from now I'll be on the retired list and I'll come back here and spend the rest of my life with you. Only a year now till I get my pension. [*Puts his newspaper in his pocket and takes out another.*] I'll come back here and turn over a new leaf. I'll be a good little boy, very considerate, and oh so well behaved.

IRINA. It's high time you did mend your ways somehow, my dear, it really is.

CHEBUTYKIN. Quite. That's how I feel. [*Sings quietly.*] Tararaboom-deay, let's have a tune today.

KULYGIN. You're incorrigible, Doctor, incorrigible.

CHEBUTYKIN. You should have taken me in hand then, you might have put me on the right lines.

IRINA. Theodore's shaved off his moustache. I can't bear to look at him.

KULYGIN. Why, what's wrong?

CHEBUTYKIN. I might tell you what your face puts me in mind of, but I'd better not.

KULYGIN. Why all the fuss? It's quite the thing these days, *modus vivendi* and all that. The head's clean shaven, so when I became second master I followed suit. No one likes it, but I don't care. I'm perfectly happy. Moustache or no moustache, I'm happy either way. [*Sits down.*]

[ANDREW *crosses the back of the stage pushing a pram with a sleeping baby in it.*]

IRINA. Doctor, be an angel—I'm awfully worried. You were in town last night. Tell me, what was this affair on the boulevard?

CHEBUTYKIN. What affair? It was nothing. Lot of poppycock. [*Reads his paper.*] Nothing that matters anyway.

KULYGIN. What I heard is, Solyony and the baron met on the boulevard outside the theatre yesterday——

TUZENBAKH. Please stop. Oh, what's the use—? [*Makes a gesture as if to dismiss the subject and goes into the house.*]

KULYGIN. It happened outside the theatre. Solyony started picking on the baron and the baron lost his temper and insulted him.

CHEBUTYKIN. I don't know anything about it. It's a lot of bunkum.

KULYGIN. A schoolmaster once wrote 'bunkum' on a pupil's essay and the boy thought it was Latin and started declining it. *Bunkum, bunkum, bunkum, bunki, bunko, bunko.* [*Laughs.*] Terribly funny that. Solyony's said to be in love with Irina and he seems to have got it in for the baron. Well, that's only natural. Irina's a very nice girl, she's even a bit like Masha, always wrapped up in her own thoughts. But you're more easy-going than Masha, Irina. Though actually Masha's very good-natured too. Oh, I do love Masha.

[*From off stage at the back comes a cry*: Hallo there! Halloo-oo!]

IRINA [*shudders*]. The least thing seems to frighten me today. [*Pause.*] I've packed everything and I'm sending my stuff on after luncheon. The baron and I are getting married tomorrow, then we're going straight off to that brick-works. Next day I start work at school and a new life begins, God willing. When I sat for my teacher's diploma I was actually crying for joy. [*Pause.*] The carter will be here for our things in a minute.

KULYGIN. This is all very well, but it doesn't add up to much, does it? It's just a lot of hot air, there's precious little sense in it. Anyway I wish you luck, I really do.

CHEBUTYKIN [*deeply moved*]. My darling child, my splendid little girl, you're so far ahead of me I'll never catch up with you now. I've been left behind like a bird that's too old to fly away with the flock. Fly away, my dears, fly away and the best of luck to you. [*Pause.*] It's a pity you shaved your moustache off, Kulygin.

KULYGIN. That's quite enough of that. [*Sighs.*] Well, the army's leaving today and we'll be back where we were. They can say what they like, but Masha's a good, loyal little woman, I love her very much and I thank my lucky stars. It's all the luck of the game, you know. There's a clerk in the tax office here, fellow called Kozyrev. We were at school together, but when he was in the fifth form he was expelled because he just couldn't grasp the construction of *ut* and the subjunctive. He's ill these days and terribly hard up, and when I run across him I always say, 'Hallo there, *ut* and the subjunctive.' 'Yes,' he always says. 'That's just my trouble, *ut* and the subjunctive.' Then he starts coughing. Now I've been lucky all my life, I'm very fortunate, I even have the Order of St. Stanislaus second class. And now I teach other people this *ut* and the subjunctive business. Of course I'm no fool, I am brighter than average. But there's more to happiness than that.

[*The* Maiden's Prayer *is played on a piano in the house.*]

IRINA. Tomorrow night I shan't have to hear that *Maiden's Prayer* any more or keep meeting Protopopov. [*Pause.*] Do you know, Protopopov's in the drawing-room. He's even turned up today.

KULYGIN. Isn't our headmistress here yet?

IRINA. No. We've sent for her. You can't imagine what a bore I find it living here on my own without Olga. Now she's headmistress, she lives in at school and she's on the go all day, while I'm lonely and depressed with nothing to do and I hate my room in this house. But I've made up my mind. If I can't go to Moscow, well, I can't, and that's that. It's just the way things have turned out. It can't be helped, it's all God's will and that's the truth. Nicholas asked me to marry him. Well, I thought it over and decided to say yes. He's a good man, he really is—unbelievably good. I suddenly felt as if I'd grown wings. I cheered up and felt so much easier in my mind, and the old urge came over me to work, work, work. But then there was this incident yesterday, whatever it was, and I feel as if something awful's going to happen to me.

CHEBUTYKIN. Stuff and nonsense. *Bunki, bunko, bunko.*

NATASHA [*through a window*]. The headmistress.

KULYGIN. The headmistress has come. Let's go in.

[*Goes indoors with* IRINA.]

CHEBUTYKIN [*reads the paper and sings softly*]. Tararaboomdeay, let's have a tune today.

[MASHA *comes up to him.* ANDREW *crosses the back of the stage pushing the pram.*]

MASHA. Taking it nice and easy, aren't you?

CHEBUTYKIN. What's wrong with that?

MASHA [*sits down*]. Oh, nothing. [*Pause.*] Were you in love with my mother?

CHEBUTYKIN. Very much so.

MASHA. Did she love you?

CHEBUTYKIN [*after a pause*]. That I don't recall.

MASHA. Is my man here? That's what our cook Martha used to call her policeman—'my man'. Is my man here?

CHEBUTYKIN. Not yet.

MASHA. When you have to snatch what crumbs of happiness you can and then lose it all, as is happening to me, you gradually grow hard and bad-tempered. [*Points at her breast.*] I feel I'm going to burst. [*Looking at* ANDREW *as he pushes the pram.*] There goes brother Andrew. All our hopes have come to nothing. Imagine thousands of people hoisting up a huge bell. Then after all the effort and money spent on it, it suddenly falls and is smashed to pieces. Suddenly, for no reason at all. That's how it's been with Andrew.

ANDREW. I say, when are we going to have some quiet round here? What an awful row.

CHEBUTYKIN. It won't be long now. [*Looks at his watch.*] I've got an old-fashioned watch, a repeater. [*Winds the watch. It rings.*] One, Two and Five Battery are leaving at one o'clock sharp. [*Pause.*] And I'm off tomorrow.

ANDREW. Will you ever come back?

CHEBUTYKIN. I don't know, I may be back next year. Damned if I know. Or care either.

[*There is the sound of a harp and violin somewhere far away.*]

ANDREW. This town will be quite dead, it'll be like living in a museum. [*Pause.*] Something happened outside the theatre yesterday, I've no idea what, but everyone's talking about it.

CHEBUTYKIN. Oh, it was nothing. Lot of nonsense. Solyony started annoying the baron, the baron lost his temper and insulted him, and the upshot was Solyony had to challenge him to a duel. [*Looks at his watch.*] It must be pretty well time. It's to be at half past twelve in that bit of crown forest over there on the other side of the river. Bang, bang! [*Laughs.*] Solyony sees himself as a Lermontov. Even writes poetry. Joking apart though, this is his third duel.

MASHA. Whose?

CHEBUTYKIN. Solyony's.

MASHA. What about the baron?

CHEBUTYKIN. What about the baron? [*Pause.*]

MASHA. I'm in a complete daze. I still say they shouldn't be allowed to fight. He might wound the baron or even kill him.

CHEBUTYKIN. The baron's a nice enough fellow, but one baron more or less in the world—what does that matter? Let them get on with it. Who cares? [*Shouts are heard from the other side of the garden: 'Yoo-hoo! Halloo-oo!'*] You can just wait a minute. That's Skvortsov shouting, one of the seconds. He's there in a boat. [*Pause.*]

ANDREW. If you ask me, duelling or attending a duel, even as a doctor, is downright immoral.

CHEBUTYKIN. That's only the way you see it. We're not real, neither is anything else in the world. We aren't here at all actually, we only think we are. And who cares anyway?

MASHA. Talk, talk, talk. Nothing but talk the whole blessed day. [*Moves off.*] As if this climate wasn't quite enough, with snow liable to fall any minute, there has to be all this chit-chat as well. [*Stops.*] I'm not going indoors, I can't bear it there. Please let me know when Vershinin gets here. [*Moves off down the avenue.*] Look, the birds are flying off already. [*Looks up.*] They're swans or geese. Dear, happy birds. [*Goes off.*]

ANDREW. Our house is going to seem awfully empty. The officers are going, you're going, Irina's getting married, and I'll be all on my own here.

CHEBUTYKIN. What about your wife?

[FERAPONT *comes in with some papers.*]

ANDREW. My wife is—well, she's my wife. She's loyal and decent—kind too, if you like—but there's something degrading about her too, as if she was some kind of blind, groping, scruffy little animal. She's not a human being anyway. I'm speaking to you as a friend. There's no one else I can really talk to. I love Natasha, yes I do, but there are times when I find her thoroughly vulgar, and then I don't know what to think and I've no idea why I do love her so much—or anyway used to.

CHEBUTYKIN [*stands up*]. I'm leaving tomorrow, old boy, and we may never meet again, so here's a word of advice. You just put your hat on, pick up a walking stick and go. Go on and on and on, and don't ever look back. And the further you go the better.

[SOLYONY *crosses the back of the stage with two officers. Seeing* CHEBUTYKIN, *he turns towards him while the officers walk on.*]

SOLYONY. It's time, Doctor. Half past twelve. [*Greets* ANDREW.]

CHEBUTYKIN. All right then, confound you all. [*To* ANDREW.] If anyone wants me, Andrew, would you mind saying I'll be back in a minute? [*Sighs.*] Ah me!

SOLYONY. 'Before he'd time to turn a hair
          He'd been knocked over by a bear.' [*Moves off with* CHEBU-TYKIN.] What are you moaning about, Grandad?

CHEBUTYKIN. Oh, go away.

SOLYONY. How are you feeling?

CHEBUTYKIN [*angrily*]. Don't ask silly questions and you won't get silly answers.

SOLYONY. The old boy needn't get hot under the collar. I shan't overdo it, I'll only wing him like a woodcock. [*Takes out a bottle and sprinkles scent on his hands.*] I've used up a whole bottle today, but my hands still smell. They smell like a corpse. [*Pause.*] Yes indeed. Do you remember those lines of Lermontov's?

'Restless, he seeks the raging storm,
As if the storm could give him rest.'

CHEBUTYKIN. Yes.

'Before he'd time to turn a hair
He'd been knocked over by a bear.' [*Goes out with* SOLYONY.]

[*Shouts are heard*: 'Halloo-oo! Yoo-hoo!' ANDREW *and* FERAPONT *come in.*]

FERAPONT. Some papers to sign——

ANDREW [*irritably*]. Leave me alone for heaven's sake, do leave me alone. [*Goes out with pram.*]

FERAPONT. But that's what papers are for, isn't it? To be signed. [*Goes to the back of the stage.*]

[*Enter* IRINA *and* TUZENBAKH, *who is wearing a straw hat.* KULYGIN *crosses the stage shouting,* 'Hallo there, Masha, hallo!']

TUZENBAKH. He must be the only person in town who's glad the army's leaving.

IRINA. That's only natural. [*Pause.*] The town will be half dead now.

TUZENBAKH. I'll be back in a minute, my dear.

IRINA. Where are you going?

TUZENBAKH. I must go into town and—see some of my friends off.

IRINA. That isn't true. Your thoughts seem far away this morning, Nicholas. Why? [*Pause.*] What did happen outside the theatre last night?

TUZENBAKH [*with an impatient gesture*]. I'll be back in an hour, back with you again. [*Kisses her hands.*] Darling. [*Gazes into her eyes.*] It's five years since I first fell in love with you and I still can't get used to it, I find you more beautiful every day. You have such marvellous, wonderful hair, such lovely eyes. I'll take you away tomorrow, we'll work, we'll be rich and all my dreams will come true. And you'll be happy. There is just one thing wrong though. You don't love me.

IRINA. I can't help that. I'll be your wife, I'll honour and obey you, but I don't love you and I can't help it. [*Cries.*] I've never been in love, never. Oh, I've longed for love, dreamed about it so much day and night, but my heart is like a wonderful grand piano that can't be used because it's locked up and the key's lost. [*Pause.*] You look worried.

TUZENBAKH. I couldn't sleep last night. Not that there's anything alarming or particularly frightening in my life, but the thought of that lost key torments me and keeps me awake. Say something to me. [*Pause.*] Say something.

IRINA. Why, what am I to say?

TUZENBAKH. Anything.

IRINA. Oh, please don't talk like that. [*Pause.*]

TUZENBAKH. It's funny the way stupid, trivial little things sometimes loom up out of the blue and affect one's life. You still laugh at them, still think of them as trivial, but you somehow get carried away by them and don't seem able to stop yourself. Anyway let's not talk about that. I feel marvellous. I feel as if I'm seeing all these fir-trees, maples and silver birches for the first time. All these things seem to be watching me as if wondering what was going to happen next. What beautiful trees. And when you come to think of it, what a beautiful thing life ought to be with trees like this around. [*Shouts of*: 'Yoo-hoo! Halloo-oo!'] I have to go now. Look at that dead tree. It's withered, but it still sways in the breeze with all the others. It's the same with me, I feel I'll still be part of life somehow or other even if I die. Good-bye, Irina. [*Kisses* IRINA'*s hands.*] I've put those papers you gave me under a calendar on my table.

IRINA. I'm coming with you.

TUZENBAKH [*alarmed*]. Oh no, no! [*Moves off quickly and stops some way down the avenue.*] Irina!

IRINA. What?

TUZENBAKH [*not knowing what to say*]. I haven't had any coffee this morning. Would you ask them to make me some? [*Goes off quickly.*]

[IRINA *stands lost in thought, then goes to the back of the stage and sits on the swing.* ANDREW *comes in pushing the pram.* FERAPONT *appears.*]

FERAPONT. Mr. Andrew, these papers aren't mine, you know, they're official documents. I didn't invent them.

ANDREW. Where is my past life, oh what has become of it—when I was young, happy and intelligent, when I had such glorious thoughts and visions, and my present and future seemed so bright and promising? Why is it we've hardly started living before we all become dull, drab, boring, lazy, complacent, useless and miserable? This town's two hundred years old and we've a hundred thousand people living here, but the trouble is, every man jack of them's exactly like every other one, and no one here does anything really worth while. Or ever has. We've never produced a single scholar or artist or anyone else with a touch of originality to make us envy him, or decide we were damn well going to go one better ourselves. All these people do is eat, drink and sleep till they drop down dead. Then new ones are born to carry on the eating, drinking and sleeping. And to save themselves getting bored to tears and put a bit of spice in their lives, they go in for all this sickening gossip, vodka, gambling, litigation. Wives deceive their husbands and husbands tell lies and pretend they're deaf and blind to what's going on, and all the time the children are crushed by vulgarity, lose any spark of inspiration they might ever have had, and—like their fathers and mothers before them—turn into a lot of miserable living corpses, each one exactly like his neighbour. [*To* FERAPONT, *angrily.*] What do *you* want?

FERAPONT. Eh? Papers for you to sign.

ANDREW. You're a nuisance.

FERAPONT [*handing over the papers*]. The porter at the tax office was on about something just now, says they had two hundred degrees of frost in St. Petersburg last winter.

ANDREW. I loathe our present life, but thinking about the future makes me feel really good. I feel so easy and relaxed, I see a light glimmering in the distance, I have a vision of freedom. I see myself and my children freed from idleness and drinking kvass and stuffing ourselves with goose and cabbage, freed from our after-dinner naps and this vile habit of trying to get something for nothing.

FERAPONT. Two thousand people froze to death, he says. He says everyone was scared stiff. It was either St. Petersburg or Moscow, I don't rightly remember.

ANDREW [*in a sudden access of tenderness*]. My dear sisters, my wonderful sisters. [*Through tears.*] Masha, my sister——

NATASHA [*appearing in a window*]. Who's making all that noise? Is that you, Andrew? You'll wake up little Sophie. *Il ne faut pas faire du bruit, la Sophie est dormée déjà. Vous êtes un ours.* [*Flaring up.*] If you can't keep your mouth shut you'd better give the pram to someone else. Ferapont, take that pram from Mr. Prozorov.

FERAPONT. Very well, madam. [*Takes the pram.*]

ANDREW [*embarrassed*]. I wasn't making much noise.

NATASHA [*from behind the window, speaking lovingly to her little boy*]. Bobik! Naughty Bobik! Bad, bad Bobik!

ANDREW [*glancing over the papers*]. All right, I'll look through this lot and sign the ones that need signing, and you can take them back to the office. [*Goes indoors reading the papers.* FERAPONT *wheels the pram off into the garden.*]

NATASHA [*from behind the window*]. Bobik! What's Mummy's name? Oh, isn't he sweet? And who's this? It's Aunty Olga. Say, 'Hallo, Aunty Olly.'

[*Two street musicians, a man and a girl, come in playing a violin and a harp.* VERSHININ *comes out of the house with* OLGA *and* ANFISA. *They listen for a while in silence.* IRINA *goes up to them.*]

OLGA. Our garden's like a public highway with people coming and going all the time. Nanny, give these people something.

ANFISA [*gives the musicians money*]. Run along then and God be with you, my dears. [*The musicians bow and go off.*] Poor things, they must be half starved. Why else would they do it? Good morning, Irina dear. [*Kisses her.*] I'm having a lovely time, child, I really am. I'm living with Olga at the high-school in a school flat. The good Lord's found me a little place of my own in my old age and I'm having the time of my life, old sinner that I am. It's a great big flat belonging to the school, and I've a little room of my own and my own little bed, all rent free. I sometimes wake up in the middle of the night and think—Lord and Holy Mother of God, I'm the happiest woman in the world.

VERSHININ [*with a glance at his watch*]. We're just leaving, Olga. I have to go. [*Pause.*] I wish you every, every—. Where's Masha?

IRINA. Somewhere in the garden. I'll go and find her.

VERSHININ. That's very kind, I am in rather a hurry.

ANFISA. I'll go and look as well. [*Shouts.*] Masha, are you there? [*Goes off into the garden with* IRINA.] Hallo there, hallo!

VERSHININ. Everything comes to an end some time, and here we are saying good-bye. [*Looks at his watch.*] The town gave us a sort of farewell lunch, we had champagne and the mayor made a speech. I ate my lunch and listened to the mayor, but I was here with you in spirit. [*Glances round the garden.*] I've grown so fond of you all.

OLGA. Shall we ever meet again?

VERSHININ. I shouldn't think so. [*Pause.*] My wife and the girls are staying on here for a couple of months. If anything should happen or they need anything, please——

OLGA. Yes, yes of course, set your mind at rest. [*Pause.*] Tomorrow there won't be a single soldier left in town. We shall stay behind with our memories, and of course things will be very different for us now. [*Pause.*] Nothing ever works out as we want it. I never wanted to be a headmistress, but I am one. So it's obvious I'll never get to Moscow now.

VERSHININ. Ah well, thank you for everything. And if there's been anything at all amiss, please forgive me. I've talked much too much. Please forgive that too. Don't think too badly of me.

OLGA [*wiping her eyes*]. Why doesn't Masha come?

VERSHININ. What else is there to say before I go? Shouldn't I hold forth about something? [*Laughs.*] Life isn't a bed of roses. A lot of us think it's a hopeless dead end. Still, you must admit things are getting brighter and better all the time, and it does look as if we'll see a real break in the clouds before very long. [*Looks at his watch.*] It really is time for me to go. In the old days people were always fighting wars and their lives were one long round of campaigns, invasions and victories, but those things are all past history now. They've left a great gap behind them and so far there's been nothing to put in their place, but people are desperately trying to find something and in the end they're bound to succeed. Oh, if that could only happen soon. [*Pause.*] If we could only combine education with hard work, you know, and hard work with education. [*Looks at his watch.*] Well, I really must be on my way——

OLGA. Here she is.

[MASHA *comes in.*]

VERSHININ. I came to say good-bye. [OLGA *moves a little to one side so that they can say good-bye.*]

MASHA [*looking into his eyes*]. Good-bye, dear. [*A long kiss.*]

OLGA. Don't, don't, please.

[MASHA *sobs loudly.*]

VERSHININ. Write to me, darling. Don't forget me. Now let me go, I must go—. You take her, Olga, I really—have to go. I'm late. [*Deeply moved, kisses* OLGA'*s hands, then embraces* MASHA *again and quickly leaves.*]

OLGA. Don't cry, Masha. Do stop, dear.

[KULYGIN *comes in.*]

KULYGIN [*embarrassed*]. Never mind, let her cry, let her. Dear Masha, good, kind Masha, you're my wife, and I'm still happy in spite of everything. I'm not complaining or blaming you at all, as Olga here can witness. Let's go back to living as we used to, and I won't breathe so much as a word or hint——

MASHA [*choking back her sobs*].
'A green oak by a curving shore,
And on that oak a chain of gold—
And on that oak a chain of gold.'
I'm going crazy. A green oak—by a curving shore.

OLGA. There, there, Masha. Calm yourself. Get her some water.

MASHA. I've stopped crying now.

KULYGIN. She's stopped crying. She's a good girl.

[*The muffled sound of a distant shot is heard.*]

MASHA.   'A green oak by a curving shore,
And on that oak a chain of gold.'
A green cat. A green oak. I've got it all mixed up. [*Drinks some water.*] I've made a mess of my life. I don't want anything now. I'll be all right in a moment—. It doesn't matter. What does it mean, 'by a curving shore'? Why can't I get those words out of my head? Oh, my thoughts are in such a whirl.

[IRINA *comes in.*]

OLGA. Calm yourself, Masha. That's right, there's a sensible girl. Let's go indoors.

MASHA [*angrily*]. I'm not going in there. [*Starts sobbing again, but stops at once.*] I don't go in that house any more. I'm not going in now.

IRINA. Let's all sit here for a bit, there's no need to talk. I'm leaving tomorrow, you know. [*Pause.*]

KULYGIN. Yesterday I took this false beard and moustache off a boy in the third form. [*Puts on the beard and moustache.*] I look like our German master. [*Laughs.*] I do, don't I? Those boys are really priceless.

MASHA. I say, you really do look like the German master.

OLGA [*laughs*]. Yes, he does.

[MASHA *cries.*]

IRINA. Please don't, Masha.

KULYGIN. A striking resemblance.

[NATASHA *comes in.*]

NATASHA [*to the* MAID]. Now what was it? Oh yes. Mr. Protopopov's going to keep an eye on Sophie and my husband may as well push Bobik's pram. Children do make such a lot of work. [*To* IRINA.] What a shame you're leaving tomorrow, Irina. Why don't you stay on another week? [*Sees* KULYGIN *and shrieks. He laughs and removes the beard and moustache.*] Oh, you awful man, you did give me a shock. [*To* IRINA.] I'm used to having you around and I'll find it quite a wrench, you know, now you're leaving. I'll move Andrew into your room along with his violin. He can scrape away in there as much as he likes and we'll put Sophie in his room. What a heavenly little girl. Isn't she a wonderful child? She gave me such a sweet look today and said 'Mummy'.

KULYGIN. She is a lovely baby, no doubt about it.

NATASHA. So I'll be all on my own here tomorrow. [*Sighs.*] The first thing I'll do is have that avenue of firs cut down and that maple-tree. It looks so hideous in the evening. [*To* IRINA.] That sash doesn't suit you at all, dear, in fact it's in very poor taste. You need something nice and bright. And I'll have lots and lots of nice flowers planted all over the place, and they'll make ever such a lovely perfume. [*Sternly.*] What's this fork doing on the bench here? [*Going indoors, to the* MAID.] I asked what this fork was doing on the bench. [*Shouts.*] You dare answer me back!

KULYGIN. She's off again.

[*A band is heard playing a march off stage. Everyone listens.*]

OLGA. They're leaving.

[CHEBUTYKIN *comes in.*]

MASHA. Our friends are leaving. Oh well, may they have a happy journey. [*To her husband.*] We'd better go home. Where's my hat and coat?

KULYGIN. I took them indoors. I'll go and get them.

OLGA. Yes, now we can all go off home. It's high time.

CHEBUTYKIN. Olga!

OLGA. What is it? [*Pause.*] What's happened?

CHEBUTYKIN. Nothing. I don't know how to tell you. [*Whispers in her ear.*]

OLGA [*aghast*]. No, no, it can't be true.

CHEBUTYKIN. Yes. What a business! I'm tired out, absolutely done in, I don't want to say another word. [*Annoyed.*] Anyway, what does it all matter?

MASHA. What happened?

OLGA [*embraces* IRINA]. This has been a terrible day. Darling, I don't know how to tell you——

IRINA. What is it? Tell me at once, for God's sake—what is it? [*Cries.*]

CHEBUTYKIN. The baron's just been killed in a duel.

IRINA [*weeps quietly*]. I knew it, I knew it.

CHEBUTYKIN [*sits down on a bench at the back of the stage*]. I'm worn out. [*Takes a newspaper out of his pocket.*] They may as well have a cry. [*Sings softly.*] Tararaboomdeay, let's have a tune today. Anyway, what does it all matter?

[*The three sisters stand close together.*]

MASHA. Oh, listen to the band. They're all leaving us, and one has gone right away and will never, never come back, and we shall be left alone to begin our lives again. We must go on living, we must.

IRINA [*puts her head on* OLGA'*s breast*]. What is all this for? Why all this suffering? The answer will be known one day, and then there will be no more mysteries left, but till then life must go on, we must work and work and think of nothing else. I'll go off alone tomorrow to teach at a school and spend my whole life serving those who may need me. It's autumn now and it will soon be winter, with everything buried in snow, and I shall work, work, work.

OLGA [*embraces both her sisters*]. Listen to the band. What a splendid, rousing tune, it puts new heart into you, doesn't it? Oh, my God! In time we shall pass on for ever and be forgotten. Our faces will be forgotten and our voices and how many of us there were. But our sufferings will bring happiness to those who come after us, peace and joy will reign on earth, and there will be kind words and kind thoughts for us and our times. We still have our lives ahead of us, my dears, so let's make the most of them. The band's playing such cheerful, happy music, it feels as if we might find out before long what our lives and sufferings are for. If we could only know! If we could only know!

[*The music becomes fainter and fainter.* KULYGIN, *smiling cheerfully, brings the hat and coat, while* ANDREW *pushes the pram with* BOBIK *sitting in it.*]

CHEBUTYKIN [*singing softly*]. Tararaboomdeay, let's have a tune to-day. [*Reads the newspaper.*] None of it matters. Nothing matters.

OLGA. If we could only know, oh if we could only know!

CURTAIN

THE CHERRY ORCHARD

[Вишнёвый сад]

A COMEDY IN FOUR ACTS

(1903–1904)

CHARACTERS

MRS. LYUBA RANEVSKY, an estate-owner
ANYA, her daughter, aged 17
VARYA, her adopted daughter, aged 24
LEONID GAYEV, Mrs. Ranevsky's brother
YERMOLAY LOPAKHIN, a businessman
PETER TROFIMOV, a student
BORIS SIMEONOV-PISHCHIK, an estate-owner
CHARLOTTE, a governess
SIMON YEPIKHODOV, a clerk
DUNYASHA, a maid
FIRS, a manservant, aged 87
YASHA, a young manservant
A passer-by
A stationmaster
A post office clerk
Guests and servants

The action takes place on Mrs. Ranevsky's estate

ACT ONE

A room which is still known as 'the nursery'. One of the doors leads to ANYA's *room. Dawn is breaking and the sun will soon be up. It is May. The cherry trees are in bloom, but it is cold and frosty in the orchard. The windows of the room are shut.*

Enter DUNYASHA *carrying a candle, and* LOPAKHIN *with a book in his hand.*

LOPAKHIN. The train's arrived, thank God. What time is it?

DUNYASHA. Nearly two o'clock. [*Blows out the candle.*] It's already light.

LOPAKHIN. How late was the train then? A couple of hours at least. [*Yawns and stretches himself.*] And a prize idiot I am, making an ass of myself like this. I come out here specially so I can go and meet them at the station, then suddenly fall asleep and wake up too late. Dropped off in the chair. What a nuisance. You might have woken me.

DUNYASHA. I thought you'd gone. [*Listens.*] It sounds as if they're coming.

LOPAKHIN [*listening*]. No, they're not. There's the luggage to be got out and all that. [*Pause.*] Mrs. Ranevsky's been living abroad for five years and I've no idea what she's like now. She was always such a nice woman, unaffected and easy to get on with. I remember when I was a lad of fifteen and my father—he's not alive now, but he kept the village shop in those days—punched me in the face and made my nose bleed. We'd come round here for something or other and he had a bit of drink inside him. Mrs. Ranevsky—I can see her now—was still quite a slip of a girl. She brought me over to the wash-stand here in this very room, the nursery as it was. 'Don't cry, little peasant,' she said. 'You'll soon be right as rain.' [*Pause.*] Little peasant. It's true my father was a peasant, but here am I in my white waistcoat and brown boots, barging in like a bull in a china shop. The only thing is, I am rich. I have plenty of money, but when you really get down to it I'm just another country bumpkin. [*Turns the pages of his book.*] I was reading this book and couldn't make sense of it. Fell asleep over it. [*Pause.*]

DUNYASHA. The dogs have been awake all night, they can tell the family are coming.

LOPAKHIN. What's up with you, Dunyasha?

DUNYASHA. My hands are shaking. I think I'm going to faint.

LOPAKHIN. You're too sensitive altogether, my girl. You dress like a lady and do your hair like one too. We can't have that. Remember your place.

[YEPIKHODOV *comes in carrying a bunch of flowers. He wears a jacket and brightly polished high boots which make a loud squeak. Once inside the room he drops the flowers.*]

YEPIKHODOV [*picking up the flowers*]. The gardener sent these, says they're to go in the dining-room. [*Hands the flowers to* DUNYASHA.]

LOPAKHIN. And you might bring me some kvass.

DUNYASHA. Yes sir. [*Goes out.*]

YEPIKHODOV. There are three degrees of frost this morning and the cherry trees are in full bloom. I can't say I think much of our climate. [*Sighs.*] That I can't. It isn't exactly co-operative, our climate isn't. Then if you'll permit a further observation, Mr. Lopakhin, I bought these boots the day before yesterday and, as I make so bold to assure you, they squeak like something out of this world. What could I put on them?

LOPAKHIN. Leave me alone. I'm tired of you.

YEPIKHODOV. Every day something awful happens to me. Not that I complain, I'm used to it. Even raise a smile.

[DUNYASHA *comes in and hands* LOPAKHIN *the kvass.*]

YEPIKHODOV. I'll be off. [*Bumps into a chair and knocks it over.*] You see. [*With an air of triumph.*] There you are, if you'll pardon my language, that's just the kind of thing I mean, actually. Quite re-markable really. [*Goes out.*]

DUNYASHA. The fact is Yepikhodov has proposed to me, Mr. Lopa-khin.

LOPAKHIN. Oh yes.

DUNYASHA. I really don't know what to do. He's the quiet type, only sometimes he gets talking and you can't make head or tail of what he says. It sounds ever so nice and romantic, but it just doesn't make sense. I do sort of like him, and he's crazy about me. He's a most unfortunate man, every day something goes wrong. That's why he gets teased here. They call him 'Simple Simon'.

LOPAKHIN [*pricking up his ears*]. I think I hear them coming.

DUNYASHA. They're coming! Oh, whatever's the matter with me? I've gone all shivery.

LOPAKHIN. Yes, they really are coming. Let's go and meet them. I wonder if she'll know me, we haven't seen each other for five years.

DUNYASHA [*agitated*]. I'm going to faint. Oh dear, I'm going to faint.

[*Two carriages are heard driving up to the house.* LOPAKHIN *and* DUNYASHA *hurry out. The stage is empty. Noises begin to be heard from the adjoining rooms.* FIRS, *who has been to meet* MRS. RANEVSKY *at the station, hurries across the stage leaning on a stick. He wears an old-fashioned servant's livery and a top hat. He mutters something to himself, but not a word can be understood. The noises off stage become louder. A voice is heard*: 'Let's go through here'. *Enter, on their way through the room,* MRS. RANEVSKY, ANYA *and* CHARLOTTE, *with a small dog on a lead, all dressed in travelling clothes,* VARYA, *wearing an overcoat and a scarf over her head,* GAYEV, SIMEONOV-PISHCHIK, LOPAKHIN, DUNYASHA *carrying a bundle and an umbrella, and other servants with luggage.*]

ANYA. Let's go through here. You remember this room, don't you, Mother?

MRS. RANEVSKY [*happily, through tears*]. The nursery!

VARYA. How cold it is, my hands are quite numb. [*To* MRS. RANEVSKY.] Your rooms are just as they were, Mother, the white one and the mauve one.

MRS. RANEVSKY. The nursery! My lovely, heavenly room! I slept in here when I was a little girl. [*Weeps.*] And now I feel like a little girl again. [*Kisses her brother and* VARYA, *and then her brother again.*] Varya hasn't changed a bit, she still looks like a nun. And I recognized Dunyasha. [*Kisses* DUNYASHA.]

GAYEV. The train was two hours late. Pretty good, eh? What price that for efficiency?

CHARLOTTE [*to* PISHCHIK]. My dog eats nuts too.

PISHCHIK [*with surprise*]. Extraordinary thing.

[*All go out except* ANYA *and* DUNYASHA.]

DUNYASHA. We've been longing for you to get here. [*Helps* ANYA *off with her overcoat and hat.*]

ANYA. I've travelled four nights without sleep, and now I'm frozen.

DUNYASHA. You left before Easter in the snow and frost. What a difference now. Darling Anya! [*Laughs and kisses her.*] I've been longing to see you again, my precious angel. I must tell you at once, I can't keep it to myself a minute longer——

ANYA [*listlessly*]. Whatever is it this time?

DUNYASHA. Yepikhodov—you know, the clerk—proposed to me just after Easter.

ANYA. Can't you talk about something else? [*Tidying her hair.*] I've lost all my hair-pins. [*She is very tired and is actually swaying on her feet.*]

DUNYASHA. I really don't know what to think. He loves me so much, he really does.

ANYA [*fondly, looking through the door into her room*]. My own room, my own windows, just as if I'd never been away. I'm home again! I'll get up tomorrow and run straight out into the orchard. Oh, if I could only go to sleep. I didn't sleep at all on the way back, I was so worried.

DUNYASHA. Mr. Trofimov arrived the day before yesterday.

ANYA [*joyfully*]. Peter!

DUNYASHA. He's sleeping in the bath-house, in fact he's living there. Afraid of being in the way, he says. [*With a glance at her pocket-watch.*] Someone ought to wake him up, but your sister said not to. 'Don't you wake him,' she said.

[VARYA *comes in. She has a bunch of keys on her belt.*]

VARYA. Dunyasha, go and get some coffee quickly. Mother wants some.

DUNYASHA. I'll see to it at once. [*Goes out.*]

VARYA. Well, thank heavens you're back. You're home again. [*Affectionately.*] My lovely, darling Anya's home again.

ANYA. I've had a terrible time.

VARYA. So I can imagine.

ANYA. I left just before Easter and it was cold then. On the way there Charlotte kept talking and doing those awful tricks of hers. Why you ever landed me with Charlotte——

VARYA. But you couldn't have gone on your own, darling. A girl of seventeen!

ANYA. It was cold and snowing when we got to Paris. My French is atrocious. I find Mother living on the fourth floor somewhere and when I get there she has visitors, French people—some ladies and an old priest with a little book. The place is full of smoke and awfully uncomfortable. Suddenly I felt sorry for Mother, so sorry, I took her head in my arms and held her and just couldn't let go. Afterwards Mother was terribly sweet to me and kept crying.

VARYA [*through tears*]. Don't, Anya, I can't bear it.

ANYA. She'd already sold her villa near Menton and had nothing left, nothing at all. I hadn't any money either, there was hardly enough for the journey. And Mother simply won't understand. If we have a meal in a station restaurant she asks for all the most expensive things and tips the waiters a rouble each. And Charlotte's no better. Then Yasha has to have his share as well, it was simply awful. Mother has this servant Yasha, you know, we've brought him with us——

VARYA. Yes, I've seen him. Isn't he foul?

ANYA. Well, how is everything? Have you paid the interest?

VARYA. What a hope.

ANYA. My God, how dreadful.

VARYA. This estate is up for sale in August.

ANYA. Oh my God!

LOPAKHIN [*peeping round the door and mooing like a cow*]. Moo-oo-oo. [*Disappears.*]

VARYA [*through tears*]. Oh, I could give him such a —. [*Shakes her fist.*]

ANYA [*quietly embracing* VARYA]. Has he proposed, Varya? [VARYA *shakes her head.*] But he does love you. Why can't you get it all settled? What are you both waiting for?

VARYA. I don't think anything will come of it. He's so busy he can't be bothered with me, he doesn't even notice me. Wretched man, I'm fed up with the sight of him. Everyone's talking about our wedding and congratulating us, when there's nothing in it at all actually and the whole thing's so vague. [*In a different tone of voice.*] You've got a brooch that looks like a bee or something.

ANYA [*sadly*]. Yes, Mother bought it. [*Goes to her room, now talking away happily like a child.*] Do you know, in Paris I went up in a balloon.

VARYA. My lovely, darling Anya's home again.

[DUNYASHA *has returned with the coffee-pot and is making coffee.*]

VARYA [*standing near the door*]. You know, darling, while I'm doing my jobs round the house I spend the whole day dreaming. I imagine marrying you off to a rich man. That would set my mind at rest and I'd go off to a convent, then on to Kiev and Moscow, wandering from one holy place to another. I'd just wander on and on. What bliss!

ANYA. The birds are singing in the orchard. What time is it?

VARYA. It must be nearly three. Time you were asleep, dear. [*Going into* ANYA'*s room.*] What bliss!

[*Enter* YASHA *with a rug and a travelling bag.*]

YASHA [*crossing the stage and speaking in a refined manner*]. Is one permitted to pass this way?

DUNYASHA. I wouldn't have known you, Yasha. You've changed so much since you've been abroad.

YASHA. H'm! And who might you be?

DUNYASHA. When you left here I was no bigger than this. [*Shows her height from the floor.*] I'm Dunyasha, Theodore Kozoyedov's daughter. You won't remember me.

YASHA. H'm! Tasty little morsel. [*Looks round, then embraces her. She gives a squeak and drops a saucer.* YASHA *hurries out.*]

VARYA [*in the doorway, speaking angrily*]. What is it now?

DUNYASHA [*through tears*]. I've broken a saucer.

VARYA. That's supposed to be lucky.

ANYA [*coming out of her room*]. Someone ought to let Mother know that Peter's here.

VARYA. I told them not to wake him up.

ANYA [*thoughtfully*]. It's six years since Father died. And a month after that our brother Grisha was drowned in the river. He was a lovely little boy, only seven years old. It was too much for Mother, she went away, just dropped everything and went. [*Shudders.*] How well I understand her, if only she knew. [*Pause.*] Peter Trofimov was Grisha's tutor, he might bring back memories.

[FIRS *comes in wearing a jacket and a white waistcoat.*]

FIRS [*goes to the coffee-pot, anxiously*]. The mistress is going to have her coffee here. [*Puts on white gloves.*] Is it made? [*To* DUNYASHA, *sternly.*] You there! What about the cream?

DUNYASHA. Oh, goodness me. [*Goes out quickly.*]

FIRS [*fussing around the coffee-pot*]. The girl's a nincompoop. [*Muttering to himself.*] They've come from Paris. There was a time when the old master used to go to Paris, went by carriage. [*Laughs.*]

VARYA. What is it, Firs?

FIRS. Beg pardon, Miss Varya? [*Happily.*] The mistress is home. Home at last. Now I can die happy. [*Weeps with joy.*]

[*Enter* MRS. RANEVSKY, GAYEV *and* SIMEONOV-PISHCHIK, *the last wearing a sleeveless coat of fine cloth and wide trousers tucked inside his boots. As he comes in,* GAYEV *moves his arms and body as if making billiard shots.*]

MRS. RANEVSKY. How does it go now? Let me remember. 'Pot the red in the corner. Double into the middle.'

GAYEV. Screw shot into the corner. At one time, dear sister, we both used to sleep in this room. And now I'm fifty-one, unlikely as it may sound.

LOPAKHIN. Yes, time marches on.

GAYEV. What's that?

LOPAKHIN. Time. It marches on, I was saying.

GAYEV. This place smells of cheap scent.

ANYA. I'm going to bed. Good night, Mother. [*Kisses her mother.*]

MRS. RANEVSKY. My own beautiful little baby. [*Kisses* ANYA'*s hands.*] Are you glad to be home? I still can't get used to it.

ANYA. Good night, Uncle.

GAYEV [*kissing her face and hands*]. God bless you. You look so like your mother. [*To his sister.*] You were just like her at that age, Lyuba.

[ANYA *shakes hands with* LOPAKHIN *and* PISHCHIK, *goes out and shuts the door behind her.*]

MRS. RANEVSKY. She's completely worn out.

PISHCHIK. Yes, it must have been a long journey.

VARYA [*to* LOPAKHIN *and* PISHCHIK]. Well, gentlemen? It's nearly three o'clock. Time you were on your way.

MRS. RANEVSKY [*laughing*]. Varya, you haven't changed a bit. [*Draws* VARYA *towards her and kisses her.*] I'll just drink this coffee, then we'll all go. [FIRS *puts a hassock under her feet.*] Thank you, my dear. I've got used to coffee, I drink it day and night. Thank you, dear old friend. [*Kisses* FIRS.]

VARYA. I'll go and see if they've brought all the luggage. [*Goes out.*]

MRS. RANEVSKY. Is it really me sitting here? [*Laughs.*] I feel like dancing and waving my arms about. [*Covers her face with her hands.*] But perhaps I'm only dreaming. God knows, I love my country, I love it dearly. I couldn't see anything from the train, I was crying so much. [*Through tears.*] But I must drink my coffee. Thank you, Firs. Thank you, dear old friend. I'm so glad you're still alive.

FIRS. The day before yesterday.

GAYEV. He's a bit deaf.

LOPAKHIN. I have to leave for Kharkov soon, about half past four. What a nuisance. I'd like to have seen a bit more of you and had a talk. You're just as wonderful as ever.

PISHCHIK [*breathes heavily*]. Even prettier. In that Parisian outfit. Well and truly bowled me over, and no mistake.

LOPAKHIN. This brother of yours calls me a lout of a peasant out for what I can get, but that doesn't bother me a bit. Let him talk. You just believe in me as you used to, that's all I ask, and look at me in the old way, with those wonderful, irresistible eyes. Merciful heavens! My father was a serf, belonged to your father and your grandfather before him. But you—you've done so much for me in the past that I've forgotten all that and love you as a brother. Or even more.

MRS. RANEVSKY. I can't sit still, I really can't. [*Jumps up and walks about in great excitement.*] I'll die of happiness. Laugh at me if you want, I'm silly. My own dear little book-case. [*Kisses the book-case.*] My own little table——

GAYEV. Nanny died while you were abroad.

MRS. RANEVSKY [*sitting down and drinking her coffee*]. Yes, God rest her soul. Someone wrote to me about it.

GAYEV. Anastasy has died too. Petrushka—remember the chap with the squint?—left me for another job, he's with the chief of police in town now. [*Takes a packet of sweets from his pocket and sucks one.*]

PISHCHIK. My daughter Dashenka sends her regards.

LOPAKHIN. I feel I want to tell you something nice and cheerful. [*With a glance at his watch.*] I'm just leaving and there isn't time to say much. Anyway, I'll be brief. As you know, the cherry orchard's being sold to pay your debts and the auction's on the twenty-second of August. But you needn't worry, dear friend, you can sleep in peace because there's a way out. Here's my plan. Please listen carefully. Your estate's only twelve miles or so from town and the new railway isn't far away. If you divide the cherry orchard and the land along the river into building plots and lease them out for summer cottages you'll have a yearly income of at least twenty-five thousand roubles.

GAYEV. Oh really, what rubbish.

MRS. RANEVSKY. I don't quite follow you, Yermolay.

LOPAKHIN. You'll get at least ten roubles an acre from your tenants every year. And if you advertise right away I bet you anything you won't have a scrap of land left by autumn, it'll all be snapped up. In fact I congratulate you. You're saved. The situation's magnificent and there's a good depth of river. But of course you will have to do a spot of tidying and clearing up. For instance, you'll have to pull down all the old buildings, let's say, and this house—it's no more use anyway, is it?—and cut down the old cherry orchard——

MRS. RANEVSKY. Cut it down? My dear man, forgive me, you don't know what you're talking about. If there's one interesting, in fact quite remarkable, thing in the whole county it's our cherry orchard.

LOPAKHIN. The only remarkable thing about that orchard is its size. It only gives a crop every other year and then no one knows what to do with the cherries. Nobody wants to buy them.

GAYEV. This orchard is even mentioned in the Encyclopaedia.

LOPAKHIN [*with a glance at his watch*]. If we don't make a plan and get something decided, that orchard—and the whole estate with it— is going to be auctioned on the twenty-second of August, you can make up your minds to that. There's no other way out, you can take it from me. And that's flat.

FIRS. In the old days, forty or fifty years ago, the cherries used to be dried, preserved and bottled. They used to make jam out of them, and time was——

GAYEV. Be quiet please, Firs.

FIRS. Time was when dried cherries used to be sent to Moscow and Kharkov by the wagon-load. They fetched a lot of money. Soft and juicy those dried cherries were, sweet and tasty. People had the knack of it in those days.

MRS. RANEVSKY. But where's the recipe now?

FIRS. Forgotten. No one remembers it.

PISHCHIK [*to* MRS. RANEVSKY]. How are things in Paris, eh? Eat any frogs?

MRS. RANEVSKY. I ate crocodiles.

PISHCHIK. Extraordinary thing.

LOPAKHIN. Until lately everyone in the countryside was a gentleman or a peasant, but now there are these holiday visitors as well. All our towns, even the smallest, are surrounded by summer cottages nowadays. And it looks as though in twenty years or so there are going to be fantastic numbers of these holiday-makers. So far your holiday-maker only has his tea on the balcony, but he may very well start growing things on his bit of land and then this cherry orchard will become a happy, rich, prosperous place.

GAYEV [*indignantly*]. That's all rubbish.

[*Enter* VARYA *and* YASHA.]

VARYA. Two telegrams came for you, Mother. [*Picks out a key and unlocks the old-fashioned book-case with a jingling noise.*] Here you are.

MRS. RANEVSKY. They're from Paris. [*Tears them up without reading them.*] I've finished with Paris.

GAYEV. Lyuba, do you know how old this book-case is? Last week I pulled out the bottom drawer and saw some figures burnt on it. This book-case was made exactly a hundred years ago. Not bad, eh?

We might celebrate its centenary. It's an inanimate object, but all the same it is a book-case, you can't get away from that.

PISHCHIK [*in amazement*]. A hundred years. Extraordinary thing.

GAYEV. Yes, this really is quite something. [*Feeling round the book-case.*] Dear and most honoured book-case. In you I salute an existence devoted for over a hundred years to the glorious ideals of virtue and justice. In the course of the century your silent summons to creative work has never faltered, upholding [*through tears*] in several genera-tions of our line confidence and faith in a better future and fostering in us the ideals of virtue and social consciousness. [*Pause.*]

LOPAKHIN. Yes.

MRS. RANEVSKY. Dear Leonid, you haven't changed a bit.

GAYEV [*somewhat embarrassed*]. In off on the right into the corner. Screw shot into the middle.

LOPAKHIN [*after a glance at his watch*]. Well, time for me to go.

YASHA [*handing some medicine to MRS. RANEVSKY*]. Would you care to take your pills now?

PISHCHIK. Don't ever take medicine, dear lady, it doesn't do any good. Or harm, if it comes to that. Here, give it to me, dearest lady. [*Takes the pills, pours them out on the palm of his hand, blows on them, puts them in his mouth and washes them down with kvass.*] There you are.

MRS. RANEVSKY [*terrified*]. You must be crazy!

PISHCHIK. I've taken the lot.

LOPAKHIN. You greedy pig. [*Everyone laughs.*]

FIRS. The gentleman was here at Easter. Ate over a gallon of pickled gherkins. [*Mutters.*]

MRS. RANEVSKY. What's he saying?

VARYA. He's been muttering like this for three years now. We've got used to it.

YASHA. It's a case of *anno domini*.

[CHARLOTTE *crosses the stage wearing a white dress. She is very thin and tightly laced and has a lorgnette attached to her belt.*]

LOPAKHIN. I'm sorry, Miss Charlotte, I haven't had a chance to say hallo. [*Tries to kiss her hand.*]

CHARLOTTE [*withdrawing her hand*]. If I let you kiss my hand it'll be my elbow next, then my shoulder——

LOPAKHIN. This is my unlucky day. [*Everyone laughs.*] Do us a trick, Charlotte.

MRS. RANEVSKY. Yes, do us a trick, Charlotte.

CHARLOTTE. Not now. I want to go to bed. [*Goes out.*]

LOPAKHIN. We'll meet again in three weeks. [*Kisses* MRS. RANEVSKY's *hand.*] Good-bye for now. I must go. [*To* GAYEV.] Fare you well [*kisses* PISHCHIK] for I must leave you. [*Shakes hands with* VARYA, *then with* FIRS *and* YASHA.] I don't really feel like going. [*To* MRS. RANEVSKY.] Think it over about those cottages, let me know if you decide to go ahead and I'll get you a loan of fifty thousand or so. Give it some serious thought.

VARYA [*angrily*]. Oh, do for heaven's sake *go*.

LOPAKHIN. All right, I'm going. [*Goes.*]

GAYEV. Ill-bred lout. Oh, I beg your pardon, Varya's going to marry him. He's Varya's 'young man'.

VARYA. Don't overdo it, Uncle.

MRS. RANEVSKY. But I should be only too pleased, Varya. He's such a nice man.

PISHCHIK. A most worthy fellow. Got to hand it to him. My daughter Dashenka says so too. She says all sorts of things actually. [*Gives a snore, but wakes up again straight away.*] By the way, dear lady, can you lend me two hundred and forty roubles? I've interest to pay on a mortgage tomorrow.

VARYA [*terrified*]. We haven't got it. Really.

MRS. RANEVSKY. Honestly, I've no money at all.

PISHCHIK. It'll turn up. [*Laughs.*] Never say die. The times I've thought, 'This is the end of me, I'm finished.' And then, lo and behold, they run a railway line over my land or something and I get some money. And sooner or later something will turn up this time, you'll see. Dashenka will win two hundred thousand. She has a ticket in the lottery.

MRS. RANEVSKY. I've finished my coffee. Now for some rest.

FIRS [*reprovingly, brushing* GAYEV's *clothes*]. You've got the wrong trousers on again. What am I to do with you?

VARYA [*in a low voice*]. Anya's asleep. [*Quietly opens a window.*] The sun's up now and it's not cold. Look, Mother, what marvellous trees! And the air is glorious. The starlings are singing.

GAYEV [*opening another window*]. The orchard is white all over. Lyuba, you haven't forgotten that long avenue, have you? It runs on and on, straight as an arrow. And it gleams on moonlit nights, remember? You can't have forgotten?

MRS. RANEVSKY [*looking through the window at the orchard*]. Oh, my childhood, my innocent childhood! This is the nursery where I slept and I used to look out at the orchard from here. When I woke up every morning happiness awoke with me, and the orchard was just the same in those days. Nothing's changed. [*Laughs happily.*] White! All white! Oh, my orchard! After the damp, dismal autumn and the cold winter here you are, young again and full of happiness. The angels in heaven have not forsaken you. If I could only shake off the heavy burden that weighs me down, if only I could forget my past.

GAYEV. Yes, and now the orchard's to be sold to pay our debts, unlikely as it may sound.

MRS. RANEVSKY. Look! Mother's walking in the orchard. In a white dress. [*Laughs happily.*] It's Mother.

GAYEV. Where?

VARYA. Really, Mother, what things you say!

MRS. RANEVSKY. There's no one there, I just imagined it. On the right at the turning to the summer-house there's a little white tree which has leant over, it looks like a woman.

[*Enter* TROFIMOV. *He is dressed in a shabby student's uniform and wears spectacles.*]

MRS. RANEVSKY. What a superb orchard! The great banks of white blossom, the blue sky——

TROFIMOV. Mrs. Ranevsky! [*She looks round at him.*] I'll just pay my respects and go away at once. [*Kisses her hand with great feeling.*] I was told to wait till later in the morning, but I was too impatient.

[MRS. RANEVSKY *looks at him in bewilderment.*]

VARYA [*through tears*]. This is Peter Trofimov.

TROFIMOV. I'm Peter Trofimov. I was Grisha's tutor. Can I have changed so much?

[MRS. RANEVSKY *embraces him and weeps quietly.*]

GAYEV [*embarrassed*]. There, Lyuba, don't cry.

VARYA [*weeping*]. I did tell you to wait till later, Peter.

MRS. RANEVSKY. Grisha, my—my little boy. Grisha, my son——

VARYA. It can't be helped, Mother, it was God's will.

TROFIMOV [*gently, through tears*]. Don't cry. Please don't.

MRS. RANEVSKY [*weeping quietly*]. I lost my little boy—drowned. Why? Why did it happen, my dear? [*In a quieter voice.*] Anya's asleep in there and here I am raising my voice and making all this noise. Well, Peter? Why have you grown so ugly? And why do you look so old?

TROFIMOV. A woman in the train called me 'that seedy-looking gent'.

MRS. RANEVSKY. You were only a boy in those days, just a nice little undergraduate. But now you're losing your hair and wear these spectacles. You can't still be a student, surely? [*Moves towards the door.*]

TROFIMOV. I'll obviously be a student for the rest of time.

MRS. RANEVSKY [*kisses her brother and then* VARYA]. Well, go to bed then. You look older too, Leonid.

PISHCHIK [*follows her*]. So we're off to bed now. Oh dear, my gout. I'd better stay the night here. And to-morrow morning, Lyuba my sweetheart, that little matter of two hundred and forty roubles.

GAYEV. Can't he think about anything else?

PISHCHIK. Two hundred and forty roubles to pay the interest on my mortgage.

MRS. RANEVSKY. But I've no money, my dear man.

PISHCHIK. I'll pay you back, dearest lady. A trifling sum.

MRS. RANEVSKY. All right then, Leonid will let you have it. Leonid, give him the money.

GAYEV. What, me give it him? Not likely!

MRS. RANEVSKY. Let him have it, what else can we do? He needs it, he'll pay us back.

[MRS. RANEVSKY, TROFIMOV, PISHCHIK *and* FIRS *go out.* GAYEV, VARYA *and* YASHA *remain behind.*]

GAYEV. My sister hasn't lost her habit of throwing money about. [*To* YASHA.] Out of the way, my man, you smell like a farmyard.

YASHA [*with an ironical grin*]. You haven't changed a bit, Mr. Gayev sir.

GAYEV. What's that? [*To* VARYA.] What did he say?

VARYA [*to* YASHA]. Your mother's come from the village. She's been waiting in the servants' quarters since yesterday and wants to see you.

YASHA. Why can't she leave me alone?

VARYA. You—you ought to be ashamed of yourself!

YASHA. What's the big idea? Couldn't she have come tomorrow? [*Goes out.*]

VARYA. Mother's just the same as ever, hasn't changed a bit. She'd give everything away if we let her.

GAYEV. Yes. [*Pause.*] When a lot of different remedies are suggested for a disease, that means it can't be cured. I've been thinking and racking my brains. I have plenty of remedies, any amount of them, and that means I haven't really got one. It would be a good thing if somebody left us some money. It would be a good thing to marry Anya to a very rich man. And it would be a good thing to go to Yaroslavl and try our luck with our aunt the Countess. Aunty is rich, you know, very much so.

VARYA [*crying*]. May God help us.

GAYEV. Stop that crying. Aunty's rich enough, but she doesn't like us. To start with, my sister married a lawyer, a social inferior——.

[ANYA *appears in the doorway.*]

GAYEV. She married beneath her, and the way she's behaved—well, she hasn't exactly been a model of propriety, has she? She's a good, kind, splendid person and I love her very much, but make what allowances you like, she's still a loose woman and you can't get away from it. It shows in every movement she makes.

VARYA [*in a whisper*]. Anya's in the doorway.

GAYEV. What's that? [*Pause.*] Curious thing, there's something in my right eye. Can't see properly. And on Thursday when I was at the County Court——

[ANYA *comes in.*]

VARYA. Why aren't you asleep, Anya?

ANYA. I can't. I just can't get to sleep.

GAYEV. My dear child. [*Kisses* ANYA*'s face and hands.*] My little child. [*Through tears.*] You're not my niece, you're an angel, you're every-thing in the world to me. Do, do believe me.

ANYA. I do believe you, Uncle. Everyone loves and respects you. But, Uncle dear, you should keep quiet, just keep quiet. What were you saying just now about my mother, about your own sister? What made you say it?

GAYEV. Yes, yes. [*Takes her hand and covers his face with it.*] You're quite right, it was dreadful of me. Oh God! God, help me! And that speech I made to the book-case just now. How silly of me. And it was only when I'd finished that I saw how silly it was.

VARYA. It's true, Uncle dear, you oughtn't to talk. Just don't talk, that's all.

ANYA. If you stop talking you'll feel easier in your own mind.

GAYEV. I am silent. [*Kisses* ANYA*'s and* VARYA*'s hands.*] I am silent. There is something rather important, though. I was at the County Court last Thursday and—well, a lot of us got talking about this and that and about several other things as well. It seems we might manage to borrow some money and pay the interest to the bank.

VARYA. May God help us.

GAYEV. I'm going back there on Tuesday and I'll talk to them again. [*To* VARYA.] Stop that crying. [*To* ANYA.] Your mother's going to speak to Lopakhin and I'm sure he won't let her down. And when you've had a rest you can go and see your great-aunt the Countess at Yaroslavl. This way we'll be tackling the thing from three different directions at once and we simply can't fail. We shall pay that interest, I'm sure of it. [*Puts a sweet in his mouth.*] I give you my word of honour, I swear by anything you like, this estate isn't going to be sold. [*Elatedly.*] As I hope to be happy, I swear it. Here's my hand and you can call me a good-for-nothing scoundrel if I let it come to an auction. I won't, on that I'll stake my life.

ANYA [*has reverted to a calmer mood and is happy*]. What a good person you are, Uncle, you're so sensible. [*Embraces him.*] I feel calm now. Calm and happy.

[*Enter* FIRS.]

FIRS [*reproachfully*]. Mr. Leonid sir, you're past praying for. When are you going to bed?

GAYEV. At once, at once. You can go, Firs. It's all right, I'll undress myself. Well, children, bed-time. The details will keep till morning and you go to bed now. [*Kisses* ANYA *and* VARYA.] I'm a man of the eighties. No one has a good word to say for those days, but still I've suffered quite a bit for my convictions, I can tell you. Do you wonder the peasants like me so much? You have to know your peasant of course. You have to know how to——

ANYA. Uncle, you're off again.

VARYA. Uncle dear, do be quiet.

FIRS [*angrily*]. Mr. Leonid, sir!

GAYEV. I'm coming, I'm coming. Go to bed. Off two cushions into the middle. Pot the white. [*Goes off with* FIRS *tottering after him.*]

ANYA. I'm not worried now. I don't feel like going to Yaroslavl and I don't like my great-aunt, but I do feel less worried. Thanks to Uncle. [*Sits down.*]

VARYA. We must get to bed. I'm just going. Oh, something unpleasant happened here while you were away. As you know, there's no one living in the old servants' quarters except some of our old folk—Yefim, Polya, Yevstigney, oh yes, and Karp. They began letting odd tramps and people spend the night there. I kept quiet about it. But then I heard of a story they'd spread that I'd said they must be fed on nothing but dried peas. Out of meanness if you please. It was all Yevstigney's doing. All right, I thought. If that's the way things are, then you just wait. I sent for the man. [*Yawns.*] He came. 'What's all this?' I said. 'You stupid so-and-so.' [*Looks at* ANYA.] Anya, dear! [*Pause.*] She's asleep. [*Takes* ANYA *by the arm.*] Come to bed, dear. Come on. [*Leads her by the arm.*] My little darling's gone to sleep. Come on. [*They move off.*]

[*A shepherd's pipe is heard playing from far away on the other side of the orchard.* TROFIMOV *crosses the stage, catches sight of* VARYA *and* ANYA *and stops.*]

VARYA. Sh! She's asleep—asleep. Come on, my dear.

ANYA [*quietly, half asleep*]. I'm so tired. I keep hearing bells. Uncle— dear—Mother and Uncle——

VARYA. Come on, dear, come on. [*They go into* ANYA'*s room.*]

TROFIMOV [*deeply moved*]. Light of my being! My springtime!

CURTAIN

ACT TWO

In the open country. A small, tumble-down old chapel long ago abandoned. Near it a well, some large stones which look like old tombstones and an old bench. A road can be seen leading to GAYEV'*s estate. Dark poplar trees loom on one side and beyond them the cherry orchard begins. There is a row of telegraph poles in the distance and far, far away on the horizon are the dim outlines of a big town, visible only in very fine, clear weather. It will soon be sunset.* CHARLOTTE, YASHA *and* DUNYASHA *are sitting on the bench.* YEPIKHODOV *stands near them playing a guitar, while the others sit lost in thought.* CHARLOTTE *wears a man's old peaked cap. She has taken a shot-gun from her shoulder and is adjusting the buckle on the strap.*

CHARLOTTE [*meditatively*]. I haven't any proper identity papers. I don't know how old I am and I always think of myself as a young girl. When I was little, Father and Mother used to go on tour round all the fairs giving performances, and very good ones too. I used to do the dive of death and lots of other tricks. When Father and Mother died a German lady adopted me and began educating me. Well, I grew up and became a governess. But where I come from and who I am I've no idea. Who my parents were I don't know either, very likely they weren't even married. [*Takes a cucumber out of her pocket and starts eating it.*] I don't know anything. [*Pause.*] I'm longing for someone to talk to, but there isn't anyone. I'm alone in the world.

YEPIKHODOV [*playing the guitar and singing*].

'I'm tired of the world and its bustle,
I'm tired of my friends and my foes.'

How nice it is to play a mandolin.

DUNYASHA. That isn't a mandolin, it's a guitar. [*Looks at herself in a hand-mirror, and powders her face.*]

YEPIKHODOV. To a man crazed with love it's a mandolin. [*Sings softly.*]

'If only my heart were delighted
By the warmth of an ardour requited.'

[YASHA *joins in.*]

CHARLOTTE. The awful way these people sing—ugh! Like a lot of hyenas.

DUNYASHA [*to* YASHA]. You're ever so lucky to have been abroad, though.

YASHA. Yes, of course. My sentiments precisely. [*Yawns, then lights a cigar.*]

YEPIKHODOV. It stands to reason. Abroad everything's pretty comprehensive like. Has been for ages.

YASHA. Oh, definitely.

YEPIKHODOV. I'm a cultured sort of person and read all kinds of remarkable books, but I just can't get a line on what it is I'm really after. Shall I go on living or shall I shoot myself, I mean? But anyway, I always carry a revolver. Here it is. [*Shows them his revolver.*]

CHARLOTTE. Well, that's that. I'm off. [*Slings the gun over her shoulder.*] Yepikhodov, you're a very clever man and a most alarming one. Women must be quite crazy about you. Brrr! [*Moves off.*] These clever men are all so stupid, I've no one to talk to. I'm lonely, oh so lonely. I'm on my own in the world, and—and who I am and what I'm for is a mystery. [*Goes out slowly.*]

YEPIKHODOV. Actually, other considerations apart, there's something I really must explain about myself at this juncture, which is that fate treats me most unkindly, like a storm buffeting a small boat. If I'm mistaken—which I allow is possible—why is it, to take a case in point, that I wake up this morning and there, sitting on my chest, is a spider of gigantic proportions? This size. [*Uses both hands to show the size.*] Or I pick up a glass of kvass to have a drink and lo and behold there's something highly improper inside it like a black-beetle. [*Pause.*] Have you ever read Buckle's *History of Civilization*? [*Pause.*] Might I trouble you for the favour of a few words, Miss Dunyasha?

DUNYASHA. All right, carry on.

YEPIKHODOV. I should prefer it to be in private. [*Sighs.*]

DUNYASHA [*embarrassed*]. Very well then, only first go and get me my cape. You'll find it in the cupboard or somewhere. It's rather damp out here.

YEPIKHODOV. Oh certainly, I'm sure. At your service. Now I know what to do with my revolver. [*Takes the guitar and goes out strumming it.*]

YASHA. Simple Simon! The man's a fool, between you and me. [*Yawns.*]

DUNYASHA. Heavens, I hope he doesn't go and shoot himself. [*Pause.*] I've grown so nervous and I feel worried all the time. The master and mistress took me in when I was a little girl and now I've lost touch with the way ordinary people live. Look at my hands, as white as white could be, just like a lady's. Yes, I've become all soft and refined and ladylike and easily frightened. I'm scared of everything. If you deceive me, Yasha, I can't think what it'll do to my nerves.

YASHA [*kissing her*]. Tasty little morsel. A girl should know her place, mind. There's nothing I dislike so much as loose behaviour in a girl.

DUNYASHA. I'm so much in love with you. You're so educated, you can talk about anything. [*Pause.*]

YASHA [*yawning*]. That's true enough. To my way of thinking, if a girl's in love with anybody that proves she's immoral. [*Pause.*] How nice to smoke a cigar out of doors. [*Pricks up his ears.*] There's somebody coming. It's the missis and the others.

[DUNYASHA *embraces him impulsively.*]

YASHA. Go back to the house as if you'd been down to the river for a bathe. Take that path, or else you'll meet them and they'll think we've been walking out together. I can't have that.

DUNYASHA [*coughing quietly*]. Your cigar's given me an awful headache. [*Goes off.*]

[YASHA *remains behind, sitting near the chapel. Enter* MRS. RANEVSKY, GAYEV *and* LOPAKHIN.]

LOPAKHIN. You must make up your minds once and for all, time's running out. And anyway it's a perfectly simple matter. Are you prepared to lease your land for summer cottages or aren't you? You can answer it in one word—yes or no. Just one single word.

MRS. RANEVSKY. Who's smoking disgusting cigars round here? [*Sits down.*]

GAYEV. How handy it is now they've built the railway. [*Sits down.*] We've been into town for lunch. Pot the red in the middle. I must go indoors now and have a game.

MRS. RANEVSKY. There's no hurry.

LOPAKHIN. One single word. [*Imploringly.*] Do give me an answer.

GAYEV [*yawning*]. What's that?

MRS. RANEVSKY [*looking in her purse*]. Yesterday I had lots of money, but I've hardly any left today. My poor Varya tries to save by feeding us all on milk soup and the old servants in the kitchen get nothing but peas to eat, while I go round simply squandering money, I can't think why. [*Drops her purse, scattering some gold coins.*] There, now I've dropped it all. [*Is annoyed.*]

YASHA. Allow me to pick it up, madam. [*Picks up the coins.*]

MRS. RANEVSKY. Please do, Yasha. Oh, whatever made me go out to lunch? That beastly restaurant of yours with its music and table-cloths smelling of soap. Does one have to drink so much, Leonid? Or eat so much? Or talk so much? You talked much too much again in the restaurant today, all most unsuitable stuff about the seventies and the decadent movement. And just think who you were speaking to. Fancy talking about the decadents to the waiters.

LOPAKHIN. Quite so.

GAYEV [*making a gesture of dismissal with his hand*]. I'm a hopeless case, obviously. [*To YASHA, irritably.*] Why is it I always see you hanging about everywhere?

YASHA [*laughing*]. I just can't help laughing when I hear your voice.

GAYEV [*to his sister*]. Either he goes or I do.

MRS. RANEVSKY. You may leave, Yasha. Off with you.

YASHA [*returning the purse to MRS. RANEVSKY*]. I'll go at once. [*Hardly able to contain his laughter.*] This very instant. [*Goes out.*]

LOPAKHIN. Do you know who's thinking of buying your property? A rich man called Deriganov. They say he's coming to the auction himself.

MRS. RANEVSKY. Oh? Where did you hear that?

LOPAKHIN. It's what they're saying in town.

GAYEV. Our aunt in Yaroslavl has promised to send money, but when she'll send it and how much it'll be, nobody knows.

LOPAKHIN. How much is she sending? A hundred thousand roubles? Two hundred thousand?

MRS. RANEVSKY. Oh, about ten or fifteen thousand, and we're lucky to get that much.

LOPAKHIN. With due respect, I've never met anyone as scatter-brained as you two, or as odd and unbusinesslike either. I tell you in plain language that your place is up for sale and you can't even seem to take it in.

MRS. RANEVSKY. But what are we to do about it? You tell us that.

LOPAKHIN. I *do* tell you. I tell you every day. Every day I say the same thing over and over again. The cherry orchard and the rest of the land must be leased out for summer cottages. You must act at once, without delay, the auction's almost on top of us. Do get that into your heads. Once you definitely decide on those cottages you can raise any amount of money and you'll be all right.

MRS. RANEVSKY. Cottages, summer visitors. Forgive me, but all that's so frightfully vulgar.

GAYEV. I entirely agree.

LOPAKHIN. I'm going to burst into tears or scream or faint. This is too much. I've had about all I can stand! [*To* GAYEV.] You're an old woman.

GAYEV. What's that?

LOPAKHIN. I say you're an old woman. [*Makes to leave.*]

MRS. RANEVSKY [*terrified*]. No, don't go away, my dear man. Stay with us, I implore you. Perhaps we'll think of something.

LOPAKHIN. 'Think'? This isn't a question of thinking.

MRS. RANEVSKY. Don't go away, I beg you. Besides, it's more amusing with you around. [*Pause.*] I keep expecting something awful to happen, as if the house was going to collapse around our ears.

GAYEV [*deep in thought*]. Off the cushion into the corner. Across into the middle——

MRS. RANEVSKY. I suppose we've committed so many sins——

LOPAKHIN. Oh? What sins have you committed?

GAYEV [*putting a sweet in his mouth*]. People say I've wasted my substance on boiled sweets. [*Laughs.*]

MRS. RANEVSKY. Oh, my sins. Look at the mad way I've always wasted money, spent it like water, and I married a man who could do nothing but run up debts. My husband died of champagne, he drank like a fish, and then I had the bad luck to fall in love with someone else and have an affair with him. And just then came my first punishment, and what a cruel blow that was! In the river here—. My little boy was drowned and I went abroad, went right away, never meaning to return or see the river again. I shut my eyes and ran away, not knowing what I was doing, and *he* followed me. It was a cruel, brutal thing to do. I bought a villa near Menton because he fell ill there and for three years I had no rest, nursing him day and night. He utterly wore me out. All my feelings seemed to have dried up inside me. Then last year, when the villa had to be sold to pay my debts, I left for Paris where he robbed me, deserted me and took up with another woman. I tried to poison myself. It was all so stupid and humiliating. Then I suddenly longed to be back in Russia, back in my own country with my little girl. [*Dries her eyes.*] Lord, Lord, be merciful, forgive me my sins. Don't punish me any more. [*Takes a telegram from her pocket.*] This came from Paris today. He asks my forgiveness and begs me to go back. [*Tears up the telegram.*] Isn't that music I hear? [*Listens.*]

GAYEV. That's our famous Jewish band. You remember, the four fiddles, flute and double-bass?

MRS. RANEVSKY. Are they still about then? We must get them round here some time and have a party.

LOPAKHIN [*listening*]. I don't hear anything. [*Sings quietly.*]
'For a spot of cash your Prussian
Will frenchify a Russian.'

[*Laughs.*] I saw a rather good play at the theatre last night, something really funny.

MRS. RANEVSKY. I don't suppose it was a bit funny. You people shouldn't go and see plays, you should try watching your own performance instead. What drab lives you all lead and what a lot of rubbish you talk!

LOPAKHIN. Quite right. To be honest, the life we lead is preposterous. [*Pause.*] My father was a peasant, an idiot who understood nothing, taught me nothing and just beat me when he was drunk, with a stick too. As a matter of fact I'm just as big a numskull and idiot myself. I never learned anything and my handwriting's awful. A pig could write about as well as I do, I'm ashamed to let anyone see it.

MRS. RANEVSKY. You ought to get married, my friend.

LOPAKHIN. Yes, that's true enough.

MRS. RANEVSKY. Why not marry Varya? She's a very nice girl.

LOPAKHIN. True.

MRS. RANEVSKY. She's a nice simple creature. She works all day long, and the great thing is she loves you. And you've been fond of her for some time too.

LOPAKHIN. All right, I've nothing against it. She is a very nice girl. [*Pause.*]

GAYEV. I've been offered a job in a bank. At six thousand roubles a year. Had you heard?

MRS. RANEVSKY. What, you in a bank! You stay where you are.

[FIRS *comes in with an overcoat.*]

FIRS [*to* GAYEV]. Please put this on, Mr. Leonid sir. It's damp out here.

GAYEV [*putting on the overcoat*]. You are a bore, my dear fellow.

FIRS. We can't have this. Goes off in the morning without so much as a word. [*Inspects him.*]

MRS. RANEVSKY. How you have aged, Firs!

FIRS. Beg pardon, madam?

LOPAKHIN. Your mistress says you look a lot older.

FIRS. Well, I've been alive a long time. They were arranging my wedding before your Dad was so much as thought of. [*Laughs.*] And when the serfs were freed I was already head valet. But I wouldn't have any of their freedom, I stayed on with the master and mistress. [*Pause.*] As I recall, everyone was very pleased, but what they were so pleased about they'd no idea themselves.

LOPAKHIN. Oh, it was a good life all right. At least there were plenty of floggings.

FIRS [*not hearing him*]. Yes, those were the days. The serfs had their masters and the masters had their serfs, but now everything's at sixes and sevens and you can't make head or tail of it.

GAYEV. Keep quiet a minute, Firs. I have to go to town tomorrow. I've been promised an introduction to a general who might let us have a loan.

LOPAKHIN. It won't come off and you won't pay the interest either, of that you may be sure.

MRS. RANEVSKY. He's only talking nonsense. There is no such general.

[*Enter* TROFIMOV, ANYA *and* VARYA.]

GAYEV. Ah, here come the children.

ANYA. Look, there's Mother.

MRS. RANEVSKY [*affectionately*]. Come, come to me. My darling girls. [*Embracing* ANYA *and* VARYA.] If you only knew how much I love you both. Sit beside me, that's right. [*All sit down.*]

LOPAKHIN. Our eternal student never strays far from the young ladies.

TROFIMOV. Mind your own business.

LOPAKHIN. He's nearly fifty and he's still a student.

TROFIMOV. Oh, stop making these idiotic jokes.

LOPAKHIN. But why so angry, my dear fellow?

TROFIMOV. Can't you leave me alone?

LOPAKHIN [*laughing*]. Just let me ask you one question. What's your opinion of me?

TROFIMOV. My opinion of you is simply this, Lopakhin. You're a rich man. You'll soon be a millionaire. Now, as part of the process whereby one form of matter is converted into another, nature needs beasts of prey which devour everything in their path. You fulfil that need. [*Everyone laughs.*]

VARYA. Oh Peter, couldn't you tell us something about the planets instead?

MRS. RANEVSKY. No, let's go on with what we were talking about yesterday.

TROFIMOV. What was that?

GAYEV. Pride.

TROFIMOV. We talked a lot yesterday, but we didn't get anywhere. A proud man in your sense of the word has something mystical about him. You may be right in a way. But if we look at the thing quite simply and don't try to be too clever, then what room is there for pride and what's the sense of it anyway, if in fact man is a pretty poor physiological specimen and if the great majority of the human race is crude, stupid and profoundly miserable? It's time we stopped admiring ourselves. The only thing to do is to work.

GAYEV. We shall all die anyway.

TROFIMOV. Why be so sure of that? And what does it mean anyway, 'to die'? Perhaps man has a hundred senses and perhaps when he dies he loses only the five we know, while the other ninety-five live on.

MRS. RANEVSKY. How clever you are, Peter.

LOPAKHIN [*ironically*]. Oh, brilliant!

TROFIMOV. Mankind marches on, going from strength to strength. All that now eludes us will one day be well within our grasp, but, as I say, we must work and we must do all we can for those who are trying to find the truth. Here in Russia very few people do work at present. The kind of Russian intellectuals I know, far and away the greater part of them anyway, aren't looking for anything. They don't do anything. They still don't know the meaning of hard work. They call themselves an intelligentsia, but they speak to their servants as inferiors and treat the peasants like animals. They don't study properly, they never read anything serious, in fact they don't do anything at all. Science is something they just talk about and they know precious little about art. Oh, they're all very earnest. They all go round looking extremely solemn. They talk of nothing but weighty issues and they discuss abstract problems, while all the time everyone knows the workers are abominably fed and sleep without proper bedding, thirty or forty to a room—with bed-bugs everywhere, to say nothing of the stench, the damp, the moral degradation. And clearly all our fine talk is just meant to pull wool over our own eyes and other people's too. Tell me, where are those children's crèches that there's all this talk about? Where are the libraries? They're just things people write novels about, we haven't actually got any of them. What we have got is dirt, vulgarity and squalor. I loathe all these earnest faces. They scare me, and so do earnest conversations. Why can't we keep quiet for a change?

LOPAKHIN. I'm always up by five o'clock, you know. I work from morning till night, and then—well, I'm always handling money, my own and other people's, and I can see what sort of men and women I have around me. You only have to start a job of work to realize how few decent, honest folk there are about. When I can't sleep I sometimes think—the Lord gave us these huge forests, these boundless plains, these vast horizons, and we who live among them ought to be real giants.

MRS. RANEVSKY. You're calling for giants. They're all very well in fairy-tales, but elsewhere they might be rather alarming.

[YEPIKHODOV *crosses the back of the stage playing his guitar.*]

MRS. RANEVSKY [*pensively*]. There goes Yepikhodov.

ANYA [*pensively*]. There goes Yepikhodov.

GAYEV. The sun has set, my friends.

TROFIMOV. Yes.

GAYEV [*in a quiet voice, as if giving a recitation*]. Nature, glorious Nature, glowing with everlasting radiance, so beautiful, so cold— you, whom men call mother, in whom the living and the dead are joined together, you who give life and take it away——

VARYA [*imploring him*]. Uncle dear!

ANYA. Uncle, you're off again.

TROFIMOV. You'd far better pot the red in the middle.

GAYEV. I am silent. Silent.

[*Everyone sits deep in thought. It is very quiet. All that can be heard is* FIRS's *low muttering. Suddenly a distant sound is heard. It seems to come from the sky and is the sound of a breaking string. It dies away sadly.*]

MRS. RANEVSKY. What was that?

LOPAKHIN. I don't know. A cable must have broken somewhere away in the mines. But it must be a long, long way off.

GAYEV. Or perhaps it was a bird, a heron or something.

TROFIMOV. Or an owl.

MRS. RANEVSKY [*shudders*]. There was something disagreeable about it. [*Pause.*]

FIRS. The same thing happened before the troubles, the owl hooting and the samovar humming all the time.

GAYEV. What 'troubles' were those?

FIRS. When the serfs were given their freedom. [*Pause.*]

MRS. RANEVSKY. Come, let's go in, everyone. It's getting late. [*To* ANYA.] You've tears in your eyes. What is it, child? [*Embraces her.*]

ANYA. It's nothing, Mother, I'm all right.

TROFIMOV. There's somebody coming.

[*The* PASSER-BY *appears. He wears a shabby, white peaked cap and an overcoat. He is slightly drunk.*]

PASSER-BY. Excuse me asking, but am I right for the station this way?

GAYEV. Yes. Follow that road.

PASSER-BY. I'm uncommonly obliged to you. [*With a cough.*] Splendid weather, this. [*Declaiming.*] 'Brother, my suffering brother!' 'Come out to the Volga, you whose groans—.' [*To* VARYA.] Miss, could you spare a few copecks for a starving Russian?

[VARYA *takes fright and shrieks.*]

LOPAKHIN [*angrily*]. Even where you come from there's such a thing as being polite.

MRS. RANEVSKY [*flustered*]. Here, have this. [*Looks in her purse.*] I've no silver. Never mind, here's some gold.

PASSER-BY. I'm uncommonly obliged to you. [*Goes off.*]

[*Everyone laughs.*]

VARYA [*frightened*]. I'm going. I'm going away from here. Oh Mother, we've no food in the house for the servants and you gave him all that money.

MRS. RANEVSKY. What's to be done with me? I'm so silly. I'll give you all I have when we get home. Yermolay, lend me some more money.

LOPAKHIN. At your service.

MRS. RANEVSKY. Come on, everybody, it's time to go in. Varya, we've just fixed you up with a husband. Congratulations.

VARYA [*through tears*]. Don't make jokes about it, Mother.

LOPAKHIN. Amelia, get thee to a nunnery.

GAYEV. My hands are shaking. It's a long time since I had a game of billiards.

LOPAKHIN. Amelia, nymph, in thy orisons, be all my sins remembered.

MRS. RANEVSKY. Come on, all of you. It's nearly supper time.

VARYA. That man scared me. I still feel quite shaken.

LOPAKHIN. May I remind you all that the cherry orchard's going to be sold on the twenty-second of August? You must think about it. Give it some thought.

[*All go off except* TROFIMOV *and* ANYA.]

ANYA [*laughing*]. We should be grateful to that man for frightening Varya. Now we're alone.

TROFIMOV. Varya's afraid we might fall in love, so she follows us about for days on end. With her narrow outlook she can't understand that we're above love. To rid ourselves of the pettiness and the illusions which stop us being free and happy, that's the whole meaning and purpose of our lives. Forward then! We are marching triumphantly on towards that bright star shining there far away. On, on! No falling back, my friends.

ANYA [*clapping her hands*]. What splendid things you say! [*Pause.*] Isn't it heavenly here today?

TROFIMOV. Yes, it's wonderful weather.

ANYA. What have you done to me, Peter? Why is it I'm not so fond of the cherry orchard as I used to be? I loved it so dearly. I used to think there was no better place on earth than our orchard.

TROFIMOV. All Russia is our orchard. The earth is so wide, so beautiful, so full of wonderful places. [*Pause.*] Just think, Anya. Your grandfather, your great-grandfather and all your ancestors owned serfs, they owned human souls. Don't you see that from every cherry-tree in the orchard, from every leaf and every trunk, men and women are gazing at you? Don't you hear their voices? Owning living souls, that's what has changed you all so completely, those who went before and those alive today, so that your mother, you yourself, your uncle—you don't realize that you're actually living on credit. You're living on other people, the very people you won't even let inside your own front door. We're at least a couple of hundred years behind the times. So far we haven't got anywhere at all and we've no real sense of the past. We just talk in airy generalizations, complain of boredom or drink vodka. But if we're to start living in the present isn't it abundantly clear that we've first got to redeem our past and make a clean break with it? And we can only redeem it by suffering and getting down to some real work for a change. You must understand that, Anya.

ANYA. The house we live in hasn't really been ours for a long time and I mean to leave it, I promise you.

TROFIMOV. If you have the keys of the place throw them in the well and go away. Be free, free as the wind.

ANYA [*carried away*]. How beautifully you put it.

TROFIMOV. Believe me, Anya. Trust me. I'm not yet thirty. I'm young and I'm still a student, but I've had my share of hardship. In winter time I'm always half-starved, ill, worried, desperately poor. And I've been landed in some pretty queer places. I've seen a thing or two in my time, I can tell you. Yet always, every moment of the day and night, I've been haunted by mysterious visions of the future. Happiness is coming, Anya, I feel it. I already see it——

ANYA [*pensively*]. The moon is rising.

[YEPIKHODOV *is heard playing his guitar, the same sad tune as before. The moon rises. Somewhere near the poplars* VARYA *is looking for* ANYA *and calling*, 'Anya, where are you?']

TROFIMOV. Yes, the moon is rising. [*Pause.*] Here it is! Happiness is here. Here it comes, nearer, ever nearer. Already I hear its footsteps. And if *we* never see it, if *we* never know it, what does that matter? Others will see it.

VARYA [*off stage*]. Anya! Where are you?

TROFIMOV. Varya's at it again. [*Angrily.*] She really is infuriating.

ANYA. Oh well, let's go down to the river. It's lovely there.

TROFIMOV. Come on then. [*They move off.*]

VARYA [*off stage*]. Anya! Anya!

CURTAIN

ACT THREE

The drawing-room. Beyond it, through an archway, the ballroom.
The chandelier is lit. The Jewish band mentioned in Act Two is
heard playing in the entrance-hall. It is evening. In the ballroom they
are dancing a grand rond. SIMEONOV-PISHCHIK's *voice is heard:*
'Promenade à une paire!' *They come into the drawing-room, the*
first two dancers being PISHCHIK *and* CHARLOTTE. TROFIMOV
and MRS. RANEVSKY *form the second pair,* ANYA *and the* POST
OFFICE CLERK *the third,* VARYA *and the* STATIONMASTER *the*
fourth and so on. VARYA *is quietly weeping and dries her eyes as she*
dances. The last couple consists of DUNYASHA *and a partner. They*
cross the drawing-room. PISHCHIK *shouts,* 'Grand rond, balancez!'
and 'Les cavaliers à genoux et remerciez vos dames!'
      FIRS, *wearing a tail-coat, brings in soda-water on a tray.* PI-
SHCHIK *and* TROFIMOV *come into the drawing-room.*

PISHCHIK. I've got high blood pressure, I've twice had a stroke and
   it's hard work dancing. Still, as the saying goes, those who run with
   the pack must wag their tails, even if they can't raise a bark. I'm as
   strong as a horse, though. My old father—he liked his little joke,
   God bless him—sometimes spoke about the family pedigree and
   he reckoned that the ancient line of the Simeonov-Pishchiks comes
   from a horse, the one Caligula made a senator. [*Sits down.*] Trouble
   is though, I've no money. A hungry dog thinks only of his supper.
   [*Snores, but wakes up again at once.*] I'm just the same, can't think
   of anything but money.

TROFIMOV. You know, you really are built rather like a horse.

PISHCHIK. Well, and why not? The horse is a fine animal. You can
   sell a horse.

      [*From an adjoining room comes the sound of people playing billiards.*
      VARYA *appears in the ballroom beneath the archway.*]

TROFIMOV [*teasing her*]. Mrs. Lopakhin! Mrs. Lopakhin!

VARYA [*angrily*]. Seedy-looking gent!

TROFIMOV. Yes, I am a seedy-looking gent and I'm proud of it.

VARYA [*brooding unhappily*]. We've gone and hired this band, but how are we to pay them?

[*Goes out.*]

TROFIMOV [*to* PISHCHIK]. Think of all the energy you've wasted in your time looking for money to pay interest on your loans. If you'd used it on something else you might have turned the world upside down by now.

PISHCHIK. Nietzsche, the philosopher—tremendous fellow, very famous, colossally clever chap—says in his works that there's nothing wrong with forging bank-notes.

TROFIMOV. Have you read Nietzsche then?

PISHCHIK. Well, Dashenka told me about it actually. And the way I'm fixed now, forging a few bank-notes is about my only way out. I have to pay three hundred and ten roubles the day after to-morrow. So far I've got a hundred and thirty. [*Feels his pockets in alarm.*] My money's gone! I've lost my money! [*Through tears.*] Where is it? [*Happily.*] Oh, here it is in the lining. That gave me quite a turn.

[MRS. RANEVSKY *and* CHARLOTTE *come in.*]

MRS. RANEVSKY [*hums a Caucasian dance tune, the* Lezginka.] Why is Leonid so long? What can he be doing in town? [*To* DUNYASHA.] Dunyasha, ask the band if they'd care for some tea.

TROFIMOV. Most likely the auction didn't even take place.

MRS. RANEVSKY. What a time to have the band here and what a time to give a party! Oh well, never mind. [*Sits down and hums quietly.*]

CHARLOTTE [*handing* PISHCHIK *a pack of cards*]. Here's a pack of cards. Think of a card.

PISHCHIK. All right.

CHARLOTTE. Now shuffle the pack. That's fine. Now give them to me, my dearest Mr. Pishchik. *Ein, zwei, drei!* And now look in your coat pocket. Is it there?

PISHCHIK [*taking a card out of his coat pocket*]. The eight of spades, you're quite right. [*In amazement.*] Extraordinary thing.

CHARLOTTE [*holding the pack of cards on the palm of her hand, to* TROFIMOV]. Tell me quick, what's the top card?

TROFIMOV. Well, say the queen of spades.

CHARLOTTE. And here she is! [*To* PISHCHIK.] Right. What's the top card now?

PISHCHIK. The ace of hearts.

CHARLOTTE. Correct. [*Claps her hand on the pack of cards, which disappears.*] What fine weather we've had today. [*She is answered by a mysterious female voice which seems to come from under the floor:* 'Oh yes, magnificent weather, madam.'] Oh you're so nice, quite charming in fact. [*The voice*: 'I likes you very much too, madam.']

STATIONMASTER [*clapping his hands*]. Hurrah for our lady ventriloquist!

PISHCHIK [*astonished*]. Extraordinary thing. Miss Charlotte, you're utterly bewitching, I've quite fallen in love with you.

CHARLOTTE. In love? [*Shrugging her shoulders.*] As if you were capable of love. *Guter Mensch, aber schlechter Musikant.*

TROFIMOV [*claps* PISHCHIK *on the shoulder*]. Good for the old horse.

CHARLOTTE. Your attention, please. Another trick. [*Takes a rug from a chair.*] Here's a very fine rug, I'd like to sell it. [*Shakes it.*] Doesn't anyone want to buy?

PISHCHIK [*astonished*]. Extraordinary thing.

CHARLOTTE. *Ein, zwei, drei!* [*Quickly snatches up the rug, which she had allowed to fall down, to reveal* ANYA *standing behind it.* ANYA *curtsies, runs to her mother and embraces her, then runs back into the ballroom amid general enthusiasm.*]

MRS. RANEVSKY [*claps*]. Well done, well done!

CHARLOTTE. Now for another. *Ein, zwei, drei!* [*Raises the rug. Behind it stands* VARYA, *who bows.*]

PISHCHIK [*astonished*]. Extraordinary thing.

CHARLOTTE. The performance is over. [*Throws the rug at* PISHCHIK, *curtsies and runs off into the ballroom.*]

PISHCHIK [*hurries after her*]. What a naughty girl! Not bad, eh? Not bad at all. [*Goes out.*]

MRS. RANEVSKY. And still no sign of Leonid. I can't think what he's been up to in town all this time. The thing must be over by now. Either the estate's sold or the auction didn't take place, so why keep us in suspense all this time?

VARYA [*trying to console her*]. Uncle's bought it, he must have.

TROFIMOV [*with a sneer*]. Oh, of course.

VARYA. Our great-aunt sent him the authority to buy it in her name and transfer the mortgage to her. She's doing it for Anya's sake. Uncle will buy it, God willing, I'm sure of that.

MRS. RANEVSKY. Your great-aunt in Yaroslavl sent fifteen thousand to buy the estate in her name—she doesn't trust us—but that much wouldn't even pay the interest. [*Covers her face with her hands.*] My fate, my whole future is being decided today.

TROFIMOV [*teasing* VARYA]. Mrs. Lopakhin!

VARYA [*angrily*]. Hark at the eternal student. He's already been sent down from the university twice.

MRS. RANEVSKY. Why are you so cross, Varya? If he teases you about Lopakhin, what of it? If you want to marry Lopakhin, do—he's a nice, attractive man. And if you don't want to, don't. Nobody's forcing you, darling.

VARYA. I'm perfectly serious about this, Mother, I must tell you quite plainly. He is a nice man and I do like him.

MRS. RANEVSKY. Well, marry him then. What are you waiting for? That's what I can't see.

VARYA. I can't very well propose to him myself, can I? Everyone's been talking to me about him for the last two years. Everyone goes on and on about it, but he either says nothing or just makes jokes. And I see his point. He's making money, he has his business to look after and he hasn't time for me. If I had just a bit of money myself—even a hundred roubles would do—I'd drop everything and go right away. I'd go to a convent.

TROFIMOV. What bliss!

VARYA [*to* TROFIMOV]. Our student must show how witty he is, mustn't he? [*In a gentle voice, tearfully.*] Oh, you have grown ugly, Peter, and you do look old. [*She has stopped crying and speaks to* MRS. RANEVSKY.] But I can't stand having nothing to do, Mother, I must be doing something every minute of the day.

[*Enter* YASHA.]

YASHA [*hardly able to restrain his laughter*]. Yepikhodov's broken a billiard cue. [*Goes out.*]

VARYA. What is Yepikhodov doing here? And who said he could play billiards? I can't make these people out. [*Goes out.*]

MRS. RANEVSKY. Don't tease her, Peter. Don't you see she's unhappy enough already?

TROFIMOV. She's a great deal too officious. Why can't she mind her own business? She's been pestering me and Anya all summer, afraid we might have a love affair. What's it got to do with her? Not that I ever gave her cause to think such a thing, anyway, I'm beyond such trivialities. We are above love.

MRS. RANEVSKY. While I'm supposed to be beneath it, I imagine. [*Greatly agitated.*] Why isn't Leonid back? If only I knew whether the estate's been sold or not. I feel that such an awful thing just couldn't happen, so I don't know what to think, I'm at my wits' end. I'm liable to scream or do something silly. Help me, Peter. Oh, say something, do, for heaven's sake speak.

TROFIMOV. What does it matter whether the estate's been sold today or not? All that's over and done with. There's no turning back, that avenue is closed. Don't worry, my dear. But don't try and fool yourself either. For once in your life you must face the truth.

MRS. RANEVSKY. What truth? *You* can see what's true or untrue, but I seem to have lost my sight, I see nothing. You solve the most serious problems so confidently, but tell me, dear boy, isn't that because you're young—not old enough for any of your problems to have caused you real suffering? You face the future so bravely, but then you can't imagine anything terrible happening, can you? And isn't that because you're still too young to see what life's really like? You're bolder, more honest, more profound than we are, but try and put yourself in our place, do show a little generosity and spare my feelings. You see, I was born here, my father and mother lived here, and my grandfather too. I love this house. Without the cherry orchard life has no meaning for me and if it really must be sold then you'd better sell me with it. [*Embraces* TROFIMOV *and kisses him on the forehead.*] My little boy was drowned here, you know. [*Weeps.*] Don't be too hard on me, my good kind friend.

TROFIMOV. As you know, I feel for you with all my heart.

MRS. RANEVSKY. Well, that isn't the way to say it, it really isn't. [*Takes out her handkerchief. A telegram falls to the floor.*] I'm so depressed today, you just can't imagine. I hate all this noise. Every sound sends a shiver right through me. I'm trembling all over, but I can't go to my room, the silence frightens me when I'm on my own. Don't think too badly of me, Peter. I love you as my own son. I'd gladly let Anya marry you, I honestly would, only you really must study, dear boy, you must take your degree. You never do anything, you just drift about from place to place, that's what's so peculiar. Well, it is, isn't it? And you should do something about that beard, make it grow somehow. [*Laughs.*] You do look funny.

TROFIMOV [*picks up the telegram*]. I don't pretend to be particularly good-looking.

MRS. RANEVSKY. That telegram's from Paris. I get one every day. One came yesterday and there's another today. That crazy creature is ill and in trouble again. He asks my forgiveness, begs me to come to him, and I really ought to go over to Paris and be near him for a bit. You look very disapproving, Peter, but what else can I do, my dear boy, what else can I do? He's ill, he's lonely and unhappy, and who'll look after him there? Who'll stop him making a fool of himself and give him his medicine at the right time? And then, why make a secret of it, why not say so? I love him, that's obvious. I love him, I love him. He's a millstone round my neck and he's dragging me down with him, but I love my millstone and I can't live without it. [*Presses* TROFIMOV's *hand.*] Don't think badly of me, Peter, and don't say anything, don't talk.

TROFIMOV [*through tears*]. Excuse me being so blunt, for heaven's sake, but he did rob you.

MRS. RANEVSKY. No, no, no, you mustn't say that. [*Puts her hands over her ears.*]

TROFIMOV. Why, the man's a swine and you're the only one who doesn't know it. He's a little swine, a nobody——

MRS. RANEVSKY [*angry, but restraining herself*]. You're twenty-six or twenty-seven, but you're still a schoolboy.

TROFIMOV. What if I am?

MRS. RANEVSKY. You should be more of a man. At your age you should understand people in love. And you should be in love yourself, you should fall in love. [*Angrily.*] Yes, I mean it. And you're not all that pure and innocent either, you're just a prig, a ridiculous freak, a kind of monster——

TROFIMOV [*horrified*]. She can't know what she's saying!

MRS. RANEVSKY. 'I am above love!' You're not above love, you're just what our friend Firs calls a nincompoop. Fancy being your age and not having a mistress!

TROFIMOV [*horrified*]. This is outrageous. She can't know what she's saying! [*Goes quickly into the ballroom clutching his head.*] It's outrageous. I can't stand it, I'm going. [*Goes out, but immediately comes back.*] All is over between us. [*Goes out into the hall.*]

MRS. RANEVSKY [*shouting after him*]. Peter, wait a minute. Don't be silly, I was only joking. Peter!

[*There is a sound of rapid footsteps on the staircase in the hall and then of someone suddenly falling downstairs with a crash.* ANYA *and* VARYA *scream, but this is at once followed by laughter.*]

MRS. RANEVSKY. What's going on out there?

[ANYA *runs in.*]

ANYA [*laughing*]. Peter fell downstairs. [*Runs out.*]

MRS. RANEVSKY. What a funny boy Peter is.

[*The* STATIONMASTER *stands in the middle of the ballroom and begins to declaim* The Sinful Woman *by Aleksey Tolstoy. The others listen, but he has only recited a few lines when the sound of a waltz comes from the hall and the recitation is broken off. Everyone dances.* TROFIMOV, ANYA, VARYA *and* MRS. RANEVSKY *pass through from the hall.*]

MRS. RANEVSKY. Now, Peter. There now, my dear good boy. Please forgive me. Let's dance. [*Dances with* PETER.]

[ANYA *and* VARYA *dance together.* FIRS *comes in and stands his walking-stick near the side door.* YASHA *has also gone in from the drawing-room and is watching the dancing.*]

YASHA. How goes it, old boy?

FIRS. I don't feel so good. We used to have generals, barons and admirals at our dances in the old days, but now we send for the post office clerk and the stationmaster and even they aren't all that keen to come. I feel so frail somehow. The old master, Mr. Leonid's grandfather, used to dose us all with powdered sealing-wax no matter what was wrong with us. I've been taking sealing-wax every day for the last twenty years or more. Maybe that's what's kept me alive.

YASHA. Granddad, you make me tired. [*Yawns.*] It's time you were dead.

FIRS. Get away with you. Nincompoop! [*Mutters.*]

[TROFIMOV *and* MRS. RANEVSKY *dance in the ballroom, then in the drawing-room.*]

MRS. RANEVSKY. Thank you. I think I'll sit down a bit. [*Sits down.*] I'm tired.

[*Enter* ANYA.]

ANYA [*excitedly*]. There was someone in the kitchen just now saying the cherry orchard's been sold today.

MRS. RANEVSKY. Sold? Who to?

ANYA. He didn't say. He's gone away now. [*She and* TROFIMOV *dance off into the ballroom.*]

YASHA. It was only some old man's gossip. Nobody from here.

FIRS. And Mr. Leonid hasn't come yet, he's still not back. He's only got his light overcoat on and he'll catch cold, like as not. These young people never stop to think.

MRS. RANEVSKY. Oh, I shall die. Yasha, go and find out who bought it.

YASHA. But he's been gone some time, that old fellow. [*Laughs.*]

MRS. RANEVSKY [*somewhat annoyed*]. Well, what's so funny? What are you so pleased about?

YASHA. Yepikhodov really is a scream. The man's so futile. Simple Simon!

MRS. RANEVSKY. Firs, if the estate's sold where will you go?

FIRS. I'll go wherever you tell me.

MRS. RANEVSKY. Why do you look like that? Aren't you well? You ought to be in bed, you know.

FIRS. Oh yes. [*With amusement.*] I go off to bed and then who'll do the serving and look after everything? There's only me to run the whole house.

YASHA [*to* MRS. RANEVSKY]. Mrs. Ranevsky, may I ask you something, please? If you go back to Paris, do me a favour and take me with you. I can't stay here, that's out of the question. [*Looks round, in an undertone.*] It goes without saying, you can see for yourself, this is an uncivilized country and no one has any morals. Besides it's boring, the food they give you in the kitchen is something awful and on top of that there's old Firs wandering round mumbling and speaking out of turn. Do take me with you. Please.

[*Enter* PISHCHIK.]

PISHCHIK. May I have the pleasure of a little waltz, you ravishing creature? [MRS. RANEVSKY *goes with him.*] But I'll have a hundred and eighty roubles off you, my bewitching friend. That I will. [*Dances.*] Just a hundred and eighty roubles, that's all. [*They go into the ballroom.*]

YASHA [*singing softly*]. 'Couldst thou but sense the trembling of my heart——'

[*In the ballroom a woman in a grey top hat and check trousers is seen jumping and waving her arms about. Shouts are heard*: 'Well done, Charlotte!']

DUNYASHA [*stops to powder her face*]. Miss Anya told me to join in the dancing. There are lots of gentlemen and only a few ladies. But I get giddy when I dance and it makes my heart beat so. I say, Mr. Firs, the man from the post office has just told me something that gave me quite a turn.

[*The music becomes quieter.*]

FIRS. What was that?

DUNYASHA. 'You're like a flower,' he said.

YASHA [*yawning*]. Shockin' ignorance. [*Goes out.*]

DUNYASHA. Like a flower. I'm such a sensitive girl and I like it ever so when people say such nice things.

FIRS. You'll end up in a real old mess.

[*Enter* YEPIKHODOV.]

YEPIKHODOV. You don't seem to want to see me, Miss Dunyasha, I might be an insect or something. [*Sighs.*] Oh, what a life!

DUNYASHA. What do you want?

YEPIKHODOV. Undoubtedly you may be right. [*Sighs.*] But of course, if one looks at things from a certain angle, as I venture to assert if you'll excuse my frankness, you've finally reduced me to a state of mind. I know what I'm up against. Every day something goes wrong, but I got used to that long ago, so I just smile at my fate. You gave me your promise, and though I ——

DUNYASHA. Please! Can't we talk about it some other time? And you leave me alone now. I'm in a sort of dream. [*Plays with her fan.*]

YEPIKHODOV. Every day something goes wrong, but, as I make so bold to assert, I just smile. Even raise a laugh.

[VARYA *comes in from the ballroom.*]

VARYA. Are you still here, Simon? Really, you don't listen to anything you're told. [*To* DUNYASHA.] Be off with you, Dunyasha. [*To* YEPIKHODOV.] First you play billiards and break a cue, and now you wander round the drawing-room as if you were a guest.

YEPIKHODOV. You've no right to tell me off, permit me to inform you.

VARYA. I'm not telling you off, I'm just telling you. All you do is drift about from one place to another, you never do a stroke of work. Goodness knows why we keep a clerk at all.

YEPIKHODOV [*offended*]. Whether I work or drift about and whether I eat or play billiards, these are questions for older and wiser heads than yours.

VARYA. How dare you talk to me like that! [*Flaring up.*] How dare you! So I don't know what I'm talking about, don't I? Then get out of here! This instant!

YEPIKHODOV [*cowed*]. I must ask you to express yourself in a more refined manner.

VARYA [*losing her temper*]. Get out of here this instant! Out you go! [*He moves towards the door, and she follows him.*] Simple Simon! You clear out of here! Out of my sight! [YEPIKHODOV *goes out. His voice is heard from behind the door:* 'I shall lodge a complaint.'] Oh, so you're coming back, are you? [*Picks up the stick which* FIRS *left near the door.*] Come on then. All right—. Come on, I'll teach you. Ah, so you are coming, are you? Then take that. [*Lashes out just as* LOPAKHIN *comes in.*]

LOPAKHIN. Thank you very much.

VARYA [*angrily and derisively*]. I'm extremely sorry.

LOPAKHIN. Not at all. Thank you for such a warm welcome.

VARYA. Oh, don't mention it. [*Moves away, then looks round and asks gently.*] I didn't hurt you, did I?

LOPAKHIN. No, it's all right. I'm going to have a whacking great bruise, though.

[*Voices in the ballroom:* 'Lopakhin's arrived! Yermolay! Mr. Lopakhin!']

PISHCHIK. As large as life and twice as natural. [*Embraces* LOPAKHIN.] There's a slight whiff of brandy about you, dear old boy. We're having a pretty good time here too.

[MRS. RANEVSKY *comes in.*]

MRS. RANEVSKY. Is it you, Yermolay? Why have you been so long? Where's Leonid?

LOPAKHIN. We came together. He'll be along in a moment.

MRS. RANEVSKY [*agitated*]. Well? Did the auction take place? For heaven's sake speak!

LOPAKHIN [*embarrassed and fearing to betray his delight*]. The auction was over by four o'clock. We missed our train and had to wait till half past nine. [*Gives a heavy sigh.*] Oh dear, I feel a bit dizzy. [*Enter* GAYEV. *He carries some packages in his right hand and wipes away his tears with his left.*]

MRS. RANEVSKY. What happened, Leonid? Leonid, please! [*Impatiently, in tears.*] Hurry up! Tell me, for God's sake!

GAYEV [*not answering her and making a gesture of resignation with his hand. To* FIRS, *weeping*]. Here, take this, some anchovies and Black Sea herrings. I haven't eaten all day. I've had a frightful time. [*The door into the billiard room is open. The click of billiard balls is heard and* YASHA's *voice:* 'Seven and eighteen!' GAYEV's *expression changes and he stops crying.*] I'm terribly tired. Come and help me change, Firs. [*Goes off through the ballroom to his own room followed by* FIRS.]

PISHCHIK. What happened at the sale? For heaven's sake tell us!

MRS. RANEVSKY. Was the cherry orchard sold?

LOPAKHIN. It was.

MRS. RANEVSKY. Who bought it?

LOPAKHIN. I did. [*Pause.*]

[MRS. RANEVSKY *is overwhelmed and would have fallen if she had not been standing near an armchair and a table.* VARYA *takes the keys from her belt, throws them on the floor in the middle of the drawing-room and goes out.*]

LOPAKHIN. I bought it. Just a moment, everybody, if you don't mind. I feel a bit muddled, I can't talk. [*Laughs.*] When we got to the auction Deriganov was already there. Gayev only had fifteen thousand, and straight off Deriganov bid thirty on top of the arrears on the mortgage. I saw how things were going, so I weighed in myself and bid forty. He bid forty-five. I went up to fifty-five. He kept raising his bid five thousand, you see, and I was going up in tens. Anyway, it finished in the end. I bid ninety thousand roubles plus the arrears. And I got it. And now the cherry orchard is mine. Mine! [*Gives a loud laugh.*] Great God in heaven, the cherry orchard's mine! Tell me I'm drunk or crazy, say it's all a dream. [*Stamps his feet.*] Don't laugh at me. If my father and grandfather could only rise from their graves and see what happened, see how their Yermolay—Yermolay who was always being beaten, who could hardly write his name and ran round barefoot in winter—how this same Yermolay bought this estate, the most beautiful place in the world. I've bought the estate where my father and grandfather were slaves, where they weren't even allowed inside the kitchen. I must be dreaming, I must be imagining it all. It can't be true. This is all a figment of your imagination wrapped in the mists of obscurity. [*Picks up the keys, smiling fondly.*] She threw away the keys to show she's not in charge here now. [*Jingles the keys.*] Oh well, never mind. [*The band is heard tuning up.*] Hey, you in the band, give us a tune, I want to hear you. Come here, all of you, and you just watch Yermolay Lopakhin get his axe into that cherry orchard, watch the trees come crashing down. We'll fill the place with cottages. Our grandchildren and our great-grandchildren will see a few changes round here. Music, boys!

[*The band plays.* MRS. RANEVSKY *has sunk into a chair and is weeping bitterly.*]

LOPAKHIN [*reproachfully*]. But why, oh why, didn't you listen to me before? My poor dear friend, you can't put the clock back now. [*With tears.*] Oh, if all this could be over quickly, if our miserable, mixed-up lives could somehow hurry up and change.

PISHCHIK [*taking him by the arm, in an undertone*]. She's crying. Come into the other room and leave her alone. Come on. [*Takes him by the arm and leads him into the ballroom.*]

LOPAKHIN. Hey, what's up? You in the band, let's have you playing properly. Let's have everything the way *I* want it. [*Ironically.*] Here comes the new squire, the owner of the cherry orchard! [*Accidentally jogs a small table, nearly knocking over the candelabra.*] I can pay for everything. [*Goes out with* PISHCHIK.]

[*There is no one left in the ballroom or drawing-room except* MRS. RANEVSKY, *who sits hunched up, weeping bitterly. The band plays quietly.* ANYA *and* TROFIMOV *come in quickly.* ANYA *goes up to her mother and kneels down in front of her.* TROFIMOV *stays by the entrance to the ballroom.*]

ANYA. Mother! Mother, are you crying? My lovely, kind, good mother. My precious, I love you. God bless you. The cherry orchard's sold, it's gone. That's true, quite true, but don't cry, Mother, you still your life to live. You're still here with your kind and innocent heart. Come with me, dear, come away. We shall plant a new orchard, more glorious than this one. And when you see it everything will make sense to you. Your heart will be filled with happiness—deep happiness and peace, descending from above like the sun at evening time. And then you'll smile again, Mother. Come, my dear, come with me.

CURTAIN

ACT FOUR

The scene is the same as in Act One. There are no window-curtains or pictures. Only a few pieces of furniture are left and have been stacked in one corner as if for sale. There is a feeling of emptiness. Suitcases, travelling bags and so on have been piled up near the outside door and at the back of the stage. The voices of VARYA *and* ANYA *can be heard through the door, left, which is open.* LOPAKHIN *stands waiting.* YASHA *is holding a tray with glasses of champagne on it.* YEPIKHODOV *is roping up a box in the hall. There is a murmur off stage at the rear, the voices of peasants who have come to say good-bye.* GAYEV's *voice is heard:* 'Thank you, my good fellows, thank you very much.'

YASHA. Some village people have come to say good-bye. If you ask my opinion, sir, the lower orders mean well, but they haven't got much sense.

[*The murmur of voices dies away.* MRS. RANEVSKY *and* GAYEV *come in through the hall. She is not crying, but she is pale, her face is working and she cannot speak.*]

GAYEV. You gave them your purse, Lyuba. You shouldn't do such things, you really shouldn't.

MRS. RANEVSKY. I couldn't help it, just couldn't help it.

[*Both go out.*]

LOPAKHIN [*calling through the door after them*]. Come along, please, come on. Let's have a little glass together before we go. I didn't think of bringing any from town and I could only get one bottle at the station. Come on. [*Pause.*] What's the matter? None of you want any? [*Comes back from the door.*] I wouldn't have bought it if I'd known. All right then, I won't have any either. [YASHA *carefully places the tray on a chair.*] You have some, Yasha, anyway.

YASHA. Here's to those that are leaving. And good luck to them that aren't. [*Drinks.*] This champagne isn't the genuine article, you can take it from me.

LOPAKHIN. And at eight roubles a bottle. [*Pause.*] It's damn cold in here.

YASHA. The stoves haven't been lit today. Never mind, we're going away. [*Laughs.*]

LOPAKHIN. What's the joke?

YASHA. I feel so pleased.

LOPAKHIN. It's October now, but it might be summer, it's so fine and sunny. Good building weather. [*Glances at his watch and calls through the door.*] I say, don't forget the train leaves in forty-seven minutes. So we must start for the station twenty minutes from now. Better get a move on.

[TROFIMOV *comes in from outside. He wears an overcoat.*]

TROFIMOV. I think it's time we were off. The carriages are at the door. Damn it, where are my galoshes? They've disappeared. [*Through the door.*] Anya, I've lost my galoshes. I can't find them anywhere.

LOPAKHIN. I've got to go to Kharkov. We're all taking the same train. I'm spending the winter in Kharkov—I've been kicking my heels round here quite long enough and I'm fed up with doing nothing. I can't stand not working—look, I don't know what to do with my arms. See the absurd way they flop about as if they belonged to someone else.

TROFIMOV. We'll soon be gone and then you can get back to your useful labours again.

LOPAKHIN. Come on, have a drink.

TROFIMOV. Not for me, thank you.

LOPAKHIN. So you're off to Moscow, are you?

TROFIMOV. Yes, I'm seeing them as far as town and going on to Moscow tomorrow.

LOPAKHIN. I see. Ah well, I daresay the professors haven't started lecturing yet, they'll be waiting for you to turn up.

TROFIMOV. Oh, mind your own business.

LOPAKHIN. How many years is it you've been at the university?

TROFIMOV. Can't you say something new for a change? That joke's played out. [*Looks for his galoshes.*] Look here, you and I may never meet again, so let me give you a word of advice before we say good-bye. Stop waving your arms about. Cure yourself of that stupid habit. What's more, all this stuff about building cottages and working out that the owners will end up as smallholders—that's just as stupid as waving your arms about. Anyway, never mind, I still like you. You have sensitive fingers like an artist's and you're a fine, sensitive person too, deep down inside you.

LOPAKHIN [*embracing him*]. Good-bye, Peter. Thanks for everything. Let me give you some money for the journey, you may need it.

TROFIMOV. I don't. Why should I?

LOPAKHIN. Because you haven't any.

TROFIMOV. Yes I have, thank you very much. I got some for a translation, it's here in my pocket. [*Anxiously.*] But I still can't find my galoshes.

VARYA [*from another room*]. Oh, take the beastly things. [*Throws a pair of galoshes on to the stage.*]

TROFIMOV. Why are you so angry, Varya? I say, these aren't my galoshes.

LOPAKHIN. I put nearly three thousand acres down to poppy in the spring and made a clear forty thousand roubles. And when my poppies were in flower, that was a sight to see. What I'm trying to say is, I've made forty thousand and I'd like to lend it you because I can afford to. So why turn it down? I'm a peasant, I put it to you straight.

TROFIMOV. Your father was a peasant and mine worked in a chemist's shop, all of which proves precisely nothing. [LOPAKHIN *takes out his wallet.*] Oh, put it away, for heaven's sake. If you offered me two hundred thousand I still wouldn't take it. I'm a free man. And all the things that mean such a lot to you all, whether you're rich or poor —why, they have no more power over me than a bit of thistledown floating on the breeze. I can get on without you, I can pass you by. I'm strong and proud. Mankind is marching towards a higher truth, towards the greatest possible happiness on earth, and I'm in the vanguard.

LOPAKHIN. Will you get there?

TROFIMOV. I shall. [*Pause.*] I'll either get there or show others the way.

[*There is the sound of an axe striking a tree in the distance.*]

LOPAKHIN. Well, good-bye, my dear fellow. It's time to go. You and I look down our noses at each other, but life goes on without bothering about us. When I work for a long time at a stretch I feel a bit calmer, and I too seem to know why I exist. But there are lots of people in Russia, old boy, and why some of them exist is anyone's guess. Oh well, never mind, that's not what makes the world go round. I hear Gayev's taken a job at the bank at six thousand a year. He'll never stick it out, though, he's too lazy.

ANYA [*in the doorway*]. Mother says would you mind waiting till she's gone before cutting down the orchard.

TROFIMOV. Yes, you really might have shown more tact, I must say. [*Goes out through the hall.*]

LOPAKHIN. Right, I'll see to it. Those people are the limit. [*Goes out after him.*]

ANYA. Has Firs been taken to hospital yet?

YASHA. I told them to this morning. They must have taken him, I reckon.

ANYA [*to* YEPIKHODOV, *who is passing through the ballroom*]. Simon, please find out if Firs has been taken to hospital.

YASHA [*offended*]. I told Yegor this morning. Why keep on and on about it?

YEPIKHODOV. The aged Firs, or so I have finally concluded, is beyond repair. It's time he was gathered to his fathers. As for me, I can only envy him. [*Has placed a suitcase on a hat box and squashed it.*] Oh look, that had to happen. I knew it. [*Goes out.*]

YASHA [*with a sneer*]. Simple Simon.

VARYA [*from behind the door*]. Has Firs been taken to hospital?

ANYA. Yes.

VARYA. Then why didn't they take the letter to the doctor?

ANYA. Well, we'll have to send it on after him. [*Goes out.*]

VARYA [*from the next room*]. Where's Yasha? Tell him his mother's come to say good-bye.

YASHA [*with an impatient gesture*]. Oh, this is too much.

[*All this time* DUNYASHA *has been busy with the luggage. Now that* YASHA *is alone she goes up to him.*]

DUNYASHA. You might at least look at me, Yasha. You're going away, deserting me. [*Weeps and throws her arms round his neck.*]

YASHA. Why all the tears? [*Drinks champagne.*] I'll be back in Paris in a week. Tomorrow we catch the express and then you won't see us for smoke. I can hardly believe it somehow. *Veev la France!* It doesn't suit me here, this isn't the life for me and that's that. I've seen enough ignorance to last me a lifetime. [*Drinks champagne.*] So why the tears? You be a good girl and then you won't have anything to cry about.

DUNYASHA [*powders her face, looking in a hand-mirror*]. Write to me from Paris. You know, I did love you Yasha, I loved you so much. Oh Yasha, I'm such a soft-hearted girl.

YASHA. Somebody's coming. [*Attends to the suitcases, humming quietly.*]

[MRS. RANEVSKY, GAYEV, ANYA *and* CHARLOTTE *come in.*]

GAYEV. We ought to be going, there's not much time left. [*Looks at* YASHA.] Someone round here smells of herring.

MRS. RANEVSKY. We'd better be getting into the carriages in about ten minutes. [*Looks round the room.*] Good-bye, house. Good-bye, dear old place. Winter will pass, spring will come again and then you won't be here any more, you'll be pulled down. These walls have seen a few sights in their time. [*Kisses her daughter with great feeling.*] My treasure, you look radiant, your eyes are sparkling like diamonds. Are you very pleased? You are, aren't you?

ANYA. Oh yes, I am. This is the start of a new life, Mother.

GAYEV [*happily*]. It's quite true, everything's all right now. Before the cherry orchard was sold we were all worried and upset, but when things were settled once and for all and we'd burnt our boats, we all calmed down and actually cheered up a bit. I'm working at a bank now, I'm a financier. Pot the red in the middle. And you can say what you like, Lyuba, you're looking a lot better, no doubt about it.

MRS. RANEVSKY. Yes. I'm not so much on edge, that's true. [*Someone helps her on with her hat and coat.*] And I'm sleeping better. Take my things out, Yasha, it's time. [*To* ANYA.] We'll soon be seeing each other again, child. I'm going to Paris and I'll live on the money your great-aunt sent from Yaroslavl to buy the estate—good old Aunty! Not that it'll last very long.

ANYA. You'll come back soon, Mother. You will, won't you? I'm going to study and pass my school exams and then I'll work and help you. We'll read together, won't we, Mother—all sorts of books? [*Kisses her mother's hands.*] We'll read during the autumn evenings.

We'll read lots of books and a wonderful new world will open up before us. [*Dreamily.*] Do come back, Mother.

MRS. RANEVSKY. I will, my precious. [*Embraces her daughter.*]

[LOPAKHIN *comes in.* CHARLOTTE *quietly hums a tune.*]

GAYEV. Charlotte's happy, she's singing.

CHARLOTTE [*picking up a bundle which looks like a swaddled baby*]. Rock-a-bye, baby. [*A baby's cry is heard.*] Hush, my darling, my dear little boy. [*The cry is heard again.*] You poor little thing! [*Throws the bundle down.*] And please will you find me another job? I can't go on like this.

LOPAKHIN. We'll find you something, Charlotte, don't worry.

GAYEV. Everyone's deserting us. Varya's going, suddenly no one wants us any more.

CHARLOTTE. I haven't anywhere to live in town. I shall have to go away. [*Sings quietly.*] Anyway, I don't care.

[PISHCHIK *comes in.*]

LOPAKHIN. Oh, look who's come! Wonders will never cease.

PISHCHIK [*out of breath*]. Phew, I say, let me get my breath back. I'm all in. My good friends—. Give me some water.

GAYEV. Wants to borrow money, I'll be bound. I'll keep out of harm's way, thank you very much. [*Goes out.*]

PISHCHIK. Haven't been here for ages, dearest lady. [*To* LOPAKHIN.] You here too? Glad to see you. Tremendously clever fellow you are. Here. Take this. [*Gives* LOPAKHIN *money.*] Four hundred roubles. That leaves eight hundred and forty I owe you.

LOPAKHIN [*amazed, shrugging his shoulders*]. I must be seeing things. Where can you have got it?

PISHCHIK. Just a moment, I'm so hot. Most extraordinary occurrence. Some Englishmen came along and found a kind of white clay on my land. [*To* MRS. RANEVSKY.] And there's four hundred for you, you ravishing creature. [*Hands over the money.*] You'll get the rest later. [*Drinks some water.*] A young fellow on the train was just saying that some great philosopher advises everyone to go and jump off a roof. 'Just you jump,' he tells them, 'and you'll find that solves your problem.' [*With astonishment.*] Extraordinary thing. More water, please.

LOPAKHIN. But what Englishmen?

PISHCHIK. I've leased them this land with the clay on it for twenty-four years. But now you must excuse me, I can't stay. Must be running along. Going to see Znoykov. And Kardamonov. Owe them all money. [*Drinks.*] And the very best of luck to you. I'll look in on Thursday.

MRS. RANEVSKY. We're just leaving for town and I'm going abroad tomorrow.

PISHCHIK. What! [*Deeply concerned.*] Why go to town? Oh, I see, the furniture and luggage. Well, never mind. [*Through tears.*] It doesn't matter. Colossally clever fellows, these English. Never mind. All the best to you. God bless you. It doesn't matter. Everything in this world comes to an end. [*Kisses* MRS. RANEVSKY'*s hand.*] If you should ever hear that my end has come, just remember—remember the old horse, and say, 'There once lived such-and-such a person, a certain Simeonov-Pishchik, may his bones rest in peace.' Remarkable weather we're having. Yes. [*Goes out in great distress, but at once returns and speaks from the doorway.*] Dashenka sends her regards. [*Goes out.*]

MRS. RANEVSKY. Well, now we can go. I'm leaving with two worries. One is old Firs, who's ill. [*With a glance at her watch.*] We still have about five minutes.

ANYA. Firs has been taken to hospital, Mother. Yasha sent him off this morning.

MRS. RANEVSKY. My other worry's Varya. She's used to getting up early and working, and now she has nothing to do she's like a fish out of water. She's grown thin and pale and she's always crying, poor thing. [*Pause.*] As you know very well, Yermolay, I had hoped—to see her married to you, and it did look as if that was how things were shaping. [*Whispers to* ANYA, *who nods to* CHARLOTTE. *They both go out.*] She loves you, you're fond of her, and I haven't the faintest idea why you seem to avoid each other. It makes no sense to me.

LOPAKHIN. It makes no sense to me either, to be quite honest. It's a curious business, isn't it? If it's not too late I don't mind going ahead even now. Let's get it over and done with. I don't feel I'll ever propose to her without you here.

MRS. RANEVSKY. That's a very good idea. Why, it won't take more than a minute. I'll call her at once.

LOPAKHIN. There's even champagne laid on. [*Looks at the glasses.*] They're empty, someone must have drunk it. [YASHA *coughs.*] That's what I call really knocking it back.

MRS. RANEVSKY [*excitedly*]. I'm so glad. We'll go out. Yasha, *allez!* I'll call her. [*Through the door.*] Varya, leave what you're doing and come here a moment. Come on! [*Goes out with* YASHA.]

LOPAKHIN [*with a glance at his watch*]. Yes. [*Pause.*]

[*Suppressed laughter and whispering are heard from behind the door. After some time* VARYA *comes in.*]

VARYA [*spends a long time examining the luggage*]. That's funny, I can't find it anywhere.

LOPAKHIN. What are you looking for?

VARYA. I packed it myself and I still can't remember. [*Pause.*]

LOPAKHIN. Where are you going now, Varya?

VARYA. Me? To the Ragulins'. I've arranged to look after their place, a sort of housekeeper's job.

LOPAKHIN. That's in Yashnevo, isn't it? It must be fifty odd miles from here. [*Pause.*] So life has ended in this house.

VARYA [*examining the luggage*]. Oh, where can it be? Or could I have put it in the trunk? Yes, life has gone out of this house. And it will never come back.

LOPAKHIN. Well, I'm just off to Kharkov. By the next train. I have plenty to do there. And I'm leaving Yepikhodov in charge here, I've taken him on.

VARYA. Oh, have you?

LOPAKHIN. This time last year we already had snow, remember? But now it's calm and sunny. It's a bit cold though. Three degrees of frost, I should say.

VARYA. I haven't looked. [*Pause.*] Besides, our thermometer's broken. [*Pause.*]

[*A voice at the outer door:* 'Mr. Lopakhin!']

LOPAKHIN [*as if he had long been expecting this summons*]. I'm just coming. [*Goes out quickly.*]

[VARYA *sits on the floor with her head on a bundle of clothes, quietly sobbing. The door opens and* MRS. RANEVSKY *comes in cautiously.*]

MRS. RANEVSKY. Well? [*Pause.*] We'd better go.

VARYA [*has stopped crying and wiped her eyes*]. Yes, Mother, it's time. I can get to the Ragulins' today so long as I don't miss my train.

MRS. RANEVSKY [*calling through the door*]. Put your things on, Anya.

[ANYA *comes in followed by* GAYEV *and* CHARLOTTE. GAYEV *wears a warm overcoat with a hood. Servants and coachmen come in.* YEPIKHODOV *attends to the luggage.*]

MRS. RANEVSKY. Now we really can be on our way.

ANYA [*joyfully*]. On our way!

GAYEV. My friends, my dear good friends! As I leave this house for the last time, how can I be silent? How can I refrain from expressing as I leave the feelings that overwhelm my entire being?

ANYA [*beseechingly*]. Uncle.

VARYA. Uncle dear, please don't.

GAYEV [*despondently*]. Double the red into the middle. I am silent.

[TROFIMOV *comes in followed by* LOPAKHIN.]

TROFIMOV. Well everybody, it's time to go.

LOPAKHIN. My coat please, Yepikhodov.

MRS. RANEVSKY. I'll just stay another minute. I feel as though I'd never really looked at the walls or ceilings of this house before and now I can hardly take my eyes off them, I love them so dearly.

GAYEV. I remember when I was six years old sitting in this window on Trinity Sunday and watching Father go off to church.

MRS. RANEVSKY. Have they taken all the luggage out?

LOPAKHIN. It looks like it. [*Putting on his coat, to* YEPIKHODOV.] Make sure everything's all right, Yepikhodov, will you?

YEPIKHODOV [*speaking in a hoarse voice*]. Don't worry, Mr. Lopakhin!

LOPAKHIN. What's wrong with your voice?

YEPIKHODOV. I've just had some water, I must have swallowed something.

YASHA [*contemptuously*]. Shockin' ignorance.

MRS. RANEVSKY. When we've gone there will be no one left here. No one at all.

LOPAKHIN. Not till spring.

VARYA [*pulls an umbrella out of a bundle in such a way that it looks as if she meant to hit someone with it.* LOPAKHIN *pretends to be frightened*]. Oh, don't be silly, I didn't do it on purpose.

TROFIMOV. Come on, everyone, let's get into the carriages. It's time. The train will be in soon.

VARYA. There your galoshes are, Peter, just by that suitcase. [*Tearfully.*] And what dirty old things they are.

TROFIMOV [*putting on his galoshes*]. Come on, everyone.

GAYEV [*greatly distressed, afraid of bursting into tears*]. The train. The station. In off into the middle, double the white into the corner.

MRS. RANEVSKY. Come on then.

LOPAKHIN. Is everyone here? Nobody left behind? [*Locks the side door on the left.*] There are some things stored in there, so I'd better keep it locked. Come on.

ANYA. Good-bye, house. Good-bye, old life.

TROFIMOV. And welcome, new life. [*Goes out with* ANYA.]

[VARYA *looks round the room and goes out slowly.* YASHA *and* CHARLOTTE, *with her dog, follow.*]

LOPAKHIN. Till the spring then. Come along, everyone. Till we meet again. [*Goes out.*]

[MRS. RANEVSKY *and* GAYEV *are left alone. They seem to have been waiting for this moment and fling their arms round each other, sobbing quietly, restraining themselves, afraid of being heard.*]

GAYEV [*in despair*]. My sister, my dear sister——

MRS. RANEVSKY. Oh, my dear, sweet, beautiful orchard. My life, my youth, my happiness, good-bye. Good-bye.

ANYA [*off stage, happily and appealingly*]. Mother!

TROFIMOV [*off stage, happily and excitedly*]. Hallo there!

MRS. RANEVSKY. One last look at the walls and the windows. Our dear mother loved to walk about this room.

GAYEV. Oh Lyuba, my dear sister——

ANYA [*off stage*]. Mother!

TROFIMOV [*off stage*]. Hallo there!

MRS. RANEVSKY. We're coming. [*They go out.*]

[*The stage is empty. The sound of all the doors being locked, then of carriages leaving. It grows quiet. In the silence a dull thud is heard, the noise of an axe striking a tree. It sounds lonely and sad. Footsteps are heard.* FIRS *appears from the door, right. He is dressed as always in jacket and white waistcoat, and wears slippers. He is ill.*]

FIRS [*goes up to the door and touches the handle*]. Locked. They've gone. [*Sits on the sofa.*] They forgot me. Never mind, I'll sit here a bit. And Mr. Leonid hasn't put his fur coat on, I'll be bound, he'll have gone off in his light one. [*Gives a worried sigh.*] I should have seen to it, these young folk have no sense. [*Mutters something which cannot be understood.*] Life's slipped by just as if I'd never lived at all. [*Lies down.*] I'll lie down a bit. You've got no strength left, got nothing left, nothing at all. You're just a—nincompoop. [*Lies motionless.*]

[*A distant sound is heard. It seems to come from the sky and is the sound of a breaking string. It dies away sadly. Silence follows, broken only by the thud of an axe striking a tree far away in the orchard.*]

CURTAIN

THE WOOD-DEMON

[*Леший*]

A COMEDY IN FOUR ACTS

(1889–1890)

CHARACTERS

ALEXANDER SEREBRYAKOV, a retired professor

HELEN, his wife, aged 27

SONYA, his daughter by his first wife, aged 20

MRS. VOYNITSKY, widow of a high official and mother of the professor's first wife

GEORGE VOYNITSKY, her son

LEONID ZHELTUKHIN, a very wealthy man, once a student of technology

JULIA, his sister, aged 18

IVAN ORLOVSKY, a landowner

THEODORE, his son

MICHAEL KHRUSHCHOV, a landowner with a medical degree

ILYA DYADIN

VASILY, Zheltukhin's manservant

SIMON, a labourer employed at Dyadin's flour-mill

ACT ONE

The garden on ZHELTUKHIN'*s estate. The house and terrace. In the open space in front of the house are two tables, a large one laid for lunch, and a smaller one with hors d'œuvres. It is between two and three o'clock in the afternoon.*

SCENE I

[ZHELTUKHIN *and* JULIA *come out of the house.*]

JULIA. I wish you'd wear your nice grey suit. That one looks all wrong.

ZHELTUKHIN. Oh, who cares? I don't.

JULIA. Don't be such a bore, Leo. And on your birthday too. You *are* a naughty boy. [*Lays her head on his chest.*]

ZHELTUKHIN. Go easy on the love and kisses, will you?

JULIA [*through tears*]. Leo!

ZHELTUKHIN. Instead of all these boring kisses and loving looks of one kind or another, not to mention gadgets for standing my watch on that are no damn use to me, why don't you try doing what I ask you? Why didn't you write to the Serebryakovs?

JULIA. But I did, Leo.

ZHELTUKHIN. Which of them did you write to?

JULIA. Sonya. I told her to be sure to be here by one o'clock today. I did write. Honestly.

ZHELTUKHIN. But here it is past two and still no sign of them. Anyway, let them please themselves, I don't care. I must drop all that business. There's no future in it. It only means being humiliated and feeling one's behaved badly. That's all there is to it. She doesn't even notice me. I'm ugly, unattractive and not a bit romantic, and if she does marry me it'll only be because she has an eye on the main chance and is after my money.

JULIA. Unattractive! How can you tell what you're really like?

ZHELTUKHIN. Oh come, I do have eyes in my head. Look how my beard grows out of my neck here unlike any self-respecting beard. Then there's my moustache, damn it, and my nose.

JULIA. What are you holding your cheek for?

ZHELTUKHIN. I have that pain below my eye again.

JULIA. Yes, there is a bit of a swelling. Let me kiss it and make it better.

ZHELTUKHIN. Don't be so silly.

[IVAN ORLOVSKY *and* VOYNITSKY *come in.*]

SCENE II

[*The above,* ORLOVSKY *and* VOYNITSKY.]

ORLOVSKY. When do we get lunch, dear? It's after two.

JULIA. I know, but the Serebryakovs haven't turned up yet.

ORLOVSKY. Well, how much longer do we have to wait? I'm hungry, my dear, and so is George here.

ZHELTUKHIN [*to* VOYNITSKY]. Is your family really coming?

VOYNITSKY. Helen was dressing as I left the house.

ZHELTUKHIN. Does that mean we can count on them?

VOYNITSKY. I wouldn't say we could count on anything. The great man might have gout or one of his moods, in which case they'll stay put.

ZHELTUKHIN. Let's eat then. Why wait? [*Shouts.*] Come on, Dyadin. You too, Sergey Nikodimovich.

[DYADIN *and two or three other guests come in.*]

SCENE III

[*The above,* DYADIN *and guests.*]

ZHELTUKHIN. Come and start then. Please help yourselves. [*Attends to the table with the hors d'œuvres.*] The Serebryakovs haven't turned up, Theodore Orlovsky isn't here and the Wood-Demon hasn't come either. They've forgotten us.

JULIA. Some vodka for you, Godfather?

ORLOVSKY. Just a drop. That's right, thank you.

DYADIN [*tying his napkin round his neck*]. You do have things running splendidly here, Julia. When I go for a drive in your fields, or stroll in the shade of your garden or just gaze at this table here, everywhere I see the mighty power of your enchanting little hand. Your very good health!

JULIA. It's an awful lot of trouble, you know. For instance, last night Nazarka forgot to put the young turkeys in the shed, they were out in the garden all night and this morning five of them died.

DYADIN. He shouldn't have done that. Your turkey is a sensitive bird.

VOYNITSKY [*to* DYADIN]. Cut me a slice of ham, will you, Waffles?

DYADIN. With the greatest pleasure. What a splendid ham! Fabulous, like something out of the *Arabian Nights*. [*Cuts some.*] I'll slice it according to the book of rules, Georgie. Beethoven and Shakespeare couldn't have put more art into it. This knife's a bit blunt, though. [*Sharpens the knife on another knife.*]

ZHELTUKHIN [*shuddering*]. Brr! Steady on, Waffles, I can't stand that.

ORLOVSKY. Come on, George, tell us what's going on at your place.

VOYNITSKY. Nothing's going on.

ORLOVSKY. What's new?

VOYNITSKY. Nothing. It's the same old story, no different this year from last. I talk a lot as usual and don't get much done. And my dear mother, the old chatterbox, still keeps burbling on about the emancipation of women. She has one foot in the grave, but she still reads all those solemn pamphlets and thinks they'll lead her to a new life.

ORLOVSKY. What about Alexander?

VOYNITSKY. The professor? The moths haven't got him yet, I'm sorry to say. He still sits in his study writing from morning till last thing at night.

> 'With harassed brain and furrowed brow
> We pen heroic lays.
> But neither we nor they till now
> Have had one word of praise.'

I pity the paper he writes on. Sonya's just the same too, still reads serious books and keeps a most formidable diary.

ORLOVSKY. Ah, my darling Sonya.

VOYNITSKY. With my powers of observation I ought to write a novel. What a subject. It's just asking to be written up. A retired professor, an old fossil, a sort of academic stuffed trout. He suffers from gout, rheumatism, migraine, liver trouble and all the rest of it. He's as jealous as Othello. He lives on his first wife's estate, not that he wants to live there, but he can't afford to live in town. He's forever moaning about his misfortunes, though he's actually been pretty lucky.

ORLOVSKY. Oh, come.

VOYNITSKY. Of course he has. Just think what luck he's had. We won't say anything about him being the son of an ordinary parish clerk, who was educated at a church school, collected academic degrees and a university chair, became a person of consequence, married a senator's daughter and so on and so forth. None of that matters. But you note my next point. For precisely twenty-five years the man's been lecturing and writing about art. And what does he understand about art? Nothing. For precisely twenty-five years he's been chewing over other people's ideas on realism, tendentiousness and every other kind of tomfoolery. For twenty-five years he's been lecturing and writing about things which every intelligent person has known all along, and which don't interest fools anyway. In other words he's spent precisely twenty-five years chasing his own shadow. And all the time what fantastic success! What colossal fame! Why? What's it in aid of? What right has he to it?

ORLOVSKY [*guffaws*]. You're jealous, you're jealous.

VOYNITSKY. All right then, I'm jealous. And what success with women! Casanova himself couldn't have done better. His first wife, my own sister—a beautiful, gentle creature as pure as the blue sky above us, a fine, generous girl who had more admirers than he had pupils—she loved him as only angels in heaven can love beings as pure and lovely as themselves. My own mother, his mother-in-law, still idolizes him, still goes in awe of him. His second wife—you've seen her—is a beautiful, intelligent woman, and she married him when he was already an old man and gave him her youth, her beauty, her freedom, her radiance. Whatever for? Why? And she's so gifted, you know, a real artist. She plays the piano superbly.

ORLOVSKY. It's a very gifted family. There aren't many like it.

ZHELTUKHIN. I agree. Sonya, for instance, has quite a voice, a magnificent soprano. I've never heard anything to match it even in St. Petersburg. But you know, she is inclined to force her top notes. It's a great pity. Let me have those top notes. I must have them. Oh, if she only had the top notes, I bet you anything you like she'd really hit the heights, if you see what I mean. Sorry, all of you, I must have a word with Julia. [*Takes* JULIA *on one side.*] Send someone over there with a message. Tell them if they can't come now they must come to dinner. [*In a lower voice.*] And don't do anything silly or let me down by making spelling mistakes. Dinner is spelt with two ens. [*In a loud voice, affectionately.*] Please, darling.

JULIA. All right. [*Goes out.*]

DYADIN. I hear that Mrs. Helen Serebryakov, the professor's good lady, whom I have not had the honour of meeting, is distinguished not merely by spiritual beauty, but by the beauty of her physical attributes as well.

ORLOVSKY. Yes, she's a wonderful woman.

ZHELTUKHIN. Is she faithful to her professor?

VOYNITSKY. Yes, I'm sorry to say.

ZHELTUKHIN. Why sorry?

VOYNITSKY. Because she's faithful in a way that's so thoroughly bogus. Oh, it sounds impressive enough, but it just doesn't make sense. To be unfaithful to an elderly husband you can't stand, that's immoral. But if you make these pathetic efforts to stifle your own youth and the spark of life inside you, that isn't immoral at all. Where's the sense of that, damn it?

DYADIN [*in a tearful voice*]. Georgie, I hate it when you talk like that. Well, really. I'm actually trembling. I do not possess the gift of flowery expression, gentlemen, but allow me to give you my honest opinion without oratorical flourishes. Gentlemen, anyone who betrays a wife or husband could easily be unreliable enough to betray his country as well.

VOYNITSKY. Oh, turn the tap off.

DYADIN. No, let me go on, Georgie. Orlovsky, Leonid, my dear friends, you must remember the vicissitudes of my fate. There's no secret about it, nothing obscure or mysterious—the day after we were married my wife ran away with another man because of my unprepossessing appearance.

VOYNITSKY. Well, can you blame her?

DYADIN. Let me go on, please. Since that episode I've always done my duty. I still love her, I'm still faithful to her, I help her as much as I can and I've made a will leaving everything I possess to her children by this other man. I've done my duty and I'm proud of it. Proud of it, I tell you. I've lost my happiness, but I've kept my pride. What about her, though? She's no longer young, she's lost her looks—as was bound to happen sooner or later—and her lover is dead, poor chap. So what has she got left? [*Sits down.*] I'm perfectly serious and you laugh at me.

ORLOVSKY. You're a good chap, a splendid fellow in fact, but you do go on and on so, and wave your arms about.

[THEODORE *comes out of the house wearing a sleeveless coat of fine cloth and high boots. On his chest there are medals, decorations, and a massive gold chain with trinkets hanging from it. He wears expensive rings on his fingers.*]

SCENE IV

[*The above and* THEODORE.]

THEODORE. Hallo there, one and all.

ORLOVSKY [*delightedly*]. Theo, my dear boy!

THEODORE [*to* ZHELTUKHIN]. Happy birthday. You'll be a big man one day. [*Greets everyone.*] My revered parent! Waffles, hallo there! And may you all enjoy your meal. Let's hope it does you good.

ZHELTUKHIN. Where did you get to? You shouldn't be so late.

THEODORE. It's hot, I could do with a spot of vodka.

ORLOVSKY [*giving him an admiring look*]. You and your beard, dear boy, you look magnificent. I say, isn't he handsome? Look at him, the handsome devil.

THEODORE. Happy birthday. [*Drinks.*] Aren't the Serebryakovs here?

ZHELTUKHIN. They haven't turned up.

THEODORE. H'm! Where's Julia then?

ZHELTUKHIN. I don't know what's keeping her. It's time to serve the pie, I'll just go and call her. [*Goes out.*]

ORLOVSKY. What's up with friend Leo? It's baby's birthday, but he seems to have got out of bed on the wrong side. A bit down in the mouth——

VOYNITSKY. The man's a swine.

ORLOVSKY. His nerves have gone to pieces, he can't help it.

VOYNITSKY. He thinks too much of himself, hence the nerves. If you told him this herring tasted good he'd be up in arms at once because you praised the herring instead of him. Ghastly little squirt! Here he comes.

[JULIA *and* ZHELTUKHIN *come in.*]

SCENE V

[*The above,* ZHELTUKHIN *and* JULIA.]

JULIA. Good afternoon, Theo. [*They kiss.*] Help yourself, dear. [*To* ORLOVSKY.] Look what I'm giving Leo for his birthday. [*Shows him the watch-stand.*]

ORLOVSKY. My darling child! A watch-stand. Isn't that lovely!

JULIA. The gold thread alone came to eight-and-a-half roubles. And look at the edges, rows and rows and rows of tiny little pearls. And here's his name, 'Leonid Zheltukhin'. And look at this silk embroidery: 'To him I love.'

DYADIN. I say, let me have a look. Charming!

THEODORE. Oh, do pack it in, that's quite enough of that. Julia, tell them to bring in the champagne.

JULIA. But that's for this evening, Theo.

THEODORE. This evening, she tells me. You get going on it right now, or else I'm leaving. I really mean it, I shall go away. Where do you keep it? I'll go and get it myself.

JULIA. You're always turning the house upside down, Theo. [*To* VASILY.] Vasily, here's the key. The champagne's in the larder. You know, in a basket near the bag of raisins in the corner. And mind you don't break anything.

THEODORE. Bring three bottles, Vasily.

JULIA. You'd never learn to run a house, Theo. [*Serves everyone with pie.*] Mind you have plenty to eat, everybody. You won't get dinner for some time, not till about half past five. You'll never add up to anything in this world, Theo, you're hopeless.

THEODORE. Dear me, we are putting people in their places, aren't we?

VOYNITSKY. I think someone's just arrived. Can you hear anything?

ZHELTUKHIN. Yes, it's the Serebryakovs. Here at last.

VASILY. Mr. and Mrs. Serebryakov are here together with Miss Sonya.

JULIA [*shrieks*]. Sonya! [*Runs out.*]

VOYNITSKY [*sings*]. Come and meet them, come and meet them. [*Goes out.*]

THEODORE. Quite overjoyed, aren't they?

ZHELTUKHIN. Some people are tactless, I must say. He's carrying on with the professor's wife and can't even keep it to himself.

THEODORE. Who is?

ZHELTUKHIN. Why, George of course. The way he was singing her praises just before you came, it was downright improper.

THEODORE. How do you know he's carrying on with her?

ZHELTUKHIN. I'm not exactly blind. Anyway it's the talk of the whole neighbourhood.

THEODORE. Stuff and nonsense. No one's carrying on with her—yet. But I soon shall be. Do you hear me? *I* shall!

SCENE VI

[*The above, together with the following, who now come in:* SERE-BRYAKOV, MRS. VOYNITSKY, VOYNITSKY *with* HELEN *on his arm,* SONYA *and* JULIA.]

JULIA [*kissing* SONYA]. Darling, darling!

ORLOVSKY [*going to meet them*]. Hallo, Alexander, hallo, old boy. [*They kiss each other.*] Are you fit? Splendid!

SEREBRYAKOV. What about you, old man? You look terrific. De-lighted to see you. Have you been back long?

ORLOVSKY. Since Friday. [*To* MRS. VOYNITSKY.] Mrs. Voynitsky! How are you keeping, madam? [*Kisses her hand.*]

MRS. VOYNITSKY. My dear—. [*Kisses him on the head.*]

SONYA. Godfather!

ORLOVSKY. Sonya, my dear. [*Kisses her.*] My darling little canary.

SONYA. You look just the same as ever, you nice sentimental old thing.

ORLOVSKY. Aren't you a big girl now! And you're as pretty as a picture, my pet.

SONYA. How are you getting on? Are you well?

ORLOVSKY. Fit as a fiddle.

SONYA. Good for you. [*To* THEODORE.] Oh, I didn't notice his lordship. [*They kiss.*] All sunburnt and covered with hair like a great spider.

JULIA. Darling!

ORLOVSKY [*to* SEREBRYAKOV]. How's life, old man?

SEREBRYAKOV. Oh, so so. How are you?

ORLOVSKY. How am I doing? I'm having quite a time. I've made over my estate to my son, found decent husbands for all my daughters and now I'm the freest man in the world. I'm having a whale of a time.

DYADIN [*to* SEREBRYAKOV]. I'm afraid you're a little on the late side, sir. The temperature of the pie has diminished considerably. May I introduce myself? Ilya Dyadin or, as certain persons have wittily nicknamed me on account of my pock-marked face, Waffles.

SEREBRYAKOV. How do you do?

DYADIN. *Madame! Mademoiselle!* [*Bows to* HELEN *and* SONYA.] These people are all friends of mine, Professor. I was pretty well off at one time. But domestic circumstances or, as people in intellectual circles put it, considerations for which the editor accepts no responsibility, compelled me to make over my share to my brother, who once had the bad luck to find himself short of seventy thousand roubles of government money. My profession is exploiting the stormy elements. I compel the tempestuous waves to turn the wheels of a flour-mill which I rent from my friend the Wood-Demon.

VOYNITSKY. Turn the tap off, Waffles.

DYADIN. I always bow down with reverence [*bows*] to the learned luminaries who shed lustre on our country's horizons. Forgive my audacity, sir, in hoping to pay you a visit and enjoy the spiritual pleasures of conversing about the latest findings of scholarship.

SEREBRYAKOV. Please do. Delighted.

SONYA. Come on, tell us what you've been up to, Godfather. Where did you spend the winter? Where did you get to?

ORLOVSKY. I've been in Gmunden, I've been in Paris, Nice, London. My dear I've been——

SONYA. Marvellous! You lucky man.

ORLOVSKY. Why don't you come with me this autumn? What do you say?

SONYA [*sings*]. 'Lead me not into temptation——'

THEODORE. Don't you sing at table, or your husband will find he has a silly wife.

DYADIN. It would be interesting to have a bird's eye view of this table. Such a charming floral arrangement, a combination of grace, beauty, profound erudition, distinc——

THEODORE. What a charming way to talk, dammit. You speak as if someone was running a carpenter's plane along your back. [*Laughter.*]

ORLOVSKY [*to* SONYA]. So you aren't married yet, dear?

VOYNITSKY. Have a heart! Who is she to marry? Humboldt's dead, Edison's in America, Lassalle's dead too. The other day I found her diary on the table, a thing this size. I opened it and read, 'No, I shall never fall in love. Love is an egoistic attraction of my person towards an object of the opposite sex.' She has a bit of everything there, dammit. 'Transcendental, culminating point of the integrating principle.' I ask you! Where did you get hold of that stuff?

SONYA. Spare us the irony, Uncle George, it's hardly your strong point.

VOYNITSKY. Why so annoyed?

SONYA. If you say another word one of us will have to go home. Either you or me.

ORLOVSKY [*gives a loud laugh*]. I say, what a girl!

VOYNITSKY. Yes, she's quite a handful, and no mistake. [*To* SONYA.] Give me your hand. Come on. [*Kisses her hand.*] Let peace and harmony reign, I'll behave myself in future.

SCENE VII

[*The above and* KHRUSHCHOV.]

KHRUSHCHOV [*coming out of the house*]. A pity I don't paint, you make such a marvellous group.

ORLOVSKY [*delighted*]. Michael! My dear godson.

KHRUSHCHOV. Many happy returns to Leo. Hallo there, Julia, you do look pretty today. Godfather. [ORLOVSKY *and he embrace.*] Sonya. [*Greets everybody.*]

ZHELTUKHIN. But why so late? Where have you been?

KHRUSHCHOV. Attending a patient.

JULIA. The pie's quite cold.

KHRUSHCHOV. Never mind, Julia, I'll eat it cold. Where do you want me to sit?

SONYA. Come and sit here. [*Points to the place next to her.*]

KHRUSHCHOV. What wonderful weather, and I'm absolutely ravenous. Just a moment, I'll have some vodka. [*Drinks.*] Happy birthday. Now for a spot of pie. Julia, give it a little kiss to make it taste better. [*She kisses it.*] Thank you. [*To* ORLOVSKY.] Well how are things with you? Haven't seen you for ages.

ORLOVSKY. Yes, it's been quite a while, hasn't it? I've been abroad, you know.

KHRUSHCHOV. So I heard, so I heard. Felt quite envious too. And how are you, Theodore?

THEODORE. Not so bad, thanks to your prayers, our ever-present help in trouble.

KHRUSHCHOV. And how's business?

THEODORE. I can't complain, I'm getting along very nicely. Only there's so much travelling, old boy, I'm quite worn out. From here to the Caucasus, back here again, then off back to the Caucasus. There's no end of this mad dashing about. I have two estates down there, you know.

KHRUSHCHOV. I do indeed.

THEODORE. I run my little colony and catch tarantulas and scorpions. On the whole things are really moving, but when we come to 'be still, ye raging passions' and all that, there's no change to report.

KHRUSHCHOV. You're in love, I take it.

THEODORE. We must have a drink on that, Mr. Wood-Demon. [*Drinks.*] Never fall in love with married women, gentlemen. Better have a bullet clean through the shoulder and another through the leg like your humble servant than be in love with a married woman, believe you me. It's more trouble than it's——

SONYA. Have you no hope?

THEODORE. Good grief, listen to her! 'No hope.' There's nothing hopeless in this world. Hopelessness, unhappy love affairs, moaning and groaning—that stuff's sheer self-indulgence. It's only a question of will-power. I don't want my shotgun to misfire and it doesn't. I do want a certain married woman to love me. And love me she will. That's the way it goes, Sonya old sport. Once I have my eye on a woman she has about as much chance of getting away as of taking a trip to the moon.

SONYA. Oh, you are a horrible man, I must say!

THEODORE. They don't escape my clutches in a hurry, oh dear me no. I haven't said more than a few words to her and she's already in my power. Yes indeed. I just told her, 'Madam, whenever you see a window anywhere, remember me. That's the way I want it.' So she thinks of me a thousand times a day. Besides, I bombard her with letters every day.

HELEN. That's pretty poor technique. She may not read the letters when she gets them.

THEODORE. You think so, do you? H'm! I've been on this earth for thirty-five years and somehow or other I've never run across any of these phenomenal women with the strength of mind not to open a letter.

ORLOVSKY [*looking at him admiringly*]. Isn't he terrific? You're a real chip off the old block, you handsome devil, you. I was just like him, you know, I was his living image. The only difference is, I was never in the war, but I did drink vodka and throw my money around like nobody's business.

THEODORE. You know, Michael, I love her damn seriously. Let her say the word and I'd give her everything I have. I'd take her off to my place in the Caucasus, in the mountains, and we'd be on top of the world. You know, Helen, I'd watch over her like a faithful hound and I'd treat her like the song one of our local big-wigs sings:

> 'Thou shalt of all the universe
> Be queen, o faithful mistress mine.'

She doesn't know her luck, believe me.

KHRUSHCHOV. And who is the lucky girl?

THEODORE. Curiosity killed the cat. But that's enough of that. Let's change the subject, shall we? I remember ten years ago when Leo was still at school and we were at his birthday party, just as we are now. I rode home with Sonya on my right arm and Julia on my left, both of them holding on to my beard. Come on, everyone, let's drink to the friends of my youth, Sonya and Julia.

DYADIN [*with a loud laugh*]. Charming, charming!

THEODORE. After the war I once got drunk with a Turkish pasha in Trebizond and he asked me whether——

DYADIN [*interrupting him*]. I say, let's drink a toast to friendliness. Long live friendship and the best of jolly good luck!

THEODORE. Stop, stop, stop! Your attention please, Sonya. I'll have a bet with you, damn it all. I'll stake three hundred roubles. Let's go and play croquet after lunch and I bet you I'll get through all the hoops and back in one go.

SONYA. I'd take you on, only I haven't got three hundred roubles.

THEODORE. Well, if you lose you must sing to me forty times.

SONYA. All right.

DYADIN. Charming, charming!

HELEN [*looking at the sky*]. What sort of bird is that?

ZHELTUKHIN. A hawk.

THEODORE. Its health, everyone! The hawk!

[SONYA *laughs loudly*.]

ORLOVSKY. I say, she *has* got a fit of the giggles. What's up?

[KHRUSHCHOV *laughs loudly*.]

ORLOVSKY. And what's got into you?

MRS. VOYNITSKY. Sonya, this is most unseemly.

KHRUSHCHOV. Oh dear, I'm sorry, everybody. I'll stop in a minute, I really will.

ORLOVSKY. This is what the Bible calls the laughter of fools.

VOYNITSKY. You only have to hold up a finger to either of those two and they burst out laughing. Sonya! [*Holds up a finger.*] See what I mean?

KHRUSHCHOV. All right, that will do. [*Looks at his watch and addresses himself.*] Well, Father Michael, your Reverence, you've had some food and drink and it's time to call it a day. Must be off.

SONYA. Where to?

KHRUSHCHOV. To see a patient. I'm sick and tired of my practice, it's like an unloved wife or a long winter.

SEREBRYAKOV. But look here, medicine is your profession after all —your business, so to speak.

VOYNITSKY [*ironically*]. He does have another profession. He digs peat on his land.

SEREBRYAKOV. What?

VOYNITSKY. Peat. Some engineer has it all worked out. There's seven hundred and twenty thousand roubles' worth of peat on his land. That's no joke.

KHRUSHCHOV. I don't dig peat to make money.

VOYNITSKY. Then what do you dig it for?

KHRUSHCHOV. To stop you cutting down the forests.

VOYNITSKY. And why shouldn't we cut them down? From the way you talk, anyone would think our forests only exist so that young lovers can bill and coo in them.

KHRUSHCHOV. I never said that.

VOYNITSKY. Whenever I've been favoured with your speeches on behalf of the forests every word has been stale, frivolous and biased. I'm sorry, but I know what I'm talking about, I know your speeches for the defence almost by heart. For instance. [*Raising his voice and making gestures as if in imitation of* KHRUSHCHOV.] O men and women, you destroy our forests, but they are the glory of our earth, they teach man to appreciate beauty and give him a sense of grandeur. Forests alleviate a harsh climate. In a mild climate less effort is spent on the struggle for existence, so that men and women are gentler and more affectionate. In countries with a mild climate, people are handsome, adaptable and sensitive, their speech is elegant and their movements are graceful. Art and learning flourish among them, their philosophy is cheerful and they treat their womenfolk with great delicacy and chivalry. And so on and so forth. That's all very charming, but so unconvincing that you must allow me to carry on burning logs in my stoves and building my barns of wood.

KHRUSHCHOV. By all means cut timber if you really need it, but it's time we stopped ruining the forests. All the forests of Russia are crashing down before the axe, millions upon millions of trees perish, the homes of birds and beasts are devastated, rivers grow shallow and dry up, wonderful scenery disappears without trace, and all because man's so lazy and hasn't the sense to bend down and take his fuel from the ground. Only an unreasoning brute could burn beauty like this [*points to the trees*] in his stove, destroying what we cannot create. Man has been granted reason and the power to create, so that he can add to what he's been given. But up to now he hasn't been a creator, only a destroyer. Forests keep disappearing, rivers dry up, wild life's become extinct, the climate's ruined and the land grows poorer and uglier every day. You look at me ironically and you find everything I say stale and frivolous, but when I walk past our village woodlands which I've saved from the axe or hear the rustle of my own saplings, planted with these hands, I feel that I too have some slight control over the climate and that if man is happy a thousand years from now I'll have done a bit towards it myself. When I plant a young birch and later see it covered with green and swaying in the breeze, my heart fills with pride at the thought that I'm helping God to create a living organism.

THEODORE [*interrupting*]. Your health, Mr. Wood-Demon.

VOYNITSKY. This is all very well, but if you looked at the thing less from a sensational and more from a scientific point of view, then——

SONYA. Uncle George, this leaves a nasty taste in the mouth. Please be quiet.

KHRUSHCHOV. Yes really, Voynitsky, let's not talk about it. Please.

VOYNITSKY. Have it your own way.

MRS. VOYNITSKY. Oh!

SONYA. What's the matter, Grandmother?

MRS. VOYNITSKY [*to* SEREBRYAKOV]. I forgot to tell you, Alexander, it slipped my mind. I had a letter today from Kharkov, from Paul Alekseyevich. He sends you his regards.

SEREBRYAKOV. Thank you, I'm delighted.

MRS. VOYNITSKY. He sent his new pamphlet and asked me to show you it.

SEREBRYAKOV. Is it interesting?

MRS. VOYNITSKY. Interesting, but rather odd. He attacks the very position he was defending seven years ago. Now isn't that so typical of our age? People have never been so ready to betray their own convictions as they are nowadays. It's dreadful.

VOYNITSKY. There's nothing dreadful about it. Have some fish, Mother.

MRS. VOYNITSKY. But I want to talk.

VOYNITSKY. For fifty years we've been talking about trends and schools of thought, and it's about time we stopped.

MRS. VOYNITSKY. For some reason you dislike the sound of my voice. I'm sorry, George, but this last year you've changed out of all recognition. You used to be a man of such firm principles, a shining example——

VOYNITSKY. Oh yes, I've been an example of something all right, but I haven't exactly shone. Do you mind if I get up? A shining example. That's a pretty poisonous sort of joke. I'm forty-seven. Until last year I was like you, I deliberately tried to befuddle myself with all sorts of abstract, pedantic humbug so as not to see life as it really is. I thought I was doing the right thing, but now—if you only knew what an ass I feel about the stupid way I've wasted time when I might have had everything I can't have now because I'm too old.

SEREBRYAKOV. Just a moment, George, you seem to be blaming your former principles for something——

SONYA. That's quite enough of that, Father. Don't be a bore.

SEREBRYAKOV. Just a moment. You seem to be blaming your former principles for something, but they're not to blame. You are. You're forgetting that principles are no good without deeds. You should have *done* something.

VOYNITSKY. 'Done something'? We can't all be non-stop writing machines.

SEREBRYAKOV. What exactly do you mean by that?

VOYNITSKY. Nothing. Let's stop talking like this. We're not at home now.

MRS. VOYNITSKY. Oh, it completely slipped my memory. Alexander, I forgot to remind you to take your medicine before lunch. I brought it with me, but I forgot to remind you.

SEREBRYAKOV. I don't want it.

MRS. VOYNITSKY. But you're not well, you know. In fact you're very ill.

SEREBRYAKOV. Well, there's no need to shout it from the roof-tops. I'm old and ill, I'm old and ill. That's all I ever hear. [*To* ZHEL-TUKHIN.] Do you mind if I get up and go indoors, Zheltukhin? It's a bit hot out here and I'm being bitten by mosquitoes.

ZHELTUKHIN. Please do, we've finished lunch anyway.

SEREBRYAKOV. I thank you. [*Goes off into the house followed by* MRS. VOYNITSKY.]

JULIA [*to her brother*]. You must go with the professor. This is most awkward.

ZHELTUKHIN [*to her*]. Oh, blast the man! [*Goes out.*]

DYADIN. Permit me to thank you from the bottom of my heart. [*Kisses her hand.*]

JULIA. Not at all. You ate so little. [*Everyone thanks her.*] Not at all, don't mention it. You've all eaten so little.

THEODORE. Well, what shall we do now, everybody? Let's go out on the croquet lawn and settle our wager. And then what?

JULIA. Then we'll have dinner.

THEODORE. And after that?

KHRUSHCHOV. You can all come over to my place. We'll go fishing on the lake this evening.

THEODORE. Splendid.

DYADIN. Charming.

SONYA. All right, come on then, everyone. We'll go and settle our bet on the croquet lawn. Then we'll have an early dinner here at Julia's, and at sevenish we'll drive over to the Wood—I mean to Mr. Khrushchov's place. Marvellous. Come on then, Julia, let's get the croquet balls. [*Goes into the house with* JULIA.]

THEODORE. Vasily, bring some wine out on to the croquet lawn. We'll drink the winners' health. Well, revered parent, shall we take part in this noble sport?

ORLOVSKY. In a moment, dear boy. I must spend five minutes or so with the professor or it would look bad. One must keep up appearances. You take my place for a bit, I'll be with you in a moment. [*Goes into the house.*]

DYADIN. I must go and sit at the feet of the learned Professor Serebryakov. Anticipating the exalted pleasure which——

VOYNITSKY. Waffles, you're a bore. Go.

DYADIN. I am going. [*Goes into the house.*]

THEODORE [*walks into the garden, singing*].

> 'Thou shalt of all the universe
> Be queen, o faithful mistress mine.' [*Goes out.*]

KHRUSHCHOV. I'm going to slip quietly away. [*To* VOYNITSKY.] Will you do me a great favour, Voynitsky? Let's never talk about forestry or medicine again. I don't know why, but when you get on to these things it leaves me with a nasty taste in my mouth for the rest of the day. I wish you a very good afternoon. [*Goes out.*]

SCENE VIII

[HELEN *and* VOYNITSKY.]

VOYNITSKY. What a narrow-minded fellow. I don't care how much nonsense people talk, but I don't like it when they put so much feeling into it.

HELEN. Once again you've behaved abominably, George. Did you have to quarrel with your mother and Alexander and bring in that stuff about non-stop writing machines? That's a pretty poor way to behave.

VOYNITSKY. But what if I hate him?

HELEN. There's no reason to hate Alexander, he's just the same as anyone else.

[SONYA *and* JULIA *cross into the garden with croquet balls and mallets.*]

VOYNITSKY. If you could only see your face and the way you move. It's as if life was too much for you, altogether too much.

HELEN. Dear me, it is, and I'm so bored too. [*Pause.*] Everyone runs down my husband to my face, just as if I wasn't there at all. Everyone looks at me as if they're sorry for me. 'Poor girl, she's married to an old man.' All of them, even the nicest ones, would like me to leave Alexander. This sympathy for me, all these pitying glances and compassionate sighs, add up to one thing. It's just what the Wood-Demon was saying just now, you all wantonly destroy the forests, and soon there won't be anything left on earth. You destroy men and women too, every bit as wantonly, and soon, thanks to your good offices, there will be no loyalty, integrity or unselfishness left on this earth. Why does it upset you so much to see a faithful wife who doesn't belong to you? Because—and the Wood-Demon's right—there's a demon of destruction in every one of you. You don't spare anything, whether it's the trees, the birds—or women or one another.

VOYNITSKY. I can't stand this sort of pretentious talk.

HELEN. And you can tell friend Theodore I'm sick and tired of his impertinence. It's thoroughly disgusting. To look me straight in the eyes and shout aloud to all and sundry about his love for some married woman, that is a bright way to behave, I must say.

[*Voices in the garden*: Hurray! Well done!]

HELEN. But isn't the Wood-Demon nice? He often comes to see us, but I'm rather shy, so we've never had a proper talk, and I've never been really friendly to him. He'll think I'm bad-tempered or proud. Do you know why you and I are such good friends, George? It must be because we're both such tiresome bores. Yes, bores! Don't look at me in that way, I don't like it.

VOYNITSKY. How else can I look at you when I love you? You are my happiness, my life, my youth. I know there's no chance of your loving me, but I don't want anything from you. Only let me look at you, listen to your voice——

SCENE IX

[*The above and* SEREBRYAKOV.]

SEREBRYAKOV [*at a window*]. Where are you, Helen?

HELEN. Here.

SEREBRYAKOV. Come and sit with us for a bit, dear. [*Disappears.*]

[HELEN *moves towards the house.*]

VOYNITSKY [*following her*]. Let me speak of my love. So long as you don't drive me away, that's all I need to be the happiest man on earth.

CURTAIN

ACT TWO

The dining-room of SEREBRYAKOV'*s house. There is a sideboard and—in the centre of the room—a dining table. It is between one and two o'clock in the morning. The watchman can be heard tapping his stick in the garden.*

SCENE I

[SEREBRYAKOV *sits dozing in an armchair by an open window while* HELEN, *also dozing, sits by his side.*]

SEREBRYAKOV [*opening his eyes*]. Who's there? Sonya, is it you?

HELEN. It's me.

SEREBRYAKOV. Oh, it's you, Helen. I'm in agony.

HELEN. Your rug's fallen on the floor. [*Wraps it round his legs.*] I'd better shut the window.

SEREBRYAKOV. No, it's too stuffy. Just now I dozed off and dreamed that my left leg didn't belong to me. I woke up with an excruciating pain. It can't be gout, it's more like rheumatism. What time is it?

HELEN. Twenty past one. [*Pause.*]

SEREBRYAKOV. You might look out Batyushkov's poems for me in the library tomorrow. I think we have them.

HELEN. What's that?

SEREBRYAKOV. Find me a Batyushkov in the morning. I seem to remember we had one. But why do I find it so hard to breathe?

HELEN. You're tired. This is the second night you've had no sleep.

SEREBRYAKOV. That's how Turgenev is supposed to have got angina, from having gout. I'm afraid it might happen to me. Old age, what a damnable, repulsive thing it is, confound it. Since I've aged so much I've even begun to disgust myself. And obviously none of you can stand the sight of me.

HELEN. The way you go on about your age, anyone would think it was all our fault.

SEREBRYAKOV. You're the one who really can't stand me.

HELEN. Don't be such a bore. [*Gets up and sits down further away.*]

SEREBRYAKOV. You're right of course. I'm not such a fool I can't see it. You're a good-looking, healthy young woman and you want a bit of life, while I'm an old man more dead than alive. Well? Do you really think I don't understand? Stupid of me of course to go on living at all. But just wait a bit, I'll soon set you all free. I shan't last much longer.

HELEN. I feel quite faint. If these sleepless nights have earned me any reward, all I ask is that you stop talking. For God's sake, stop it. That's all I ask.

SEREBRYAKOV. What it comes to is that you're all faint and weary and you're all wasting the best years of your lives on my account. While I'm the only person who's happy and enjoys life. Obvious, isn't it?

HELEN. Do stop it. You've completely worn me out.

SEREBRYAKOV. But then I've worn everybody out, haven't I? Obviously.

HELEN [*crying*]. I can't stand any more! Look here—what do you want from me?

SEREBRYAKOV. Nothing.

HELEN. Well, in that case stop talking. Please.

SEREBRYAKOV. It's a curious thing, but if George or that imbecile old mother of his ever say anything, that's perfectly in order and everyone listens. But I've only to open my mouth and everyone starts feeling miserable. Even my voice disgusts you. All right, I'm disgusting, I'm selfish, I'm a tyrant. But haven't I the right to a little selfishness in my old age? Haven't I earned it? My life hasn't been all that easy. Orlovsky and I were students together at one time. You ask him. He led a gay life, used to go off with gipsy girls and was a kind of benefactor to me, while I lived in cheap, dirty lodgings, slaving away day and night, going short of food and worrying because I was living at someone else's expense. Then I went to Heidelberg, though I saw nothing of Heidelberg while I was there. I went to Paris and saw nothing of Paris either. I was cooped up indoors the whole time working. And since I got my university chair I've spent my whole life serving faithfully, so to speak, in the ranks of scholarship, and I'm still soldiering on. I'm asking you, hasn't all

this earned me the right to a peaceful old age and a little considera-
tion from others?

HELEN. No one's disputing that right. [*The window bangs in the wind.*]
There's a wind getting up, I'd better shut that window. [*Shuts it.*]
It's going to rain. Nobody's disputing your rights.

[*Pause. The watchman in the garden is heard tapping his stick and
singing a song.*]

SEREBRYAKOV. You give your whole life to scholarship, you grow used
to your study, your lecture-room and your distinguished colleagues.
Then, God knows why, you turn up in this dead-and-alive hole
where you can't get away from second-rate people and their inane
chatter. I want some life, I like success, I like to be well known and
make a bit of a stir, but here—I might as well be exiled to the depths
of Siberia. To spend every moment regretting one's past, watching
others succeed and going in fear of death—I can't stand it. It's too
much! And now they won't even forgive me for growing old.

HELEN. Just wait and be patient. In five or six years I'll be old too.

[SONYA *comes in.*]

SCENE II

[*The above and* SONYA.]

SONYA. I can't think why there's no doctor here yet. I told Stephen to
go and fetch the Wood-Demon if the local man's out.

SEREBRYAKOV. What do I want with this Wood-Demon of yours?
He knows as much about medicine as I do about astronomy.

SONYA. We can hardly bring an entire medical faculty out here to
attend to your gout.

SEREBRYAKOV. I won't even talk to him, he's a complete crack-pot.

SONYA. Have it your own way. [*Sits down.*] I don't care.

SEREBRYAKOV. What time is it?

HELEN. Past one o'clock.

SEREBRYAKOV. It's stuffy in here. Sonya, will you get me that medicine from the table?

SONYA. Here you are. [*Hands him the medicine.*]

SEREBRYAKOV [*irritably*]. Oh, really, not that one! It's no use asking for anything.

SONYA. Please stop behaving like a child. It may appeal to some people, but don't treat me that way, thank you very much. I dislike that sort of thing.

SEREBRYAKOV. The girl's quite impossible. Why are you so angry?

SONYA. And why do you sound so dismal? Anyone might think you were really unhappy, when actually you're one of the happiest people on earth.

SEREBRYAKOV. Oh yes, of course, I couldn't be happier.

SONYA. Of course you're happy. And even if you do have gout you know perfectly well it will be gone by morning. So why all the groans? What a lot of fuss about nothing!

[*Enter* VOYNITSKY *wearing a dressing-gown and carrying a candle.*]

SCENE III

[*The above and* VOYNITSKY.]

VOYNITSKY. There's going to be a storm. [*A flash of lightning.*] Did you see that! Helen and Sonya, you go to bed. I've come to relieve you.

SEREBRYAKOV [*terrified*]. No, no! Don't leave me alone with him. No! He'll talk my head off.

VOYNITSKY. But you must let them have some rest, they were up all last night.

SEREBRYAKOV. Let them go to bed, but you go away too, thank you very much. I implore you in the name of our past friendship, don't argue. We'll talk some other time.

VOYNITSKY. Our past friendship? That's news to me, I must say.

HELEN. Please be quiet, George.

SEREBRYAKOV. My dear, don't leave me alone with him. He'll talk my head off.

VOYNITSKY. This is becoming quite ridiculous.

KHRUSHCHOV [*off stage*]. Are they in the dining-room? In here? Will you have someone look after my horse, please?

VOYNITSKY. Look, the doctor's come.

[*Enter* KHRUSHCHOV.]

SCENE IV

[The above and KHRUSHCHOV.]

KHRUSHCHOV. I say, what do you think of the weather? There was a shower coming up behind me, I only just dodged it. How are you? [*Shakes hands.*]

SEREBRYAKOV. I'm sorry you've been bothered. It wasn't my idea.

KHRUSHCHOV. Oh come, come, that's all right. But what do you mean by falling ill like this, Professor? Whatever next! This won't do, oh dear me no. What's the matter?

SEREBRYAKOV. Why do doctors always have to talk to their patients in this patronizing way?

KHRUSHCHOV [*laughs*]. You shouldn't be so observant. [*Affectionately.*] Come, we'd better go to bed. We're not comfortable here. It'll be warmer and more restful in bed. Come on. Then I'll listen to your chest and everything will be fine.

HELEN. Go on, Alexander, do what he says.

KHRUSHCHOV. If it hurts you to walk we'll carry you in your chair.

SEREBRYAKOV. It's all right, I can manage. I'll walk. [*Gets up.*] Only they shouldn't have troubled you. [KHRUSHCHOV *and* SONYA *lead him by the arms.*] Besides I haven't all that much faith in—in medicaments. Why are you helping me? I can manage on my own. [*Goes off with* KHRUSHCHOV *and* SONYA.]

SCENE V

*[*HELEN *and* VOYNITSKY.]

HELEN. He's completely worn me out, I can hardly stand.

VOYNITSKY. He wears you out and I wear myself out. This is the third night I've had no sleep.

HELEN. We are in a bad way in this house. Your mother hates everything except her pamphlets and the professor. The professor's overwrought, he doesn't trust me and he's afraid of you. Sonya's annoyed with her father and not on speaking terms with me. You loathe my husband and openly sneer at your mother. I'm a complete wet blanket and I'm so much on edge, I've been on the verge of tears a dozen times today. In fact we're all fighting each other, but what

I want to know is—what's the point of this free-for-all? What's it all in aid of?

VOYNITSKY. We can do without the moralizing, thank you.

HELEN. Yes, we are in a bad way here. You're an intelligent and civilized man, George. I should have thought you must see why the world's heading for disaster. It's not bandits and thieves, so much as all this concealed hatred, this hostility between nice people, all these sordid little squabbles. There are people who call our house a cultural haven, but they never notice these things. Do help me to make peace here. I can't do it on my own.

VOYNITSKY. First help me make peace with myself. My darling——.

[*Bends down and kisses her hand.*]

HELEN. Leave me alone. [*Removes her hand.*] Go away.

VOYNITSKY. Soon the rain will be over. All living things will revive and breathe more freely. Except me. The storm won't revive me. Day and night my thoughts choke me, haunt me with the spectre of a life hopelessly wasted. I've never lived. My past life has been thrown away on stupid trivialities and the present is so futile, it appals me. My life and my love—well, there you have it. What can I do with them? What can I make of them? My feelings are wasted like a ray of sunlight falling in a well, and I'm running to waste too.

HELEN. When you talk about love I somehow can't think or feel— words fail me. I'm sorry, but I've nothing to say to you. [*Makes to leave.*] Good night.

VOYNITSKY [*barring her way*]. And if you only knew how it hurts me to think that in this very house another life is wasting away besides my own. I mean yours. What are you waiting for? What's stopping you, dammit? Some wretched theory or other? You may suppress your youthful high spirits or even try to bury them alive. But that's not what being moral means in the best sense of the word, so get that into your head.

HELEN [*stares at him*]. George, you're drunk.

VOYNITSKY. Possibly, very possibly.

HELEN. Is Theodore with you?

VOYNITSKY. He's sleeping in my room tonight. Possibly, very possibly. Anything's possible.

HELEN. So you've been celebrating again today, have you? What do you do it for?

VOYNITSKY. It at least gives one the illusion of being alive. Don't try and stop me, Helen.

HELEN. You never used to drink. And you never used to talk so much as you do now. Go to bed. You bore me. And tell your friend Theodore Orlovsky that if he doesn't stop annoying me I intend to do something about it. Now go.

VOYNITSKY [*bending down to kiss her hand*]. My darling. Wonderful woman!

[KHRUSHCHOV *comes in.*]

SCENE VI

[*The above and* KRUSHCHOV.]

KHRUSHCHOV. Your husband's asking for you.

HELEN [*snatching her hand away from* VOYNITSKY]. Right, I'm coming. [*Goes out.*]

KHRUSHCHOV [*to* VOYNITSKY]. Is nothing sacred to you? You might remember, you and that dear lady who's just gone out, that her husband was once married to your sister. And that you have a young girl living under the same roof. Your affair's already the talk of the whole county. You should be thoroughly ashamed of yourselves. [*Goes off to his patient.*]

VOYNITSKY [*alone*]. She's gone. [*Pause.*] Ten years ago I used to meet her at my sister's. She was seventeen then and I was thirty-seven. Why didn't I fall in love then and ask her to marry me? It would have been the most natural thing in the world. And she'd be my wife now. Yes. And tonight the storm would have woken us both. She'd be scared of the thunder and I'd hold her in my arms and whisper, 'Don't be afraid. I'm here.' Oh, what wonderful thoughts, I could laugh for sheer joy. But oh God, my head's in such a whirl. Why am I so old? Why can't she understand me? The affected way she talks, her languid moralizing, those trivial, tired ideas about the world heading for disaster—how utterly I loathe it all. [*Pause.*] Why am I such an awful character? How I envy that gay spark Theodore or that stupid Wood-Demon! They're natural, sincere and stupid —and free from this damned irony that poisons everything.

[*Enter* THEODORE ORLOVSKY *wrapped in a blanket.*]

SCENE VII

[VOYNITSKY *and* THEODORE ORLOVSKY.]

THEODORE [*speaking through the door*]. Here on your own? None of the ladies about? [*Comes in.*] The storm woke me up. Quite a shower. What time is it?

VOYNITSKY. How the hell should I know?

THEODORE. I thought I heard Helen speaking.

VOYNITSKY. She was in here a moment ago.

THEODORE. Gorgeous creature. [*Looks at the medicine bottles on the table.*] What are those? Peppermints? [*Eats some.*] Yes indeed, a gorgeous creature. Is the professor ill then?

VOYNITSKY. Yes, he is.

THEODORE. That kind of existence makes no sense to me. It's said the ancient Greeks used to throw weak and sickly babies over a precipice on Mont Blanc. That's the way to treat his sort.

VOYNITSKY [*irritably*]. It wasn't Mont Blanc, it was the Tarpeian Rock. What gross ignorance!

THEODORE. All right, make it a rock then. What the hell does it matter? And why so mournful tonight? Feeling sorry for the professor or something?

VOYNITSKY. Leave me alone. [*Pause.*]

THEODORE. Or could it be that you're in love with Mrs. Professor? Eh? Oh well, there's nothing wrong with that. Languish away. But just get this straight. If I find there's one grain of truth in the gossip that's going round the place you can expect no mercy. I'll chuck you off the Tarpeian Rock.

VOYNITSKY. She's a friend of mine.

THEODORE. Already?

VOYNITSKY. What do you mean, 'already'?

THEODORE. A woman can become a man's friend only under the following conditions—first an acquaintance, next a mistress, and only then a friend.

VOYNITSKY. That's a pretty cheap line of talk.

THEODORE. Then let's have a drink on it. Come on, I think I still have a bit of Chartreuse. Let's have a drink. And as soon as it gets light we'll drive over to my place. Wodger say? I have a manager on one of my estates called Luke, who can't say 'what do you', always says 'wodger'. A frightful rogue. So wodger say? [*Seeing* SONYA, *who is coming in.*] Heavens alive, excuse me, I haven't got a tie on. [*Runs out.*]

SCENE VIII

[VOYNITSKY *and* SONYA.]

SONYA. So you've been drinking champagne with Theo again, have you, Uncle George? And driving about in a troika? The boys *have* been getting together, haven't they? All right then, he's quite hopeless, he's been a rake since the day he was born, but what's got into you? It doesn't suit you at your time of life.

VOYNITSKY. My time of life is neither here nor there. When people aren't really alive they live on illusions. It's better than nothing anyway.

SONYA. We haven't got the hay in yet. Gerasim told me today it would all rot in the rain, and you spend your time on illusions. [*Alarmed.*] Uncle, you have tears in your eyes!

VOYNITSKY. What do you mean, tears? Nothing of the sort. Rubbish. The way you looked at me just now, your poor dear mother used to look like that. My darling—. [*Eagerly kisses her hands and face.*] My sister, my darling sister—. Where is she now? If she only knew! Oh, if she only knew!

SONYA. Knew what? What do you mean, Uncle?

VOYNITSKY. It's so painful, such a wretched business. Never mind. [KHRUSHCHOV *comes in.*] I'll tell you later. It doesn't matter—I'll go. [*Goes.*]

SCENE IX

[SONYA *and* KHRUSHCHOV.]

KHRUSHCHOV. Your father won't listen to me at all. I tell him it's gout, he says it's rheumatism, and if I ask him to lie down he sits up. [*Picks up his peaked cap.*] It's all nerves.

SONYA. He's spoilt. Put your hat down and wait till the rain stops. Do you want something to eat?

KHRUSHCHOV. Well, yes perhaps.

SONYA. I like eating in the middle of the night. We have some food in the sideboard, I think. [*Rummages in the sideboard.*] What does he want with a doctor? What he wants is a dozen women sitting round him, gazing into his eyes and groaning, 'Professor!' Here, have some cheese.

KHRUSHCHOV. That's not the way to talk about your father. I agree, he is difficult, but compared with other people—why, all these Uncle Georges and Ivan Orlovskys aren't worth his little finger.

SONYA. Here's a bottle of something. I wasn't speaking of him as a father, but as a great man. I love my father, but I'm bored stiff with great men and all the oriental ceremonial that goes with them. [*They sit down.*] What a downpour! [*Lightning.*] I say!

KHRUSHCHOV. The storm's passing over, we shall pretty well miss it.

SONYA [*pouring out*]. Have something to drink.

KHRUSHCHOV. Your very good health. [*Drinks.*]

SONYA. Are you angry with us for bringing you out in the middle of the night?

KHRUSHCHOV. Not a bit. If you hadn't sent for me I'd be asleep now, and it's so much nicer to see you in the flesh than in my dreams.

SONYA. Then why do you look angry?

KHRUSHCHOV. Because I happen to be angry. There's no one about, so I can speak frankly. Oh, Sonya, how I'd love to take you away from here this very instant. I simply can't breathe the air in this house and I think it's poisoning you. Your father, so obsessed with his gout and his books and refusing to notice anything else, your Uncle George, and then your step-mother——

SONYA. What about my step-mother?

KHRUSHCHOV. There are some things one doesn't talk about, one can't. My dear, wonderful girl, there's so much I don't understand about people. People should be beautiful in every way—in their faces, in the way they dress, in their thoughts and in their innermost selves. Oh, I've seen plenty of pretty faces and dresses, been quite swept off my feet at times. But the mind and spirit that go with them, well, the less said about those the better. A pretty face can conceal a nature so black that no amount of make-up could hide it. I'm sorry, I'm rather worked up. You're very precious to me, you know.

SONYA [*drops a knife*]. Oh dear, I've dropped it.

KHRUSHCHOV [*picks it up*]. Never mind. [*Pause.*] When you walk in a wood on a dark night there's sometimes a glimmer of light shining in the distance, isn't there? Then you somehow feel so wonderful that you don't notice how tired you are or how dark it is or how the thorns and twigs hit you in the face. I work from morning till night with never a moment's peace, winter or summer, battling away against people who don't understand me, and things sometimes get too much for me. But now at last I've found my light shining in the distance. I'm not going to make out I love you more than anything in the world. Love isn't the whole of my life, it's my reward. But my darling, there's no higher reward for anyone who works, struggles and suffers.

SONYA [*most upset*]. I'm sorry. Can I ask you something, Michael?

KHRUSHCHOV. What is it? Tell me quickly.

SONYA. Well, look, you come here pretty often, and I sometimes go over to your place with my family. And you feel terribly guilty about it all, don't you?

KHRUSHCHOV. What do you mean?

SONYA. I mean this—your democratic feelings are offended by your friendship for us. I went to an exclusive school, Helen comes from a titled family and we dress fashionably, while you hold these democratic views——

KHRUSHCHOV. Well, really! Don't let's talk about that. This isn't the time.

SONYA. The point is, you go round digging up peat and planting trees. Well, it is a bit odd. In fact you're a kind of socialist.

KHRUSHCHOV. 'Democratic, socialist.' Sonya, don't tell me you can use such words seriously. Why, you even sound quite worked up about it.

SONYA. Well, I am serious. Very much so.

KHRUSHCHOV. Oh really, you can't be.

SONYA. I'll tell you something else and I'll bet you anything you like it's true. Suppose I had a sister and suppose you fell in love with her and asked her to marry you, you'd never forgive yourself. You'd be ashamed to show yourself to your doctor friends, including those women, in the council health department—ashamed of loving someone who went to a fashionable girls' school, a namby-pamby young lady who never learned anything useful and who dresses according to the latest fashion. I know you would, I can see it in your eyes. In fact, to put it in a nutshell, those woods of yours, your peat and your embroidered shirts, they're all an affectation, a pretentious piece of play-acting and nothing more.

KHRUSHCHOV. What have I done to deserve this? Why do you insult me, child? Anyway, I'm a fool, it serves me right for not knowing my place. Good-bye. [*Moves towards the door.*]

SONYA. Good-bye. I was rude, please forgive me.

KHRUSHCHOV [*returning*]. If you only knew what an oppressive, stuffy atmosphere you have here. You're surrounded by people who come crawling up to a man, look at him sideways on and try to discover in him a socialist, a psychopath or an idle chatterbox—anything you like except a human being. 'Oh, he's a psychopath,' they say. And they're delighted. Or, 'He talks a lot of hot air.' And they're as pleased as if they'd discovered America. And when they don't understand me and don't know what label to stick on me, they don't blame themselves. They blame me and say, 'He's an odd fellow, odd.' You're only twenty, but you're already as old and canny as your father and your Uncle George, and I wouldn't be the least surprised if you were to call me in to cure your gout. That's no way to live. Never mind who I am, you should look me straight in the eye—openly, without reservations or preconceived ideas—and above all try to see me as a human being, or else you'll never really get on with people. Good-bye. And just remember this. With calculating, suspicious eyes like yours you'll never fall in love.

SONYA. That's not true.

KHRUSHCHOV. Oh yes, it is.

SONYA. It's not true. Well, just to show you—I am in love, so there. I'm in love and I'm terribly, terribly unhappy. Now leave me alone. Go away, for heaven's sake. And stop coming here, don't you come here any more.

KHRUSHCHOV. I wish you a very good night. [*Goes off.*]

SONYA [*alone*]. Oh, I *have* made him angry. I hope to God I never have a temper like that. [*Pause.*] He speaks very well, but who can be sure it's not a lot of hot air? Then he has those woods on the brain, he can talk of nothing else, and he plants trees. That's all very well, but it could so easily turn out to be psychopathic. [*Covers her face with her hands.*] I can't make him out at all. [*Cries.*] He studied medicine, but his interests are right outside medicine. It's all very odd, it really is. Lord, help me to make some sense of it.

[HELEN *comes in.*]

SCENE X

[SONYA *and* HELEN.]

HELEN [*opens the windows*]. The storm's over. What wonderful air. [*Pause.*] Where's the Wood-Demon?

SONYA. Gone home. [*Pause.*]

HELEN. Sonya.

SONYA. What?

HELEN. When are you going to stop sulking? We've done each other no harm, so why should we be enemies? Can't we call it off?

SONYA. I've wanted to myself. [*Embraces her.*] Darling!

HELEN. That's splendid. [*Both are very moved.*]

SONYA. Has Father gone to bed?

HELEN. No, he's in the drawing-room. We don't speak to each other for a whole month and heaven knows why. It's high time we did call it off. [*Looks at the table.*] What's this?

SONYA. The Wood-Demon has been having some supper.

HELEN. There's wine too. Let's drink to our friendship.

SONYA. Yes, let's.

HELEN. From the same glass. [*Fills it.*] That's better. So we're friends now, Sonya?

SONYA. Friends, Helen. [*They drink and kiss each other.*] I've wanted to make it up for ages, but I felt too embarrassed somehow. [*Cries.*]

HELEN. But why are you crying?

SONYA. Never mind, it's nothing.

HELEN. There, there, that'll do. [*Cries.*] You silly girl, now you've made me cry. [*Pause.*] You're angry with me because you think I married your father for selfish reasons. I give you my word of honour, if that means anything to you, that I married him for love. He attracted me as a scholar and public figure. It wasn't real love, it was quite artificial, but it seemed real enough at the time. It wasn't my fault. But since the day we were married you've been tormenting me by looking at me with those calculating, suspicious eyes.

SONYA. Please, please, remember we're friends now. Let's forget all that. That's the second time today I've been told about my calculating, suspicious eyes.

HELEN. You shouldn't look so calculating then, it doesn't suit you. You must trust people or life becomes impossible.

SONYA. Once bitten, twice shy. I've been let down so often.

HELEN. Who by? Your father's a good, honest man and he works hard. You were on at him today about being happy. If he's really been happy then he hasn't noticed it himself because he's been working too hard. I've never tried to hurt either you or your father. Your Uncle George is a very kind, honest man, but he's unhappy and discontented. So who is it you can't trust? [*Pause.*]

SONYA. Tell me honestly as a friend. Are you happy?

HELEN. No.

SONYA. I knew it. Another question. Tell me frankly, do you wish you were married to somebody younger?

HELEN. What a child you are. Of course I do. [*Laughs.*] All right, ask me something else, go on.

SONYA. Do you like the Wood-Demon?

HELEN. Yes I do, very much.

SONYA [*laughs*]. I have a foolish expression on my face, haven't I? He's just left, but I can still hear his voice and footsteps. And if I look into a dark window I seem to see his face in it. Let me finish what I have to say. But I can't say it out loud like this, I feel too embarrassed. Let's go to my room and talk there. Do you think I'm silly? You do, don't you? Is he a good man?

HELEN. Yes, indeed he is.

SONYA. I'm puzzled by this forestry and peat business. I can't make sense of it.

HELEN. There's a bit more to it than forestry, you know. Don't you see, my dear? He's a brilliant man! You know what that means? It means he has courage, flair, tremendous vision. When he plants a tree or digs up half a hundredweight of peat he's already working out what the result will be in a thousand years' time, already dreaming of man's happiness. People like that are precious and should be cherished. God bless you both. You're decent, courageous, honest people. He's a bit unhinged, but you're clear-headed and sensible. You'll make a very good match. [*Stands up.*] As for me, I'm just a tiresome character and not a very important one. In my music, in my husband's house, in all your romantic affairs—in everything, that is— I've always played a minor role. Come to think of it, Sonya, I really must be very, very unhappy. [*Walks agitatedly up and down the stage.*] There's no happiness for me in this world. None at all. What are you laughing at?

SONYA [*laughing and hiding her face*]. I'm so happy. Oh, how happy I am!

HELEN [*wringing her hands*]. Oh, really, how unhappy I am!

SONYA. I'm happy—happy.

HELEN. I feel like playing the piano. I'd like to play something now.

SONYA. Yes, do. [*Embraces her.*] I can't sleep. Do play something.

HELEN. Just a minute, your father's still awake. Music annoys him when he's unwell. Go and ask him and I'll play something if he doesn't mind. Go on.

SONYA. All right. [*Goes out.*]

[*The watchman is heard tapping his stick in the garden.*]

HELEN. It's ages since I played anything. I'll play and cry, cry my eyes out like a silly girl. [*Through the window.*] Is that you knocking, Yefim?

WATCHMAN [*off stage*]. Hallo there!

HELEN. Stop it then. The master's unwell.

WATCHMAN [*off stage*]. I'm just going. [*Whistles under his breath.*] Hey there, good dogs. Come on, dogs! [*Pause.*]

SONYA [*returning*]. He says no.

CURTAIN

ACT THREE

The drawing-room of SEREBRYAKOV'*s house. There are three doors—right, left and centre. Afternoon.* HELEN *can be heard playing the piano off stage. She is playing Lensky's aria which precedes the duel in* Eugene Onegin.

SCENE I

[ORLOVSKY, VOYNITSKY *and* THEODORE, *the latter in Circassian costume and carrying a fur cap.*]

VOYNITSKY [*listening to the music*]. Helen's playing my favourite aria. [*The music stops.*] Yes, it's a lovely thing. I don't think it's ever been quite so boring here before.

THEODORE. You don't know the meaning of the word boredom, old boy. When I was with the volunteers in Serbia we had the genuine article there all right, what with the stifling heat and the dirt and your head practically splitting in two because you had a hangover. I remember once sitting in some filthy little shed along with a Captain Kashkinazi. We'd long ago said all we had to say, there was nowhere to go and nothing to do, and we didn't want a drink. It was sickening, you know, enough to drive you round the bend. We sit there like a couple of snakes trying to hypnotize each other. He stares at me and I stare at him. I stare at him and he stares at me, and we go on staring like that without knowing why. Well, an hour passes, you see, and then another, and there we are still staring at each other. Then suddenly, God knows why, he jumps to his feet, whips out his sabre and goes for me. How do you like that! Well of course, I draw my own sabre pretty smartly—no point in being killed—and then the fun begins. Bim bam bim bam! They had a job separating us. I didn't get hurt, but Captain Kashkinazi's still going round with a scar on his cheek. It shows how crazy people can be.

ORLOVSKY. Yes, such things happen.

[*Enter* SONYA.]

SCENE II

[The above and SONYA.]

SONYA *[aside]*. I don't know what to do with myself. [*Laughs as she crosses the stage.*]

ORLOVSKY. Where are you off to, Kitten? Sit with us for a bit.

SONYA. Come here a moment, Theo. [*Takes* THEODORE *on one side.*] Come over here.

THEODORE. What do you want? What do you look so happy about?

SONYA. Promise you'll do what I ask.

THEODORE. Well, what is it?

SONYA. Drive over to the—Wood-Demon's.

THEODORE. What for?

SONYA. Oh, nothing. Just drive over and ask him why he hasn't been near us for so long. It's been a whole fortnight.

THEODORE. She's blushing. You should be ashamed of yourself. I say, everyone, Sonya's in love.

EVERYONE. Shocking. You should be ashamed of yourself.

[SONYA *covers her face with her hands and runs out.*]

THEODORE. She drifts around from one room to another as if she was half dead and doesn't know what to do with herself. She's in love with the Wood-Demon.

ORLOVSKY. She's a splendid child, I'm very fond of her. I did think you might marry her, Theo. You couldn't find a better wife. Ah well, things haven't worked out that way. But it would have given me such pleasure, I'd have been delighted. I'd have come to see you, and there you'd have been with your young wife in the bosom of your family with the good old samovar on the boil.

THEODORE. That's not my line of country. But if I ever was crazy enough to get married I'd marry Julia anyway. She is at least small, and one should always choose the lesser of two evils. And she does know how to run a house. [*Claps his forehead.*] I've had an idea.

ORLOVSKY. What's that?

THEODORE. Let's have some champagne.

VOYNITSKY. It's a bit early and it's too hot. Let's leave it a bit.

ORLOVSKY [*with an admiring look*]. My own boy, handsome devil! Wants champagne, the dear fellow.

[*Enter* HELEN.]

SCENE III

[*The above and* HELEN. HELEN *crosses the stage.*]

VOYNITSKY. Look at that. There she goes, nearly falling over from sheer laziness. A charming sight, I must say.

HELEN. Stop it, George. Things are quite boring enough without you going on all the time.

VOYNITSKY [*barring her way*]. Our brilliant pianist! But you don't look much like one. Lazy, indolent, sluggish and so virtuous that I can't bear to look at you.

HELEN. Then don't look at me, let me go.

VOYNITSKY. Why so downhearted? [*Vigorously.*] No really, my dear, splendid creature, do be sensible. There's mermaid's blood flowing in your veins. So go on, be a mermaid.

HELEN. Leave me alone.

VOYNITSKY. Let yourself go for once in your life and fall madly in love with a river god——

THEODORE. And dive head first into deep water with him and leave the learned professor and the rest of us gasping on the shore.

VOYNITSKY. A mermaid, eh? How about a little love affair before it's too late?

HELEN. Why are you telling me what to do? If I had my way, I wouldn't need you to show me how to live. I'd fly away, free as a bird, far away from you all, away from your sleepy faces and your dull, boring talk. I'd forget that you so much as exist, and then no one would dare to tell me what to do. But I have no will of my own. I'm such a coward, I'm so shy. I keep feeling that if I was unfaithful all other wives would do the same and leave their husbands. I feel that God would punish me and my conscience would torment me, otherwise I'd show you a thing or two about leading a free life. [*Goes out.*]

ORLOVSKY. My dear, my beautiful——

VOYNITSKY. I think I'll soon find myself despising that woman. She's as bashful as a young girl, but she lays down the law like some stuffy old parish clerk who's never done anything wrong in his life. What sickly, wishy-washy stuff!

ORLOVSKY. All right, that will do. Where's the professor now?

VOYNITSKY. In his study, writing.

ORLOVSKY. He wrote and asked me to come and talk over some business matter. You don't know what it's all about, I suppose?

VOYNITSKY. He has no business affairs. All he ever does is write nonsense, grumble and feel jealous.

[ZHELTUKHIN *and* JULIA *come in through the door, right.*]

SCENE IV

[*The above,* ZHELTUKHIN *and* JULIA.]

ZHELTUKHIN. Hallo, everybody. [*Greets everyone.*]

JULIA. Hallo, Godfather. [*They kiss.*] Hallo, Theo. [*They kiss.*] Hallo, Mr. Voynitsky. [*They kiss.*]

ZHELTUKHIN. Is Professor Serebryakov in?

ORLOVSKY. Yes, he's in his study.

ZHELTUKHIN. I must go and see him. He wrote and told me he wanted to talk business. [*Goes out.*]

JULIA. Mr. Voynitsky, that barley you ordered—did you get it yesterday?

VOYNITSKY. Yes, thank you. What do I owe you? We had something from you in the spring as well, I don't remember what. We must settle up. I can't bear having my accounts in a mess or neglecting them.

JULIA. In the spring you had sixty-four bushels of rye, two heifers and one calf. And the people from your farm sent for some butter.

VOYNITSKY. Then what do I owe you?

JULIA. I can't tell you. Not without my counting frame.

VOYNITSKY. Well, I'll go and get it for you if you need it.

[*Goes out and returns at once with the counting frame.*]

ORLOVSKY. How's big brother Leo, my dear?

JULIA. Fine, thanks. I say, where did you buy that lovely tie?

ORLOVSKY. In town. At Kirpichov's.

JULIA. It's jolly nice. I must get one like that for Leo.

VOYNITSKY. Here's your counting frame.

[JULIA *sits down and rattles the beads on the frame.*]

ORLOVSKY. Leo should thank his lucky stars he has Julia to run the place. A tiny little thing, so small you can hardly see her, but look at the way she works! Not bad, eh?

THEODORE. While all he does is walk round clutching his cheek, the lazy so-and-so.

ORLOVSKY. My dearest beggar maid. Do you know, she goes round wearing an old-fashioned cloak? While I drive round the market on a Friday she walks about among the carts wearing this cloak.

JULIA. Now you've put me off.

VOYNITSKY. Let's go somewhere else, everybody. How about the ballroom? I'm fed up with being in here. [*Yawns.*]

ORLOVSKY. Whatever you say. I don't mind.

[*They go out through the door, left.*]

JULIA [*alone, after a pause*]. Theo's wearing Caucasian dress. That's what happens when parents don't discipline their children properly. He's the best-looking man in the county, he's clever, he's rich, but he's just no good. He's a complete ass. [*Rattles the counting frame.*]

[*Enter* SONYA.]

SCENE V

[JULIA *and* SONYA.]

SONYA. You here, Julia? I didn't know.

JULIA [*they kiss each other*]. Darling!

SONYA. What are you up to? Doing some sums? You look so efficient, I feel quite envious. My dear, why don't you get married?

JULIA. Oh, I don't know. Approaches have been made, but I've turned them down. No real man would ever want to marry me. [*Sighs.*] That's impossible.

SONYA. But why not?

JULIA. I'm uneducated. I was taken away from school in the second form, you know.

SONYA. Whatever for?

JULIA. I just wasn't any good.

[SONYA *laughs.*]

JULIA. Why do you laugh?

SONYA. I have a funny sort of feeling. I'm so happy today, oh so happy, I'm almost bored with my own happiness. I don't know what to do with myself. Well, come on, let's talk about something, shall we? Have you ever been in love?

[JULIA *nods her head.*]

SONYA. Really? With someone attractive?

[JULIA *whispers in her ear.*]

SONYA. Who? Theodore?

JULIA [*nods her head*]. And what about you?

SONYA. Yes, me too. Only not with Theodore. [*Laughs.*] Go on then, tell me more.

JULIA. I've wanted to talk to you for ages, Sonya.

SONYA. Well, carry on then.

JULIA. I want to clear things up. You see, I've always liked you. I've plenty of girl friends, but you're the nicest of the lot. If you asked me to give you ten horses or two hundred sheep, say, I'd be delighted. I'd do anything for you.

SONYA. But why be so embarrassed about it?

JULIA. I feel ashamed. I—like you so much. You're the nicest friend I have, you're not the least bit proud. What a lovely dress you're wearing!

SONYA. Let's leave my dress till later. Go on.

JULIA [*agitatedly*]. I don't know how to put it in clever language. May I propose to you—that you should make me happy. I mean, er, I mean—you must marry Leo. [*Covers her face.*]

SONYA [*getting up*]. Let's not say any more about that, Julia. Don't let's talk about it, please.

[HELEN *comes in.*]

SCENE VI

[The above and HELEN.]

HELEN. There's absolutely nowhere to go in this house. George and the two Orlovskys are wandering round and wherever I go I find them. It really is depressing. What do they want here? Why don't they go off somewhere?

JULIA [*through tears*]. Hallo, Helen. [*Is about to kiss her.*]

HELEN. Hallo, Julia. I'm sorry, I don't like kissing all the time. What's your father doing, Sonya? [*Pause.*] Sonya, why don't you answer me? I asked you what your father's doing. [*Pause.*] Why don't you answer me? Sonya!

SONYA. So you want to know, do you? Come here then. [*Takes her slightly to one side.*] All right, I'll tell you. I feel so honest today, I just can't keep up the usual pretence while talking to you. Here, take this. [*Hands over a letter.*] I found it in the garden. Come on, Julia. [*Goes out with* JULIA *through door, left.*]

SCENE VII

[HELEN *and—later—*THEODORE.]

HELEN [*alone*]. What's all this? A letter from George to me. But what have I done wrong? Why, how rude and heartless of her! She feels so honest that she can't talk to me. My God, what an insult! My head's going round, I think I'm going to faint.

THEODORE [*comes through the door, left, and starts crossing the stage*]. Why do you always shudder when you see me? [*Pause.*] H'm! [*Takes the letter out of her hands and tears it to pieces.*] You must give all this up. You must only think of me. [*Pause.*]

HELEN. What do you mean?

THEODORE. I mean that if I have my eye on a girl she doesn't get out of my clutches in a hurry.

HELEN. No, what you really mean is that you're stupid and insolent.

THEODORE. You'll wait for me by the bridge on the other side of the garden at half past seven this evening. All right? That's all I have to say. Till half past seven then, my angel. [*Tries to take her hand.*]

[HELEN *slaps his face.*]

THEODORE. You put it rather forcibly.

HELEN. Get out of here.

THEODORE. Very well then. [*Moves off and then comes back.*] I'm most touched. Let's discuss the thing calmly. You see, I've experienced everything in this world. I've even eaten goldfish soup a couple of times. But I've still never been up in a balloon or run off with the wife of a learned professor.

HELEN. Please go away.

THEODORE. Certainly, at once. I've experienced everything, that's why I'm so full of impudence I don't know what to do with it. Anyway, the point is, if you ever need a friend or a faithful hound, apply to me. My feelings have been profoundly touched.

HELEN. I don't require any hounds. Please go away.

THEODORE. All right. [*Deeply moved.*] Still, I'm very touched all the same. Of course I am. Yes indeed. [*Goes out hesitantly.*]

HELEN [*alone*]. I have a headache. Every night I have nightmares and I feel as if something terrible was going to happen. What a loathsome business, though. These young people were born here and brought up together, they're close friends, they're always embracing, and they ought to be on the best of terms. But they look ready to eat one another alive. The Wood-Demon's saving our forests, but what about people? There's no one to save them.

[*Moves off towards the door, left, but seeing* ZHELTUKHIN *and* JULIA *advancing to meet her goes out through the centre door.*]

SCENE VIII

[ZHELTUKHIN *and* JULIA.]

JULIA. How unlucky we are, Leo. Dear me, we are unlucky.

ZHELTUKHIN. But who asked you to speak to her? Who do you think you are, a village match-maker? Now you've spoilt everything. She'll think I can't speak up for myself and—and oh, how vulgar and provincial! I've told you a thousand times we ought to drop the whole thing. It brings nothing but humiliation and these hints of one kind and another. It's a dirty, rotten business. The old man must have guessed I'm in love with her and he's already taking advantage of my feelings. He'd like me to buy this estate from him.

JULIA. How much does he want for it?

ZHELTUKHIN. Sh! Someone's coming.

[*Enter through the door, left,* SEREBRYAKOV, ORLOVSKY *and* MRS. VOYNITSKY, *the last reading a pamphlet as she comes in.*]

SCENE IX

[*The above,* SEREBRYAKOV, ORLOVSKY *and* MRS. VOYNITSKY.]

ORLOVSKY. I don't feel too grand myself, old boy. I've had this headache for two days and I ache all over.

SEREBRYAKOV. But where are the others? I hate this house. It's such a labyrinth, twenty-six enormous rooms with people wandering off in all directions so you can never find anyone. [*Rings.*] Ask George and my wife to come here.

ZHELTUKHIN. Julia, you're not doing anything. Go and find George and Helen.

[JULIA *goes out.*]

SEREBRYAKOV. One can put up with ill health. What does it matter anyway? But what I can't stand is my present state of mind. I feel as if I was already dead or had left the earth entirely and got stuck on some strange planet.

ORLOVSKY. It all depends on your point of view.

MRS. VOYNITSKY [*reading*]. Give me a pencil, someone. Here's another contradiction, I must mark it.

ORLOVSKY. Here you are, dear madam. [*Gives her a pencil and kisses her hand.*]

[VOYNITSKY *comes in.*]

SCENE X

[*The above,* VOYNITSKY *and—later—*HELEN.]

VOYNITSKY. Do you want me?

SEREBRYAKOV. Yes I do, George.

VOYNITSKY. What exactly do you require of me?

SEREBRYAKOV. 'Require of you'? But what are you so annoyed about? [*Pause.*] If I've offended you somehow, please forgive me.

VOYNITSKY. Oh, don't be so pompous, and let's get down to business. What do you want?

[HELEN *comes in.*]

SEREBRYAKOV. Ah, here is Helen. Sit down, ladies and gentlemen. [*Pause.*] Ladies and gentlemen, I have invited you here to announce that a government inspector is on his way. Actually, joking apart, I do have something serious to say. I have gathered you all here to ask for your help and advice. And, aware as I am of your unfailing kindness, I trust I shall receive the same. I'm an academic person, a man of books, and I've always been out of my depth in practical affairs. I cannot manage without the guidance of competent persons, so I appeal to you, Orlovsky, to you, Zheltukhin, and to you, George. The thing is that *manet omnes una nox.* In other words none of us is going to live for ever. I'm old and ill, so it seems to me high time to put my property and affairs in order in so far as they affect my family. My own life is over and I'm not thinking of myself, but I do have a young wife and an unmarried daughter. They simply cannot go on living in the country.

HELEN. It makes no difference to me.

SEREBRYAKOV. We are not cut out for country life. But we can't live in town either on the income from this estate. The day before yesterday I sold some woodland for four thousand roubles, but that's an abnormal measure which can't be repeated every year. We must find some procedure that guarantees us a constant, more or less stable income. Such a procedure has occurred to me and I have the honour to submit it for your consideration. I'll leave out the details and explain it in general terms. Our estate gives an average return of no more than two per cent on its capital value. I propose we sell it. If we invest the proceeds in securities we should get from four to five per cent on them. There may even be a few thousand roubles to spare, so that we can buy a cottage near St. Petersburg.

VOYNITSKY. Just a moment. My ears must be deceiving me. Say that again.

SEREBRYAKOV. Invest the money in securities and buy a cottage near St. Petersburg.

VOYNITSKY. No, it wasn't the bit about St. Petersburg. It was something else you said.

SEREBRYAKOV. I propose selling the estate.

VOYNITSKY. Ah, that was it. You're going to sell the estate. Wonderful. A very bright idea. And what do you suggest my old mother and I should do with ourselves?

SEREBRYAKOV. We'll discuss that all in good time. One can't do everything at once.

VOYNITSKY. Just a moment. It looks as if I've never had a scrap of ordinary common sense. Till now I've been stupid enough to think this estate belonged to Sonya. This estate was bought by my father as a dowry for my sister. So far I've been simple-minded enough to imagine that our laws weren't made in Turkey and I thought the estate had passed from my sister to Sonya.

SEREBRYAKOV. Yes, the estate does belong to Sonya. Nobody denies that. Without Sonya's consent I shouldn't venture to sell it. What's more, I'm acting in the girl's own best interests.

VOYNITSKY. But this is fantastic, utterly fantastic. Either I've gone stark, staring mad or—. Or else——

MRS. VOYNITSKY. Don't contradict the professor, George. He knows better than we do what's right and what's wrong.

VOYNITSKY. Oh, give me some water. [*Drinks water.*] Say what you like then, I give up.

SEREBRYAKOV. I don't know why you're so worked up, George. I'm not claiming my scheme is ideal. If you all decide it's no good I shan't insist on it.

[DYADIN *comes in wearing a tail-coat, white gloves and a broad-brimmed top hat.*]

SCENE XI

[The above and DYADIN.*]*

DYADIN. A very good day to you all. Excuse me venturing in here unannounced. I'm guilty, but I deserve to be let off lightly as there wasn't a single domestic in your hall.

SEREBRYAKOV [*embarrassed*]. Delighted. Do come in.

DYADIN [*bowing and scraping*]. Professor Serebryakov! Dear ladies! My intrusion on these premises has a double motive. I am here in the first place to visit you, sir, and pay my humble respects. Secondly, I've come to invite you all on an expedition to my part of the world to celebrate this excellent weather. I live at the water-mill which I rent from our mutual friend, the Wood-Demon. It's a secluded and romantic spot where you can hear water-nymphs splashing about at night, and in the daytime——

VOYNITSKY. One moment, Waffles, this is serious. Hold it, you can tell us later. [*To* SEREBRYAKOV.] Here, ask him. This estate was bought from his uncle.

SEREBRYAKOV. Oh really, and why should I ask him? Where would that lead us?

VOYNITSKY. This estate was bought for ninety-five thousand roubles as prices went in those days. My father paid only seventy thousand down and left twenty-five thousand on mortgage. Now listen to me. The estate would never have been bought at all if I hadn't given up my own share of the inheritance to my sister, of whom I was very fond. What's more, I slaved away for ten years and paid off the whole mortgage.

ORLOVSKY. What are you getting at, old boy?

VOYNITSKY. This estate is free from debt and in good order solely through my own personal efforts. And now I've grown old I'm to be pitched out of it neck and crop!

SEREBRYAKOV. I don't know what you're getting at.

VOYNITSKY. For twenty-five years I've run this estate. I've worked and sent the money to you. The best manager in the world couldn't have done more. And all this time you haven't thanked me once. All this time, when I was young and just the same today, I've been getting a salary of five hundred roubles a year from you—a miserable pittance! And not once has it occurred to you to give me a single extra rouble.

SEREBRYAKOV. But how was I to know, George? I'm an unpractical person, I don't understand these things. You could have helped yourself to as much as you liked, couldn't you?

VOYNITSKY. Why didn't I steal, you mean? Why don't you all despise me for not stealing? It would have been only fair if I had, and I shouldn't be a pauper now.

MRS. VOYNITSKY [*sternly*]. George!

DYADIN [*agitatedly*]. Do stop it, Georgie, for heaven's sake. I'm trembling all over. Why spoil good relations? [*Kisses him.*] Please don't.

VOYNITSKY. For twenty-five years I've been cooped up in this place with her—with this mother of mine. All our thoughts and feelings were for you alone. In the daytime we talked of you and your writings, we were proud of your reputation and spoke your name with reverence. And we wasted our nights reading books and journals that I utterly despise.

DYADIN. Oh Georgie, stop it, please. I can't stand this.

SEREBRYAKOV. What are you driving at? That's what I don't see.

VOYNITSKY. We thought of you as a superior being and we knew your articles by heart. But now my eyes have been opened. Everything's perfectly clear. You write about art, but you haven't the faintest idea what art is all about. Your entire works, which once meant so much to me, aren't worth a brass farthing.

SEREBRYAKOV. My friends, can't you stop him? Really! I'll go away.

HELEN. George, I insist you keep quiet. Do you hear me?

VOYNITSKY. I will not keep quiet. [*Barring* SEREBRYAKOV's *way.*] Wait, I haven't finished yet. You've ruined my life! I've not lived—not lived, I tell you. Thanks to you the best years of my life have been thrown down the drain. You are my worst enemy!

DYADIN. I can't stand this—I really can't. I'm going into another room. [*Goes out of the door, right, in terrible agitation.*]

SEREBRYAKOV. What do you want from me? And what right have you to talk to me like that? Nonentity! If the estate is yours, take it. I don't want it.

ZHELTUKHIN [*aside*]. I say, the sparks are flying! I'm off. [*Goes.*]

HELEN. If you won't keep quiet I shall get out of this madhouse this instant. [*Shouting.*] I've had about as much as I can take.

VOYNITSKY. My life's ruined! I'm gifted, intelligent and courageous. If I'd had a normal life I might have been a Schopenhauer or a Dostoyevsky. But I'm talking nonsense, I'm going mad. Mother dear, I'm desperate. Mother!

MRS. VOYNITSKY. Do as the professor says.

VOYNITSKY. Mother! What am I to do? Never mind, don't tell me. I know what to do all right. [*To* SEREBRYAKOV.] I'll give you something to remember me by! [*Goes out through centre door.*]

[MRS. VOYNITSKY *follows him.*]

SEREBRYAKOV. Really, everybody, what on earth is all this? Rid me of this maniac!

ORLOVSKY. It's quite all right, Alexander, just let him simmer down a bit. And don't you get so worked up.

SEREBRYAKOV. I cannot live under the same roof with him. His room is here [*points to the centre door*], almost next to mine. Let him move into the village, into a cottage in the grounds, or I'll move out myself, but I can't stay here with him.

HELEN [*to her husband*]. If anything like this happens again I'm leaving.

SEREBRYAKOV. Oh, don't try and frighten me, please.

HELEN. I'm not trying to frighten anyone, but you all seem to have conspired to make my life hell. I shall go away.

SEREBRYAKOV. Everyone knows perfectly well that you're young and I'm old and that you're doing me a great favour by living here at all.

HELEN. Go on, finish what you have to say.

ORLOVSKY. Oh come, come, my friends——

[KHRUSHCHOV *comes in hurriedly.*]

SCENE XII

[*The above and* KHRUSHCHOV.]

KHRUSHCHOV [*agitatedly*]. Oh, I am glad to find you in, Professor. Sorry if I've come at the wrong time or am being a nuisance, but that's not the point. How are you?

SEREBRYAKOV. What exactly do you want?

KHRUSHCHOV. I'm sorry, I'm rather distraught. Been riding so fast. Professor, I hear you sold your woods to Kuznetzov for timber the day before yesterday. If this is true and not just a rumour, then I say, please don't do it.

HELEN. My husband isn't in the mood to talk business just now. Let's go into the garden.

KHRUSHCHOV. But I must talk about it now.

HELEN. As you wish. I can't cope with this. [*Goes out.*]

KHRUSHCHOV. Let me go over and see Kuznetsov. Let me tell him you've changed your mind. How about it? You're going to fell a thousand trees. And what are you destroying them for? Just for two or three thousand roubles to buy a few miserable dresses for your wife and indulge yourself in a little luxury! Why destroy them? So that posterity may curse us as a lot of savages? If you, a scholar and a distinguished man, can be so cruel, what about those who haven't your advantages? This is quite appalling.

ORLOVSKY. We can talk about it later, Michael.

SEREBRYAKOV. Come on, Orlovsky, we'll never hear the end of this.

KHRUSHCHOV [*barring* SEREBRYAKOV's *way*]. In that case I'll tell you what, Professor. Hold off a bit, and I'll get some money and buy it myself in three months' time.

ORLOVSKY. I'm sorry, Michael, but this is decidedly odd. All right, we all know you're a man of principle. We thank you humbly and respect you for it. [*Bows.*] But why all the fuss?

KHRUSHCHOV [*flaring up*]. Hark at the universal uncle! There are plenty of easy-going people in this world, and that's always struck me as suspicious. Because why are they all so easy-going? It's just that they don't care.

ORLOVSKY. You came here to pick a quarrel, old boy, and that's rather a poor show. Principles are all right in their way, but you need this little gadget as well, old sport. [*Points to his heart.*] Without this little contraption, old boy, all your woods and your peat aren't worth a damn. Don't take it the wrong way, but you've got a lot to learn, dear me, you have.

SEREBRYAKOV [*brusquely*]. And another time be kind enough not to come in unannounced. I must also ask you to spare me these psycho-pathic outbursts. You've all been trying to make me lose my temper and you've finally succeeded. Be so good as to leave me alone. In my opinion this stuff about woods and peat is all sheer raving lunacy. Come on, Orlovsky. [*Goes out.*]

ORLOVSKY [*following him*]. That was a bit steep, Alexander. No need to be quite so outspoken. [*Goes out.*]

KHRUSHCHOV [*alone, after a pause*]. 'Raving lunacy.' So I'm a madman according to this distinguished academic figure. I bow to your pro-fessorial authority and I'm going straight home to shave my head. I must say, it's the earth itself that's mad for still putting up with us.

[*Goes quickly towards the door, right. Enter* SONYA *through the door, left, where she has been eavesdropping throughout the whole of* SCENE XII.]

SCENE XIII

[KHRUSHCHOV *and* SONYA.]

SONYA [*runs after him*]. Just a moment. I heard all that. Hurry up and say something or else I'll break down and say a thing or two myself.

KHRUSHCHOV. I've already said my piece. I begged your father to spare those trees. I know I was right, but he insulted me and called me a madman. All right then, I'm mad.

SONYA. Oh, don't go on like that, please.

KHRUSHCHOV. But those who hide their cruel, stony hearts behind a façade of learning, those who try to pass off their own insensitivity as the height of wisdom—they aren't mad, oh dear no! Nor, I suppose, are those who marry old men with the sole purpose of blatantly deceiving them and of buying themselves fashionable, elegant dresses on the proceeds of destroying our trees.

SONYA. Do listen to me, please. [*Presses his hands.*] Do let me tell you——

KHRUSHCHOV. That's quite enough of that. We've nothing in common. I know what you think of me already, and there's no place for me here any more. So good-bye. Our friendship has meant a lot to me and I'm sorry I shall now only be left with the memory of your father's gout and your remarks about my democratic sentiments. But that's not my fault. It's not I who——

[SONYA *weeps, covers her face and quickly goes out of the door, left.*]

KHRUSHCHOV. I was rash enough to fall in love here and that will be a lesson to me. I must get out of this dump.

[*Goes towards the door, right. Enter* HELEN *through the door, left.*]

SCENE XIV

[KHRUSHCHOV *and* HELEN.]

HELEN. Are you still here? Wait a moment. Mr. Orlovsky has just told me that my husband was rather sharp with you. I'm sorry, he's in a bad temper today and he didn't understand you. As for me, I'm entirely on your side. I think most highly of you, believe me, I really mean it. I sympathize with you and I feel for you, so allow me to offer you my sincere friendship. [*Holds out both her hands.*]

KHRUSHCHOV [*with aversion*]. Get away from me. I despise your friendship! [*Goes out.*]

HELEN [*alone, groans*]. What was that for? Why?

[*A shot is heard off stage.*]

SCENE XV

[HELEN, MRS. VOYNITSKY *and—later—*SONYA, SEREBRYAKOV, ORLOVSKY *and* ZHELTUKHIN. MRS. VOYNITSKY *staggers through the door, centre, shrieks and falls down in a faint.* SONYA *comes in and runs out through the door, centre.*]

SEREBRYAKOV.

ORLOVSKY. } What's the matter?

ZHELTUKHIN.

[SONYA *is heard to scream. She comes back and shouts,* 'Uncle George has shot himself!' SONYA, ORLOVSKY, SEREBRYAKOV *and* ZHELTUKHIN *run out of the next door.*]

HELEN [*groans*]. What for? What ever for?

[DYADIN *appears in the doorway, right.*]

SCENE XVI

[HELEN, MRS. VOYNITSKY *and* DYADIN.]

DYADIN [*in the doorway*]. What's the matter?

HELEN [*to him*]. Take me away from here. Throw me off a precipice or kill me if you like, but I can't stay here any longer. Quickly, quickly—please! [*Goes out with* DYADIN.]

CURTAIN

ACT FOUR

The forest and the house by the mill which DYADIN *rents from* KHRUSHCHOV.

SCENE I

[HELEN *and* DYADIN *are sitting on a bench beneath a window.*]

HELEN. I wonder if you'd mind driving over to the post office again tomorrow.

DYADIN. Not in the slightest.

HELEN. I'll wait another three days. If my brother hasn't answered my letter by then I'll borrow some money from you and go to Moscow myself. After all I can't spend the rest of my life at your mill, can I?

DYADIN. No, of course not. [*Pause.*] It's not for me to advise you, dear lady, but all these letters and telegrams and my daily trips to the post office—well, they're all a waste of time, I'm sorry. Whatever your brother tells you, you'll still go back to your husband in the end.

HELEN. Oh no I shan't. Let's be rational, shall we? I don't love my husband. I did like those young people, but they've been unfair to me all along. So why should I go back? You'll say it's my duty. I know that all right, but I repeat, we must be rational. [*Pause.*]

DYADIN. Yes indeed. The great Russian poet Lomonosov ran away from Archangel Province to seek his fortune in Moscow. A fine thing to do, of course. But you—why did you run away? Quite frankly, there's no happiness for you in this world. A canary should sit in its cage and watch others being happy. It should stay put, in fact.

HELEN. Perhaps I'm not a cage-bird. Perhaps I'm free to fly where I like.

DYADIN. Don't you believe it. With due respects, you must expect to be judged by results like anyone else. This last fortnight another woman in your position might have popped up in a dozen different towns and had everyone running round in small circles, but you've only got as far as this mill and even that's been too much for you. Oh, come down to earth, can't you? You'll stay on here a bit till you've calmed down and then back you'll go to your husband. [*Pricks up his ears.*] I hear a carriage coming. [*Gets up.*]

HELEN. I'll go away.

DYADIN. I won't venture to impose on you further. I'll go into my mill and have a little snooze. I was up with the lark today.

HELEN. Come back here when you wake up and we'll have tea. [*Goes into the house.*]

DYADIN [*alone*]. If I lived somewhere with a bit of cultural life, I can see a caricature of myself appearing in a magazine. It could have a most amusing satirical caption. Just think of someone as old and unattractive as me running off with the young wife of a distinguished professor. Charming! [*Goes out.*]

SCENE II

[SIMON, *carrying buckets, and* JULIA, *coming in.*]

JULIA. Good afternoon, Simon. Nice to see you. Is Mr. Dyadin in?

SIMON. Yes, he's down at the mill.

JULIA. Would you mind calling him?

SIMON. Not at all, miss. [*Goes out.*]

JULIA [*alone*]. He's probably having a nap. [*Sits down on the bench beneath the window and gives a deep sigh.*] Some of them sleep, others enjoy themselves, but I'm run off my feet all day long. Ah well, no peace for the wicked. [*Gives an even deeper sigh.*] Heavens, how can anyone be as stupid as old Waffles? I was driving past his barn just now and a little black pig came out of the door. If other people's pigs start getting at his corn sacks it will just serve him right. [DYADIN *comes in.*]

SCENE III

[JULIA *and* DYADIN.]

DYADIN [*putting on a frock-coat*]. Is that you, Julia? Excuse my *déshabillé*, I was going to rest awhile in the arms of Morpheus.

JULIA. How are you?

DYADIN. I'm sorry I can't ask you in, the house isn't tidy and all that. Would you care to come over to the mill?

JULIA. No, I'm all right here for a bit. Let me tell you why I came. Leo and the professor have decided on an outing and they'd like to picnic at your mill this afternoon.

DYADIN. Delighted.

JULIA. I've come on ahead. The others will be here soon. Could you have a table brought out—oh, and a samovar too of course? And would you mind telling Simon to get the picnic baskets out of my carriage?

DYADIN. Very well. [*Pause.*] Well, what news? How are things?

JULIA. Bad. I'm sick with worry, I can tell you. You know the professor and Sonya are staying with us now, don't you?

DYADIN. Yes.

JULIA. They can't bear their own house since George's suicide. They were scared. It wasn't too bad during the day, but at night they all used to sit huddled in one room till dawn, terrified of George's ghost appearing in the dark.

DYADIN. That's all superstition. Do they ever mention Helen?

JULIA. Of course they do. [*Pause.*] She's cleared out.

DYADIN. Yes, it's a subject worthy of the brush of Ayvazovsky. She just cleared out.

JULIA. And now no one knows where she is. Perhaps she's gone away or perhaps she was desperate enough to——

DYADIN. God is merciful, my dear. It'll be all right.

[KHRUSHCHOV *comes in carrying a portfolio and a drawing-case.*]

SCENE IV

[*The above and* KHRUSHCHOV.]

KHRUSHCHOV. Hey! Is anyone here? Simon!

DYADIN. Try looking this way.

KHRUSHCHOV. Ah! Good afternoon, Julia.

JULIA. Good afternoon.

KHRUSHCHOV. Well, I came out here to do some work again, Dyadin. I don't feel like staying at home. Would you ask them to put my table under this tree the way I had it yesterday, and tell them to have two lamps ready? It's getting dark.

DYADIN. At your service, sir. [*Goes out.*]

KHRUSHCHOV. How are you, Julia?

JULIA. Oh, all right. [*Pause.*]

KHRUSHCHOV. The Serebryakovs are staying with you, aren't they?

JULIA. Yes.

KHRUSHCHOV. H'm! And what's brother Leo up to?

JULIA. He stays at home, spends his time with Sonya.

KHRUSHCHOV. I'll bet he does. [*Pause.*] Why doesn't he marry the girl?

JULIA. Why indeed? [*Sighs.*] I only wish he would. He's educated, he's a gentleman, and she comes of a good family too. I've always wanted it.

KHRUSHCHOV. She's a fool.

JULIA. Don't say such things.

KHRUSHCHOV. And your Leo's a bright specimen, I must say. You and your friends are a pretty prize collection one way and another. Quite a glut of intellect there, and no mistake.

JULIA. You must have missed your lunch today.

KHRUSHCHOV. Oh? Why?

JULIA. You're in such a bad temper.

[DYADIN *and* SIMON *come in carrying a small table.*]

SCENE V

[*The above,* DYADIN *and* SIMON.]

DYADIN. You do know how to look after yourself, Michael. You've picked a splendid place to work. It's an oasis. Yes, I mean it. Can't you see yourself surrounded by palm trees? Julia's a gentle doe, you're a lion and I'm a tiger.

KHRUSHCHOV. You're a very nice fellow, Dyadin, but why carry on like this? These sugary words, all this foot-scraping and shoulder-twitching—anyone who didn't know you wouldn't take you for a human being at all. Devil knows what he'd think of you. Pity.

DYADIN. It must be the way I'm made. Such are the dictates of destiny.

KHRUSHCHOV. There you go again, 'dictates of destiny'. Can't you drop that stuff? [*Pins a chart on the table.*] I think I'll stay the night here.

DYADIN. Delighted. You're in a bad temper, but I feel inexpressibly cheerful as though there was a dear little bird inside me singing a song.

KHRUSHCHOV. Well, make the most of it. [*Pause.*] You may have a dear little bird inside you. I haven't. Quite the opposite in fact. It's been just one damn thing after another. Shimansky's sold his wood for timber for a start. And then Helen's run away from her husband and no one knows where she's got to. And thirdly, I feel I'm becoming stupider, cheaper and more second-rate every day. There was something I wanted to tell you yesterday, but couldn't—couldn't pluck up the courage. You may congratulate me. George's diary turned up after his death. Mr. Orlovsky got hold of it first and I went over there and read it a dozen times.

JULIA. Yes, we read it too.

KHRUSHCHOV. George's affair with Helen had the entire district buzzing like a hive, but it turns out the whole story was a filthy pack of lies. I believed it and joined in the general mud-slinging—the hatred, the contempt, the insults.

DYADIN. That was very wrong of course.

KHRUSHCHOV. I first heard it from your brother, Julia. A prize specimen I am! I don't think much of your brother, but I believed him rather than Helen, though I only had to open my eyes to see how unselfishly she was behaving. I'd rather believe evil than good and I can't see further than the end of my own nose, which means I'm just as second-rate as the rest of them.

DYADIN [*to* JULIA]. Let's go down to the mill, child, and leave our bad-tempered friend to his work while we amuse ourselves. Come on. And you do your work, Michael. [*Goes out with* JULIA.]

KHRUSHCHOV [*alone, mixes some paint in a saucer*]. One night I saw him press his face against her hand. There's a detailed description of that night in his diary, how I came in and what I said. He quotes my words, calls me a narrow-minded fool. [*Pause.*] This colour's too dark. Must get it lighter. Then he blames Sonya for loving me. She never loved me. Now I've made a blot. [*Scrapes the paper with a knife.*] Even supposing there was something in it, there's no point in thinking about that now. It began and ended in foolishness. [SIMON *and some workmen bring in a large table.*] What are you doing? What's that for?

SIMON. Mr. Dyadin's orders. The ladies and gentlemen from the Zheltukhin estate are going to have tea here.

KHRUSHCHOV. Oh, that's just wonderful. So there's no point in me bothering about my work any more. I'll pack up and go home.

[ZHELTUKHIN *comes in with* SONYA *on his arm.*]

SCENE VI

[KHRUSHCHOV, ZHELTUKHIN *and* SONYA.]

ZHELTUKHIN [*sings*]. 'Against my will to these sad shores
An unknown force has drawn me.'

KHRUSHCHOV. Who's there? Oh! [*Hurriedly puts his drawing materials away in their cases.*]

ZHELTUKHIN. One more question, Sonya. Do you remember lunching with us on my birthday? You thought I looked funny, didn't you? You laughed at me.

SONYA. Oh, please stop it. How can you? I wasn't laughing at anything in particular.

ZHELTUKHIN [*catching sight of* KHRUSHCHOV]. I say, who's this I see? You here as well? Hallo.

KHRUSHCHOV. Hallo.

ZHELTUKHIN. Working? Splendid. Where's Waffles?

KHRUSHCHOV. Over there.

ZHELTUKHIN. Where's over there?

KHRUSHCHOV. I should have thought I'd made myself clear. Over there at the mill.

ZHELTUKHIN. I must go and call him. [*Goes off singing.*] 'Against my will to these sad shores—' [*Goes out.*]

SONYA. Good afternoon.

KHRUSHCHOV. Good afternoon. [*Pause.*]

SONYA. What are you drawing?

KHRUSHCHOV. Oh, nothing of any interest.

SONYA. Is it a plan?

KHRUSHCHOV. No, it's a map of the forests in our district. I made it. [*Pause.*] The green colouring shows the forests of our grandfathers' time and before. Light green shows where they've been felled during the last twenty-five years—oh, and the blue shows where they're still standing. Yes. [*Pause.*] Well now, how are you? Happy?

SONYA. This is no time to think about happiness.

KHRUSHCHOV. Then what should we think about?

SONYA. That's what caused the tragedy, thinking too much about happiness.

KHRUSHCHOV. Just as you say. [*Pause.*]

SONYA. It's an ill wind that blows nobody any good. Misfortune has taught me to forget my own happiness and think only of others. Life should be an act of constant self-sacrifice.

KHRUSHCHOV. As you say. [*Pause.*] Mrs. Voynitsky's son shot himself. But she's still chasing contradictions in her wretched pamphlets. You've had a ghastly experience, and now you try to cripple your whole life, and call that self-sacrifice—which is just pandering to your own vanity. Everyone's heartless. You are. And so am I. All the wrong things are done and everything's going to rack and ruin. I'm just off, I don't want to be in the way of you and Zheltukhin. But why the tears? I wasn't trying to make you cry.

SONYA. Never mind, it doesn't matter. [*Wipes her eyes.*]

[*Enter* JULIA, DYADIN *and* ZHELTUKHIN.]

SCENE VII

[*The above,* JULIA, DYADIN *and* ZHELTUKHIN, *then—later—* SEREBRYAKOV *and* ORLOVSKY.]

SEREBRYAKOV [*off stage*]. Hallo there! Where are you all?

SONYA [*shouts*]. We're here, Father.

DYADIN. They're bringing the samovar. Charming. [*He and* JULIA *attend to the table.*]

[SEREBRYAKOV *and* ORLOVSKY *come in.*]

SONYA. This way, Father.

SEREBRYAKOV. All right, I can see you.

ZHELTUKHIN [*in a loud voice*]. Ladies and gentlemen, I declare the meeting open. Take out the cork, Waffles.

KHRUSHCHOV [*to* SEREBRYAKOV]. Let's forget what happened, shall we? [*Holds out his hand.*] Forgive me, please.

SEREBRYAKOV. Thank you, only too delighted. And you must forgive me. When I tried to think about that business next day and remembered what we said, I felt very bad about it. Let's be friends. [*Takes him by the arm and goes to the table.*]

ORLOVSKY. This was long overdue, old boy. A bad peace is better than a good war.

DYADIN. I am indeed happy, sir, that you have honoured my oasis with a visit. It gives me more pleasure than I can say.

SEREBRYAKOV. Thank you, my dear sir. It's really lovely out here, an oasis indeed.

ORLOVSKY. You're fond of nature, are you?

SEREBRYAKOV. Very much so. [*Pause.*] Well, come on, all of you, don't let the conversation flag. In our position it's best to keep talking. We've got to face up to our misfortunes. I'm putting a better face on things than all of you just because I'm the most unfortunate of us all.

JULIA. I say, I'm not giving you any sugar, you must all have jam with your tea.

DYADIN [*bustling about among his guests*]. I'm delighted, delighted.

SEREBRYAKOV. Recently, Michael, I've had so much to put up with and I've thought so many thoughts, I could probably write a whole treatise on the art of living for the benefit of posterity. One's never too old to learn. Misfortune is a great teacher.

DYADIN. Let bygones be bygones. With God's mercy it will turn out all right.

[SONYA *gives a start.*]

ZHELTUKHIN. What made you jump like that?

SONYA. I heard someone shout.

DYADIN. It's some of the locals catching crayfish in the river. [*Pause.*]

ZHELTUKHIN. Didn't we agree to spend the evening as if nothing had happened? Yet there's a feeling of tension somehow.

DYADIN. I revere scholarship, sir, and even have a kind of family feeling for it. My brother Gregory's wife's brother, a Mr. Konstantin Novosyolov—you may possibly know him—held a master's degree in foreign literature.

SEREBRYAKOV. I don't know him, but I know of him. [*Pause.*]

JULIA. It's exactly a fortnight since George died.

KHRUSHCHOV. Don't let's talk about it, please.

SEREBRYAKOV. Well come on, don't be downhearted.

ZHELTUKHIN. All the same, there is a feeling of tension somehow.

SEREBRYAKOV. Nature abhors a vacuum. She robbed me of two dear ones, but soon sent some new friends along to fill the gap. Your health, Zheltukhin.

ZHELTUKHIN. Thank you, Professor. Permit me in turn to drink to your fruitful academic work.

> 'Scatter the seed for a harvest of kindliness,
> Reason and goodness—and Russia will gratefully
> Offer her thanks.'

SEREBRYAKOV. I appreciate the compliment. I sincerely hope our friendship will ripen in the not too distant future.

[THEODORE *comes in.*]

SCENE VIII

[*The above and* THEODORE.]

THEODORE. So that's what's going on. A picnic.

ORLOVSKY. My dear boy—you handsome fellow, you.

THEODORE. Good evening, all. [*Kisses* SONYA *and* JULIA.]

ORLOVSKY. It's a whole fortnight since we met. What have you been up to, eh?

THEODORE. I've just been over to Leo's place and they told me you were here, so I drove out.

ORLOVSKY. Where did you get to all this time?

THEODORE. I haven't slept for three nights. I lost five thousand roubles at cards last night, Father. I've been drinking and gambling, and made half a dozen trips to town. I've gone completely off my rocker.

ORLOVSKY. Good for you! I daresay you're a bit drunk now, eh?

THEODORE. Not on your life. Julia! Tea, girl! But I'd like it on the tart side with a bit of lemon in it. What price old George, eh? Going and putting a bullet through his head like that. And what possessed him to use a French revolver? Wasn't a Smith and Wesson good enough?

KHRUSHCHOV. Hold your tongue, you swine.

THEODORE. I may be a swine, but I'm a pedigree animal. [*Strokes his beard.*] My beard alone is worth a fortune. Yes, I'm a swine, a fool, a scoundrel. But if I said the word, any young woman would marry me like a shot. Sonya, marry me. [*To* KHRUSHCHOV.] All right, I'm sorry. *Pardonnez-moi*, I'm sure.

KHRUSHCHOV. Oh, stop fooling around.

JULIA. You're hopeless, Theo. You're the worst drunkard and spend-thrift in the county. Just look at you. You're pathetic. You're the absolute limit, you wicked, wicked man.

THEODORE. Oh, don't be such a spoil-sport. Come and sit next to me. That's right. I'll come and stay with you for a fortnight. Must get some rest. [*Kisses her.*]

JULIA. You ought to be ashamed of yourself. You should comfort your father in his old age and you only disgrace him. It's a crazy way to carry on, that's all I can say.

THEODORE. I'm giving up drinking. I'm finished with that. [*Pours himself a drink.*] Is this plum wine or cherry?

JULIA. Don't drink it. Leave it alone.

THEODORE. I'm allowed one glass. [*Drinks.*] I'll give you a pair of horses and a gun, Mr. Wood-Demon. I'm going to stay at Julia's, going to spend a fortnight over there.

KHRUSHCHOV. A spot of corrective detention is more what you need.

JULIA. Come on, drink your tea, do.

DYADIN. Have some biscuits with it.

ORLOVSKY [*to* SEREBRYAKOV]. You know, old man, I lived just like young Theodore till I was forty. I once started counting how many women I'd made unhappy in my life and I got as far as seventy, old boy, and then stopped counting. Yes indeed. But something sud-denly came over me at the age of forty, old boy. I felt depressed and out of things. In fact I felt terribly mixed up inside, and that was that.

I tried everything—reading, work, travel—but it was no good. Anyway, old boy, I once went to see an old pal of mine who's not with us any longer, Prince Dmitry Pavlovich. We had dinner, hors d'œuvres and all that, and instead of a nap afterwards we laid on some target practice outside. There were masses of people there, friend Waffles among them.

DYADIN. Indeed I was, I haven't forgotten.

ORLOVSKY. You know, I felt absolutely miserable, my God I did! I couldn't stand it. I suddenly burst into tears, staggered and bellowed across the yard at the top of my voice, 'Good people, my friends, forgive me in the name of Christ!' And all at once I began to feel kind, pure and warm inside. And ever since then, old boy, I've been the happiest man in these parts. You ought to try it yourself.

SEREBRYAKOV. Try what?

[*A glow appears in the sky.*]

ORLOVSKY. Do the same as me. Surrender. Capitulate.

SEREBRYAKOV. A fine piece of homespun philosophy. You're telling me to apologize. Why should I? Let other people apologize to me.

SONYA. But it's *we* who're at fault, Father.

SEREBRYAKOV. Is it? At the moment you're all thinking of my attitude to my wife, I presume. Do you really think that's my fault? Why, that's absurd, you know. She's neglected her duty and left me just when I most needed her.

KHRUSHCHOV. Listen to me, Serebryakov. For twenty-five years you've been a professor and done academic work while I've planted trees and practised medicine. But what's the point of these things, and who gets anything out of them, if we're not kind to those we're working for? We say we're serving humanity, while all the time we're callously wrecking each other's lives. For instance, did you or I do anything to save George? Where's your wife, whom we've all insulted? Where's your peace of mind and your daughter's? Everything's gone to rack and ruin, it's all going to blazes. You people call me a wood-demon, but I'm not the only one, you know. You've all got a demon inside you, and you're all wandering in a dark wood and feeling your way. You're all just about bright enough, and have just about enough sense, to ruin your own and other people's lives.

[HELEN *comes out of the house and sits on the bench beneath the window.*]

SCENE IX

[The above and HELEN.*]*

KHRUSHCHOV. I thought I was a man of integrity and understanding, when I couldn't forgive anyone the slightest mistake, believed in gossip and joined in the general mud-slinging. And then when your wife sincerely offered me her friendship, I came down on her like a ton of hot bricks—told her to leave me alone, said I despised her friendship. That's what I'm like. There's a demon inside me, and I'm narrow-minded, blind, second-rate, but you're not all that wonderful yourself, Professor. Meanwhile everyone round here thinks I'm a hero and a man of the future. All the women certainly think so. And your name's a byword throughout Russia. Now if my sort are seriously taken for heroes and your sort are seriously regarded as celebrities—well, all I can say is we *are* in a bad way, and we haven't any real heroes or brilliant men or anyone else to lead us out of this dark wood and put right the damage we do. There are no really first-class people with a genuine right to fame and honour——

SEREBRYAKOV. I'm very sorry, I didn't come here to cross swords with you or defend my claims to distinction.

ZHELTUKHIN. We might change the subject anyway, Michael.

KHRUSHCHOV. I'll be through in a moment and then I'll go. All right, I'm not much good, but you're no great shakes yourself, Professor. And George, who couldn't find anything better to do than put a bullet through his brains, he wasn't up to much either. You're none of you very much good if it comes to that. And the women——

HELEN *[interrupting]*. And the women are no better. *[Approaches the table.]* There was a woman called Helen who left her husband, but will she make any use of her freedom? Don't worry, she'll be back. *[Sits down at the table.]* In fact here I am.

[General consternation.]

DYADIN *[with a loud laugh]*. Charming! Now, everybody, let me say a word before you all shout 'Off with his head!' Professor, it was I who ran off with your wife, as a certain Paris once carried off Helen of Troy. Yes, I did it. True, you don't get pock-marked Parises, but there are more things in heaven and earth, Horatio, than are dreamt of in your philosophy.

KHRUSHCHOV. I don't get this. Can it really be you, Helen?

HELEN. Yes, I've been staying here for the last fortnight. Well, why do you all stare at me like that? How are you all? I was sitting by the window and I could hear everything you said. [*Embraces* SONYA.] Let's be friends again. How are you, dear? Do let's be friends.

DYADIN [*rubbing his hands*]. Charming!

HELEN [*to* KHRUSHCHOV]. Michael! [*Holds out her hand.*] Can't we let bygones be bygones? How are you, Theodore? Julia——

ORLOVSKY. My dear old girl, dear wife of our dear professor, you glorious, beautiful creature. She's returned, she's come back to us.

HELEN. I've missed you all so much. Hallo, Alexander. [*Holds out her hand to her husband, who turns away.*] Alexander!

SEREBRYAKOV. You've neglected your duty.

HELEN. Alexander!

SEREBRYAKOV. I won't deny I'm glad to see you and I'm quite willing to talk to you—but at home, not here. [*Moves away from the table.*]

ORLOVSKY. Alexander! [*Pause.*]

HELEN. I see. So the solution to our problem is a very simple one. It hasn't got a solution. Oh, all right then. I admit I don't count for very much. My happiness is that of a cage-bird, the sort of happiness suitable for a woman. That means being cooped up at home for the rest of my life, eating, drinking, sleeping and listening every day to people going on about their gout, and about their merits and their rights. Why do you all look away? You're not embarrassed, are you? How about a glass of wine? Oh, come on!

DYADIN. It will turn out all right in the end. Everything's going to be fine.

THEODORE [*approaches* SEREBRYAKOV, *agitatedly*]. I feel very much moved. Do be kind to your wife, say something nice to her, and on my word of honour you can count on my loyalty and friendship for the rest of my life. I'll present you with my best troika.

SEREBRYAKOV. Thank you, but I'm afraid I don't quite understand.

THEODORE. So you don't understand, eh? One day on my way back from a shooting trip I saw a brown owl in a tree, so I loosed off at him with small shot. He stayed put, so I let him have a charge of buck-shot. And he didn't budge an inch, there was absolutely nothing doing. Just sat there blinking.

SEREBRYAKOV. What was all that directed at?

THEODORE. A brown owl. [*Goes back to the table.*]

ORLOVSKY [*pricks up his ears*]. Just a moment, everyone. Quiet, please. I think I hear bells, it must be a fire-alarm.

THEODORE [*spotting the glow in the sky*]. I say! Take a look at the sky. See that glow?

ORLOVSKY. Good heavens, while we're sitting here and missing it all!

DYADIN. Pretty good, eh?

THEODORE. Phew, I say! Quite a display! It's near Alekseyevskoye.

KHRUSHCHOV. No, Alekseyevskoye must be further to the right. It's more likely Novo-Petrovskoye.

JULIA. How awful! I'm scared of fires.

KHRUSHCHOV. Yes, of course it's Novo-Petrovskoye.

DYADIN [*shouts*]. Simon, run along to the weir and see if you can tell where the fire is. You might be able to see from there.

SIMON [*shouts*]. It's the Telibeyev Woods.

DYADIN. What?

SIMON. The Telibeyev Woods.

DYADIN. The woods——.

[*A lengthy pause.*]

KHRUSHCHOV. I must get along there to the fire. Good-bye. I'm sorry I was so rude, but I've never felt quite so depressed in my life. Things have really got me down. Anyway, what does that matter? A man should stand on his own feet, and I shan't shoot myself or throw myself under the mill-wheel. I may not be much of a hero, but I'll be one some day, I'll grow an eagle's wings and I shan't fear that glow in the sky or the devil himself. Let the woods burn. I'll plant new ones, and if the one I love won't have me I'll find myself another. [*Rushes out.*]

HELEN. Good for him!

ORLOVSKY. Yes, indeed. 'If the one I love won't have me I'll find myself another.' Now I wonder what he meant by that pronouncement.

SONYA. Take me away, I want to go home.

SEREBRYAKOV. Yes, it is time we went, it's impossibly damp out here. My rug and overcoat must be somewhere around.

ZHELTUKHIN. Your rug's in the carriage and your overcoat's here. [*Gives him the overcoat.*]

SONYA [*in great agitation*]. Take me away, for heaven's sake.

ZHELTUKHIN. At your service.

SONYA. No, I'll go with my godfather. Please take me with you, Godfather.

ORLOVSKY. Come on then, girl, come on. [*Helps her on with her coat.*]

ZHELTUKHIN [*aside*]. Damnation! This is all so sordid and degrading.

[THEODORE *and* JULIA *pack the crockery and napkins in a basket.*]

SEREBRYAKOV. I've got a pain in my left foot, it must be rheumatism. That means another sleepless night.

HELEN [*buttoning up her husband's overcoat*]. Mr. Dyadin, would you bring me my hat and cape from the house, please?

DYADIN. Certainly. [*Goes into the house and comes back with her hat and cape.*]

ORLOVSKY. So you're scared of the fire, are you, girl? Don't be afraid, it's not so bad as it was. It'll soon be out.

JULIA. We've left half a jar of cherry jam. Oh well, Mr. Dyadin can have it. [*To her brother.*] Take the basket please, Leo.

HELEN. I'm ready. [*To her husband.*] Come on then, carry me off like the statue of the Commendatore in *Don Giovanni* and let's go to hell together in your twenty-six gloomy rooms. That's all I'm good for.

SEREBRYAKOV. 'Statue of the Commendatore.' I might find the comparison more amusing were it not for the pain in my foot. [*To the whole company.*] Good-bye, everyone, and thank you for your hospitality and pleasant company. It's been a wonderful evening, the tea was excellent and everything in the garden's lovely. But there's one thing I can't accept, I'm sorry, and that's all this hedgerow philosophy and your general attitude. What we need, ladies and gentlemen, is action. We can't go on like this. We must *do* things, indeed we must. Good-bye. [*Goes out with his wife.*]

THEODORE [*to* JULIA]. Come on, my little beggar maid. [*To his father.*] Good-bye, Your Reverence. [*Goes out with* JULIA.]

ZHELTUKHIN [*following them, carrying the basket*]. This basket's heavy, damn it. How I hate picnics! [*Goes out and shouts off stage.*] Drive up there, Aleksey.

SCENE X

[ORLOVSKY, SONYA *and* DYADIN.]

ORLOVSKY [*to* SONYA]. Well, what are you waiting for? Come on, my pet. [*Moves off with* SONYA.]

DYADIN [*aside*]. And nobody said good-bye to me. Charming! [*Puts out the candles.*]

ORLOVSKY [*to* SONYA]. What's the matter?

SONYA. I just can't move. I feel too weak. I'm desperate, completely desperate. I'm so utterly miserable.

ORLOVSKY [*alarmed*]. What's all this? My pretty darling——

SONYA. Let's stay here a bit.

ORLOVSKY. First it's take me away, then it's stay here a bit. I can't make you out.

SONYA. I've lost all my happiness here today. Oh, I do feel awful. Why, oh why, am I still alive? [*Embraces him.*] Oh, if you only knew, if you did but know.

ORLOVSKY. You need a drink of water. Come and sit down. Come on.

DYADIN. What's the matter? Sonya, my dear, this is awful, I'm all of a dither. [*Tearfully.*] I can't bear to see you like this. My child——

SONYA [*to* DYADIN]. Please take me to the fire. Please!

ORLOVSKY. What do you want at the fire? What can you do there?

SONYA. For goodness' sake take me, or I'll go on my own. I'm desperate. I'm so unhappy, so unbearably unhappy. Take me to the fire.

[KHRUSHCHOV *rushes in.*]

SCENE XI

[*The above and* KHRUSHCHOV.]

KHRUSHCHOV [*shouts*]. I say, Dyadin!

DYADIN. I'm here. What do you want?

KHRUSHCHOV. I can't walk all that way. Can you let me have a horse?

SONYA [*noticing* KHRUSHCHOV, *gives a happy shout*]. Michael! [*Goes towards him.*] Michael! [*To* ORLOVSKY.] Go away please, I must talk to him. [*To* KHRUSHCHOV.] Michael, you said you'd find someone else. [*To* ORLOVSKY.] Do go away, please. [*To* KHRUSHCHOV.] Well, I *am* someone else now. I only want the truth—the truth and nothing but the truth. I love you, I love you. I love you.

ORLOVSKY. So that's the reason for all this coming and going. [*Gives a loud laugh.*]

DYADIN. Charming!

SONYA [*to* ORLOVSKY]. Please go away. [*To* KHRUSHCHOV.] Yes, yes, the truth and nothing but the truth. Speak to me, for heaven's sake, I've said all I have to say.

KHRUSHCHOV [*embracing her*]. My darling.

SONYA. Don't go away now, Godfather. Michael, when you tried to tell me you loved me I was so happy I could hardly breathe, but I had all those absurd prejudices. And what stopped me telling you how I really felt? Why, the same thing that stops Father from smiling at Helen now. Now I'm free——

ORLOVSKY [*laughs*]. Journeys end in lovers' meetings. So you're safe on shore at last. I have the honour to congratulate you. [*Bows low.*] Oh, you naughty, naughty children—the way you've dragged the thing out, chasing each other up hill and down dale.

DYADIN [*embracing* KHRUSHCHOV]. You've made me very happy, my dear fellow.

ORLOVSKY [*embracing and kissing* SONYA]. My little canary, darling Sonya. [SONYA *laughs.*] I say, she's off again.

KHRUSHCHOV. I'm in a complete daze, I'm sorry. Let me have another word with her. Please don't get in our way. Do go away, please.

[THEODORE *and* JULIA *come in.*]

SCENE XII

[*The above,* THEODORE *and* JULIA.]

JULIA. But you're always talking nonsense, Theo, you never do anything else.

ORLÓVSKY. Sh! Be quiet, children. My son's coming, the young bandit. Hurry up, everybody, let's hide somewhere. Come on.

[ORLOVSKY, DYADIN, KHRUSHCHOV *and* SONYA *hide.*]

THEODORE. I left my whip somewhere round here, and a glove.

JULIA. But you're always talking nonsense.

THEODORE. Well, what if I am? I don't want to go over to your place just yet. Let's have a stroll and then drive over.

JULIA. Oh, you are a nuisance, you're the absolute limit. [*Claps her hands together.*] I say, isn't old Waffles an ass? He hasn't even cleared the table. Someone might have stolen the samovar. Oh, Waffles, Waffles, he seems quite old, but he's got no more sense than he was born with.

DYADIN [*aside*]. Thank you.

JULIA. I heard someone laughing as we were coming along.

THEODORE. It's some of the local women bathing. [*Picks up a glove.*] Somebody's glove. It's Sonya's. I don't know what's bitten Sonya today. She's in love with the Wood-Demon. She's quite crazy about him and the silly chump can't see it.

JULIA [*angrily*]. But where are you taking me?

THEODORE. To the weir. Let's go for a walk, it's the prettiest spot in the whole neighbourhood. Beautiful!

ORLOVSKY [*aside*]. That's my own boy, the handsome devil, with that whacking great beard of his——

JULIA. I heard someone speak just then.

THEODORE. 'Oh wondrous spot, wood-demons' haunt,
          Where water-nymphs sit in the trees.'
That's the way of it, old man. [*Claps her on the shoulder.*]

JULIA. I'm not an old man.

THEODORE. Let's talk things over calmly. Listen. I've been through hell and high water. I'm thirty-five and I've no position in life except that of lieutenant in the Serbian Army and sergeant of the Russian reserve. I'm neither one thing nor the other. I must turn over a new leaf, and, well, I've got the crazy idea, you see, that if I marry my whole life will be different. So will you marry me, eh? You're the girl for me.

JULIA [*embarrassed*]. H'm. Well, you see—. Hadn't you better mend your ways first?

THEODORE. Oh come on, don't beat about the bush! Say yes or no.

JULIA. I'm too embarrassed. [*Looks round.*] Wait a moment, someone might come in or overhear us. I think Waffles is looking through the window.

THEODORE. There's nobody there.

JULIA [*throws her arms round his neck*]. Theo!

[SONYA *laughs.* ORLOVSKY, DYADIN *and* KHRUSHCHOV *laugh, clap their hands and shout,* 'Hurrah! Well done!']

THEODORE. Gosh! You frightened us. Where have you sprung from?

SONYA. Congratulations, Julia. And you can say the same to me.

[*Laughter, kisses, noise.*]

DYADIN. Charming, charming!

CURTAIN

APPENDIX I

THE WOOD-DEMON

1. The text, its composition and the first performance
2. Contemporary reception
3. The draft version

I. THE TEXT, ITS COMPOSITION AND THE FIRST PERFORMANCE

This translation is based on Rassokhina's lithographed (Moscow, 1890) version, here termed the 'final edition', as reproduced in *Works*, 1944–51, xi with the restoration of two minor changes imposed by the censorship in the 1890 edition.

The final edition was preceded by three documents of importance to the history of the play's composition:

(a) the 'programme' for the play contained in a letter of Chekhov's dated 18 October 1888,
(b) the lost draft of May 1889 and
(c) the 'censor's copy' of October, 1889.

These documents are now considered in sequence together with:
(d) the final edition.

(a) The 'programme'

The first clear reference to an unnamed and projected play, recognizable as a prototype of *The Wood-Demon*, occurs in a letter of 18 October 1888 from Chekhov to A. S. Suvorin, the well-known conservative journalist, playwright and publisher (1834–1912), a close friend of Chekhov. At this time Chekhov, who was planning to write the play in collaboration with Suvorin, refers to the 'beginning of the play' as having been already written by Suvorin and reminds Suvorin of their 'programme' (more strictly 'play-bill'—афиша in Russian) for the play. The text of the 'programme' is as follows:

'I have received the beginning of the play. Thank you. Blagosvetlov [the proto-type of Serebryakov] can go in entirely, just as he is. You've made a good job of him. From the moment he first opens his mouth he produces an exhausting and irritating impression, and if the audience listens to him for three to five minutes on end, exactly the right effect will be obtained. The audience will think, "Oh, do shut up for heaven's sake!" The man, i.e. Blagosvetlov, must impress the audience both as an intelligent, gout-ridden old codger and as a boring piece of music which has been played too long. I think you'll see how successful you've been with him when I've sketched out Act One and sent it to you.

'I shall leave Anuchin's surname and all that sort of thing, but we must lubricate his conversation a bit. Anuchin [the prototype of Ivan Orlovsky] is a flabby, oily, affectionate sort of character and his speech too is flabby and oily, whereas you've made it too staccato and not easy-going enough. This godfather must give off a whiff of old age and laziness. He is too lazy to listen to Blagosvetlov, and instead of arguing he would prefer to have a snooze and listen to stories about St. Petersburg, the Tsar, literature, learning—or to have a bite of food in good company.

'May I remind you of the programme of our play?

'1. Alexander Platonovich Blagosvetlov, member of the Council of State, who has received the Order of the White Eagle and has a pension of 7,200 roubles. Comes from a priest's family, and was educated at a church school. Attained his position by his own efforts. His past is without blemish. Suffers from gout, rheumatism, insomnia and a noise in his ears. Has received some landed property as part of his wife's dowry. Is definitely intelligent. Cannot stand mystics, visionaries, crackpots, lyric poets, prigs, doesn't believe in God and is accustomed to judge everything in this world from the point of view of deeds. Deeds, deeds, deeds. And all the rest is nonsense or charlatanism.

'2. Boris, his son, a student, a very delicate, honest youth who knows not a thing about life. Having once imagined himself to be a populist,[1] he's had the idea of dressing as a peasant and has dolled himself up like a Turk. Plays the piano excellently, sings feelingly, secretly writes plays, has an amorous disposition, wastes lots of money and always talks nonsense. Is a poor student.

'3. Blagosvetlov's daughter [the prototype of Sonya], only please let's not call her "Sasha". I've already got fed up with that name in *Ivanov*.[2] If the son's Boris, let the daughter be a Nastya. (And may we erect an everlasting monument to Boris and Nastya.) Nastya is twenty-three or twenty-four years old. Is well educated and can think for herself. Is bored with St. Petersburg and with the country too. Has never been in love. Lazy, likes abstract discussions, reads books lying down. Wants to get married only for the sake of variety and so as not to be left on the shelf. Says she can only love somebody interesting. Would be delighted to fall in love with a Pushkin or an Edison and marry them, but only boredom would lead her to marry a decent man. Will respect her husband and love her children. Having seen and heard the Wood-Demon, she gives way to passion to the ultimate degree, to the point of frenzy and stupid, senseless laughter. The powder damped down by the tundra of St. Petersburg dries in the sun and explodes with terrific force. I've thought of a phenomenal love scene.

---

[1] That is, a *narodnik*—a kind of socialist and champion of the Russian peasantry.
[2] Chekhov's play *Ivanov*, 1887–89.

'4. Anuchin, the old man. Considers himself the happiest man on earth. His sons are making their way in life, his daughters are married and he himself is free as a bird. Has never been near a doctor, gone to law or worn medals, forgets to wind up his watch and is everyone's friend. Makes a good supper, sleeps splendidly, drinks a lot without suffering from hangovers, gets angry with himself for being so old and is incapable of thinking of death. Used to grouse and suffer from melancholia, had a bad appetite and was interested in politics, but was saved by an accident. For some reason or other he once had occasion about ten years previously to ask everyone to forgive him at a county council [*zemstvo*] meeting. After that he suddenly felt cheerful and got an appetite, and, having a subjective character, being civic-minded to the marrow of his bones, came to the conclusion that absolute sincerity, as displayed in public repentance, was the cure for all diseases. Recommends this cure to everybody, Blagosvetlov included.

'5. Victor Petrovich Korovin [the prototype of Khrushchov], a landowner of between 30 and 33 years of age, the Wood-Demon. A poet and landscape painter with a tremendous feeling for nature. Once while he was still at high school he planted a silver birch in his yard. When it became green and began to sway in the breeze and to rustle and cast a small shadow, his heart filled with pride. He'd helped God to create a new birch-tree, made the world richer by one tree! This was the beginning of his peculiar form of creativity. He brings his idea to fruition not on canvas or paper, but in the ground, not in terms of dead paint, but in terms of organisms. A tree is a beautiful thing, but it also has the right to life, it is as necessary as water, sunlight and the stars. Life on this earth is unthinkable without trees. Forests condition climate, climate influences people's character etc. etc. There can be neither civilization nor happiness if the forests go crashing down beneath the axe, if the climate is cruel and rough and if people are cruel and rough as well. The future is horrible. Nastya likes him, not because of his ideas, which are foreign to her, but because of his gifts, his passion and the wide range of his thought. She likes the fact that his brain has gone striding through the whole of Russia and landed up ten centuries ahead of us. When he appeals to her father, begging him with sobs and tears not to sell his forests for timber, she laughs aloud for happiness and delight because she has at last clapped eyes on the kind of person in whom she used not to believe when she seemed to recognize his characteristics in, say, dreams and novels.

'6. Galakhov [the prototype of Zheltukhin], the same age as the Wood-Demon, but already a very senior civil servant, a very wealthy man who serves alongside Skalkovsky.[1] A bureaucrat to the marrow of his bones, he is quite unable to throw off his bureaucratic characteristics because they are part of his flesh and blood inherited from his ancestors. Wants to live by the dictates of his heart, but is unable. Tries to understand nature and music, but can't. Is an honest, sincere man who realizes that the Wood-Demon is superior to him and

[1] K. A. Skalkovsky (1843–1906), a mining engineer, high official and journalist.

openly admits this. Wants to marry for love, thinks he is in love and works himself up into a lyrical mood, but nothing comes of it. Likes Nastya only as a beautiful, intelligent girl, as a good wife, and that's all.

'7. Vasily Gavrilovich Volkov [the prototype of George Voynitsky], brother of Blagosvetlov's deceased wife. Manages Blagosvetlov's estate (he has got through his own some time previously). Regrets never having stolen anything. Did not expect his relatives from St. Petersburg to show so little appreciation of his efforts. They don't understand him and don't want to understand him, and he regrets never having stolen anything. Drinks Vichy water and grumbles. Stands on his dignity. Stresses the fact that he is not afraid of generals. Shouts.

'8. Lyuba, his daughter [prototype of Julia]. Concerned with earthly things. Hens, ducks, knives, forks, the cattle yard, the award from The Meadow[1] which has to be framed, the entertainment of guests, dinners, suppers, tea—these are her sphere. Considers it a personal affront if other people take it upon themselves to pour out tea—"So I'm not wanted in this house any more!" Dislikes people who splash their money about and don't work. Worships Galakhov because of his positive qualities. You haven't brought her on properly. Ought to come on from the far part of the garden in an agitated state and raise a shout, "How dare Mariya and Akulina leave the young turkeys out all night in the open?"—or something of that kind. Is always severe. Severe both with people and with ducks. Women who really know how to run things never delight in the work of their hands. On the contrary, they try to prove they lead a life of slavery, that—God forgive them—they've no time to rest, that everyone else sits around doing nothing while only they, poor things, work their fingers to the bone. Ticks off Nastya and Boris for not working for their living and fears Blagosvetlov.

'9. Simon, a peasant, works for the Wood-Demon as a manager.

'10. The wandering pilgrim Feodosy, an old man of eighty whose hair has not yet turned grey. Was a soldier under Nicholas I, served in the Caucasus and speaks Lezgin.[2] Has a sanguine temperament. Likes anecdotes and cheerful conversations. Bows low to everybody, kisses them on the shoulder and kisses the ladies by force. Was a novice in a monastery on Mount Athos. Has collected 300,000 roubles in his time and sent the whole lot to the monastery while remaining poor himself. Calls people fools and blackguards with no respect for office or position.

'There you have the whole programme. You will receive my material for Act One by Christmas. I shan't touch Blagosvetlov. He and Galakhov are yours, I renounce them. A good half of Nastya is yours. I can't cope with her on my own. Boris isn't important, it's not hard to master him. The Wood-Demon is mine up to Act Four, but he's all yours in Act Four up to the conversation with Blagosvetlov. In this conversation I shall have to maintain the general mood of the character, a mood which you won't manage to catch.

[1] The magazine Niva.
[2] Lezgin—a language belonging to the Daghestan group of Caucasian languages.

'As for Act Two (the guests), once again you can write the beginning.
'Feodosy is a minor character, who I think will be needed. I don't want the
Wood-Demon to be alone on the stage, I want Blagosvetlov to feel himself
surrounded by crackpots. In the programme I've left out Mlle Émilie, the elderly
Frenchwoman who is also quite crazy about the Wood-Demon. We must
show the effect that Mr. Wood-Demon and his like have on women. Émilie is
a kind old woman, a governess, who has not yet lost all her electricity. When
she gets excited she mixes up French and Russian. A patient nurse to Blagosvetlov. She's all yours. I'll leave some gaps for her in the first scene.' (*Letter to
A. S. Suvorin, 18 Oct. 1888.*)

Of the characters mentioned in the 'programme', eight are recognizable
prototypes of characters in *The Wood-Demon*, though all have different names
with the trivial exception of the manservant Simon. Of these eight, four
eventually emerged after further development in *Uncle Vanya*. These relationships are as follows:

The 'programme'	*The Wood-Demon*	*Uncle Vanya*
1. Blagosvetlov = Serebryakov	= Serebryakov
2. Boris		
3. Nastya = Sonya	= Sonya
4. Anuchin = Ivan Orlovsky	
5. Korovin = Khrushchov	= Astrov
6. Galakhov = Zheltukhin	
7. Volkov = George Voynitsky	= Vanya Voynitsky
8. Lyuba = Julia	
9. Simon = Simon	

'Feodosy' and 'Mlle Émilie' were—perhaps fortunately—abandoned.

(b) The lost draft of May 1889

Suvorin soon gave up the idea of collaborating with Chekhov on the play,
as is evident from Chekhov's letter to him of 15 November 1888 ('Why do
you refuse to write *The Wood-Demon* with me?'). And Chekhov himself tem-
porarily abandoned the project, being now busy revising his earlier play
Ivanov. But references in his correspondence show that he had not forgotten *The
Wood-Demon*. On 8 January 1889 he wrote to Suvorin: 'I think my *Wood-
Demon* will be put together with a great deal more subtlety than *Ivanov*.' In
February he made the following two conflicting statements: 'The time when
I shall get down to *The Wood-Demon* . . . seems to me to be in the far distant
future.' (*Letter to A. S. Suvorin, 6 Feb. 1889.*) 'I shall write *The Wood-Demon*
in time for the next season.' (*Letter to A. S. Suvorin, 20 Feb. 1889.*)

By March 1889 Chekhov was working on the play, but not making much
progress. 'I shall write *The Wood-Demon* in May or August. . . . I've put together the first three acts in a most satisfactory way, but I've hardly sketched

out the fourth at all. Act Three is so scandalous that when you look at it you'll say: "This was written by someone very cunning and merciless." ' (*Letter to A. S. Suvorin, 5 March 1889.*) 'I'm not writing a play, and I shan't write one soon since I've nothing to write about and am not all that keen.' (*Letter to V. A. Tikhonov, 7 March 1889.*) 'I shan't write any plays. If I have time I'll do some kind of pot-boiler, but I shall spend the autumn and winter on fiction only. As a playwright I'm out of luck.' (*Letter to A. N. Pleshcheyev, 7 March 1889.*)

However, by April Chekhov was seriously at work on *The Wood-Demon*. 'I've begun *The Wood-Demon*, having nothing better to do. The result is something terribly boring like *Nathan the Wise*.' (*Letter to A. S. Suvorin, 17 April 1889.*) 'Can you believe it, I've finished Act One of *The Wood-Demon*. It's turned out not bad, though a bit long. I feel much stronger than I did when I was writing *Ivanov*. The play will be finished by the beginning of June.' (*Letter to A. S. Suvorin, 4 May 1889.*)

By 14 May Chekhov was speaking of the play as already finished. 'The play has turned out boring and resembles a mosaic, but still it does look to me as if some hard work has gone into it. I have hit off some characters which are definitely new. In the whole play there is not one lackey, not one comic character introduced for the sake of effect, not one little widow. There are eight characters in all, of which only three have minor roles. In general I've tried to avoid overdoing things and I think I've succeeded.' (*Letter to A. S. Suvorin, 14 May 1889.*)

Chekhov now felt that the play was sufficiently advanced for him to promise it to two actors—to P. M. Svobodin, for his forthcoming benefit performance at the St. Petersburg Aleksandrinsky Theatre, and to A. P. Lensky for performance at the Moscow Maly Theatre.

However, towards the end of May Chekhov stopped work on *The Wood-Demon*. 'I began a comedy, but abandoned it after writing two acts. It's turning out boring.' (*Letter to V. A. Tikhonov, 31 May 1889.*)

(c) The 'censor's copy' of October 1889

Chekhov resumed work on *The Wood-Demon* in September 1889. 'Can you believe it, I'm writing a big romantic comedy [комедия-роман], and I've already churned out two and a half acts at a single gulp. . . . In this comedy I introduce good, healthy people who are half likeable. There is a happy ending. The general mood is one of uninterrupted lyricism. It's called *The Wood-Demon*. . . . I'll finish *The Wood-Demon* by 20 October.' (*Letter to A. N. Pleshcheyev, 30 Sept. 1889.*)

In fact Chekhov finished the play at the beginning of October. 'I've written a comedy! A bad one maybe, but I've written it! In September and at the beginning of October I worked so hard that I feel queer in the head and my eyes ache.' (*Letter to A. N. Pleshcheyev, 6 Oct. 1889.*) Though this 'censor's copy' reproduces many of the features of the 'programme' quoted above, Chekhov had started it afresh after destroying the draft version of May 1889, which has not survived. '... I've written the four-acter *The Wood-Demon*, written it afresh after destroying everything I'd written in the spring.' (*Letter to A. S. Suvorin, 13 Oct. 1889.*)

This version was submitted to the censor and passed as acceptable on 10 October 1889. As the result of objections by the censor two minor alterations were made. These alterations have been restored in the text on which this translation is based and were as follows:

(i) *In Act One, Scene VI (p. 212) the name* 'Schopenhauer' *was substituted for* 'Lassalle'.

(ii) *In Act One, Scene VII. In Khrushchov's speech (p. 217) the words* 'at the thought that I'm helping God to create a living organism' *were changed to* 'at the thought that thanks to me there's one life more on this earth.'

(d) The final edition and the first performance

In early October the actor P. M. Svobodin, who wished to appear in *The Wood-Demon* in his impending benefit performance, collected a copy of the play from Chekhov in Moscow and took it to St. Petersburg. On 9 October Svobodin read it to an unofficial committee acting on behalf of the St. Petersburg Aleksandrinsky Theatre and including the writer D. V. Grigorovich and the Director of the Russian Imperial Theatres (of which the Aleksandrinsky was one), I. A. Vsevolozhsky. The committee rejected the play. Chekhov described these proceedings as a 'field court martial' on him and *The Wood-Demon*. (*Letter to A. S. Suvorin, 13 Oct. 1889.*)

Svobodin, who did not lose his own enthusiasm for *The Wood-Demon*, wrote to Chekhov giving the committee's reasons for rejecting the play, which included its 'lack of action' and 'tedious passages'. (*Letter from P. M. Svobodin to Chekhov, 25 Oct. 1889, 'Chekhov i teatr', p. 211.*) According to another account the play was described by the committee as a 'splendid dramatized short story, but not a drama'. (*'Petersburg Gazette', 1889, no. 287, quoted in 'Works', 1944–51, xi, p. 614.*)

Chekhov was annoyed by this reaction, on which he made the following comment: 'Very nice. This means one of two things. Either I'm no good as a playwright (which I readily endorse) or we must regard certain people as hypocrites. I mean those gentlemen who love me as dearly as their own sons and beg me in God's name to be myself in my plays, to avoid stereotypes and present a complex conception.' (*Letter to A. N. Pleshcheyev, 21 Oct. 1889.*) Here Chekhov had in mind D. V. Grigorovich, who had encouraged him earlier in his career, but whose present attitude he resented.

Other discouraging reactions reached Chekhov. In early November the actor A. P. Lensky wrote: 'I'm sending you your play. . . . I've only one thing to say. Stick to stories. You're too contemptuous of the stage and of dramatic form, you respect them too little, to write a drama. This is a more difficult form than narrative, and you must excuse my saying you're too spoilt by success to study the form of the drama thoroughly—learn its ABC, as it were—and grow fond of it.' (*Letter to Chekhov from A. P. Lensky, Nov. 1889, 'Chekhov i teatr', p. 214.*)

Replying to Lensky, Chekhov expressed his intention of writing no more plays. 'I shan't revise *The Wood-Demon*, I'll sell it to one of our private theatres.' (*Letter to A. P. Lensky, 2 Nov. 1889.*)

Another early reaction was that of V. I. Nemirovich-Danchenko, who sought to encourage Chekhov. He did not agree with Lensky that Chekhov had shown contempt for the stage in writing *The Wood-Demon*. It would be truer to say that he had shown ignorance of it. 'And, as far as I can see, it is easy for you to master the stage.' (*Letter of V. I. Nemirovich-Danchenko to Chekhov, 6 Nov. 1889, 'Chekhov i teatr', p. 313.*) This reaction is particularly important in view of the fact that Nemirovich-Danchenko was later co-founder (with Stanislavsky) of the Moscow Art Theatre, with which Chekhov became closely associated.

Chekhov soon changed his decision not to revise *The Wood-Demon*: 'Thank you for reading the play. I knew myself that Act Four was no good, but when I handed over the play I did make the reservation that I would write a new act.' (*Letter to A. S. Suvorin, 12 Nov. 1889.*)

Chekhov did in fact succeed in selling *The Wood-Demon* to a private theatre, the Theatre of Abramova in Moscow. Here it was performed on 27 December 1889. The text from which it was performed formed the basis of Rassokhina's lithographed edition (Moscow, 1890) on which the present translation is based.

2. CONTEMPORARY RECEPTION

The reactions of Russian dramatic critics to the first performance of *The Wood-Demon* were almost all unfavourable. In particular Chekhov was accused of mechanically reproducing ordinary everyday life and of being ignorant of the stage.

The writer D. S. Merezhkovsky and the less well-known writer A. I. Urusov were among the few enthusiasts for *The Wood-Demon*. They advised Chekhov to submit the play for publication to the magazine *Severny vestnik*, of which his friend A. N. Pleshcheyev was literary editor. Chekhov did so reluctantly: 'I hope that when you've read the play you may share the doubts which compel me to send it to the magazine so hesitantly.' (*Letter to A. N. Pleshcheyev, 17 March 1890.*) Pleshcheyev replied that he was not satisfied with the play and Chekhov thereupon gave up the idea of publication in *Severny vestnik*.

Previously, when there had been some question of *The Wood-Demon* appearing in another magazine, *The Artist*, Chekhov had written to the publisher, F. A. Kumanin, as follows (*letter of 8 Jan. 1890*): 'I ask you [to withdraw the play from publication] *in all seriousness*. If you agree, answer quickly. If you don't agree I shall be deeply wounded and aggrieved, as I shall be deprived of the chance of doing some more work on *The Wood-Demon*. If they've started setting up the type I'll pay for the type-setting, throw myself in a lake or hang myself—whichever you like.'

Throughout his life Chekhov opposed all further attempts to stage or publish *The Wood-Demon*. In 1897 his brother Michael, who was then living in Yaroslavl, inquired about the possibility of staging the play there, but Chekhov refused permission (*letter to M. P. Chekhov, 4 Feb. 1897*). In 1899 A. I. Urusov (who, after the appearance of *Uncle Vanya*, took the eccentric view that *The Wood-Demon* was the better of the two plays) asked Chekhov's permission to publish *The Wood-Demon*. Chekhov replied: 'I beg you not to be angry, but I can't publish *The Wood-Demon*. I hate the play and I'm trying to forget it. Whether it's the fault of the play itself or of the circumstances in which it was written and staged, I don't know. But it would be a real blow to me if some unknown force were to drag it out of obscurity and bring it to life. There's a fine example of perverted parental love for you.' (*Letter to A. I. Urusov, 16 Oct. 1899.*)

Chekhov also excluded *The Wood-Demon* from the first comprehensive edition of his works, that published by A. F. Marks (1899–1901).

3. THE DRAFT VERSION

The only extant draft of *The Wood-Demon* is that of October 1889, referred to above as the 'censor's copy'. In revising this for the final version Chekhov left Act Two unchanged, but virtually rewrote Act Four and made extensive alterations to Acts One and Three. The draft version of Act Four is translated in its entirety below. So far as the drafts of Acts One and Three are concerned, an account is given of the lengthier and more important alterations only. The general effect of these alterations was to shorten the final text as compared with the draft and to tone down the element of facetiousness.

(*a*) *Act One*

Scene III

The following passage appears in the draft between
'JULIA. All right. [*Goes out.*]'
and
'DYADIN. I hear that Mrs. Helen Serebryakov' (*p. 207.*):

ZHELTUKHIN [*returns to the table*]. I've an apology to make, Orlovsky. You had a school consecrated at Grebtsov on Sunday, but I couldn't come, I honestly couldn't. I couldn't get away all day. I thank you with all my heart, my dear friend. [*Holds out his hand.*]

ORLOVSKY. What for?

ZHELTUKHIN. What do you mean, 'what for'?

> 'Scatter the seed for a harvest of kindliness,
> Reason and goodness—and Russia will gratefully
> Offer her thanks.'[1]

ORLOVSKY. Well, there you are. You don't really think I built the school, do you, old man? That really is——

Scene V

At the beginning of the scene (p. 209) the draft has the following passage which has been excluded from the final version:

VOYNITSKY. So you say you're very fond of the Wood-Demon, Orlovsky. All right, I agree. He's a splendid, likeable person.

JULIA. Good afternoon, Theo. [*They kiss.*]

THEODORE. Hallo there. Best birthday wishes.

VOYNITSKY. I like the Wood-Demon very much. He's such a generous, fair-minded person——

ZHELTUKHIN. You mean Khrushchov, the Wood-Demon? Yes indeed! He's a straightforward, honest, happy-go-lucky fellow. But you know—he's a friend of mine and I'm very fond of him, yet there are times when I just can't stand him. There's something about him, er, I can't put it into words, but it's something repulsive. If you look at him when he's standing sideways on to you, you'll find he has a strange sort of expression on his face, a mixture of a satyr and Mephistopheles. Anyway, you know what I mean.

VOYNITSKY. Yes, I do.

Scene VI

The passage on p. 212, from
'SONYA. Marvellous! You lucky man'
to
'VOYNITSKY. Where did you get hold of that stuff?'
appears in expanded form in the draft as follows:

SONYA. You lucky man! It's all right for people with lots of money. You can just get up and go.

DYADIN. Excuse me, mademoiselle. I will permit myself to paraphrase your felicitous idea as follows. It's all right for those who don't grudge their money. Not all millionaires lead a gay life and not all beggars are bored. The man who's on top of the world is the man who doesn't mind spending his money.

SONYA. But what if you haven't any money at all?

[1] This quotation from Nekrasov's poem *To the Sowers* was later incorporated in Act Four—see p. 262.

DYADIN. It would be interesting to have a bird's eye view of this table. Such a charming floral arrangement, a combination of grace, beauty, profound erudition, distinc——

THEODORE [*interrupting*]. What a charming way to talk, dammit. And you speak as if someone was running a carpenter's plane along your back. Why don't you save your breath to cool your porridge?

SEREBRYAKOV [*eating*]. 'Save your breath to cool your porridge.' In connexion with this saying a trifling episode comes to mind. A certain professor, whom I consider it unnecessary to name, once invited me to lunch at his house when I was in St. Petersburg. On the appointed day I drove over to his country villa and incidentally ran across the late Sergey Mikhaylovich Solovyov[1] there. We got there early and our host, hoping to entertain us, began talking about the phenomenon of social outcasts in early Russian history. He went on talking for a long time and completely wore us out. It looked as if he'd never be finished. When the pie was served Mr. Solovyov took a piece and said, 'Save your breath to cool your pie.' He said it quite automatically of course, without any malice, but our host took umbrage and stopped talking. It was all rather awkward.

MRS. VOYNITSKY [*with a loud laugh*]. So I should imagine.

SEREBRYAKOV. Afterwards we laughed a lot about it.

VOYNITSKY [*aside*]. Yes, very funny. [*Pause.*]

SONYA. You know, Godfather, we've been bored stiff here all winter while you've been away.

ORLOVSKY. It's your own fault. Why don't you ever go and see your neighbours?

SONYA. I do go to Julia's sometimes, but I don't visit the others, thank you very much! God forbid. I prefer boredom to your neighbours.

ORLOVSKY. Why?

SONYA. Oh, spare me the neighbours! There's not a single normal person among them, they're all museum pieces. Populists in embroidered blouses, doctors on the council welfare service who resemble Bazarov——[2]

ORLOVSKY. You're talking rubbish.

SONYA. Followers of Tolstoy who, when they visit anybody, make a point of going in through the kitchen by the servants' entrance—no, thank you very much, you can count me out. I got sick and tired of such poseurs in the town.

ORLOVSKY. You have a very lively imagination. I suppose you don't ever write articles for the newspapers?

---

[1] The historian (1820–79).
[2] The 'nihilist' Bazarov is the central character in Turgenev's novel *Fathers and Children* (1862).

VOYNITSKY. She writes a diary. A thing this size! All possible problems have been solved there.

ORLOVSKY. You ought to fall in love and get married, my dear.

VOYNITSKY. Oh, have a heart.

(b) Act Three

Scene II

Instead of the exchange (p. 238)
'THEODORE. But if I was ever crazy enough to.'
to
'THEODORE. Let's have some champagne.'
the draft has:

VOYNITSKY. He wants everything all cut and dried.

ORLOVSKY. She's a splendid little girl.

THEODORE. She drifts around more dead than alive from one room to another and she doesn't fit in anywhere. She's in love with the Wood-Demon.

VOYNITSKY. Well, she's bitten off rather more than she can chew, I can tell you.

THEODORE. Why? He's a very nice fellow.

ORLOVSKY. Then may God help them. When people are happy one should make them even happier. We ought to give the Wood-Demon some kind of present. Why don't you send him a couple of horses, Theo, eh?

THEODORE. Remind me to when we get home. I'll give him a couple of horses and a gun too perhaps. [*Stretches himself.*] Phew! I say, everyone, how about some champagne, eh?

Scene III

Instead of the passage (pp. 239-40)
'HELEN. Why are you telling me what to do?'
to
'VOYNITSKY.What sickly, wishy-washy stuff!'
the draft has:

HELEN. Get thee behind me, Satan! [*Goes out.*]

VOYNITSKY. I think I shall soon find myself despising that woman. She's as bashful as a young girl, but she lays down the law like an old parish clerk who's a model of all the virtues. If you're fed up with living, then go into the wilderness or join a convent, or go away and die in the last resort, but why make fools of people and why try to pass off something which is downright criminal as a piece of virtue? Isn't it criminal to cripple one's youth, isn't it——?

Scene VII

After

'THEODORE. You must only think of me' (*p. 243*), *the draft has, in place of the rest of Scene VII, the following much shorter passage:*

[*Goes out through the door, right.*]

HELEN. What did he just say? What has he done? He's on about windows again. The wretched man embarrasses me. I'm frightened of him, and Sonya feels so pure she can't even talk to me. [*Cries.*] If only I could get away from this dump—get out into the fields and go on walking day and night, seeing nothing, hearing nothing and thinking nothing. [*Moves off towards the door, left, but seeing* ZHELTUKHIN *and* JULIA *advancing to meet her, goes out through the centre door.*]

Scene IX

After SEREBRYAKOV's *speech* (*p. 245*) *ending* 'got stuck on some strange planet.' *the draft has the following passage, which has been excluded from* The Wood-Demon *or, in part, used in the final version of Act Four:*

ZHELTUKHIN. That's exactly how I feel too. The only ones among us who lead a happy life are money-grubbing peasants and heroes from Shchedrin.[1] And I wouldn't be the least bit surprised if you and I were to die of starvation or, or—well, anyway——

ORLOVSKY. It all depends on your point of view. You may well be right. But I interpret your mood as follows, Alexander. Before you actually retired and got stuck here you were happy and contented with yourself and other people, you weren't aware of your old age or your illnesses. But when you got stuck here against your will, everything was turned inside out. You don't like people, you don't like yourself. You don't like the way things are done here and then there are your illnesses and your age. And this of course is why you're bound to feel at odds with your own self.

SEREBRYAKOV. Yes, that's what I do feel.

ORLOVSKY. And when you're at odds with yourself you can't help yourself with words or tears or ideas of various kinds. You know, old man, I lived just like young Theodore till I was forty. I went in for drinking bouts and splashing money about. And when it came to the fair sex, well, I was no slouch there either. The other day I said to him, 'Theo, tell me honestly, how many women have you made unhappy in your life?' He thought a bit and said, 'I don't remember. About sixty or seventy maybe. One can't remember everything.'

---

[1] M. Ye. Saltykov (1826–89), the leading Russian satirist who wrote under the pen-name 'Shchedrin' and is often referred to as 'Saltykov-Shchedrin'.

Well, there were just as many in my case. But something suddenly came over me at the age of forty, old boy. I felt depressed and out of things, found myself crying, couldn't look people in the eye, was actually on the point of shooting myself. In fact I felt terribly mixed up inside, and that was that. What was I to do? I tried everything—reading, work, travel—but it was no good. Well now, old boy, I suppose you're going to ask what saved me. The merest trifle. I once went to see an old pal of mine who's not with us any longer, Prince Dmitry Pavlovich. We had dinner, hors d'œuvres and all that, and instead of a nap afterwards we laid on some target practice outside. There were masses of people there—people of our own class, peasants, huntsmen and our friend Vadolya. You know, I felt absolutely miserable, my God I did! I couldn't stand it. I suddenly burst into tears, staggered and bellowed across the yard at the top of my voice, 'Good people, my friends, forgive me in the name of Christ!' And all at once I began to feel kind, pure and warm inside. And ever since then, old boy, I've been the happiest man in these parts. You ought to try it yourself.

SEREBRYAKOV. You're an intelligent man, Orlovsky. Now why should I ask people's forgiveness? [*To* ZHELTUKHIN.] Tell me please, aren't there any ordinary, normal people here? The whole lot of them are thinkers and philosophers—people who've been out too long in the sun and started all this theorizing. One of them suddenly ups and asks everyone to forgive him while another raves about forests or something. You know, you people ought to do a job of work. This won't do. We need a bit of action.

Scene XI

Instead of the passage (p. 250)
'SEREBRYAKOV. Let him move into the village'
to
'ORLOVSKY. Oh come, come, my friends——'
the draft has:

SEREBRYAKOV. If he's needed here let him move into the village or into a cottage in the grounds, or I'll move out myself. But I can't stay here with him. I'll go away and leave this place.

HELEN. I'm tired out, Alexander. If you really consider him unhinged, then please don't answer his insults. Otherwise this feud will go on for ever. Please.

ZHELTUKHIN. I have been an involuntary witness of this disagreeable scene, so I ask permission to intervene. I'll have a talk to him today and get him to apologize.

HELEN. No, there's no need for an apology. I'm afraid of these apologies.

Scene XII

Instead of the passage (p. 251)
'ORLOVSKY. We can talk about it later, Michael'
to
'KHRUSHCHOV. Hark at the universal uncle!'
the draft has:

ZHELTUKHIN. We can talk about it later, Michael. Professor Serebryakov isn't in the mood——

KHRUSHCHOV [*to* SEREBRYAKOV]. You're turning your back on me. If you think I'm wrong in imploring you to do this so abjectly, then prove it to me. You're a professor, a distinguished scholar, you're erudite and you've lived a long life. I shall believe you. So go on and prove it.

SEREBRYAKOV. Come on, Orlovsky, we'll never hear the end of this.

ZHELTUKHIN. Excuse me, but this is naïve of you actually, Michael. What right have we to stick our noses in other people's business? [*Makes a gesture of resignation and goes out.*]

KHRUSHCHOV [*blocking* SEREBRYAKOV's *way*]. Or what about this? Just wait a bit, Professor, and in three months' time I'll get some money and buy it off you myself. Mr. Orlovsky, Godfather, won't you at least stick up for me? Do just put in a word.

ORLOVSKY. You are a funny fellow. What on earth can I say?

KHRUSHCHOV [*flaring up*]. Exactly. What can you say? So just keep quiet and don't do anything about it. Oh, Godfather . . .

The passage continues: 'There are plenty of easy-going people in this world' *etc. as on p. 251.*

(c) *Act Four*

The forest and the house by the mill which DYADIN *rents from* KHRUSHCHOV.

Scene I

[SIMON, *carrying buckets,* JULIA *and—later—*DYADIN.]

JULIA [*coming in*]. Good afternoon, Simon. Nice to see you. Is Mr. Dyadin in?

SIMON. Yes. He's asleep in the mill.

JULIA. Would you mind going and waking him up?

SIMON. Not at all, miss. [*Goes out.*]

JULIA [*alone, sits down on the bench beneath the window and gives a deep sigh*]. Ah me! Some of them sleep, others enjoy themselves, but I'm run off my feet all day long. I think I'm the unhappiest person in the world. Ah well, no peace for the wicked. [*Gives an even deeper sigh.*] Heavens, how can anyone be as stupid as old Waffles? I was driving past his barn just now and a little black pig came out of the door. If other people's pigs start getting at his corn sacks it will just serve him right.

[DYADIN *comes in, putting on a frock-coat.*]

DYADIN. Is that you, Julia? Excuse my *déshabillé*, I've just had a little after-lunch snooze in the arms of Morpheus.

JULIA. How are you?

DYADIN. I'm sorry I can't ask you in, the house isn't tidy and all that. Would you care to come over to the mill?

JULIA. No, I'm all right here for a bit. Now tell me, what do you think you're playing at? Why are you getting my sacks all mixed up?

DYADIN. What do you mean?

JULIA. We bought our sacks from Kharlamov and they're marked with a K, but you sent us some with a V on or something.

DYADIN. *Tout cela n'est qu'un* waste of time. Not important at all. I can change them for you any time.

JULIA. Then please do change them. Now let me tell you why I came. Leo and the professor have decided on an outing and they'd like to picnic at your mill this afternoon.

DYADIN. Delighted.

JULIA. I've come on ahead. The others will be here soon. Could you have a table brought out—oh, and a samovar too of course? And would you mind telling Simon to get the picnic baskets out of my carriage?

DYADIN. Very well. [*Pause.*] Well, what news? How are things?

JULIA. Bad. You've no idea how much work we have on hand. You know the professor and Sonya are staying with us now, don't you? They've been afraid to live in their own house since George's suicide. The professor's a broken man, he's grown terribly thin and he just will not speak a single word. Sonya, poor thing, cries all the time and you can't get a word out of her either. It wasn't too bad during the day, but at night they all used to sit huddled in one room till dawn, terrified of George's ghost appearing in the dark.

DYADIN. That's all superstition. I don't believe in ghosts, don't even believe in spiritualism. Do they ever mention Helen?

JULIA. Of course they do. She ran away from Theo, you know. Had you heard?

DYADIN. Yes, it's a subject worthy of the brush of Ayvazovsky. She just ran away. [*Laughs.*] What a business! All the servants in the yard and the rustics in the village saw him take her off in his carriage. He held on to her—she'd fainted right away—with one hand and used the other to whip along his horses as fast as he could like Phoebus Apollo bowling along in his chariot. And he only got about four miles. He stopped not far from here, in the Count's woods near Yakunchikha's hut, and went to get Helen a drink of water. While he was fetching the water she made herself scarce, and when he came back she'd vanished into thin air. He looked round, but couldn't find her anywhere. And what do you think next? He was so angry at the failure of this amorous exploit that he smashed all the doors and windows of Yakunchikha's hut, broke the crockery and gave Yakunchikha herself a couple of black eyes. Charming!

JULIA. Then she disappeared completely. No one knows where she is. Perhaps she's gone away or perhaps she was desperate enough to—well, you know, all sorts of things do happen.

DYADIN. God is merciful, my dear. It'll be all right. You know, I must confess I feel blissfully happy. I really do. I'm so utterly happy that, without having recourse to high-flown phrases, I can express it in the words of a certain poet——

JULIA [*interrupting*]. But why is that?

DYADIN. I don't know. Or rather, I haven't the right to put it in words. I haven't the right, though I'm burning with impatience.

[KHRUSHCHOV *comes in carrying a portfolio and a drawing-case.*]

Scene II

[*The above and* KHRUSHCHOV.]

KHRUSHCHOV. Hey! Is anyone here? Simon!

DYADIN. Try looking this way.

KHRUSHCHOV. Ah! Good afternoon, Julia.

JULIA. Good afternoon.

KHRUSHCHOV. Well, I came out here to do some work again, Dyadin. I don't feel like staying at home. Would you ask them to put my table under this tree the way I had it yesterday, and tell them to have two lamps ready? It's getting dark.

DYADIN [*moving off*]. Very well. At your service, sir.

KHRUSHCHOV. You have my box of drawing-pins over there and a saucer. Mind you don't forget them.

DYADIN. I know. [*Goes out.*]

KHRUSHCHOV. How are you, Julia?

JULIA. Oh, all right. [*Pause.*] Michael, how much are those perimid poplars in your nurseries?

KHRUSHCHOV. Not perimid poplars, Julia. Pyramid.

JULIA. That's just what I said. Perimid. How much are they?

KHRUSHCHOV. Come and choose some. We'll see about it then, we shan't quarrel about terms. The Serebryakovs are staying with you, aren't they?

JULIA. Yes.

KHRUSHCHOV. I suppose dear brother Leo stays at home all day now? He must be pleased.

JULIA. Yes, he stays at home. Spends his time with Sonya, goes for walks with her, recites poetry to her. It does make her feel a bit better. And he does recite marvellously, you know. Yesterday he even made me cry.

[DYADIN *and* SIMON *come in carrying a small table.*]

Scene III

[*The above,* DYADIN *and* SIMON.]

DYADIN. Michael, you do know how to look after yourself. You've picked a splendid place to work, it's an oasis. Yes, I mean it. Can't you see yourself surrounded by palm trees? Julia's a gentle doe, you're a lion and I'm a tiger.

KHRUSHCHOV. You're a very nice fellow, Dyadin, but why carry on like this? These sugary words, all this foot-scraping and shoulder-twitching—anyone who saw you for the first time wouldn't take you for a human being at all. Devil only knows what he'd think of you. Pity.

DYADIN. It must be the way I'm made. Such are the dictates of destiny.

KHRUSHCHOV. There you go again, 'dictates of destiny'. Can't you drop that stuff? [*Pins a chart on the table.*] I think I'll stay the night here.

DYADIN. Delighted. You're in a bad temper, but I feel inexpressibly cheerful as though there was a dear little bird inside me singing a song.

KHRUSHCHOV. Well, make the most of it. [*Pause.*] You feel cheerful, but I feel gloomier than ever. You may have a dear little bird inside you. I haven't. Quite the opposite in fact. I'm bored and fed up. I feel guilty somehow, I even feel ready to cry. It's been just one damn thing after another. Shimansky's sold his wood for timber for a start. Mr. Orlovsky is dangerously ill—he has typhus and, I think, pneumonia as well. That makes two things. Helen's run away from that ass Theodore and no one knows where she's got to. That makes three. She may have gone off somewhere, thrown herself in the river or poisoned herself, you can take your pick. But the main point, more terrible and exasperating than anything else, is that I'm unable to stay at home on my own and I'm afraid of the dark. I wanted to tell you yesterday, but couldn't—couldn't pluck up the courage. I say, did you know George's diary turned up after his death and makes it plain as a pikestaff that we're all vile slanderers? Mr. Orlovsky got hold of it first. I went over there to treat him and read it a dozen times.

JULIA. Yes, we read it too.

KHRUSHCHOV. George's affair with Helen has the entire district buzzing like a hive, but it turns out the whole story was a filthy pack of lies. I believed it and joined in the general mud-slinging—the hatred, the contempt, the insults. Why don't you say anything? Why don't you speak?

DYADIN. Michael, I swear to you by God Almighty. As I hope for salvation, Helen is a wonderful woman. She's gentle, honourable, straight-dealing, sensitive, and her nature is such that my ignorance does not permit me to put it in words. [*Cries.*] Believe me, Michael. When I received the honour of becoming more closely acquainted with her, my heart was filled with inexpressible bliss. It is pleasant to see physical beauty near one, but it is much pleasanter to see spiritual beauty.

KHRUSHCHOV. I first heard it from your brother, Julia. He was the first to tell me. He's not a very nice person, you know. Why did he mislead me?

[JULIA *cries.*]

DYADIN. Do stop, Michael, please. Sh! Don't be insulting.

KHRUSHCHOV. What's the point of crying? Tears won't make any difference.

DYADIN [*to* JULIA]. Let's go down to the mill, my children, and leave our bad-tempered friend to his work while we take a constitutional. Come on then, and you do your work, Michael.

KHRUSHCHOV [*alone, mixes some paint in a saucer*]. One night I saw him press his face against her hand. There's a detailed description of that night in his diary, how I came in and what I said. He quotes my words, calls me a narrow-minded fool. [*Pause.*] This colour's too dark. Must get it lighter. Then he blames Sonya for loving me. May you rest in peace, poor fellow, but your powers of observation let you down there. She never loved me. My hand's trembling like a drunkard's. Now I've made a blot. [*Scrapes the paper with a knife.*] Even supposing there was something in it, there's no point in thinking about that now. It began and ended in foolishness. And it was really a good thing I did burn her photograph yesterday. Oh dear, otherwise—. [SIMON *and some workmen bring in a large table.*] What are you doing? What's that for?

SIMON. Mr. Dyadin's orders. The ladies and gentlemen from the Zheltu-khin estate are going to have tea here.

KHRUSHCHOV. Oh, that's just wonderful. So there's no point in my bothering about my work any more. I can't work today anyway. I'll pack up and go home.

[ZHELTUKHIN *comes in with* SONYA *on his arm.*]

Scene IV

[KHRUSHCHOV, ZHELTUKHIN *and* SONYA.]

ZHELTUKHIN [*sings*]. 'Against my will to these sad shores
                            An unknown force has drawn me.'

KHRUSHCHOV. Who's there? Oh! [*Hurriedly puts his drawing materials away in their case.*]

ZHELTUKHIN. I know I'm in danger of annoying you, Sonya, but I've one last question. Do you remember lunching with us on my birthday? I proposed a toast and you laughed at me, didn't you?

SONYA. I wasn't laughing at anything in particular, I assure you. You shouldn't hold these grudges, Leonid.

ZHELTUKHIN [*catching sight of* KHRUSHCHOV]. Oh, are you here as well? Hallo.

KHRUSHCHOV. Hallo.

ZHELTUKHIN. Working? Splendid. Where's Waffles?

KHRUSHCHOV. Over there at the mill.

ZHELTUKHIN. I must go and call him. [*Goes off singing.*] 'Against my will to these sad shores—' [*Goes out.*]

SONYA. Good afternoon.

KHRUSHCHOV. Good afternoon. [*Pause.*]

SONYA. What are you drawing?

KHRUSHCHOV. Oh, nothing of any interest.

SONYA. Is it a plan?

KHRUSHCHOV. No, it's a map of the forests in our district. I made it. [*Pause.*] The green colouring shows the forests of our grandfathers' time and before. Light green shows where they've been felled during the last twenty-five years —oh, and the blue shows where they're still standing. There's three times as much light green as blue. [*Pause.*] I want to make a map of the whole province. [*Pause.*] Well, what about you? Are you happy? I'm sorry, that's a silly question. I didn't put it the right way.

SONYA. This is no time to think about happiness.

KHRUSHCHOV. Then what should we think about?

SONYA. That's what caused the tragedy, thinking too much about happiness.

KHRUSHCHOV [*dropping a saucer*]. I'm sorry.

SONYA. It's an ill wind that blows nobody any good. Misfortune has taught me a lesson and now I understand where I went wrong. One must forget one's own happiness and think only of the happiness of others every minute of the day. Life should be an act of constant self-sacrifice.

KHRUSHCHOV. Oh yes, of course.

SONYA. One should work for the common good, help the poor and try to like people one dislikes.

KHRUSHCHOV. Oh, yes, and marry Zheltukhin. [*Pause.*] Mrs. Voynitsky's son shot himself, but she's still burbling away about women's emancipation and chasing contradictions in her wretched pamphlets. You've had a ghastly experience, but you only pander to your own vanity with thoughts about some kind of sacrifices. Everyone's heartless. You are. And so am I. All the wrong things are done and everything's going to rack and ruin. I'm just off——

SONYA. Somebody's coming and I'm crying.

[*Enter* JULIA, DYADIN *and* ZHELTUKHIN.]

Scene V

[*The above,* JULIA, DYADIN, ZHELTUKHIN *and—later—*SEREBRYAKOV.]

SEREBRYAKOV [*off stage*]. Hallo there! Where are you all?

SONYA [*shouts*]. We're here, Father. [*Quickly wipes her eyes.*]

DYADIN. They're bringing the samovar. Charming. [*He and* JULIA *attend to the table.*]

[SEREBRYAKOV *comes in with the* MAID, *who is carrying a basket.*]

SONYA. This way, Father.

SEREBRYAKOV. All right, I can see you.

ZHELTUKHIN [*in a loud voice*]. Ladies and gentlemen, I declare the meeting open. The cordial has been uncorked.

KHRUSHCHOV [*to* SEREBRYAKOV]. Let's forget what happened, shall we? [*Holds out his hand.*] I ask your forgiveness—in all sincerity, believe me.

SEREBRYAKOV. Thank you, only too delighted. And you must forgive me. When I tried to think about that business next day and remembered what we said, I was horrified at my own cruelty. Let's be friends. [*Takes him by the arm and goes to the table.*]

DYADIN. I am indeed happy, sir, that you have come here and haven't turned up your nose at my oasis. Most delightful! Most!

SEREBRYAKOV. I thank you. Please sit down, everyone. [*Sits down at the table.*] It's really lovely out here, an oasis indeed. Well, come on, all of you, don't let the conversation flag. In our position it's best to keep talking. Our misfortunes are our own fault, so let's put up with them and keep smiling. I'm putting a better face on things than all of you just because I am the most to blame.

JULIA. I say, I'm not giving you any sugar, you must all have jam with your tea.

DYADIN [*attending to the table*]. I'm delighted, delighted. Some cordial for you. Have one of these doughnuts, Michael.

SEREBRYAKOV. Recently, Michael, I've had so much to put up with and I've thought so many thoughts, I could probably write a whole treatise on the art of living for the benefit of posterity. I repeat—the day after that incident

I was horrified at my own cruelty. I was amazed at how little I'd seen and understood up to then, while all the time I'd done so much talking. It seems strange to me now that I never talked to my wife about anything except my gout and my rights, but all that seemed to be the proper thing then. [*In a trembling, tearful voice.*] Of course I'm to blame. I say nothing about George, who, if——

ZHELTUKHIN. We did promise not to discuss that today, you know. You've forgotten our agreement.

DYADIN. Let bygones be bygones. With God's mercy it will turn out all right. Away with melancholy! We'll have a nice glass of tea and jam with rusks and a bit of lemon. We'll drink some nice cordial and Leo will recite some nice poetry.

SEREBRYAKOV. Yes, Leonid, do recite something, please. You do it so well.

ZHELTUKHIN. But what am I to recite?

SEREBRYAKOV. Something with a neutral flavour. You know any amount of these things.

ZHELTUKHIN. Very well then. [*After some thought.*] Here's a bit of Nekrasov.[1] This is rather up your street, Michael.

'The Green Noise is humming, coming,
The Green Noise, the Noise of spring!
There is the gentle rustle of cherry orchards in their milky dresses
And the merry rustle of pinewoods bathed in warm sunshine.
Near by the new green leaves of the pale lime-tree
And of the white birch with its green tresses,
Lisp a new song.
The little reed rustles,
The cheerful maple rustles.
They rustle in a new way,
In a new way to greet the spring.
The Green Noise is humming, coming,
The Green Noise, the noise of spring!
Savage thoughts grow mild,
The knife falls from the hand
And all the time in wood and meadow
I hear the same song:
"Love while you can,
Suffer while you can,
Say farewell when your time comes.
And may God be your judge." '

[SONYA *gives a start.*]

[1] N. A. Nekrasov (1821–78), the well-known poet and editor. This is the second part of his poem *The Green Spring*, 1862.

DYADIN. What made you jump like that?

SONYA. I heard someone shout.

DYADIN. It's some of the locals catching crayfish in the river. [*Pause.*]

SEREBRYAKOV. And how is Ivan Orlovsky?

KHRUSHCHOV. Not too well. [*Pause.*]

ZHELTUKHIN. Let's not be so downhearted, everybody. Didn't we agree to spend the evening as if nothing had happened? Yet there's a feeling of tension somehow.

DYADIN. I revere scholarship, sir, and even have a family feeling for it to some extent. My brother Gregory's wife's brother, a Mr. Konstantin Novosyolov— you may possibly know him—held a master's degree in foreign literature.

SEREBRYAKOV. I don't know him, but I know of him. [*Pause.*]

SONYA. It's exactly a fortnight since Uncle George died.

ZHELTUKHIN. Remember our agreement, Sonya.

SONYA. I'm sorry.

[JULIA *cries.*]

ZHELTUKHIN. What's the matter with you?

JULIA. It was Leo who brought it up in the first place.

ZHELTUKHIN. What did I say?

JULIA. It was you! You!

KHRUSHCHOV. Don't let's speak about it, Julia, I beg you.

SEREBRYAKOV. Come along, do cheer up. It's against doctor's orders, but I'm going to have a little wine. Why not follow my example, everybody? [*Drinks. Pause.*]

ZHELTUKHIN. All the same, there is a feeling of tension somehow. Come on, everybody, let's make the party go with a swing. [*Bangs his knife.*] Silence for the master of ceremonies!

SEREBRYAKOV. There's one curious psychological detail—what strange desires one sometimes has! At the moment for some reason I'm very keen to be terribly insulted or to fall ill. Obviously my soul—that is, my psychological make-up—needs to react strongly. [*Pause.*]

[KHRUSHCHOV *jumps up abruptly.*]

ZHELTUKHIN. What's the matter with you?

KHRUSHCHOV [*excitedly*]. Good God, this is more than flesh and blood can stand! I feel unbearably depressed. I'm a complete swine, a filthy slanderer. At a difficult moment of her life she held out both her hands to me and offered me her friendship. And I told her to leave me alone, said I despised her friendship. Like a complete slave I joined in with everyone else in insulting her, slandering her and hating her. You should all despise me, hate me, point your fingers at me——

DYADIN [*in alarm*]. Don't go on like this, Michael. [*Kisses him.*] Please don't.

KHRUSHCHOV. Serebyrakov, for twenty-five years you've been a professor and done academic work while I've planted trees, but what's the point of these things, and who gets anything out of them, if we're heartless and destroy each other instead of being merciful? Did you and I do anything to save George? Where's your wife whom I have foully insulted? Where's your peace of mind, where is my love? Everything's gone to rack and ruin, it's all going to blazes. Everything's ruined! All right, run round, shout——

[SONYA *and* JULIA *shriek. General consternation.*]

DYADIN. Take it easy, Michael old boy.

KHRUSHCHOV. It's terrible, just terrible! We're all done for.

JULIA [*embraces and kisses him*]. Michael, darling Michael——

SEREBRYAKOV. Give him some water.

KHRUSHCHOV. You must excuse this outburst, please. I couldn't stand the tension. I feel much better now. Let's sit down. Don't worry.

ZHELTUKHIN. All right. That will do.

DYADIN. You know, everything's going to turn out all right, I swear it. I've no right to put it in words, but—but in fact God is merciful.

SONYA. It's getting dark, Father. Let's go home.

SEREBRYAKOV. No, dear, let's stay on a bit longer. I can't bear the sight of our home. The later we get there the better.

DYADIN. My minions will be bringing the lamps in a moment, and the darkness will disperse.

[THEODORE *comes in.*]

Scene VI

[*The above and* THEODORE.]

SONYA [*terrified*]. Uncle George!

KHRUSHCHOV. Where? Where? Oh, this is too much!

SONYA. He's over there!

KHRUSHCHOV. Where? That's Theodore. I say, everyone, the best thing is to keep quiet and not answer any questions. Don't pay any attention, Professor.

SEREBRYAKOV. I have nothing against him. Let him do what he likes.

KHRUSHCHOV. Sh!

THEODORE [*approaching the table*]. Hallo there! In the bosom of nature, eh?

How very amusing! Hallo, Wood-Demon. [*Pause.*] Why won't you shake hands with me?

KHRUSHCHOV [*holding out his hand*]. All right then.

THEODORE [*sits down*]. Is that you, Professor? I didn't recognize you, I'm sorry. All the best to you. [*Pause.*] It's a stroke of luck finding you here—you and I must have a serious talk. We're all friends here, so I presume I can put my cards on the table. The point is that sooner or later I'm going to find Helen and marry her. So give me a divorce. I'll pay you as much as you like.

KHRUSHCHOV. Sh! [*Pause.*]

THEODORE. Actually, I suppose I have rather overstepped the mark. Let's discuss the thing peaceably. [*To* ZHELTUKHIN.] I really came to see you, Leo. I heard you were at the picnic and so, as you see, I've come rushing here to see my dear friend. Why wasn't I invited?

ZHELTUKHIN. What a strange thing to ask. How on earth could I invite you? In the first place I didn't know where you were, and in the second place we only had the idea—decided to have a picnic, that is—late in the afternoon. There wasn't any time and what's more, relations are such that——

THEODORE. Don't beat about the bush. You just tell me why you didn't invite me.

ZHELTUKHIN. Oh, let's drop the subject.

THEODORE. H'm! I've experienced pretty well everything in this life, my friend, except that I've never been up in a balloon or fought a duel with you. Balloons are a pretty remote prospect, but we could have a duel right now.

KHRUSHCHOV [*shouts*]. Get out of here, you offensive brute!

THEODORE. Take it easy, will you? I'm the nervous type.

KHRUSHCHOV. You just clear out!

THEODORE. Let's discuss the thing peaceably. This means I'll fight you first, Leo, and then you, Mr. Wood-Demon.

KHRUSHCHOV. Oh really, this is too absurd. Don't worry, Julia and Sonya, just stay where you are. [*To* THEODORE.] Come with me, we'll have a talk.

[TRIFON¹ *comes in quickly, goes up to the house and knocks on a window.*]

Scene VII

[*The above and* TRIFON.]

DYADIN. Who's there? What's up?

TRIFON. Is that you, Mr. Dyadin?

DYADIN. What do you want?

¹ 'TRIFON, a horse-trainer on Orlovsky's staff'—item, excluded from the final version, in the list of CHARACTERS at the beginning of the draft version.

TRIFON. Good evening. A very good appetite to your honour. Lyudmila Ivanovna sends her regards and asks me to tell you that Mr. Orlovsky passed away at dinner time today.

THEODORE. Father! My God! Who's that? Is it you, Trifon?

TRIFON. Yes, it's me, sir.

THEODORE. When did it happen?

TRIFON. At dinner time today.

THEODORE. My God, and I haven't been home for a whole week. Father— poor fellow. Come on, Trifon, hurry up. [*In a dejected voice.*] Excuse me, everybody. I had something else to say to you, Professor, I can't remember what. You were a friend of Father's—. No, that wasn't it. Oh, I know—your wife is a saint. [*Goes out with* TRIFON.]

JULIA [*after a pause*]. Poor Godfather!

SEREBRYAKOV. Let's go home, Sonya, it's time we were off.

SONYA. No, I just can't bring myself to, Father. Let's all sit here. This was our last trial. Now there won't be any more. No more. [*Pause.*]

KHRUSHCHOV. What a feeling of depression and tension! Say something, Leo. Sing or recite, can't you? Recite!

ZHELTUKHIN. What am I to recite? [*Pause.*]

[*In the house someone plays Lensky's aria from* Eugene Onegin *on the piano.*]

KHRUSHCHOV. What's that? Can that be Helen playing? Where has she come from? Where is she? And what does this mean?

DYADIN. Charming! She's staying with me, she's in my house. She escaped here from the Count's woods and she's been living in my house for the last fortnight. What a blissful existence, Michael! [*Shouts.*] Please come here, Helen, you've been in hiding quite long enough.

SONYA. So it was Helen playing the piano. That's her favourite aria.

KHRUSHCHOV. Where is she? [*Runs into the house.*]

SEREBRYAKOV. This makes no sense to me. None whatever.

DYADIN [*rubbing his hands*]. She'll be here in a second. Our misfortunes have ended.

[HELEN *comes out of the house followed by* KHRUSHCHOV.]

Scene VIII
[*The above,* HELEN *and* KHRUSHCHOV.]

KHRUSHCHOV. Say just one word, just a single word! Don't be as cruel as I was. Do forgive me, please!

HELEN. I heard everything. [*Kisses his head.*] That will do. We'll be friends. Hallo, Alexander. Hallo, Sonya.

SONYA [*throws herself on* HELEN's *neck*]. Helen!

[*They all surround* HELEN *and kisses are exchanged.*]

HELEN. These last few days I've been suffering and thinking just as much as you have. You've forgiven me and I've forgiven you, and we've all become better people. Let's start living in a new way as if this was the spring-time of our lives. Shall we go home? I've been so bored.

DYADIN. Charming!

KHRUSHCHOV. I say, what a relief! There's nothing to worry about. I feel so happy.

SEREBRYAKOV. Come on, Helen. Now I won't mind our house any more.

HELEN. I was sitting behind the window and heard everything. You poor people! All right, let's hurry up and go. [*Takes her husband by the arm.*] Let's forget the past. Shall we go to our place, Michael?

KHRUSHCHOV. At your service.

JULIA [*to her brother*]. You should apologize as well.

ZHELTUKHIN. I can't stand all this sickly sentimentality. Let's go home, it's damp here. [*Coughs.*]

HELEN. Sonya's laughing. Laugh away, my dear, I'm laughing too. And that's the way it should be. Come on, Alexander. [*Goes out with her husband.*]

ZHELTUKHIN. Come on then. [*Goes out with his sister and shouts off stage.*] Drive up, Aleksey!

KHRUSHCHOV [*to* SONYA]. When people have a clear conscience it shows in their eyes. I see everything now. Come on, my dear. [*Embraces her and follows her out.*]

DYADIN [*alone*]. I say, they've all forgotten me! Charming! Quite charming!

CURTAIN

APPENDIX II

UNCLE VANYA

1. The composition
2. The text
3. Some further comments by Chekhov
4. Contemporary reception

1. THE COMPOSITION

The conversion of *The Wood-Demon* into *Uncle Vanya* is scantily documented and it is not known with certainty when Chekhov carried out the work. That he intended further revision of *The Wood-Demon* in early 1890 is shown by his letter to F. A. Kumanin of 8 January of that year, quoted above (p. 280).

The first mention of *Uncle Vanya* occurs in a letter from Chekhov to Suvorin of 2 December 1896 referring to his collected *Plays*, a volume which was to appear in 1897: 'Two long plays remain to be set up in type: *The Seagull*, which you know, and *Uncle Vanya*, which nobody on this earth knows.'

It has generally been assumed that Chekhov converted *The Wood-Demon* into *Uncle Vanya* in 1896. However, it must be admitted that the documentary evidence is in favour of an earlier date, March–April 1890 (see N. I. Gitovich, *Letopis zhizni i tvorchestva A. P. Chekhova*, pp. 282–3). This evidence includes the following items:

(i) Writing to S. P. Diaghilev (the famous impresario, 1872–1929) on 20 December 1901 Chekhov said, in reply to a query, that he could only give an approximate answer about the dates of composition of his various works. He went on to give 1890 as the year when *Uncle Vanya* was written.

(ii) Writing to Maxim Gorky on 3 December 1898 Chekhov stated: 'Uncle Vanya was written long, long ago.'

(iii) A letter from the actor P. M. Svobodin to Chekhov, dated 9 April 1890, shows that Chekhov then intended to submit an unnamed play—by inference possibly *Uncle Vanya*—for production (see Gitovich, op. cit. p. 260).

2. THE TEXT

The translation is based on the version in the second (1902) edition of vol. vii of Chekhov's *Collected Works* as reproduced in *Works*, 1944–51, xi. The 1902 edition of *Uncle Vanya* was preceded by:

(a) A. P. Chekhov, *Plays*, St. Petersburg, 1897—a collection of Chekhov's plays, among which *Uncle Vanya* appeared for the first time in print, and (*b*) the first (1901) edition of vol. vii of the *Collected Works*, in which the play appears in the same form as in the second edition.

In revising (*a*) for the first edition of his *Collected Works* Chekhov made four minor alterations of which two are so small that they do not affect the translation. The other two are as follows:

(i) *In Act One the following exchange between Voynitsky and Astrov, which appeared in the 1897 edition, was excluded from the 1901 edition:*

VOYNITSKY [*to* HELEN]. He doesn't even eat meat.

ASTROV. Yes, I regard the killing of animals as a sin.

This exchange appeared after:

'ASTROV. However, [*drinks*] I must go' (*p. 28*).

(ii) *In Act Four of the 1897 edition the passage (p. 63) from*

'ASTROV. Yes, you'd better leave.'

to

'HELEN. I'm taking this pencil to remember you by' *appeared a few lines later—after Helen's remark (p. 63)*: 'I think someone's coming. [*Both listen.*]'

In the 1903 *Collected Works*, vol. xiv, a misprint crept into Act Four of *Uncle Vanya* and was repeated in some later Russian editions of Chekhov, hence appearing in some translations into English, including those of Stark Young and Elisaveta Fen. The incorrect version affects a phrase in Astrov's speech (p. 62) and is даже очень красиво ('it's quite beautiful in fact') instead of the correct text, даже осень красива ('it's even beautiful in autumn').

3. SOME FURTHER COMMENTS BY CHEKHOV

An exchange of comments of importance for the interpretation of *Uncle Vanya* occurs in Chekhov's correspondence with his future wife, the actress Olga Knipper, who was to appear in the Moscow Art Theatre production of *Uncle Vanya*. Knipper wrote:

'I'm rather put out by a comment of Stanislavsky's on Astrov's last scene with Helen. He wants Astrov to address Helen as an ardent lover seizing on his passion as a drowning man clutches at a straw. In my opinion if that were the case Helen would follow him and wouldn't have the courage to answer, "You really are absurd". On the contrary, he speaks to her in the most cynical way, even somehow making fun of his own cynicism. Am I right or not?' (*Letter of O. L. Knipper to Chekhov, 26 Sept. 1899.*)

As so often on later occasions, Chekhov here found Stanislavsky's interpretation over-flamboyant. He replied that Stanislavsky's interpretation as described by Knipper was 'wrong, quite wrong. Astrov is attracted by Helen, she captivates him with her beauty, but in the last act he already knows there's nothing doing. He knows Helen's going away for good so far as he's concerned and in this scene he speaks to her in the same tone as when he talks about the heat in Africa. And he kisses her quite casually [просто так] because he has nothing better to do. If Astrov makes a great to-do about this scene the entire mood of Act Four, which is quiet and apathetic, will be ruined.' (*Letter to O. L. Knipper, 30 Sept. 1899.*)

In the spring of 1900 the Moscow Art Theatre went on tour to Sevastopol and Yalta, where Chekhov was able to see a public performance of *Uncle Vanya* for the first time. He expressed himself satisfied with the production. On this occasion he gave Stanislavsky a hint on the interpretation of Astrov. 'He whistles. . . . Uncle Vanya weeps, but Astrov whistles.' Stanislavsky regarded the hint as cryptic, but took it as an indication that Astrov's lack of faith in people had reached the point of cynicism. (*'Chekhov i teatr', p. 259.*)

According to the evidence of A. M. Fyodorov, Chekhov found the Moscow Art Theatre production of *Uncle Vanya* more satisfactory than the production of any of his other plays by the same theatre. Fyodorov quotes Chekhov as saying: 'In the Art Theatre only *Uncle Vanya* seemed really to belong to me. Especially Act Two.' (*Ibid., p. 367.*)

Chekhov's objections to an over-flamboyant interpretation of *Uncle Vanya* are further attested in the reminiscences of the actress N. S. Butova. She states that in Act Three of a performance of *Uncle Vanya* witnessed by Chekhov, the actress playing Sonya went down on her knees and kissed her father's hand after saying the words (p. 56): 'Do show some understanding, Father.'

' "That was wrong. That's not what drama is," said Chekhov. "The whole meaning and drama of a person is inside, not in outward manifestations. There was drama in Sonya's life before that moment and there will be drama after it, but that's a mere accident, a continuation of the revolver shot. And the shot isn't drama either, but an accident." ' (Butova's reminiscences, quoted in *Chekhov i teatr*, p. 346. The incident in question actually precedes the shot and does not follow it as Chekhov is made to suggest.)

In early 1903 a correspondent, who was appearing in a provincial performance of *Uncle Vanya*, wrote to consult Chekhov on the interpretation of Helen. Was she the type of an average decent, intelligent woman or an apathetic, lazy woman incapable of thinking or even of loving? Chekhov replied: 'It may be that Helen does seem incapable of thinking or even of loving, but that wasn't my idea when I wrote *Uncle Vanya*.' (*Letter to M. F. Pobedimskaya, 5 Feb. 1903.*)

Several early references by Chekhov to *Uncle Vanya* suggest that he was extremely dissatisfied with the play. For instance: 'Oh why did I write plays instead of stories? I've wasted my themes, utterly wasted them, scandalously and unproductively.' (*Letter to A. S. Suvorin, 7 Dec. 1896.*)

4. CONTEMPORARY RECEPTION

When *Uncle Vanya* first appeared in print in 1897 it had never been performed on the stage, but soon after publication provincial Russian companies (in Odessa, Kiev, Nizhny-Novgorod, Saratov, Tiflis etc.) began to stage it. Though it was moderately successful, Chekhov's attitude to it remained sceptical. For instance, when writing of the success which his plays in general had enjoyed in the winter of 1897–8, he added that 'even' *Uncle Vanya* had been successful. (*Letter to A. S. Suvorin, 13 Mar. 1898*). 'My *Uncle Vanya* is running all over the provinces and is everywhere successful. . . . I wasn't counting on this play at all.' (*Letter to M. P. Chekhov, 26 Oct. 1898.*)

The play received favourable reviews in the provinces and a performance in Nizhny-Novgorod, witnessed by Maxim Gorky, led to an exchange of letters between Gorky and Chekhov. In these Gorky appears as the effusive enthusiast. ('I saw *Uncle Vanya* the other day and cried like a peasant woman . . . came home deafened and crushed by your play . . . trembled with admiration for your gifts.' *Letter of Maxim Gorky to Chekhov, late Nov. 1898, 'Chekhov i teatr', p. 359.*) Chekhov, who disliked this kind of gush, made a polite but typically dry reply in which he said: 'In general I am indifferent to my plays, have long been out of touch with the theatre and no longer want to write for the stage.' (*Letter to Maxim Gorky, 3 Dec. 1898.*) But this only provoked an even more grandiloquent reply from Gorky.

After the successful performance in October 1898 of Chekhov's *Seagull* in the opening season of the newly-founded Moscow Art Theatre, the same theatre applied for his permission to stage *Uncle Vanya* in the following season. At first Chekhov had to turn down the proposal since he had already accepted an offer by the long-established Moscow Maly Theatre to produce *Uncle Vanya*.

However, before *Uncle Vanya* could be passed for production in the Maly Theatre it had to obtain the approval of the official Theatrical and Literary Committee. This committee considered all plays submitted for performance in the state theatres, of which the Maly Theatre was one, and on 8 April 1899 it considered *Uncle Vanya*. In a lengthy report, which might have been compiled by a conclave of Professor Serebryakovs, the play was referred back to the author so that certain cuts and alterations could be made, after which it might be submitted again.

Among the committee's objections were the following (taken from the full Russian text of the report, printed in *Chekhov i teatr*, pp. 433–4):

(i) 'Nothing prepares us for the powerful explosion of passion which takes place during the conversation with Helen.' (The reference is to the scene between Astrov and Helen in Act Three. With reference to the 'explosion of passion' the words 'On whose part?' were added by Chekhov himself in the margin of the committee's report.)

(ii) The change in Uncle Vanya's attitude to Professor Serebryakov was said to be too abrupt and unmotivated. 'He [Vanya] may well have been irritated by the old man's high-handed attitude during the family council [in Act Three], but that is no reason for pursuing him with revolver shots and chasing after him in such an irresponsible way.'

(iii) Helen was said to be too 'dreary' a character to interest the audience.

(iv) The play was said to contain long, boring passages, for example the speeches of Sonya and Astrov about the woods in Act One, Astrov's theories of forestry in general, and Sonya's 'meditations' at the end of the play.

As the result of this report Chekhov withdrew the play from the Maly Theatre and gave permission for its production by the Moscow Art Theatre. He did this not only out of pique with the committee, but also because he was inclined to think that the newly founded Art Theatre would produce the play more effectively. He was present at some early rehearsals and commented: 'I've seen two acts in rehearsal, it's going splendidly.' (*Letter to G. M. Chekhov, 2 June 1899*.) In September Chekhov went to Yalta and the first performance of *Uncle Vanya* by the Moscow Art Theatre took place on 26 October 1899 in his absence. The performance met with only qualified success, as is shown by the first reviews (quoted in *Works*, 1944–51, xi, pp. 582–3) and confirmed by the comments of the two co-founders of the Art Theatre, V. I. Nemirovich-Danchenko and Konstantin Stanislavsky.

'After *Uncle Vanya* we went to a restaurant, as we always did after a first night, to wait for the morning papers and we weren't exactly in the best of moods. . . . The public in general did not immediately understand *Uncle Vanya, The Three Sisters* or *The Cherry Orchard*. Each of these three plays began to achieve real success only with its second season and thereafter maintained itself uninterruptedly.' (V. I. Nemirovich-Danchenko, as quoted in *Works*, 1944–51, xi, p. 583.)

'It's hard to believe now that after the first night of *Uncle Vanya* a whole crowd of us met in a restaurant and wept because everyone thought that the performance had been a flop. But time did its work. The performance was accepted, maintained itself in the repertoire for more than twenty years and became famous in Russia, Europe and America.' (K. S. Stanislavsky, quoted in *Chekhov i teatr*, p. 258.)

Among the comments by other contemporaries on *Uncle Vanya*, those of Leo Tolstoy, as recorded in a letter to Chekhov from A. A. Sanin, are perhaps the most amusing.

' "Where is the drama?" shouted the great genius. "What does it consist of? The play just doesn't move anywhere. . . ." Later on Tolstoy pronounced that Astrov and Uncle Vanya were a couple of idle wastrels. . . . He also said that "Astrov should take an Alyona and Uncle Vanya a Matryona" [i.e. Astrov and Uncle Vanya should get themselves a peasant girl apiece] and that "it is wrong and immoral of them to pester Helen Serebryakov".' (*Chekhov i teatr*, pp. 482–3.)

APPENDIX III

THREE SISTERS

1. The composition
2. The text
3. Some further comments by Chekhov
4. Contemporary reception

1. THE COMPOSITION

The first mention of *Three Sisters* occurs in a letter of 24 November 1899 from Chekhov to V. I. Nemirovich-Danchenko: 'I'm not writing a play. I have a theme—three sisters—but I shan't get down to the play till I've finished the short stories which have been on my conscience for a long time. The next season will go by without any play of mine, that's already decided.' In response to Nemirovich-Danchenko's requests to provide a new play for the Moscow Art Theatre to perform in the 1900-1 season, Chekhov replied: 'You want a new play for the next season without fail. But what if it doesn't get written? I'll have a try of course, but I don't guarantee anything and I'm making no promises.' (*Letter of 3 Dec. 1899*.) Again: 'Am I writing a new play? It is nibbling at the bait, but I haven't started writing, I don't feel like it and I must wait till the warm weather anyway.' (*Letter to V. I. Nemirovich-Danchenko, 10 March 1900*.)

It is in a letter to the actor A. L. Vishnevsky of 5 August 1900 that Chekhov first speaks of having settled down to serious work on *Three Sisters*: 'I'm writing a play, I've already written a lot, but I can't judge it till I'm in Moscow. Perhaps what I'm producing isn't a play, but boring Crimean rubbish. It's called *Three Sisters* (as you already know) and I've done a part for you in it, that of second master at a high school, the husband of one of the sisters. You will wear a schoolmaster's regulation frock-coat and have a medal on a ribbon round your neck. If the play turns out no good for this season I'll alter it next season.'

At about the same time the play was promised to the Moscow Art Theatre for the beginning of the 1900-1 season. On 9 August 1900 Chekhov wrote to Olga Knipper that he had received a visit from Stanislavsky and had promised to finish the play by September at the latest. The evidence of Chekhov's letters shows that he was making slow progress, interrupted by illness. On 13 September 1900 Chekhov wrote two letters (to V. F. Komissarzhevskaya and Yu. O. Gryunberg) in which he speaks of the play without enthusiasm, saying that he cannot now predict when it will be finished.

However, on 16 October Chekhov was able to report that he had finished the play. 'Can you believe it—I've written a play. As it won't be put on now, but only next season, I haven't made a fair copy of it. Let it lie around for a bit. Writing *Three Sisters* was terribly hard. There are three heroines after all, and each one has to be cut according to her own pattern. And all three are general's daughters! The action takes place in a provincial town such as Perm in an army (artillery) milieu.' (*Letter to Maxim Gorky.*)

On 23 October 1900 Chekhov reached Moscow from Yalta, bringing a copy of *Three Sisters* with him. The play was copied and read out to the Moscow Art Theatre company.

The text with which the Moscow Art Theatre first became acquainted presumably corresponded closely to that described below as the 'Yalta manuscript'. Chekhov did not regard it as the final version. 'It's being read in the Art Theatre now (one copy, there aren't any more). Next I'll take it and make another fair copy. Then we'll have several copies run off, of which I'll hasten to send you one.' (*Letter to V. F. Komissarzhevskaya, 13 Nov. 1900.*)

Chekhov was present at some early rehearsals of *Three Sisters* at the Art Theatre, but on 11 December he left Moscow for Nice. By this time he was already half-way through revising the text and he mentions further work on this in letters from Nice. 'I'm copying out the play and puzzling how I came to write the thing and what I wrote it for. . . . I'll send Act Three to Nemirovich tomorrow and Act Four the day after or both of them together. I've changed one or two things in Act Three and added one or two things, but not very much.' (*Letter to O. L. Knipper, 15 Dec. 1900.*)

In another letter to Olga Knipper (who was to take the part of Masha in *Three Sisters*) of 17 December, Chekhov wrote: 'I sent Act Three of the play to Moscow yesterday and I'll send Act Four tomorrow. I've changed only a few things in Act Three, but I've made some big changes in Act Four. I've added a lot of lines to your part.' In late December, Nemirovich-Danchenko visited Chekhov at Nice and returned to Moscow with a few further corrections to the text of the play.

Chekhov sent letters to Moscow making a number of further minor alterations to the text of *Three Sisters*. But the information about these contained in Stanislavsky's memoirs is incorrect in two particulars. It is not true that the remark 'Balzac got married in Berdichev' (see p. 100) was inserted as the result of a note sent from Nice by Chekhov. Nor is it true that a long speech by Andrew Prozorov was struck out of Act Four, again on instructions received from Chekhov at Nice, or the words 'a wife is a wife' substituted for it. (See A. R. Vladimirskaya, 'Iz tvorcheskoy istorii *Tryokh sestyor*', *Literaturnoye nasledstvo: Chekhov*, p. 14.)

Chekhov was still abroad when the first performance of *Three Sisters* took place on the stage of the Moscow Art Theatre on 31 January 1901.

2. THE TEXT

(a) The 'Moscow manuscript'

Like the other plays in this volume, *Three Sisters* is translated from *Works*, 1944–51, xi. However, in the case of *Three Sisters* the authenticity of this text has been called in question at certain points on the basis of a newly discovered manuscript of the play in Chekhov's handwriting.

This manuscript, which was found in November 1953 in a safe at the Museum of the Moscow Art Theatre, was not available to the editors of *Works*, 1944–51. It provided the evidence on which certain minor changes were introduced into the text of the twelve-volume Russian collection of Chekhov's *Works* published by Goslitizdat in 1955–6. But the new evidence was not fully exploited there, as shown in the article which forms the basis of the comments on the text here—A. R. Vladimirskaya, op. cit. above.

The evidence of the newly discovered manuscript does not involve changes of great substance in the English translation, since the passages in the previously accepted text challenged by the new version are few in number and are all brief. However, with an author of Chekhov's importance a translator cannot afford to ignore any detail, however small, and this new evidence has been taken into account here.

For convenience the manuscript which contains the new evidence and which Vladimirskaya calls the 'fair copy' (беловая рукопись) is termed here the 'Moscow manuscript' to distinguish it from the 'Yalta manuscript' which will be discussed later.

(b) The first published texts

In order to understand the impact of the new evidence provided by the 'Moscow manuscript', it is first necessary to take into account the four editions of the play published during Chekhov's lifetime:

(i) The 'Magazine Edition'—the version published in no. 2 of the magazine *Russkaya mysl* for 1901.

(ii) The 'Separate Edition'— i.e. that brought out as a separate volume in May 1901 by A. F. Marks, the first publisher of Chekhov's *Collected Works*.

(iii) The 'Supplement Edition'—published by Marks in March 1902, as a supplement to vol. vii of the first edition of Chekhov's *Collected Works*. (In addition to *Three Sisters* this volume also contains Chekhov's short plays *The Jubilee* and *The Wedding*.)

(iv) The '*Collected Works* Edition'—in vol. vii of the *Collected Works*, second edition, published by Marks (1902).

Of the above, the '*Collected Works* Edition' is virtually identical with the

'Supplement Edition' and has provided the text reproduced in later Russian editions (down to and including *Works*, 1944–51). It is this text which is now called in question at certain points by the 'Moscow manuscript'.

The Moscow manuscript (or at least a recension corresponding closely to it) provided the text from which the 'Magazine Edition' was set up. The type-setting or sub-editing was done carelessly and Chekhov, who was abroad, did not have an opportunity to correct the proofs. Only the 'Supplement Edition' and the '*Collected Works* Edition' had the benefit of Chekhov's final revision and proof-correction.

This might be thought sufficient guarantee of the authenticity of the text of those editions, were it not for the fact that certain errors in the text of the 'Magazine Edition' apparently escaped Chekhov's notice during the process of revision and slipped through into the 'Separate Edition', the 'Supplement Edition' and the '*Collected Works* Edition'—and hence into succeeding post-humous editions. The point here is that Chekhov apparently based his final revision of the text not, as might have been wiser, on his 'Moscow manuscript' (which was no longer in his possession) but on the garbled version of that manuscript published by *Russkaya mysl*. He could no doubt have obtained the 'Moscow manuscript' from the Moscow Art Theatre if he had asked for it, but since it was his normal custom to destroy his manuscripts after they had appeared in print, this possibility may not even have occurred to him.

Wherever the '*Collected Works* Edition' reproduces the wording of the 'Maga-zine Edition' at a point where the text of the latter diverges from the text of the 'Moscow manuscript', there is a possibility that Chekhov may through over-sight have perpetuated a textual aberration originated by a type-setter or sub-editor on the staff of *Russkaya mysl*. This presupposition is strengthened if (where these conditions are met) the 'Moscow manuscript' appears to offer a better reading than the '*Collected Works* Edition'.

(c) *Emendations introduced on the basis of the 'Moscow manuscript'*

On the basis of collation with the 'Moscow manuscript', Vladimirskaya proposes a number of corrections to the text of *Three Sisters* (including some already adopted in the 12-volume edition of 1955–6). These are given on pp. 16–17 of her article to which reference was made above, and although she does not pretend to have produced a definitive text, feeling that there is still room for further research, it has been decided to incorporate some of her corrections in the present translation, which is otherwise based on the text as printed in *Works*, 1944–51. The following table shows the points at which Vladimirskaya's proposed corrections affect the text of our translation.

Page	Translation of emended text reads	Translation based on text in 'Works', 1944–51, would read
73	You're wearing white	You're wearing a white dress
76	Well, I shan't for one	I shan't for one
81	It may even seem terribly sinful	It may even seem sinful
88	Don't talk to me about love, Nicholas dear	Don't talk to me about love, Nicholas
89	MASHA. I'm going to have a little glass of something	MASHA [*banging her fork on her plate*]. I'm going to have a little glass of something
96	bringing you home every evening	bringing you home every day
107	You're the only one who really understands me, no one else can	You're the only one who can understand me
112	Either I don't understand you or	Either I don't understand or
112	We must get this straight once and for all, Olga	We must get this straight, Olga
114	Masha for instance plays the piano beautifully	In my opinion Masha plays the piano beautifully
119	it's only a matter of doing one's duty	it's a matter of doing one's duty
120	Oh, you are funny, Olga	Oh, you are silly, Olga
122	My wife, in case you want to know, is a fine, decent, straightforward, honourable woman	My wife is a fine, decent, straightforward, honourable woman
127	I was actually crying for joy	I was actually crying from joy and serenity

Three emendations proposed by Vladimirskaya have not been accepted here. The first of these would involve the insertion of the following sentence in Chebutykin's speech on p. 113 (after 'I've forgotten it all, it's all gone'):

My head's empty, my feelings have withered away.

The second emendation would involve the insertion of the following exchange after Tuzenbakh's speech beginning 'I couldn't sleep' and ending 'Say something' (p. 132):

IRINA. But what? What? Everything around us is so mysterious, the old trees stand there so silently. [*Lays her head on his chest.*]

TUZENBAKH. Say something to me.

The third emendation would involve a slight expansion of a sentence ('It looks so hideous in the evening') spoken by Natasha on p. 137:

It's so frightening in the evening and looks so hideous.

(*d*) The 'Yalta manuscript'

Shortly after the discovery of the 'Moscow manuscript' another manuscript with an important bearing on the composition of *Three Sisters* came to light in the Museum of the Moscow Art Theatre. This is the copy passed for performance by the censor and marked 'Admitted for performance, St. Petersburg, 18 December 1900'. This manuscript had been on show in the Museum without anyone realizing that it represented the earliest extant recension of *Three Sisters*, though the date should have made this obvious (Act Four of the 'Moscow manuscript' did not reach the Moscow Art Theatre from Chekhov at Nice until 24 December 1900).

The censor's copy turned out on examination to be a typed copy of the (lost) manuscript of *Three Sisters* completed by Chekhov at Yalta. Now that this document, here termed the 'Yalta manuscript', is available, Chekhov's revision of *Three Sisters* can be studied in two stages:

(i) by comparison of the 'Yalta manuscript' with the 'Moscow manuscript', both of which are published in *Literaturnoye nasledstvo: Chekhov*, pp. 19–86.

(ii) by comparison of the 'Moscow manuscript' with the '*Collected Works* Edition' of 1902—with the qualification that in certain instances (as shown above) a superior reading can arguably be restored in the *Collected Works* text from the 'Moscow manuscript'.

(e) Some features of Chekhov's revision

Though (i) and (ii) above represent the two main stages in the final revision of the play, it must be realized that no big changes were involved at either stage. The changes affect style and tone rather than content and are best thought of as a pre-final and final polish given by Chekhov to *Three Sisters*. They do not involve fundamental revision, such as was found for instance in the process whereby the first extant draft of *The Wood-Demon* was converted into *Uncle Vanya*.

Stage One (comparison of the 'Yalta manuscript' with the 'Moscow manuscript').

The changes of greatest interest are those in which Chekhov modifies the conception of individual characters.

Masha, who had been conceived as a 'slightly vulgar . . . "daughter of the regiment" ' (Vladimirskaya), is made a little gentler, though her dialogue retains its 'racy' touch. Examples of this toning down are her (repeated) use of the quotation 'A green oak by a curving shore . . .' ('Moscow manuscript') in places where she had formerly quoted a bluff dispatch sent by General Suvorov, which may be rendered:

'Thanks to us and God on high,
The army's taken Turtukay.'

Similarly (see p. 98) Masha's comment on Chebutykin, 'He looks so pompous sitting there', had a more 'dashing' flavour in the 'Yalta manuscript': 'Good for the doctor!'

Chebutykin. The detail about the woman patient at Zasyp for whose death he was responsible (see p. 113), absent in the 'Yalta manuscript', is introduced in the 'Moscow manuscript'. Likewise the sentence (see p. 115) 'No doubt it was your mother's if you say so' is introduced in the 'Moscow manuscript', as is (see p. 129) 'The baron's a nice enough fellow, but one baron more or less in the world—what does that matter? Let them get on with it.' The force of the latter two changes was to emphasize the element of cynicism in Chebutykin's character.

Vershinin. The changes serve to emphasize his lack of interest in what anyone else has to say. Thus, in answer to Tuzenbakh's speech on p. 82, he replies with the casual 'Yes, yes of course' ('Moscow manuscript') in place of the former 'That may well be so' ('Yalta manuscript').

Solyony. Amongst other details enriching the characterization of Solyony in the 'Moscow manuscript' is the comparison between him and Lermontov (as on p. 104), which does not appear in the 'Yalta manuscript'.

Stage Two (comparison of the 'Moscow manuscript' with the *Collected Works* text).

The most important changes here affect the last scene of the play and were accepted by Chekhov after consultation with Stanislavsky and Olga Knipper on the basis of rehearsals for the first performance.

(i) Masha's last speech (p. 138) was considerably shortened. After the words 'to begin our lives again' it continues as follows in the 'Moscow manuscript':

> I shall go on living, my dears. One must live. [*Looks upwards.*] There are migrating birds up there, they fly past every spring and autumn, they've been doing it for thousands of years and they don't know why. But they fly on and they'll go on flying for ages and ages, for many thousand years, until in the end God reveals his mysteries to them.

This was cut by Chekhov at the request of Olga Knipper. 'Does it matter if I make a cut in my last speech? If I find it difficult to say?' (*Letter of O. L. Knipper to Chekhov, quoted by A. R. Vladimirskaya, op. cit., p. 13.*)

(ii) The following item was cut out of the stage directions at the end of the play (after '*The music becomes fainter and fainter*', p. 139):

> There is a noise at the back of the stage. A crowd can be seen watching as the body of the baron, who has been killed in the duel, is carried past.

Stanislavsky found these instructions awkward. 'The sisters have got to see the corpse. What are they to do?' he asked. Chekhov replied: 'You're absolutely right. Tuzenbakh's body must not be shown at all. I felt that as I was writing it and told you so, as you may remember.' (*Letter to K. S. Stanislavsky, 15 Jan. 1901.*)

Other changes in the final stage of revision involved the exclusion from the final version of a number of short passages, among which were the following:

Act One

(i) *The following sentence, which occurred in Chebutykin's speech on p. 77 after the words* 'I can't say I greatly care either', *was excluded from the final version:*

I've done nothing all my life and I've never had time to do anything all my life.

(ii) *The following passage was excluded from Masha's speech on p. 82:*

You come from Moscow and you can understand. I can't bear the way people dress here and it offends me to look at the smart girls of the neighbourhood.

(iii) *The following passage previously took the place of the words* '[*Laughs.*] You know much too much' *in Vershinin's speech on p. 84:*

In the first place I doubt whether any of us holds a sufficiently correct viewpoint to distinguish what is superfluous from what is really necessary. And in the second place

Act Two

(i) *The following passage, which followed Andrew's words on p. 94,* 'You might come and fetch some papers tomorrow morning', *was excluded from the final version:*

You see, I remember everything. I haven't forgotten anything. I have a colossal memory and in my place any other man with such a memory would long ago have stretched himself over the whole of Moscow, like your rope. Or across all Russia.

(ii) *The following words, which followed Tuzenbakh's* 'Now how can I convince you?' *on p. 99, were excluded from the final version:*

We live our present lives and the future will live its life—one exactly like ours, no better and no worse.

Act Three

The following words, which appeared in Andrew's speech on p. 122 after 'sheer childishness', *were excluded from the final version:*

or rather the childish tricks of old maids. Old maids don't like their sisters-in-law and never have liked them, that's always the case.

Act Four

The following words, which appeared in Masha's speech on p. 128, after 'I feel I'm going to burst', *were excluded from the final version:*

The person I'd like to give a jolly good hiding to is brother Andrew. The stuffed dummy!

3. SOME FURTHER COMMENTS BY CHEKHOV

'I've absolutely got to be present at rehearsals, I've got to! Four responsible female parts, four educated young women, I can't leave them to Stanislavsky, with all my respect for his talent and understanding. I must at least look in on rehearsals.' (*Letter to O. L. Knipper, 15 Sept. 1900.*)

'Do describe at least one rehearsal of *Three Sisters* for me. Doesn't anything need adding or taking away? Are you yourself acting well, darling? But do watch out. Don't look sad in any of the acts. You can look angry, that's all right, but not sad. People who have been unhappy for a long time, and grown used to it, don't get beyond whistling and are often wrapped up in their thoughts. So mind you look thoughtful fairly often on the stage during the conversations. Do you understand?' (*Letter to O. L. Knipper, 2 Jan. 1901.* Olga Knipper took the part of Masha in *Three Sisters.*)

'You write that Natasha, making her rounds of the house at night in Act Three, puts out the lights and looks for burglars under the furniture. But it seems better to me for her to cross the stage in a straight line without looking at anybody or anything, like Lady Macbeth, with a candle. It's quicker and more frightening that way.' (*Letter to K. S. Stanislavsky, 2 Jan. 1901.*)

'Here are the answers to your questions:

'1. Irina doesn't know that Tuzenbakh is going off to fight a duel, but she guesses that some awkward incident occurred on the previous day, an incident which may have important consequences, and bad ones at that. But when a woman guesses something she always says, "I knew it, I knew it."

'2. Chebutykin sings only the words, "Be so good as to accept one of these dates." These words come from an operetta which was once performed at the Hermitage Theatre. I don't remember what it was called.... Chebutykin mustn't sing anything else, otherwise his exit will take too long.

'3. Solyony really does think he looks like Lermontov, but of course he doesn't, it's absurd even to think of such a thing.... He must be made up to look like Lermontov. He has a great resemblance to Lermontov, but this resemblance exists only in Solyony's mind.' (*Letter to I. A. Tikhomirov, 14 Jan. 1901.*)

'That the end [of *Three Sisters*] reminds people of *Uncle Vanya* doesn't matter very much. After all, *Uncle Vanya* is my play and not someone else's, and it's thought to be a good thing to remind people of oneself in one's works.' (*Letter to K. S. Stanislavsky, 15 Jan. 1901.*)

'Of course you can come in wearing a service-dress jacket in Act Three, that's quite all right. But why do you come into the drawing-room wearing a fur coat in Act Two? Why? Perhaps it does come off all right actually. Have it your own way.' (*Letter to A. L. Vishnevsky, 17 Jan. 1901.* Vishnevsky took the part of Vershinin in *Three Sisters.*)

'Of course Act Three must be conducted quietly on the stage to convey the feeling that people are tired and want to go to bed. What's all the noise about? The points at which the bells are to be rung off stage are shown.' (*Letter to O. L. Knipper, 17 Jan. 1901*. She had written to Chekhov on 11 Jan. 1901, saying that Stanislavsky, in a rehearsal of Act Three, had 'created a terrible hulla-baloo on the stage with everyone running in all directions and getting excited'.)

'Well, how's *Three Sisters* getting on? Judging by your letters you're all talking outrageous rubbish. "Noise in Act Three"—but why noise? The noise is only in the distance—off stage, a vague, muffled noise—while everyone here on stage is tired and almost asleep. If you spoil Act Three you'll ruin the play and I shall be hissed off the stage in my old age. . . . Vershinin pronounces his "Ti tum ti tum ti" as a question, and you appear to answer it. And you think this is such an interesting trick that you bring out your "tum tum tum" as if it amuses you. . . . You bring out your "tum tum tum" and give a laugh, but not a loud one, just a little one. And while you're about it you don't want to look as you do in *Uncle Vanya* [Olga Knipper took the part of Sonya in *Uncle Vanya*]. You should look younger and more lively. Remember, you're fond of laughing and easily get angry. Anyway, I put my trust in you, darling, you're a good actress.

'I said at the time that it would be awkward to carry Tuzenbakh's body past on your stage, but Stanislavsky insisted he couldn't do without the body. I wrote to him that the body wasn't to be carried past. I don't know whether he got my letter.' (*Letter to O. L. Knipper, 20 Jan. 1901.*)

'Darling, Masha's repentance in Act Three isn't repentance at all, it's no more than a frank talk. Act it with feeling, but not desperately. Don't shout, put in some smiles, even if only a few, and in general act it so that people feel the tiredness of the night. And make them feel you're cleverer than your sisters —or at least that you think yourself cleverer. About your "tum tum tum", do as you like. You're a clever girl.' (*Letter to O. L. Knipper, 21 Jan. 1901.*)

'I've heard from you that you're leading Irina round by the arm in Act Three. Why is that? Is that consistent with your mood? You mustn't leave the sofa. Don't you think Irina can get about on her own?' (*Letter to O. L. Knipper, 24 Jan. 1901.*)

Stanislavsky on the first reading of *Three Sisters* to the Art Theatre Company: Chekhov 'was convinced that he had written a gay comedy, but at the reading everyone took the play for a drama and wept as they listened to it. This made Chekhov think the play was incomprehensible and had failed.' (*K. S. Stanislavsky, 'My Life in Art', quoted in 'Chekhov i teatr', p. 260.*)

Stanislavsky also reports that Chekhov, on going abroad in the middle of rehearsals by the Moscow Art Theatre for the first performance of *Three Sisters*, left behind 'his military representative, a charming colonel whose job it was to see that no slackness occurred in matters relating to the uniform, bearing or habits of the officers, their way of life etc. Chekhov paid particular attention to this aspect of things, as rumours were going round the city that he had written a play directed against the army—which had aroused indignation, bad feeling and forebodings of alarm in military circles. In actual fact Chekhov was particularly anxious not to offend the services. He was well disposed to them, especially to the army, which according to him was carrying out a cultural mission by going into outlandish parts of the country and taking with it . . . knowledge, art, happiness and joy.' (*Ibid., pp. 261–2.*)

'On returning from abroad Chekhov was satisfied with us [with the Moscow Art Theatre performance of *Three Sisters*] and only regretted that during the fire [in Act Three] we didn't make the right noise when ringing the bell and sounding the military alarm signals. He was continually worrying about this and complaining to us about it. We invited him to rehearse the noises of the fire himself and put all the stage apparatus at his disposal for this purpose. Chekhov delightedly took on the part of producer and went at the thing with great enthusiasm, giving us a whole list of stuff which was supposed to be got ready for his noise experiment. I wasn't at the rehearsal as I was afraid of being in his way, so I don't know what happened there.' (*Ibid., p. 262.*)

'The thing which struck him most, a thing he couldn't put up with until his dying day, was the fact that his *Three Sisters*—and after that *The Cherry Orchard* —was a tragedy [тяжёлая драма—literally "a heavy drama"] of Russian life. He was sincerely convinced that it was a gay comedy, almost a farce. I can't remember that he ever defended any of his opinions with such feeling as he defended this one at the meeting where he first heard such a comment on his play.' (*K. S. Stanislavsky, 'A. P. Chekhov v Khudozhestvennom teatre', quoted in 'Chekhov i teatr', p. 278.*)

'Amidst all his agitation about the fate of his play, he was no little worried about how the alarm would be sounded in Act Three during the fire off stage. He wanted to demonstrate to us the jarring noise made by a provincial [church] bell. On every convenient occasion he would come up to one or other of us and try by use of his hands, by rhythm and gesticulation to impress on us the mood evoked by this soul-searing provincial fire alarm.

'He attended almost all the rehearsals of his play, but only occasionally expressed his own opinion, cautiously and almost timidly. There was only one thing he insisted on with particular emphasis. Both in *Uncle Vanya* and here he was afraid of provincial life being exaggerated and caricatured, of his officers being turned into the usual heel-clickers with jingling spurs. He wanted us to play simple, charming, decent people, dressed in worn, untheatrical uniforms, without any theatrical military mannerisms, throwing back of shoulders, bluff remarks and the like.

' "That sort of thing just doesn't happen, you know," he insisted with great heat. "The services have changed, you know. They've become more cultured, you know, and many of them are even beginning to understand that their peacetime job is to carry culture with them into out-of-the-way spots." ' (*Idem, in 'Chekhov i teatr', p. 279.*)

'In the Theatre the play [*Three Sisters*] was read out in his presence. He was struggling with indignation and several times repeated, "But what I wrote was a farce." Later on he would say the same thing about *The Cherry Orchard* too, that he'd written a farce. In the last resort we just couldn't understand why he called the play a farce, when even in the manuscript *Three Sisters* was called a "drama". All the same, fifteen or twenty years afterwards various irresponsible persons would juggle with this phrase of his.

'When the actors, after listening to the play, asked him for explanations, he usually answered with phrases which explained very little—"Andrew wears slippers in this scene", or "Here he simply whistles." He was more exact on these matters in his letters.' (*V. I. Nemirovich-Danchenko, 'Iz proshlogo', quoted in 'Chekhov i teatr', p. 309.*)

'The first performances of *Three Sisters* took place . . . in Chekhov's absence. He first began to see the play at rehearsals in the autumn of the following season and made observations so detailed that he actually produced the scene of the fire in Act Three personally. He was dissatisfied with me [in the part of Andrew Prozorov] at rehearsals, sent for me and went through Andrew's part with me in great detail with pauses and explanations. . . . He insisted that Andrew should be very excited in his last speech. "He must be just about ready to threaten the audience with his fists!" ' (*V. V. Luzhsky, from his recollections, quoted in 'Chekhov i teatr', p. 353.*)

4. CONTEMPORARY RECEPTION

'At the end of Act One . . . there were about a dozen shattering curtain-calls. After Act Two there was one. After the Third Act only a few people timidly applauded and the actors could not appear, and after Act Four they got one very thin curtain-call. . . . It took a long time for Chekhov's art in this play to reach the theatre-goer.' (*K. S. Stanislavsky, 'My Life in Art', quoted in 'Works', 1944–51, xi, p. 593.*)

'Success? It was not as shattering as *The Seagull* had received, but in my opinion it was more valuable and significant because we, the audience, reacted with profound thoughtfulness and attention. In general the success was colossal. When you read it it seems an excellent literary work, but when it's interpreted on the stage things which had not been visible emerge brightly, in sharp relief and with merciless inevitability.' (*Letter to Chekhov from V. M. Lavrov, 1 Feb. 1901.*)

'*Three Sisters* is going splendidly, brilliantly, much better than the play itself is written. I've done a bit of producing and have exercised my author's influence on one or two of them and the play is now said to be going better than it did last season.' (*Letter from Chekhov to L. V. Sredin, 24 Sept. 1901.*)

APPENDIX IV

THE CHERRY ORCHARD

1. The composition
2. The text
3. Some further comments by Chekhov
4. Contemporary reception

1. THE COMPOSITION

(a) First intimations

According to Stanislavsky the idea of *The Cherry Orchard* first presented itself to Chekhov in vague form in 1901 during the period of rehearsals for the first performance of *Three Sisters* (see *Works*, 1944–51, xi, pp. 595–6). Letters from Chekhov to Olga Knipper shortly after the first performance of *Three Sisters* show that he intended to write a farce or comedy for the Moscow Art Theatre. 'The next play I write will definitely be funny, very funny—at least in intention.' (*Letter of 7 March 1901.*) 'There are moments when an overwhelming desire comes over me to write a four-act farce [водевиль] or comedy for the Art Theatre. And I shall write one if nothing prevents me, only I shan't deliver it to the theatre before the end of 1903.' (*Letter of 22 April 1901.*)

In view of Chekhov's later repeated insistence that *The Cherry Orchard* was a comedy or farce, it seems likely that these early intimations have some bearing on the play. The same is true of the following passage in a letter to Olga Knipper of 20 January 1902: 'The reason I haven't written to you about my forthcoming play is not that I don't trust you, as you say in your letter, but that I don't yet trust the play. It's just a faint glimmering in the brain, like the earliest moment of the dawn, and I don't yet know myself what it's like or what will come of it, and it changes its shape every day.' Similarly Chekhov wrote to Stanislavsky about an unnamed play on 1 October 1902: 'I'll be in Moscow on 15 October and I'll explain to you why my play still isn't ready. I have a subject, but so far I haven't got steam up.'

The first recorded mention of the title *The Cherry Orchard* occurs in December 1902: 'My *Cherry Orchard* will be in three acts. That's what I think, but actually I haven't yet made up my mind definitely.' (*Letter to O. L. Knipper, 24 Dec. 1902.*) References in Chekhov's letters of January and February 1903 show that he had not yet started writing the play, but that he was turning it over in his mind. Two characters, who can be equated with Mrs. Ranevsky and Varya respectively, an 'old woman' and a 'silly girl', had occurred to him.

'I wanted to do *The Cherry Orchard* in three long acts, but I may do it in four. It makes no difference to me, because the play will be just the same any-way whether it's in three or four acts.' (*Letter to O. L. Knipper, 3 Jan. 1903.*)

'With regard to the play, I can tell you the following:

'It's true that I've thought of a play and I already have a name for it (*The Cherry Orchard*, but this is a secret for the moment), and I shall probably get down to writing it no later than the end of February, if I'm well, of course.

'The central part in this play is that of an old woman [Mrs. Ranevsky], to the author's great regret!' (*Letter to V. F. Komissarzhevskaya, 27 Jan. 1903.*)

'I'm counting on getting down to the play after 20 February and I shall finish it by 20 March. It's already completed in my head. It's called *The Cherry Orchard*, it has four acts and in Act One cherry trees can be seen in bloom through the windows, the whole orchard a mass of white. And ladies in white dresses.' (*Letter to K. S. Stanislavsky, 5 Feb. 1903.*)

'I shall start writing the play on 21 February. You'll play the silly girl [Varya]. But who's going to play the old mother? Who indeed? We'll have to ask M. F. [Mariya Fyodorovna Andreyeva]' (*Letter to O. L. Knipper, 11 Feb. 1903.*)

'Your part is a complete fool of a girl. Do you want to play a silly girl [Varya]? A kind-hearted simpleton.' (*Letter to O. L. Knipper, 22 Feb. 1903.*)

(b) *First phase of writing, March–April 1903*

Chekhov started writing *The Cherry Orchard* in March 1903. 'I've laid out the paper for the play and written down the title.' (*Letter to O. L. Knipper, 1 March 1903.*) During March and the first half of April he worked on the play, breaking off in mid-April to visit Moscow and St. Petersburg.

'If the play doesn't work out the way I've planned it, you must punch my head. There's a comic part [Lopakhin] for Stanislavsky, and one for you too.' (*Letter to O. L. Knipper, 5 and 6 March 1903.*)

'Incidentally, I'm not getting on all that well with the play. One of the main parts isn't sufficiently worked out yet and is causing trouble. But I think the character will be clear by Easter and I shall be out of the wood.' (*Letter to O. L. Knipper, 18 March 1903.*)

'There will be a *Cherry Orchard* and I shall try to have as few characters as possible, that makes it more intimate.' (*Letter to O. L. Knipper, 21 March 1903.*)

'Will you [the Moscow Art Theatre] have an actress for the part of the elderly lady in *The Cherry Orchard*? If not there won't even be any play, I won't even write it.' (*Letter to O. L. Knipper, 11 April 1903.*)

'I don't very much want to write for your theatre [the Moscow Art Theatre], mainly because you haven't got an old woman. They'll start trying to foist the part of the old woman [Mrs. Ranevsky] on you, but there's another part for you and anyway you've already played an old lady in *The Seagull*.' (*Letter to O. L. Knipper, 15 April 1903.*)

'The play is coming on bit by bit, but I'm afraid I've rather lost my touch. (*Letter to O. L. Knipper, 17 April 1903.*)

(*c*) *Second phase of writing, July–October 1903*

On returning to Yalta in July 1903, Chekhov resumed work on *The Cherry Orchard*. The following quotations from his letters record progress from then to mid-October, when he sent the completed draft to the Moscow Art Theatre.

'My play isn't ready. It's moving rather sluggishly, which I put down to laziness, the marvellous weather and the difficulty of the subject. When the play is ready, or before it's ready, I'll write to you or better still send a telegram. Your part [Lopakhin] has come off quite well, I think, though actually I don't take it upon myself to judge, for I understand precious little about plays in general when I read them.' (*Letter to K. S. Stanislavsky, 28 July 1903.*)

'Now, as regards my . . . play *The Cherry Orchard*, everything's fine so far. I'm getting on with the work bit by bit. Even if I am a bit late with it, it won't matter all that much. I've reduced the décor side of the play to the minimum, no special sets will be needed and no special displays of ingenuity required.

'In Act Two of my play I've substituted an old chapel and a well for the river. It's more peaceful that way. Only in Act Two you must give me some proper green fields and a road and a sense of distance unusual on the stage.' (*Letter to V. I. Nemirovich-Danchenko, 22 Aug. 1903.*)

'My play (if I carry on working as I've worked until today) will be finished soon, don't worry. Writing Act Two was difficult, very much so, but I think it's turned out all right. I shall call the play a comedy.

'Olga [Knipper] will take the part of the mother in my play. But who's going to play the daughter aged seventeen or eighteen, a slender young girl, I don't take it upon myself to decide. Anyway, we'll see about that when the time comes.' (*Letter to V. I. Nemirovich-Danchenko, 2 Sept. 1903.*)

'Dear Mariya Petrovna, don't believe what anyone says. Not a single living soul has read my play yet. The part I've written for you [Varya] isn't that of a "prig", but of a very charming girl with whom you, or so I hope, will be quite satisfied. I've almost finished the play, but fell ill just over a week ago, started coughing and became very weak. In fact it was as if last year's business had started again. Now, i.e. today, it's warm and my health seems to have got better, but I still can't write because I have a headache. Olga [Knipper] won't bring the play with her, I'll send all four acts as soon as I have the chance to get down to it again for a whole day. It hasn't turned out as a drama, but as a comedy, in places even a farce, and I'm afraid I may get into hot water with Vladimir Ivanovich [Nemirovich-Danchenko]. Konstantin Sergeyevich [Stanislavsky] has a big part. There aren't many parts altogether.' (*Letter to M. P. Alekseyeva [Lilina], 15 Sept. 1903.*)

'My splendid little wife, I feel a bit more comfortable today. Obviously

I'm getting back to normal. I can look at my manuscript without being angry now, I'm writing already, and when I've finished I'll send you a telegram at once. The last act will be gay. Actually the whole play is gay and frivolous.' (*Letter to O. L. Knipper, 21 Sept. 1903.*)

'Act Four of my play will be thin in content compared with the other acts, but effective. The end of your part seems not bad to me. In general don't be down-hearted. Everything's fine.

'My regards to Vishnevsky, and tell him to stock up with gentleness and elegance for a part [Gayev] in my play.' (*Letter to O. L. Knipper, 23 Sept. 1903.*)

'You'll probably get this letter after you've had my telegram about finishing the play. Act Four is proving easy to write, it all seems to go very smoothly, and if I haven't finished it quickly it's because I keep falling ill.

'However boring my play may be, I think there's something new about it. Incidentally, there's not a single pistol shot in the whole play. There's a good part [Trofimov] for Kachalov. Do keep an eye open for someone to play the seventeen-year-old girl and write to me about it.' (*Letter to O. L. Knipper, 25 Sept. 1903.*)

'My darling little horse, I've already sent you a telegram telling you the play's finished and all four acts are written. I'm already copying it. It's true that my characters have turned out as living people, but what the play is like as a play I don't know. When I send it you'll read it and find out.' (*Letter to O. L. Knipper, 27 Sept. 1903.*)

'The play's finished already, but I'm copying it slowly as I have to revise it and rethink it. I'll just send two or three passages unfinished, I'm putting them off till later. You must excuse me. . . .

'Oh, if only you could take the part of the governess in my play! It's the best part. I don't like the others.' (*Letter to O. L. Knipper, 29 Sept. 1903.*)

'I write every day. Only a bit maybe, but I still do write. When I send the play you'll read it and see what might have been made out of the subject under favourable circumstances—that is, given good health. As it is the whole thing is quite disgusting, you write a couple of lines a day and get used to what's been written etc. etc.' (*Letter to O. L. Knipper, 2 Oct. 1903.*)

'My play is moving, and I'm finishing copying Act Three today and starting Act Four. Act Three is the least boring, but the second act is as boring and as monotonous as a cobweb.

'Who, oh who, will play my governess?' (*Letter to O. L. Knipper, 8 Oct. 1903.*)

'I'm in splendid form. I'm copying the play and I'll soon be finished, darling, I swear it. When I send it off I'll let you have a telegram. I assure you that every extra day is only to the good, for my play is getting better and better and the characters are now quite clear. Only I'm afraid there are passages which the censor may strike out. That will be terrible.' (*Letter to O. L. Knipper, 9 Oct. 1903.*)

'The play's finished now, finally finished, and tomorrow evening, or at the latest on the morning of the 14th, will be sent to Moscow. At the same time I'll send you one or two comments. If any alterations are needed I think they'll be very small ones. The worst thing about the play is that I didn't write it at a sitting, but spent a long, long time over it, so it's bound to seem a bit spun out. Anyway, we'll see what happens.' (*Letter to O. L. Knipper, 12 Oct. 1903.*)

2. THE TEXT

(a) The earliest published texts and extant manuscripts

The present translation is made from the text of *The Cherry Orchard* as it appears in *Works*, 1944–51, xi. This reproduces the text of the play as first published in St. Petersburg almost simultaneously in June 1904 in:

(i) a separate edition by A. F. Marks, and
(ii) vol. 2 of a collection published by the *Znaniye* Company.

It should be noted, however, that the text in *Works*, 1944–51, xi, as translated here, differs from the above two editions at two points in Act Two where Chekhov's original version has been restored in place of the wording which he inserted as a substitute for material cut out by the censor (see below, pp. 321–2).

A manuscript of the play, in Chekhov's handwriting and including some author's corrections, is preserved in the State (Lenin) Library of the U.S.S.R. It represents an earlier recension and contains variants which are discussed below (pp. 322–4).

(b) Alterations imposed by the censorship

The Cherry Orchard was submitted to the theatrical censorship in November 1903 and objection was taken to two passages in Act Two. In place of these passages Chekhov supplied alternative versions, inserted in the manuscript in his handwriting. The offending passages were enclosed in brackets in the manuscript, but were not crossed out. The two passages are as follows:

(i) *Restored original text as translated here* (see Trofimov's speech, p. 170, above):

everyone knows the workers are abominably fed and sleep without proper bedding, thirty or forty to a room—with bed-bugs everywhere, to say nothing of the stench, the damp, the moral degradation.

Alternative version supplied by Chekhov and incorporated in the 1904 editions:

the great majority of us, ninety-nine out of a hundred, live like savages, cursing and punching people's heads on the slightest excuse, eat revolting food, sleep in dirt and bad air.

(ii) *Restored original text as translated here* (see Trofimov's speech, p. 173, above):

Owning living souls, that's what has changed you all so completely, those who went before and those alive today, so that your mother, you yourself, your uncle—you don't realize that you're actually living on credit. You're living on other people, the very people you won't even let inside your own front door.

Alternative version supplied by Chekhov and incorporated in the 1904 editions:

Oh, it's terrible! Your orchard frightens me. When you walk through it in the evening or at night the old bark on the trees gives out a dim glow and the cherry-trees seem to be dreaming of what happened one or two hundred years ago, and painful visions oppress them. What's the point of talking about it?

(c) Alterations made in the Lenin Library manuscript

The manuscript mentioned above as preserved in the Lenin Library contains some insertions and alterations made by Chekhov at points where an earlier, rejected version remains legible. Among these the following involve the only alterations of significance:

(i) *In Act One, in Lopakhin's speech (p. 153), the present text from* 'I feel I want to tell you something nice and cheerful' *to* 'Here's my plan' *was inserted in the manuscript in place of the following earlier version:*

Only I just want to tell you before I go. [*Looks at his watch.*] It's about the estate, just a couple of words. I want to offer you a means of escape. To stop your estate running at a loss you must get up at four o'clock in the morning every day and work all day. For you of course this is impossible, I can see that. But there is another way out. Listen to me.

(ii) *The following exchange, which appears in the manuscript after* 'ANYA. There goes Yepikhodov' *(see p. 171), was cut out of the final version:*

VARYA. Why do we have him in the house? He only eats all the time and drinks tea all day.

LOPAKHIN. And he's preparing to shoot himself.

MRS. RANEVSKY. But I like Yepikhodov. When he talks about his misfortunes it's really funny. Don't give him his notice, Varya.

VARYA. I must, Mother. He must be dismissed, the worthless fellow.

(d) Variants found in the Lenin Library manuscript

The following are some of the variants found in the Lenin Library manuscript and superseded in the final version on which this translation is based:

(i) *Act One.* Minor alterations only are involved, and include the removal of one of Charlotte's 'tricks' (see p. 156).

In the final version Charlotte's words 'Not now. I want to go to bed' *were substituted for the following speech, found in the manuscript:*

CHARLOTTE [*going up to the door*]. Someone's standing behind the door. Who's there? [*There is a knock on the other side of the door.*] Who's that knocking? [*A knock.*] That's the gentleman to whom I'm engaged.

(ii) *Act Two.* It was in Act Two that the most extensive alterations were made.

1. *In the manuscript Charlotte does not appear at all at the beginning of the act, which continues as follows after the words* 'It will soon be sunset' (*see p. 162*):

[YASHA *and* DUNYASHA *are sitting on the bench.* YEPIKHODOV *stands near them.* TROFIMOV *and* ANYA *pass by on the road from the estate.*]

ANYA. Our great-aunt is lonely and very rich. She doesn't like Mother. During my first few days at her house I was in low spirits and she talked to me very little. It was all right later and she laughed. She promised to send some money and gave me and Charlotte some for the journey. But what an eerie sensation. How depressing to feel oneself a poor relation.

TROFIMOV. I think there's someone here already, someone sitting here. In that case let's go on a bit further.

ANYA. I've been away from home for three weeks. How I've missed it.

[*They go off.*]

The manuscript then continues as the final version with 'DUNYASHA [*to* YASHA]. You're ever so lucky to have been abroad, though' (*see p. 163*).

2. *The following passage, which was cut out of the final version, appears in the manuscript after* 'MRS. RANEVSKY. Perhaps we'll think of something' (*see p. 166*):

[VARYA *and* CHARLOTTE *pass along the road from the estate.* CHARLOTTE *is wearing man's clothing and carries a gun.*]

VARYA. She's an intelligent girl and well brought up, and nothing can happen to her. Still, it's not right for her to be left alone with a young man. Supper's at nine o'clock, Charlotte. Mind you're not late.

CHARLOTTE. I'm not hungry. [*Quietly sings a song.*]

VARYA. That's not important. You must have some as a matter of form. Look, you see—they're sitting there on the bank.

[VARYA *and* CHARLOTTE *go off.*]

3. Act Two has a different ending in the manuscript from that in the final version. It includes some of the material given to Charlotte at the beginning of the act in the final version.

In the manuscript the end of Act Two, after Anya's speech (*p. 174*) 'How beautifully you put it', *reads as follows:*

TROFIMOV. Sh! There's somebody coming. Varya's at it again. [*Angrily.*] She really is infuriating.

ANYA. Oh well, let's go down to the river. It's lovely there.

TROFIMOV. Come on then.

ANYA. The moon will soon be up. [*They go off.*]

[*Enter* FIRS *followed by* CHARLOTTE. FIRS, *muttering, looks for something on the ground near the bench and lights a match.*]

FIRS [*mutters*]. Oh, get away with you, you nincompoop!

CHARLOTTE [*sits on the bench, and removes her peaked cap*]. Is that you, Firs? What are you looking for?

FIRS. The mistress has lost her purse.

CHARLOTTE [*helping him to look*]. Here's a fan. And here's a handkerchief. It smells of scent. [*Pause.*] There's nothing else. Mrs. Ranevsky's forever losing things. She's thrown away her life as well. [*Quietly sings a song.*] I haven't any proper identification papers, old man, I don't know how old I am and I think of myself as a little girl. [*Puts her cap on* FIRS's *head. He sits there without moving.*] Oh, I love you, my dear old gentleman. [*Laughs.*] Ein, zwei, drei! [*Takes the cap off* FIRS's *head and puts it on her own.*] When I was little, Father and Mother used to go on tour round all the fairs giving performances.

[*The passage continues almost exactly as on p. 162 down to* 'I don't know anything', *after which it continues as follows:*]

FIRS. When I was about twenty or twenty-five I was walking along with the son of our priest and Vasily the cook, and there was a man sitting on the stone right here in this very spot—no one from these parts, a stranger. I was scared for some reason and went away, and after I'd gone the two of them went and killed him—he had some money.

CHARLOTTE. Well then? *Weiter!*

FIRS. Well, then the legal people turned up, started asking questions. They ran them in and me along with them. I spent a couple of years in prison. It was all right after that, they let me out. Ages ago, it was. [*Pause.*] You can't remember everything.

CHARLOTTE. It's time you were dead, Granddad. [*Eats a gherkin.*]

FIRS. Eh? [*Mutters to himself.*] So then we all drove off together and then we got held up. The old chap jumped off the cart, picked up a sack. And inside that sack there was another sack. He looks at it and then something suddenly gives a jerk, jerk, jerk!

CHARLOTTE [*laughing, quietly*]. A jerk, jerk, jerk! [*Carries on eating the gherkin.*]

[*Someone is heard walking quietly along the road and quietly playing a balalaika. The moon rises. Somewhere near the poplars* VARYA *is looking for* ANYA *and calling*: 'Anya! Where are you?']

Note on the alterations to Act Two. The 'supplementary' manuscript. The alterations to Act Two, made after the play had been passed by the censorship, were so extensive that they had to be submitted for supplementary censorship. The text of the relevant passages in Chekhov's handwriting (the 'supplementary' manuscript) is preserved in the archives of the Moscow Art Theatre Museum. It has been published in *Literaturnoye nasledstvo: Chekhov*, pp. 141–6, with an introductory note by A. R. Vladimirskaya. A comparison of the text in this supplementary manuscript with that of the final version reveals a number of minor variants of interest to students of Chekhov's technique of revision, but the individual variants are not of sufficient substance to call for translation.

(iii) *Acts Three and Four.* Only a few minor alterations are involved, including the following:

1. *In Act Three (see p. 184) the stage direction 'Lashes out just as* LOPAKHIN *comes in' reads as follows in the manuscript:*

[*The blow strikes* LOPAKHIN, *who comes in at that moment.*]

2. *The passage (see p. 190) from* 'Anyway, never mind' *to* 'deep down inside you' *is not in the manuscript and was inserted in the final version.*

3. SOME FURTHER COMMENTS BY CHEKHOV

(a) *From October 1903 to the first performance*

Between mid-October 1903, when Chekhov sent the completed *Cherry Orchard* to the Moscow Art Theatre, and 17 January 1904, when the first performance took place, the play remained his constant preoccupation. This is shown by the following comments from his letters and elsewhere, made during the period and dealing in detail with problems of interpretation and casting. The letters tail off at the end of November because Chekhov left for Moscow on 2 December, and was able to be present at rehearsals of *The Cherry Orchard* at the Moscow Art Theatre.

'You will play Lyuba Ranevsky since there's nobody else to. She's not dressed luxuriously, but with great taste. She's intelligent, very kind and absent-minded. She's nice to everybody and always has a smile on her face.

'Anya absolutely must be played by a young actress. . . .

'Gayev is for Vishnevsky. Ask Vishnevsky to listen to people playing billiards and write down as many billiard terms as possible. I don't play billiards, or rather I did play at one time and have forgotten all about it now, and everything about it in the play is haphazard. I'll settle the thing with Vishnevsky later on and make the necessary insertions. . . .

'Charlotte—a question mark. I'll put in some more lines for her in Act Four —yesterday I had a stomach-ache when I was copying Act Four and couldn't make any new insertions. In Act Four Charlotte plays a trick with Trofimov's galoshes. Rayevskaya won't be able to play it. What we need here is an actress with a sense of humour. . . .

'I must admit I'm terribly bored with the play. If anything about it isn't clear, write and tell me.

'It's an old manor house. At one time people lived there in great style and this must be conveyed by the set. There is an atmosphere of riches and comfort.

'Varya's a bit crude and a bit stupid, but very kind-hearted.' (*Letter to O. L. Knipper, 14 Oct. 1903.*)

'I must revise and polish off a few odd things about the play. I don't think it'll take more than a quarter of an hour. Act Four hasn't received its final polish, I must move one or two things around in Act Two and perhaps change two or three words at the end of Act Three. As it is, it's perhaps like the end of *Uncle Vanya*.' (*Letter to O. L. Knipper, 17 Oct. 1903.*)

'The thing that frightened me most was the sluggishness of Act Two and a certain unfinished quality about the student Trofimov. You see, Trofimov is in exile off and on and gets chucked out of the university every so often, and how is one to depict that kind of thing?' (*Letter to O. L. Knipper, 19 Oct. 1903.*)

'I had a telegram from Stanislavsky today in which he calls my play a work of genius, which is to over-praise the play and rob it of a good half of the success which it might achieve under favourable conditions. Nemirovich hasn't yet sent me a list of the actors who are taking part in the play, but I'm still scared. He's already sent me a telegram saying that Anya resembles Irina [in *Three Sisters*]. . . . But Anya's about as much like Irina as I'm like Burdzhalov [an actor and producer at the Art Theatre]. Anya is above all a child who remains gay right up to the end, doesn't know life and never cries except in Act Two, where she only has tears in her eyes. But, you know, M. F. [Andreyeva] will make the whole part into one long whine, and what's more she's too old. Who's playing Charlotte?' (*Letter to O. L. Knipper, 21 Oct. 1903.*)

'You write that Vishnevsky can't play Gayev. Then who can? Stanislavsky? In that case who's to play Lopakhin? It can't be given to Luzhsky on any account, he'll either make a very colourless job of it or ham it. He must play Yepikhodov. No, don't you be too hard on Vishnevsky.

'Nemirovich writes that there are lots of tears in my play and some crudities. Darling, write and tell me what you find to be wrong and what people are saying, and I'll change it. It's not too late, after all, I can still revise a whole act.

'So the actors have taken to Pishchik, have they? I'm delighted.' (*Letter to O. L. Knipper, 23 Oct. 1903.*)

'I'd very much like to look in on rehearsals. I'm afraid Anya might be a bit weepy (for some reason you find her similar to Irina) and I'm afraid of her being played by an actress who isn't young. Anya doesn't cry once in my text, she nowhere talks in a weepy tone of voice. She does have tears in her eyes in Act Two, but the mood is gay and lively. What's this in your telegram about the play being full of people crying? Where are they? Varya's the only one, but that's because Varya's a cry-baby by nature, and her tears shouldn't depress the audience. You'll often find the stage-direction 'through tears' in my text, but that only shows the mood of the characters and not their tears. There isn't a cemetery in Act Two.' (*Letter to V. I. Nemirovich-Danchenko, 23 Oct. 1903.*)

'My darling little horse, what's the point of translating my play into French? Why, it's a mad idea. The French won't understand anything about Yermolay [Lopakhin] or about the sale of the estate and will only be bored. It's a bad idea, darling, there's no point in it.' (*Letter to O. L. Knipper, 24 Oct. 1903.*)

'No, I never wanted to make Mrs. Ranevsky a person who has calmed down. Nothing less than death can calm a woman like that. But perhaps I don't understand what you mean. It's not hard to play Ranevsky. It's only necessary to strike the right note from the very beginning. It's necessary to invent a smile and a way of smiling, and it's necessary to know how to dress. Anyway, you'll manage all that with a little good will and good health.' (*Letter to O. L. Knipper, 25 Oct. 1903.*)

'If Mariya Petrovna [Lilina] would agree to play Charlotte, what could be better than that? I had it in mind, but didn't dare say so. The fact that she's frail and short doesn't matter, she's too old for Anya. . . . Konstantin Sergeyevich [Stanislavsky] and no one else must play the merchant [Lopakhin]. After all, he's not a merchant in the vulgar sense of the word, that must be borne in mind.' (*Letter to O. L. Knipper, 28 Oct. 1903.*)

'Stanislavsky will make a most excellent and original Gayev, but in that case who's to play Lopakhin? After all, the part of Lopakhin is the central one. If it doesn't come off the whole play will be a flop. Lopakhin mustn't be played by anyone rowdy, and he doesn't inevitably have to be a [typical] merchant. He's a gentle person.' (*Letter to O. L. Knipper, 30 Oct. 1903.*)

'Many thanks for your letter and thanks for your telegram too. Letters are very precious to me now, firstly because I'm stuck here on my own and, secondly, I sent off the play three weeks ago and I only had your letter yesterday. If it hadn't been for my wife I wouldn't have known a thing, and heaven knows what I might have imagined. When I wrote the part of Lopakhin I thought of it as your part. If you don't like the look of it for some reason, then take Gayev. True, Lopakhin is a merchant, but he's a decent person in the full sense of the words and his bearing must be that of a completely dignified and intelligent man. There must be nothing petty about him, no tricks, and my idea was that you'd make a brilliant success of this part, which is the central one in the play. If you take Gayev, give Lopakhin to Vishnevsky. He won't make an artistic Lopakhin, but at least he won't be a petty one. Luzhsky would be only a cold foreigner in this part. Leonidov would make a typical profiteering peasant [кулачок] of him. When choosing an actor for this part it must not be forgotten that Lopakhin was loved by Varya, a serious and religious girl. She wouldn't love some wretched money-grubbing peasant.' (*Letter to K. S. Stanislavsky, 30 Oct. 1903.*)

'I don't know why Mariya Petrovna [Lilina] is so keen on playing Anya. After all it's a short part and not a very interesting one. My idea is that Varya suits her much better. Nemirovich writes that she's afraid of the resemblance between Varya and Sonya in *Uncle Vanya*. But what resemblance is there? Varya's a nun, a silly girl.' (*Letter to O. L. Knipper, 1 Nov. 1903.*)

'Anya can be played by anyone you like, a completely unknown actress even, as long as she's young and looks like a little girl and talks in a young, ringing voice. This isn't one of the important parts.

'Varya is a more serious part—that is, if Mariya Petrovna [Lilina] should take it. Without M.P. this part will turn out flat and crude, and it will be necessary to revise it and tone it down. Mariya Petrovna is unable to repeat herself, firstly because she's a talented person, and secondly because Varya does not resemble Sonya and Natasha. She's a figure in a black dress, a nun, a silly girl, a cry-baby, etc. etc.

'Gayev and Lopakhin—let Konstantin Sergeyevich [Stanislavsky] choose between these parts and try them out. If he should pick Lopakhin and succeed in this role the play would succeed. You see, if Lopakhin's colourless and is played by a colourless actor both the part and the play will fail. . . .

'Charlotte is an important part. . . . This is the part for Miss Knipper.[1] . . .

'The stationmaster who declaims *The Sinful Woman* in Act Three should be an actor with a bass voice.

'Charlotte talks good—not broken—Russian. Only she occasionally mixes up hard and soft consonants at the end of a word and confuses adjectives of the masculine and feminine gender. Pishchik is a Russian, an old man crippled with gout, old age and good living. He is stout and is dressed in a peasant's sleeveless coat . . . with heelless high boots. Lopakhin has a white waistcoat and brown boots, he waves his arms about as he walks, takes long strides and meditates while walking about—walking in a straight line. His hair isn't short and so he often throws back his head. He absent-mindedly combs his beard from back to front—i.e. from his neck in the direction of his mouth. Trofimov's quite clear, I think. Varya wears a black dress with a broad belt.

'I spent three years preparing to write *The Cherry Orchard* and for three years I've been telling you to engage an actress for the part of Lyuba Ranevsky. So don't complain if you now find yourselves playing a game of patience which just won't come out.' (*Letter to V. I. Nemirovich-Danchenko, 2 Nov. 1903.*)

'The house in the play has two stories and is large. After all there is a mention in Act Three of a staircase going downstairs.

'The house must be large and solid. Whether it's made of wood . . . or stone, that doesn't matter. It's very old and large. Summer holiday-makers don't rent that kind of house. That kind of house is usually pulled down and the material is used to build summer cottages. The furniture is old-fashioned, of good style and solid. The furniture and fittings haven't been affected by financial ruin and debts.

---

[1] Olga Knipper in fact took the part of Mrs. Ranevsky.

'When people buy a house of this kind they argue as follows: it's cheaper and easier to build a smaller new one than to repair this old one.' (*Letter to K. S. Stanislavsky, 5 Nov. 1903.*)

'Nemirovich sent me an express telegram asking me to reply by express telegram. Who, he asks, is to play Charlotte, Anya and Varya? There were three names opposite Varya, two unknown ones and Andreyeva. I had to choose Andreyeva. Very cunningly rigged.' (*Letter to O. L. Knipper, 7 Nov. 1903.*)

'Tell her [Muratova] to be funny in the part of Charlotte, that's the main thing. I doubt whether Lilina will succeed with Anya, she'll just be an old-fashioned girl with a squeaky voice and no more.' (*Letter to O. L. Knipper, 8 Nov. 1903.*)

'Of course you can use the same set for Acts Three and Four, the one with a hall and staircase. In general please don't stint yourself with the scenery—I defer to you. In your theatre I'm always stunned and usually sit with my mouth wide open. There's nothing more to be said about this. Whatever you do will be splendid, a hundred times better than anything I could think of.

'Dunyasha and Yepikhodov stand in the presence of Lopakhin, they don't sit down. After all, Lopakhin is very much at his ease, behaves like a squire and calls the servants "thou", while they call him "you".' (*Letter to K. S. Stanislavsky, 10 Nov. 1903.*)

'I've received the plan of Act One. The house will have two stories, which means that the garden-room also has two stories. But you know, there won't be much sunlight in the little patio formed by this garden-room, and cherries wouldn't grow there.' (*Letter to O. L. Knipper, 20 Nov. 1903.*)

'Haymaking usually takes place between 20 and 25 June, at which time I think the corncrake no longer cries, and frogs also are silent at this time of year. Only the golden oriole sings then. There isn't a cemetery. There *was* one a long time ago. Two or three gravestones lying around any old how, that's all that's left. The bridge is a very good idea. If you can show a train without any noise, without a single sound, then carry on. I haven't anything against a single set for Acts Three and Four as long as the entrances and exits are convenient in Act Four.' (*Letter to K. S. Stanislavsky, 23 Nov. 1903.*)

'Konstantin Sergeyevich [Stanislavsky] wants to bring on a train in Act Two, but I think he must be restrained. He also wants frogs and corncrakes.' (*Letter to O. L. Knipper, 23 Nov. 1903.*)

'I'm deeply convinced that my *Cherry Orchard* doesn't suit you at all. The central female part in this play is that of an old woman bound up with the past, who has nothing to do with the present, and the other parts, at least the women's, are rather petty and crude and not interesting for you.' (*Letter to V. F. Komissarzhevskaya, 6 Jan. 1904.*)

'I think my play will be performed on 17 January. I don't expect any particular success, things are pretty slack.' (*Letter to V. K. Kharkeyevich, 13 Jan. 1904.*)

'He [Chekhov] told me that Lopakhin must look like a cross between a merchant and a professor of medicine at Moscow University. Later at rehearsal, after Act Three, he said to me: "Listen, Lopakhin doesn't shout. He's a rich man, and rich men never shout." ' (*The actor L. M. Leonidov, quoted in 'Chekhov i teatr', p. 351.*)

(b) After the first performance

The comments made by Chekhov between the first performance of *The Cherry Orchard* on 17 January 1904 and his death in July of the same year are dispirited, frustrated, and often irritable in tone. Evidently he was dissatisfied with the interpretation of his play by the Moscow Art Theatre, but the state of his health during the months shortly before his death no doubt coloured his comments.

'My play was put on yesterday, so I'm not feeling too good. I want to slip off somewhere and I'll probably go to France by February, or at least to the Crimea.' (*Letter to I. L. Leontyev, 18 Jan. 1904.*)

'If you arrive at carnival time, that's fine. Only as far as I can see, it will be carnival time at least before our actors come to themselves and start playing *The Cherry Orchard* less confusedly and flamboyantly than now.' (*Letter to F. D. Batyushkov, 19 Jan. 1904.*)

'*The Seagull* and *Three Sisters* have long ago been translated into German (I haven't had a single farthing from them), and *The Cherry Orchard* is already being translated for Berlin and Vienna, and it won't come off there at all as they haven't got billiards, Lopakhins or students à la Trofimov.' (*Letter to O. L. Knipper, 4 March 1904.*)

'Tell Nemirovich that the sound in Acts Two and Four of *The Cherry Orchard* must be shorter, a lot shorter, and must be felt as coming from a great distance. What a lot of fuss about nothing—not being able to cope with a trifle like this, a mere noise, although it's so clearly described in the play.' (*Letter to O. L. Knipper, 18 March 1904.*)

'Tell the actress who plays the maid Dunyasha to read *The Cherry Orchard* in the *Znaniye* edition or in proof. Then she'll be able to see where she has to powder her face etc. etc. Do make sure she reads it. In your notebooks the whole thing's a complete mess.' (*Letter to O. L. Knipper, 24 March 1904.*)

'Lulu and K. L. [relatives of O. L. Knipper] saw *The Cherry Orchard* in March. Both of them say that Stanislavsky [as Gayev] plays repulsively in Act Four and drags things out most painfully. This is really dreadful! An act which ought to last for a maximum of twelve minutes—you're dragging it out for forty. The only thing I can say is that Stanislavsky has ruined my play. Oh, well, the less said about him the better.' (*Letter to O. L. Knipper, 29 March 1904.*)

'Why do they so obstinately call my play a "drama" in play-bills and news-paper advertisements? What Nemirovich and Stanislavsky see in my play definitely isn't what I wrote and I'm ready to swear anything you like that neither of them has read through my play carefully once. I'm sorry to say so, but I assure you I'm right.' (*Letter to O. L. Knipper, 10 April 1904.*)

4. CONTEMPORARY RECEPTION

Whether by accident or design, the first performance of *The Cherry Orchard* had been fixed for 17 January 1904, which was Chekhov's name-day and birthday. That this might well be the last birthday of Chekhov's life was a thought which nobody liked to put into words, but which could not help occurring to all who saw him in his present utterly exhausted and emaciated condition. His friends in the Art Theatre decided to take what might be their last opportunity to express their love and admiration by making the première of *The Cherry Orchard* the occasion for a public celebration in his honour. The pretext was the twenty-fifth anniversary of his début as a writer, although this particular date was at least a year premature.

An impressive programme of speeches and presentations was arranged to take place in the interval between the third and fourth acts of the play, and a large number of prominent people, representing literary, theatrical and learned associations, arrived with gifts in their hands and the manuscripts of speeches in their pockets. *The Cherry Orchard* was well under way when a startling dis-covery was made. Chekhov was not in the theatre! The reason for his absence was not only ill-health. He had always been embarrassed to the point of genuine suffering by official honours, even when the recipients were other people. 'They spend twenty years running a man down,' he once told Bunin when discussing jubilee celebrations, 'and then present him with an aluminium goose-quill pen, and spend a whole day churning out solemn clap-trap to the accompaniment of kisses and tears.' Now that his own turn had come he simply could not face it, and his friends almost had to use force to make him leave his lodgings.

The third act was finishing when he reached the theatre. Pale and weak, he took up his position on the stage and the applause which broke out was such as to leave him in no doubt of the place which he held in the affections of the audience. It is difficult for anyone except a Russian to appreciate the warm personal feeling with which he was greeted that night by people who, although many of them had never seen him before, knew and loved him for his writings, and who, moreover, still had the words of *The Cherry Orchard* ringing in their ears.

He had hardly taken his place on the stage when he was seized by a fit of uncontrollable coughing. People in the audience began to shout, 'Sit down, Anton Pavlovich', 'A chair for Anton Pavlovich', but he insisted on remaining on his feet. The speeches and presentations began. There was an address on behalf of the Lovers of Russian Literature by Professor A. N. Veselovsky, and another on behalf of the Moscow Little Theatre by the actress Fedotova. There were many other speeches, including some by representatives of the liberal press in which Chekhov had published much of his best work. Finally Nemirovich-Danchenko rounded things off with an eloquent tribute in which he expressed what all his colleagues in the Art Theatre felt: 'Our theatre is so much indebted to your talent, to your tender heart and pure soul, that you have every right to say "This is my theatre".'

Knowing that his friends and admirers were sincerely trying to please him, Chekhov listened with great attention and seriousness. All the same there were times when those who knew him best caught a glint of ironical humour in his expression. One of these points occurred when a new speaker began his oration with the words 'Dear and most honoured Anton Pavlovich'. Stanislavsky, who, as Gayev in *The Cherry Orchard*, had to deliver a speech to an old book-case beginning 'Dear and most honoured book-case', caught Chekhov's eye at this moment. The exchange of glances showed him that Chekhov was as much amused by the coincidence as he was.

Despite the personal acclaim which Chekhov received at the first performance of *The Cherry Orchard*, it was some time, according to Nemirovich-Danchenko, before the play really 'got through to its audience' (*Works*, 1944-51, xi, p. 605). Contemporary reviews tended to dwell on the social commentary contained in the play. Dissatisfaction was expressed with certain characters, especially with Trofimov (for being too vague a representative of the rising generation) and with Lopakhin, who was found surprising because he did not conform with preconceived ideas about the typical Russian merchant.

NOTES

The following notes, which have been kept as brief as possible, are designed to explain references in the text of the plays which might be obscure to English-speaking readers, and to point out certain difficulties which have occurred in translation.

Page

22. 'With harassed brain and furrowed brow ....' The lines come from the satire *Other People's Views* (1794) by I. I. Dmitriyev (1760–1837), in which the hero is an untalented writer of verse.

30. '*The watchman can be heard tapping his stick in the garden.*' In order to warn thieves that they were alert and show their masters that they were awake, Russian watchmen used to make a banging noise with a stick against a board or with some kind of improvised rattle.

30. 'Batyushkov's poems ....' K. N. Batyushkov (1787–1855) was a well-known Russian poet of the beginning of the nineteenth century, and an important forerunner of Pushkin.

52. '... a government inspector is on his way.' The reference is to the well-known comedy *The Inspector-General* (1836) by N. V. Gogol (1809–52), in which the Mayor announces the imminent arrival of a government inspector.

58. '... worthy of the brush of Ayvazovsky.' I. K. Ayvazovsky (1817–1900) was renowned for his paintings of tempestuous seas and naval battles. It is tempting to translate this sentence: 'It was as good as a storm at sea.'

77. '... someone called Dobrolyubov ....' N. A. Dobrolyubov (1836–61) was a leading Russian radical literary critic.

77. 'A green oak by a curving shore ....' These are the opening lines of the long romantic and mock-heroic poem *Ruslan and Lyudmila* (1820) by A. S. Pushkin (1799–1837).

78. 'Before he'd time to turn a hair ....' The lines come from the fable *The Peasant and the Workman* by I. A. Krylov (1769–1844).

81. 'In the Novo-Devichy cemetery.' The reference is to the famous cemetery of the Novo-Devichy Convent in Moscow, where Chekhov himself is buried.

94. '... drop in at Testov's ....' Testov's was a well-known Moscow restaurant.

100. 'As Gogol said ....' Masha is quoting the last words of Gogol's story *How Ivan Ivanovich quarrelled with Ivan Nikiforovich* (1835).

100. 'Balzac got married in Berdichev.' Berdichev is a town in the Ukraine.

101. 'Tsitsihar.' A town in north-east China.

102. '... over the Panama swindle.' Reference is to the notorious fraudulent dealings, involving important politicians, of the French company which was formed to build the Panama Canal and went bankrupt in 1888.

103. 'I may be odd, but who is not?' From a speech by Chatsky in Act Three of the verse play *Woe from Wit* (1822–24) by A. S. Griboyedov (1795–1829).

103 and 104. 'Aleko, be not angry' and '... Forget, forget your dreams.' Aleko is the name of the hero of Pushkin's poem *The Gipsies* (1824). Though Aleko does get angry in the poem, the words 'quoted' here do not actually occur in it.

104. '... the Lermontov type.' M. Yu. Lermontov (1814–41), the leading Russian romantic poet, was a notoriously moody, introverted person. He shared Solyony's fondness for duelling, and was himself killed in a duel. See also Chekhov's letter to I. A. Tikhomirov of 14 January 1901, quoted above, p. 313.

104. 'Oh, my porch . . . .' A well-known Russian folk song.

110. '... the French did get a surprise.' The reference is to the invasion of Russia by Napoleon in 1812.

113. 'Zasyp.' This is presumably intended to be understood as a place in the locality. Untraced.

115. 'Be so good as to accept one of these dates.' See Chekhov's letter to I. A. Tikhomirov, quoted above, p. 313.

116. 'As everyone has always found . . . .' The lines come from Pushkin's novel in verse, *Yevgeny* (Eugene) *Onegin* (1823–31).

116. 'Ti tum ti tum ti—' For this passage, see Chekhov's letter to O. L. Knipper of 20 January 1901, quoted above, p. 314.

117. 'I could develop my idea . . . .' The lines are from Krylov's fable *The Geese*.

121. '... like the madman in Gogol's story.' The reference is to Gogol's *Memoirs of a Madman* (1835).

131. 'Restless, he seeks the raging storm . . .'. These are the last two lines of Lermontov's well-known lyric *The Sail*.

147. 'Simple Simon.' Literally, 'twenty-two misfortunes'.

151. 'Pot the red . . . ,' etc. Gayev's imaginary billiard strokes, which recur throughout the play, do not seem to correspond with any known game of billiards. After some inquiry the present translator has failed to discover what rules of billiards Chekhov had in mind, and agrees with the comment of Mr. Davidson: 'The rules of Gayev's game must remain a mystery, but presumably correspond to one of the games mentioned in the *Entsiklopedichesky slovar* (1891).' (This mentions four games—the five-ball game known as 'Russian billiards', the three-ball game known as 'Berlin billiards', the pyramid, in which fifteen balls are used, and the cannon

game, known as 'French billiards'. See *A. P. Chekhov, The Cherry Orchard*, edited by J. M. C. Davidson, p. 74.) Cf. also Chekhov's own comment: 'I don't play billiards . . . and everything about it in the play is haphazard' (quoted above, p. 325). In view of the above, and of the evident failure of earlier translators to penetrate these mysteries, a compromise has been aimed at here, in translating Gayev's references to billiards, between literal faithfulness to the Russian and the game of billiards as played nowadays in English-speaking countries. In particular, where Gayev speaks of the 'yellow' ball, this has been rendered 'red' to avoid creating unnecessary confusion.

151. 'LOPAKHIN. Yes, time marches on.' No provision has been made in the stage directions for Lopakhin's return. Presumably he is supposed to have come in with Mrs. Ranevsky, Gayev, and Simeonov-Pishchik a few lines earlier on.

159. 'Yaroslavl.' An old Russian town on the Volga.

162. 'I'm tired of the world and its bustle . . .' and 'If only my heart were delighted. . . .' The quatrain comes from a well-known drawing-room ballad of the period.

163. 'Buckle.' Henry Thomas Buckle (1821–62), the English historian.

165. '. . . about the seventies and the decadent movement.' The name 'decadent' was sometimes given to the symbolist movement in literature and art of the end of the nineteenth century.

167. 'For a spot of cash your Prussian . . . .' Untraced.

168 and 171. 'And when the serfs were freed . . .' and 'When the serfs were given their freedom.' The references are to the Emancipation of the Serfs in Russia in 1861.

172. 'Brother, my suffering brother!' From a poem by S. Ya. Nadson (1862–87). 'Come out to the Volga . . . .' From a poem by N. A. Nekrasov (1821–78).

172. 'Amelia . . . .' The Russian has Охмелия—i.e. a pun, whereby the name Ophelia is distorted to incorporate the Russian word хмель, 'hops, intoxication'. It is tempting to translate: 'Ophelia—hop along and get thee to a nunnery' and: 'Nymph, in thy orisons be all my sins—and double gins—remembered.'

181. 'The Sinful Woman.' A poem by A. K. Tolstoy (1817–75). The opening lines are, in translation:

> 'A bustling crowd with happy laughter,
> With twangling lutes and cymbals' clash,
> With flowers and foliage all around
> The colonnaded portico . . . .'

214 and 220. 'Thou shalt of all the universe . . . .' The lines are from Lermontov's

poem *The Demon* (1839). Chekhov has substituted the word 'faithful' for the word 'first', which occurs in the original.

237. *'Lensky's aria* . . . Eugene Onegin.' The reference is to the opera *Eugene Onegin* (1877–8) by P. I. Tchaikovsky (1840–93), based on Pushkin's verse novel with the same title.

237. '. . . the volunteers in Serbia . . . .' When Serbia declared war on Turkey in 1876, many Russians sympathized with the Serbs as fellow-Slavs and volunteered to fight in the Serbian army. In the following year Russia declared war on Turkey, thus beginning the Russo-Turkish War of 1877–8.

254. 'Lomonosov.' M. V. Lomonosov (1711–65) was the son of a fisherman in the north Russian port of Archangel. He ran away to Moscow at the age of 17 and became famous as a scientist, educationist, poet and grammarian.

256. 'Ayvazovsky.' See note to p. 58, above.

259. 'Against my will to these sad shores . . . .' This couplet comes from Pushkin's dramatic poem *The Mermaid* (1832).

262. 'Scatter the seed . . . .' From Nekrasov's poem *To the Sowers* (1876–7).

271. 'O wondrous spot, wood-demons' haunt . . . .' The lines occur near the beginning of Pushkin's poem *Ruslan and Lyudmila* (1820).

271. '. . . lieutenant in the Serbian army . . . .' See note to p. 237, above.

THE PRONUNCIATION OF RUSSIAN PROPER NAMES

English-speaking actors do not usually attempt a phonetically accurate reproduction of Russian proper names on the stage. And rightly so. It is probably
better to make 'Boris' and 'Ivan' rhyme with 'Horace' and 'enliven' respectively,
than to say 'Bah-reess' and 'Ee-vahn'.

On the other hand, where less familiar proper names are concerned it is
probably worth trying at least to preserve the Russian stress accent, and so an
alphabetical list is appended of the proper names in the text, the stressed
syllable being indicated by an acute accent over the relevant vowel. It should
be borne in mind that:

(i) stressed 'i' is pronounced 'ee' as in 'cheese'—thus, 'Yefim' is pronounced
roughly as if written 'Yefeem', and
(ii) stressed 'e' is pronounced 'ay' as in 'play'—thus 'Telegin' is pronounced
roughly as if written 'Telaygin'.

Aléko	Fedótik	Kulýgin
Aleksándr	Ferapónt	Kuznetsóv
Alekséy	Fyódor	Lakedemónov
Alekséyevich	[Galétin]	Lénsky
Alekséyevskoye	Gáyev	Leoníd
Anastásy	Gerásim	Lérmontov
Andréy	Gógol	Lezgínka
Anfísa	Grísha	Lomonósov
Ánya	Ilyá	Lopákhin
Ástrov	Irína	Luká
Ayvazóvsky	Iván	Lyúba
Basmánny	Ivánovna	Lyudmíla
Bátyushkov	Kardamónov	Málitskoye
Berdíchev	Kashkinázi	Marína
Bóbik	Khárkov	Másha
Borís	Kharlámov	Mikhaíl
Chebutýkin	Khrushchóv	Natásha
Dáshenka	Kíev	Nazárka
Derigánov	Kirpichóv	Nekrásov
Dmítry	Kirsánovsky	Nemétsky
Dobrolyúbov	Kolotílin	Nikodímovich
Dostoyévsky	Konstantín	Nikoláy
Dunyásha	Kozoyédov	Novo-Dévichy
Dyádin	Kózyrev	Novo-Petróvskoye

Ólga
Onégin
Orlóvsky
Ostróvsky
Pável
Pávlovich
Petrúshka
Pólya
Protopópov
Prózorov
Pýzhikov
Ragúlin
Ranévsky
Rozhdéstvennoye
Sarátov
Semyón
Serebryakóv
Sergéy
Sharlótta

Shimánsky
Simeónov-Píshchik
Skvortsóv
Solyóny
Sónya
Stanisláv
Stepán
Telégin
Telibéyev
Téstov
Tolstóy
Trífon
Trofímov
Túla
Turgénev
Túzenbakh
Ványa
Várya
Vasíly

Vershínin
Vladímir
Vólga
Voynítsky
Yaroslávl
Yásha
Yáshnevo
Yefím
Yegór
Yeléna
Yepikhódov
Yermoláy
Yevgény
Yevstignéy
Yúliya
Zásyp
Zheltúkhin
Znóykov

SELECT BIBLIOGRAPHY

I. BIBLIOGRAPHIES IN ENGLISH

Two most useful bibliographies, published by the New York Public Library and containing in all nearly five hundred items, give a comprehensive picture of the literature relating to Chekhov published in English—translations of his writings, biographical and critical studies, memoirs, essays, articles etc. They are:

> *Chekhov in English: A List of Works by and about him.* Compiled by Anna Heifetz. Ed. and with a Foreword by Avrahm Yarmolinsky (New York, 1949) and
> *The Chekhov Centennial Chekhov in English: A Selective List of Works by and about him, 1949–60.* Compiled by Rissa Yachnin (New York, 1960).

Bibliographies in English will also be found in the books by David Magarshack (*Chekhov: a Life*), Ernest J. Simmons and Ronald Hingley mentioned in Section III, below. Magarshack provides a bibliographical index of Chekhov's writings in alphabetical order of their English titles, Simmons includes a list of bibliographies in Russian, and Hingley gives a list of Chekhov's translated stories in chronological order.

II. TRANSLATIONS INTO ENGLISH OF THE PLAYS IN THIS VOLUME

(a) IN COLLECTIONS

Two plays by Tchekhof. The Seagull, The Cherry Orchard. Tr. with an Introduction and Notes by George Calderon (London, 1912).

Plays by Anton Tchekoff. Uncle Vanya, Ivanoff, The Seagull, The Swan Song. Tr. with an Introduction by Marian Fell (New York, 1912).

Plays by Anton Tchekoff, Second Series: *On the High Road, The Proposal, The Wedding, The Bear, A Tragedian in spite of himself, The Anniversary, The Three Sisters, The Cherry Orchard.* Tr. with an Introduction by Julius West (New York, 1916).

> Some of the plays in this and the preceding volume were republished in 1939 and 1949 as *Five Famous Plays by Anton Tchekoff* and *Six Famous Plays by Anton Tchekoff.* See below.

The Moscow Art Theatre Series of Russian Plays. Ed. Oliver M. Sayler, tr. Jennie Covan (New York, 1922).

> Includes, in addition to two translated plays by other Russian authors, Chekhov's *The Cherry Orchard, The Three Sisters* and *Uncle Vanya.*

Plays from the Russian. Tr. Constance Garnett (London, 1923; New York,

1924). Vol. 1: *The Cherry Orchard, Uncle Vanya, The Sea-gull, The Bear, The Proposal.* Vol. 2: *Three Sisters, Ivanov, Swan Song, An Unwilling Martyr, The Anniversary, On the High Road, The Wedding.*

Plays and stories, Anton Tchekhov. Tr. S. S. Koteliansky (London, 1937; New York, 1938).

> Contains the following plays: *The Cherry Orchard, The Seagull, The Wood Demon, Tatyana Riepin, On the Harmfulness of Tobacco.*

Five Famous Plays by Anton Tchekoff. The Bear, The Three Sisters, The Cherry Orchard, tr. Julius West; *Uncle Vanya, The Seagull,* tr. Marian Fell (London, 1939).

Six Famous Plays by Anton Tchekoff (London, 1949).

> As preceding item, but with the addition of *The Proposal,* tr. Julius West.

Three plays: The Cherry Orchard, Three Sisters, Ivanov. Tr. and with an Introduction by Elisaveta Fen (Harmondsworth, 1951).

The Seagull and Other Plays: The Seagull, Uncle Vania, The Bear, The Proposal, A Jubilee. Tr. and with an Introduction by Elisaveta Fen (Harmondsworth, 1954).

Plays by Anton Chehov: Ivanov, The Seagull, Uncle Vania, Three Sisters, The Cherry Orchard, The Bear, The Proposal, A Jubilee. Tr. and with an Introduction by Elisaveta Fen (Harmondsworth, 1959).

> A reissue of the preceding two items in one volume.

Six plays of Chekhov. New English Versions and Introduction by Robert W. Corrigan. Foreword by Harold Clurman (New York, 1962).

> Contains: *Ivanov, The Wood Demon, The Sea Gull, Uncle Vanya, The Three Sisters, The Cherry Orchard.*

(*b*) SEPARATE TRANSLATIONS OF THE FOUR PLAYS IN THIS VOLUME

(i) *Uncle Vanya*

Uncle Vania: Scenes from Country Life in Four Acts. Tr. Frances Arno Saphro (Boston, 1922).

Uncle Vanya. Tr. and adapted by Rose Caylor (New York, 1930).

Uncle Vanya: Scenes from Village Life in Four Acts. Tr. Stark Young (New York, 1956).

The Storm and other Russian Plays. Tr. and introduced by David Magarshack (London, 1960).

> Includes *Uncle Vanya.*

(ii) *Three Sisters*

A Treasury of Russian Literature. Ed. Bernard Guilbert Guerney (New York, 1934; London, 1948).

> Includes *Three Sisters,* tr. B. G. Guerney.

The Three Sisters: a Drama in Four Acts. Tr. Stark Young (New York, 1941).

(iii) *The Cherry Orchard*

The Cherry Garden: a Comedy in Four Acts. Tr. Max. S. Mandell, with an Introduction by the translator (New Haven, Conn., 1908).

Masterpieces of the Russian Drama. Ed. George Rapall Noyes (New York, 1933).
Includes *The Cherry Orchard*, tr. Camilla Chapin Daniels and G. R. Noyes.

The Cherry Orchard: a Play in Four Acts. Tr. Hubert Butler, Introduction by Tyrone Guthrie (London, 1934).

The Cherry Orchard: a Play in Four Acts. Tr. Kenneth James (London, 1943).

The Heritage of European Literature. By E. H. Weatherly, A. P. Wagener, E. H. Zeydel, and A. Yarmolinsky. Vol. 2 (Boston, 1948–9).
Includes *The Cherry Orchard*, tr. Irina Skariatina.

The Portable Chekhov. Ed. and with Introduction by Avrahm Yarmolinsky (New York, 1947).
Includes *The Cherry Orchard*.

The Cherry Orchard: a Drama in Four Acts. Tr. Stark Young (New York, 1947).

(iv) *The Wood-Demon*

The Wood Demon: a Comedy in Four Acts. Tr. S. S. Koteliansky (London, 1926).

III. BIOGRAPHICAL AND CRITICAL STUDIES

Leon Shestov, *Anton Tchekhov and Other Essays* (Dublin and London, 1916).

William Gerhardi, *Anton Chehov: a Critical Study* (London, 1923).

Oliver Elton, *Chekhov* (The Taylorian Lecture, 1929; Oxford, 1929).

Nina Andronikova Toumanova, *Anton Chekhov: the Voice of Twilight Russia* (London, 1937).

W. H. Bruford, *Chekhov and his Russia: a Sociological Study* (London, 1948).

Ronald Hingley, *Chekhov: a Biographical and Critical Study* (London, 1950).

Irene Nemirovsky, *A Life of Chekhov.* Tr. from the French by Erik de Mauny (London, 1950).

David Magarshack, *Chekhov: a Life* (London, 1952).

David Magarshack, *Chekhov the Dramatist* (London, 1952).

Vladimir Yermilov [Ermilov], *Anton Pavlovich Chekhov, 1860–1904.* Tr. Ivy Litvinov (Moscow, 1956; London, 1957).

W. H. Bruford, *Anton Chekhov* (London, 1957).

T. Eekman, ed., *Anton Chekhov, 1860–1960* (Leiden, 1960).

Beatrice Saunders, *Tchehov the Man* (London, 1960).

Ernest J. Simmons, *Chekhov: a Biography* (Boston, Toronto, 1962; London, 1963).

Kornei Chukovsky. *Chekhov the Man.* Tr. Pauline Rose (London, n.d.).

IV. LETTERS AND MEMOIR MATERIAL, ETC.

Letters of Anton Tchehov to his Family and Friends. Tr. Constance Garnett (London, 1920).

The Note-books of Anton Tchekhov together with Reminiscences of Tchekhov by Maxim Gorky. Tr. S. S. Koteliansky and Leonard Woolf (Richmond, 1921).

Letters on the Short Story, the Drama and Other Literary Topics. By Anton Chekhov. Selected and ed.' Louis S. Friedland (New York, 1924).

Konstantin Stanislavsky, *My Life in Art.* Tr. J. J. Robbins (London, 1924; New York, 1956).

The Life and Letters of Anton Tchekhov. Tr. and ed. S. S. Koteliansky and Philip Tomlinson (London, 1925).

The Letters of Anton Pavlovitch Tchehov to Olga Leonardovna Knipper. Tr. Constance Garnett (London, 1926).

Anton Tchekhov. Literary and Theatrical Reminiscences. Tr. and ed. S. S. Koteliansky (London, 1927).

Vladimir Nemirovitch-Dantchenko, *My Life in the Russian Theatre.* Tr. John Cournos (London, 1937).

The Personal Papers of Anton Chekhov. Introduction by Matthew Josephson (New York, 1948).

Lydia Avilov, *Chekhov in my Life: a Love Story.* Tr. with an Introduction by David Magarshack (London, 1950).

Konstantin Stanislavsky, *Stanislavsky on the Art of the Stage.* Tr. with an introductory essay on Stanislavsky's 'System' by David Magarshack (London, 1950).

The Selected Letters of Anton Chekhov. Ed. Lillian Hellman, tr. Sidonie Lederer (New York, 1955).

V. WORKS IN RUSSIAN USED IN THE PREPARATION OF THIS VOLUME

Polnoye sobraniye sochineny i pisem A. P. Chekhova ['Complete Collection of the Works and Letters of A. P. Chekhov'], ed. S. D. Balukhaty, V. P. Potyomkin, N. S. Tikhonov, A. M. Yegolin. 20 vols. (Moscow, 1944–51).

N. I. Gitovich, *Letopis zhizni i tvorchestva A. P. Chekhova* ['Chronicle of the Life and Literary Activity of A. P. Chekhov'] (Moscow, 1955).

M. Stroyeva, *Chekhov i Khudozhestvenny teatr* ['Chekhov and the Art Theatre'] (Moscow, 1955).

Literaturnoye nasledstvo: Chekhov ['Literary Heritage: Chekhov'], ed. V. V. Vinogradov and others (Moscow, 1960).

A. P. Chekhov: rukopisi, pisma, biograficheskiye dokumenty, vospominaniya, teatralnyye postanovki, risunki, fotografii ['A. P. Chekhov: Manuscripts, Letters, Biographical Documents, Memoirs, Theatrical Performances, Drawings, Photographs'], compiled by V. P. Nechayev and Yu. M. Mirkina, ed. Yu. A. Krasovsky (Moscow, 1960).

Chekhov i teatr: pisma, felyetony, sovremenniki o Chekhove-dramaturge ['Chekhov and the Theatre: Letters, Articles and the Comments of Contemporaries on Chekhov as Playwright'], ed. E. D. Surkov (Moscow, 1961).

A. P. Chekhov, *Dyadya Vanya* ['Uncle Vanya'], ed. J. M. C. Davidson (London, 1961).

A. P. Chekhov, *Tri sestry* ['Three Sisters'], ed. J. M. C. Davidson (London, 1962).

A. P. Chekhov, *Vishnyovy sad* ['The Cherry Orchard'], ed. J. M. C. Davidson (London, 1962).

A. Tove, 'Konstantsiya Garnet—perevodchik i propagandist russkoy literatury' ['Constance Garnett, Translator and Propagandist of Russian Literature'], *Russkaya literatura* (Moscow), 1958, no. 4, pp. 193–9.

A. Tove, 'Perevody Chekhova v Anglii i SSHA' ['Translations of Chekhov in Britain and the U.S.A.'], *Nauchnyye doklady vysshey shkoly: Filologicheskiye nauki* (Moscow), 1963, no. 1, pp. 144–51.

PRINTED IN GREAT BRITAIN
AT THE UNIVERSITY PRESS, OXFORD
BY VIVIAN RIDLER
PRINTER TO THE UNIVERSITY